Arab Nationalism

Arab nationalism has been one of the dominant ideologies in the Middle East and North Africa since the early twentieth century. However, a clear definition of Arab nationalism, even as a subject of scholarly inquiry, does not yet exist.

Arab Nationalism sheds light on cultural expressions of Arab nationalism and the sometimes contradictory meanings attached to it in the process of identity formation in the modern world. It presents nationalism as an experienceable set of identity markers – in stories, visual culture, narratives of memory, and struggles with ideology, sometimes in culturally sophisticated forms, sometimes in utterly vulgar forms of expression. Drawing upon various case studies, the book transcends a conventional history that reduces nationalism in the Arab lands to a pattern of political rise and decline. It offers a glimpse at ways in which Arabs have constructed an identifiable shared national culture, and it critically dissects conceptions about Arab nationalism as an easily graspable secular and authoritarian ideology modeled on Western ideas and visions of modernity.

This book offers an entirely new portrayal of nationalism and a crucial update to the field, and as such, is indispensable reading for students, scholars, and policymakers looking to gain a deeper understanding of nationalism in the Arab world.

Peter Wien teaches at the University of Maryland in College Park and currently serves as President of The Academic Research Institute in Iraq (TARII).

Arab Nationalism

The Politics of History and Culture in the Modern Middle East

Peter Wien

Routledge
Taylor & Francis Group

LONDON AND NEW YORK

First published 2017
by Routledge
2 Park Square, Milton Park, Abingdon, Oxon OX14 4RN

and by Routledge
711 Third Avenue, New York, NY 10017

Routledge is an imprint of the Taylor & Francis Group, an informa business

British Library Cataloguing-in-Publication Data
A catalogue record for this book is available from the British Library

Library of Congress Cataloging-in-Publication Data
Names: Wien, Peter, author.
Title: Arab nationalism: the politics of history and culture in the
modern Middle East / Peter Wien.
Description: Milton Park, Abingdon, Oxon: Routledge, 2017. | Includes
bibliographical references and index.
Identifiers: LCCN 2016025769 | ISBN 9780415499378 (hardback) |
ISBN 9780415499385 (pbk.) | ISBN 9781315412214 (ebook)
Subjects: LCSH: Arab nationalism. | Arab countries—Civilization.
Classification: LCC DS63.6 .W54 2017 | DDC 320.540917/4927—dc23
LC record available at https://lccn.loc.gov/2016025769

ISBN: 978-0-415-49937-8 (hbk)
ISBN: 978-0-415-49938-5 (pbk)
ISBN: 978-1-315-41221-4 (ebk)

Typeset in Times New Roman
by codeMantra
Printed and bound by CPI Group (UK) Ltd, Croydon, CR0 4YY

Meinen Söhnen

Contents

Figures

Avant-Propos

First, a warning to the esteemed reader: This book is a study of cultural manifestations of Arab Nationalism, and not a survey text of modern Arab history, or of Arab Nationalism in general. Nor does it put a lot of emphasis on broad theoretical inquiries about nationalism. It is assumed that the reader is familiar with the basic tenets of these subject areas. Information on further readings offering either broad background or further specifics about certain areas covered in this book can be found in the extensive reference section.

It is a time-honored custom to start a book with expressions of thanks to the many persons and institutions who lent support in the realization of such a project. I would like to thank my friends, mentors, and scholarly companions Israel Gershoni, Orit Bashkin, Eve Trout Powell, Madeline Zilfi, and Ahmet Karamustafa, who read the manuscript, as well as Jennifer Dueck, Dina Khoury, Elizabeth Thompson, Yoav Alon, Jonathan Wyrtzen, Michael Provence, James McDougall, Stefan Hoerdler, Stefan Weber, Umar (Amr) Ryad, David Motadel, Mark Baer, Mehdi Sajid, Goetz Nordbruch, Olivier Wieviorka, Albrecht Fuess, Jordi Tejel, Anja Pistor-Hatam, Stefan Leder, Thomas Scheffler, Manfred Sing, and Stefan Wild. They all helped me at various stages of this project, giving me comments and ideas, or hosting me and inviting me to participate in conferences or on panels, or simply by being brilliant partners in conversation. I would like to thank specifically Ulrike Freitag for many years of support, and for hosting me at the Zentrum Moderner Orient (ZMO, Centre for Modern Oriental Studies) in Berlin during a sabbatical in 2013. Everyone at the ZMO welcomed me so warmly to the Mittelhof and its unique community of scholars, again. Thomas Ripper, the ZMO's librarian and archivist, has been tremendously helpful. A special thanks is also due to Emad Ahmed Helal of the Dar al-Watha'iq al-Qawmiyya (Egyptian National Archives) in Cairo and his invaluable support during my visit in 2012. I am also grateful to Stephan Seidlmayer and Ralph Bodenstein for generously hosting me at the German Archaeological Institute during that visit. Stephan Seidlmayer was also there in times of need when my family and I had to leave Cairo at an earlier sojourn during the Tahrir Revolution of 2011.

My deep gratitude goes to the people of the Africa and Middle East Division of the Library of Congress (LOC) in Washington D.C. AMED has been a scholarly home for nearly a decade now. Mary Jane Deeb, Fawzi Tadros, Muhannad Salhi,

Hirad Dinavari, and Abdulahi Ahmed have been the most generous hosts. With similar fondness I would like to thank the people of the LOC's Kluge Center, which offered me a fellowship in 2012. Thank you, Carolyn Brown, Mary Lou Reker, Jason Steinhauer, and my fellow scholars for the unique atmosphere of the Center. I would like to thank especially Basil Bastaki, who did invaluable work for me as a research assistant and intern during my time at the Kluge.

I would also like to thank the staff and personnel of the Institut Français du Proche Orient, the Dar al-Watha'iq al-Qawmiyya and the Assad Library in Damascus for their support, especially Amr Soumar. I hope they are all well. The staff at the Centre des Archives Diplomatiques de Nantes (CADN) was especially helpful. Like often before, the German Orientinstitut in Beirut hosted me graciously during a short visit in the early stages of this project.

In its latest stages, Thomas Pierret and Mouaz al-Khatib gave me important information and advice. I would also like to thank Joe Whiting and his team at Routledge for their great support and patience in the realization of this book. Thanks are due, too, to the anonymous readers who made the effort to recommend my manuscript to the publisher.

A special thanks goes to my dear friends and colleagues at the University of Maryland for their many years of encouragement, and for giving me time to work on this book. Madeline and Ahmet again, Phil Soergel, Richard Price, Antoine Borrut, James Gilbert, Valerie Anishchenkova – thank you for the inspiration and the companionship.

Chapters 5 and 7 contain extracts from articles that I published earlier. I received kind permission to use them again for this book from Cambridge University Press for the *International Journal of Middle East Studies*, from Stefan Reichmuth, editor of *Die Welt des Islams*, and the editorial team of *Geschichte und Gesellschaft*.[1]

I am also grateful for the financial support that I received from the Kluge Center, the National Endowment for the Humanities, the ZMO, as well as the Graduate School, the History Department, the College of Arts and Humanities, and the Office of International Programs at the University of Maryland.

My joy and my strength is in my family. I would like to thank, before all, Imke, Benno, Franz, Lukas and Felix for being in my life.

The transcription of Arabic follows the rules of the *International Journal of Middle East Studies*, with the exception that diacritical markers have been avoided altogether, even in technical terms. Apostrophes " ' " and " ' " represent 'Ayn and Hamza, respectively. All translations are my own unless otherwise indicated.

1 Introduction

A critique of Arab nationalism

Nationalism explains the order of the world. Other than, for instance, communism, or economic liberalism, it has no recourse to pure theory or doctrine with global validity, however. Instead, nationalism is a compartmentalized perception of the superiority of a particular community of people, based on ideas of ethnic origin or other variants of rationalizing the bonds that bind a community together. Sometimes, mere physical borders create these bonds, even if they were more or less arbitrarily drawn. The lack of doctrine, however, is compensated in stories. Nationalism is of a narrative nature because its ideas about the shared origins of a community have to be communicated in order to be of value. Stories of a shared origin, but also stories about the glorious deeds of the forefathers, of *Great Men* who saved or shaped the nation, or stories of injustice and humiliation, communicate the imaginary of the nation to which one belongs. Nationalism does not tolerate a pluralism of stories and ideas. It is an ideology because it postulates a hegemonic version of the story of the origin and evolution of the community, and it is modern because it uses the means of the modern nation state – education, media, bureaucratic coercion, or mass mobilization – to disseminate and enforce the hegemonic narrative. Besides that, there is no rationale for belonging to a nation. It consists of a certain narrative heritage that one considers one's own. Efforts to present it as superior to other nationalisms are secondary to this acceptance of identity, and consequently, there is no way to rationalize individual adherence to one nationalism over another, except through the continuity of exposure to a particular set of stories. In contrast, the individual endorsement of ideologies such as communism or free market capitalism can be the result of an intellectual effort and a rational choice. It is, however, not impossible to switch from one nationalism to another, but difficult because the act would compel the individual to throw a whole set of collective images, themes and stories overboard in order to adopt new ones. In certain cases, a particular nationalism might become utterly discredited through defeat in war or association with a particularly heinous crime, as happened in post-World War II Germany, but even that involves a slow and conflict laden process of unlearning. Most of the time, to turn away from one nationalism therefore means to turn away from all.[1]

Nationalism is thus a reference system for the shaping of collective identities, and as such it is an intrinsic part of twentieth-century culture. Politics and socio-economic transformations, such as the creation of urban mass societies and coercive state systems that practice social engineering, or the demands of an industrializing society to oversee and rationalize the workforce, created the foundations for the emergence of nationalism. On another level, political agendas evolved from it. But in its essence, nationalism is a cultural reference system that creates belonging.

Over the past 50 years or so, works that aimed to synthesize Arab nationalism throughout the twentieth century often focused on the evolution of regimes and on the formulation of ideology by the letter. In scholarly works, conceptual epithets such as "crisis of ..., the problem of ..., the predicament of ..." abound. Until the 1960s, Western observers described the emergence of the post-World War II Middle Eastern state system according to modernization theory, postulating that the new nation states were on an irreversible route towards democratization and the development of secular societies. The upheavals after the 1967 Arab–Israeli war, however, made popular a four-fold periodization that was divided into "the rise of Arab nationalism," followed by the "formative years" of nationalist ideology, shaped by the likes of Sati' al-Husri and Michel 'Aflaq, and its "flowering" in the 1950s under Nasser, which, again, was followed, according to this periodization, by a steep "decline" in the 1960s where nationalism became a delusory propagandistic tool to discipline societies and divert attention from the parochial activities of cliques whose only concern was to remain in power, only to be replaced in the 1970s by Islamism as an alternative popular political ideology. Beyond this broad-brush approach, and beyond the obvious shortcomings of Arab leaders and ideologists, it remains to be shown how, and to what extent, the ideas and practices of Arab Nationalism became, and perhaps remain meaningful for ordinary people in the Arab world.[2]

The present book builds on an approach that first received prominence in 1997 in a volume edited by Israel Gershoni and James Jankowski, who assembled an array of individual studies shedding light on aspects of cultural and intellectual history as well as biography related to Arab nationalism, all within the framework of individual countries. The editors pointed to the lack of theoretical sophistication in Arab nationalism research that is still present even in more recent publications. The contributions to their volume offered examples for what Gershoni called a "New Narrative" of Arab nationalism built on a primary source base that transcended the level of big politics and great thinkers. This volume shares similar perspectives and adds a transnational point of view, as well as non-textual representations in festivals and nationalist liturgy, along with institutions in the cultural inquiry. It examines all these with regard to their social and political meanings.[3]

Even today, Arab nationalism as a framework of cultural references circumscribes an imaginary space between the Atlantic Ocean, the southern and eastern rim of the Mediterranean, and the Tigris River. To try to grasp it means to enquire into the real and imaginary movements of people – dead or alive – their words and ideas in this space, between locations and in time. It also means to look for their manifestations in particular places and at particular times. While the space is imagined, only these manifestations make it experienceable; the people who moved in this space were at times excited about its promises, as well as disappointed about its corruption and containment. The following chapters address the questions of if and in what ways this virtual pan-Arab community ever existed, transcending the borders of nation states, or to what extent local agendas actually confirmed borders and fissures, even if they were presented in the language of nationalism. In the case studies, Arab nationalism is not presented as a political agenda of unification and cooperation first of all, but rather with a focus on the roots, the establishment, and the evolution of imaginative, symbolic, or "lived" ties between people(s) who claimed to belong to an Arab national community.[4] At the same time, however, Arab nationalism was never the exclusive frame of reference for people living in the Arab lands. As usual, it only offered one of a wide variety of options that people could choose from in the process of constructing and negotiating their identities. It is therefore important to describe nationalism as fractured and conflicted, and as gaining shape in contradictory ways and out of specific contexts. It would be a misunderstanding therefore to speak of only one Arab nationalism. Rather, there is a conglomerate of sometimes contradictory, sometimes complementary Arab nationalisms that take different forms in the different Arab lands and are deeply rooted in local contexts. They do, however, share a common reference to a vaguely defined and delineated Arabness. This study about Arab Nationalism is therefore also about shifting boundaries – between countries and their peoples, between elites and the populace, between the Ottoman and Mandate eras in the Middle East, and between various ideological commitments.[5]

Before going into a number of case studies to illustrate these points, a few conceptual remarks are necessary to highlight leading problems in Arab nationalism research – to dissect Arab nationalism as a multifaceted subject of investigation.

How modern is Arab nationalism?

Nationalism as a worldview emerged together with the modern nation state and the societal transformations that it accompanied. It is considered a product of European modernity. An outdated, but still popular, narrative about Middle Eastern history describes the advent of modernity in the region as a rupture, brought by imperialism as Napoleon Bonaparte embodied it when he disembarked at Alexandria in 1798. According to more recent scholarship, however, the French conquest of Egypt, though definitely a break politically, only served as a catalyst of trends that had taken root in Middle Eastern societies some time before. The debate follows two lines of inquiry. One disproves the notion that modern, "enlightened" ways of thinking only appeared in the Ottoman lands as a consequence of the encounter with Western science. Some researchers have identified signs of a rudimentary autochthonous Islamic Enlightenment in the Middle East of the eighteenth century or even earlier – a controversial notion that ushered in fierce debates. In the second line, more cautious researchers have argued that a growing economic middle class in places such as Cairo developed individualized forms of literary expression and critical approaches to textual debate that thrived regionally, building on an expanding book market based on the output of specialized workshops that produced manuscripts for export and local consumption.[6] Altogether, these phenomena prepared a momentous shift in worldviews away from concrete and locally limited perceptions of community adherence towards abstract notions of allegiance to broader groups based on shared ethnic, religious, and cultural markers.

In this context, Islamic Studies scholarship has put a great deal of emphasis on the alleged emergence of Neo-Sufi trends, based on a revival of Hadith studies in eighteenth- and early nineteenth-century Sufi circles, and the new networks that evolved from the heightened scholarly activities in the Haramain cities (Mecca and Medina), combined with a new level of mobility among scholars and their disciples throughout a broad region of Islam, spanning from West Africa and Morocco to the Indian Ocean region. An equal amount of energy has been spent on the refutation of such theses – especially the related arguments about an Islamic Enlightenment. According to the *Neo-Sufism* concept, the unquestionable surge in activist Sufi organization throughout Africa, north and south of the Sahara, and the Middle East that occurred in the nineteenth century was due to a shift in Sufism away from localized mystical and superstitious practices to a more rational and worldly way of organizing and linking people, especially men, together. Neo-Sufism re-focused Muslim spirituality away from a distant deity to the person of the prophet as a go-between of the divine and the worldly spheres. The Sufi way thus took a turn towards a *tariqa Muhammadiyya* (a "Muhammadan path") in the eighteenth century, which proponents of the Islamic Enlightenment thesis interpret as a step towards the endorsement of an anthropocentric worldview. At least, Sufi organization provided assets that became useful in anti-colonial resistance throughout the nineteenth century, such as the strict hierarchical order of a master's charismatic leadership and his disciples' obedience, the missionary activities of the orders, and the resulting wide spatial distribution of a network of lodges, and not least the esprit de corps founded on an awareness of shared genealogies, common practices and a distinctive belief system. In addition, the increased focus of Neo-Sufism on the Prophet as a pathway to the divine either led to, or at least coincided with, a revival of Hadith studies in the academies of Mecca and Medina where legal scholars, who were at the same time Sufi masters, had already argued in the eighteenth century that their students should go back to the sources of Islamic law that were the closest in time to the life of the prophet. They should use individual intellect and reason (*ijtihad*) to adjust Islamic law to current circumstances instead of practicing *taqlid*, which is the principle of mere emulation of century-old authorities in Islamic jurisprudence that conservative adherents of orthodoxy among the legal scholars ('*ulama*') propagated.[7]

Critics of Neo-Sufism reject the idea that the described phenomena were new. Many of the supposedly novel positions of these leaders had been formulated by others centuries earlier, and the authoritative writings of alleged Neo-Sufi leaders such as the Moroccan Ibn Idris (1760–1837) banned free-wheeling *ijtihad* rather than promoting it.[8] The fiercest critics of Neo-Sufism have tended to rely on close textual arguments without much sense for historical contextual source critique. For instance, Ibn Idris' emphasis on normative behavior in his writings might have been a reaction precisely to increased transgression among his disciples. Another argument weighs more heavily, however, namely that Neo-Sufism might be a mere invention of nineteenth-century colonialism and a product of the surprise of French, British, or later Italian authorities when they encountered resistance against their endeavors from various well organized Sufi movements. Arguably, the effectiveness of this resistance ran counter to the Orientalist prejudice that the Sufi maraboutism of North African peoples was particularly passive and otherworldly. The unexpected experiences to the contrary called for a new explanatory paradigm, which was then passed down and readily accepted by twentieth-century scholars.[9]

Critics of Neo-Sufism have been ready to concede that the new organizational forms and the mobilizing power of Sufi orders in the nineteenth century were indeed a novelty, as evident, for instance, in the swift organization of anti-French resistance in Eastern Algeria by 'Abd al-Qadir al-Jaza'iri in the 1830s, or the respective role of the Sanusi brotherhood in Libya and the central Sahara.[10] In contrast, the assertion that aspects of Neo-Sufism related to doctrine and philosophy constituted a rudimentary form of autochthonous Islamic Enlightenment has been attacked, sometimes with fierce conviction. Terminology has been a problem, because the occurrence of the Enlightenment epithet itself with its baggage of ideological usages in a European *Geistesgeschichte*, was sure to give rise to misunderstandings, even if, at times, they tended to smack of traditional Orientalist perceptions as if Islamic cultural manifestations, including Sufism, belonged to an a-historical continuum and were incapable of an autochthonous Enlightenment unless they had been poked and impregnated by European modernity driving them to frantic activism.[11]

Even if there is still substantial controversy over the Enlightenment theory, scholars indeed do offer strong arguments supporting the dissemination of an increasingly anthropocentric worldview with the Prophet as the lead model in Sufi circles during the eighteenth century.[12] The result was, arguably, that individual members of increasingly activist Sufi orders were ultimately considered to be individually responsible for the application of the norms put forward in scripture. They were compelled to give up inherited patterns of orientation that were bound to the societal bonds of local tradition and authority, especially if this re-orientation took place in the context of the highly transformative and mobile networks of masters, their deputies, and the disciples in the expanding brotherhoods. The new – or Neo – Sufis found themselves part of wider and more abstract networks of belief and identity.

These trends preceded and thus maybe facilitated the occurrence of other markers of change and transformation in the Arab world during the nineteenth century that help explain how Arabs became *modern*, in a recognizable European sense, so swiftly. Such markers are rudimentary capitalist market conditions, the emergence of a quasi-bourgeois elite, the development of a book production

industry, and a move towards individualism even before European encroachment. At least some Arabs were much better prepared to handle the encounter
with Europe than the aforementioned rupture theory insinuates. Individuals ad-
justed their identities and adherences as a consequence of new notions of space
and the position of the individual within it, resulting from new patterns of movement that Neo-Sufism pioneered – building wide networks that bound people
together – beyond the scholarly class that had had the sole privilege of traveling
widely in the Islamic realm for centuries. In the nineteenth century, these trends
concurred with the integration of the southern and eastern rim of the Mediterranean into the imperialist world economic system, as well as the intensification of
global trade throughout the Atlantic world and the Indian Ocean, which resulted
in labor-driven movements of rural populations that followed the re-direction of
trade routes to the exponentially expanding port cities, as well as to the administrative hubs of the emerging bureaucracies of nascent nation states and colonial
administrations. The ensuing re-direction of group allegiances and emergence of
new social norms among heterogeneous urban populations produced new ways
of social mobilization that influenced both contents and language of political as
well as religious debates, but also the shape of communal behavior (both violent and non-violent). The economic classes that formed did not supersede older
allegiances, but at times, the process of uprooting as a consequence of the new
mobility paradoxically threw them into stronger relief because differences became essential when removed from their inherited local contexts. City life and
shared economic hardships provided new contexts that called for explanation, so
the legacy of discourses of difference based on, for example, sectarian or ethnic
background, turned into ideology and means of mobilization.[13]

When tangible group identities (family, clan, tribe, village, town quarter,
or religious denomination) ceased to serve as exclusive points of reference for
the individual, the state tried to interfere with – and discipline – individual life
stories, too. The reform movements of the nineteenth century – the Tanzimat,
Mehmet Ali's Egyptian military reforms, Tunisia's constitutional movement –
set out to redefine the relationship between the state and the citizen. It is true
that both political reforms and intellectual trends of the nineteenth and early
twentieth centuries called for individualism (both in terms of individual liber-
ties and accountabilities), but in fact they often demanded nothing but conform-
ity and individual submission under rules defined by others. During the period
between the two World Wars, these rules became subsumed under the terms
of national cohesion.[14] However, disciplinary politics and the de-localization of
individual identities did not only occur in the secular sphere of the state, but
also in the context of Islamic revivalism and reformism as outlined above. But
only the encounter with Western imperialism forced members of Middle Eastern
Societies to redefine their positions vis-à-vis their traditions and localities on a
grand scale. Shared experiences of hardships, dislocation, bureaucratization, the
loss of inherited support networks, but also the streamlining of education and
the influence of circulating media and means of propaganda turned people into
individuals – certainly with rights and responsibilities, but also as citizens of

abstract communities such as the nation, class, or Islamic *umma*. The disintegration of Algerian society in the wake of the French conquest, the pan-Islamic propaganda of Ottoman Sultan Abdülhamit II, and the destructive effects of World War I on the Syrian lands are cases in point.[15]

Hence, modernity indeed had autochthonous roots in the countries of the Middle East, but these roots have long been overshadowed by the deep and lasting impact of the encounter with Western imperialism and the hegemonic imprint that it left on the way that Arabs relate to themselves and the world. It remains important to inquire into the historical roots of modernization in Muslim societies as scholars continue to do in the Neo-Sufism or Islamic Enlightenment debates. Contemporary Arab perceptions of the origins of Arab modernity are different, though, and much more in line with the Napoleonic rupture thesis. A lead example for the orientation of Arab intellectuals is the Averroes (Ibn Rushd) reception in the Arab world. Twentieth-century intellectuals tended to derive their knowledge about the thought of the Muslim Andalusian philosopher rather from translations of the works of the influential French Orientalist Ernest Renan than from original texts. The latter stipulated that medieval Europeans like Thomas Aquinas received and cultivated Averroes' rationalism, while Muslims largely ignored the Arab philosopher's legacy after his death in the year 1198, which therefore allegedly marks the beginning of a period of decline in Arab thought until the West made contact with the Arabs in 1798 – conspicuously exactly 600 years later. Not only left-leaning Arab philosophers have accepted this *paradox of Averroes* along with the adoption of radical Western-oriented rationalism. Even Islamist doctrinaires propagate the need to return to the "authentic" religion and "authentic" Arabism of the early days of Islam, the days of the forefathers (salaf). The Salafists of our time endorse the rupture thesis indirectly when they promote a fundamentalist return to the roots disregarding continuities of Islamic thought.[16]

To add an example, this image of decline and awakening runs counter to scholarly findings about the intellectual efforts of reformist Sufi circles in Middle Eastern cities during the second half of the nineteenth century. The activities of 'Abd al-Qadir al-Jaza'iri in Damascus – both a Sufi and a scholar, whose posthumous fame is the subject of a chapter of this book – might constitute a missing link between the Ottoman and post-Ottoman intellectual worlds. According to the broad lines of this story, 'Abd al-Qadir and his circle acted as incubators for new ways of thinking about Islam that combined adherence to Islamic legal principles and spirituality with a call for a rational re-consideration of the sources of Islamic jurisprudence in light of the advancement of the sciences in the Western world – promoting an openness to *ijtihad* just like the new trends in Sufism had done earlier.[17] 'Abd al-Qadir was the perfect figure to represent this synthesis due to his biography as a devout Sufi practitioner and sheikh, his leadership of the early Algerian resistance to French colonization, and his intensive experiences with Europe, which he gained during his detention in France after his surrender in North Africa in 1847. When 'Abd al-Qadir took up residence in Damascus in 1855 after a short stint in Bursa, he turned into a notable of the city with substantial landed property. His international reputation increased considerably in the context of the 1860 sectarian riots in Lebanon and Syria when he protected scores of Christian families in his palace. 'Abd al-Qadir spent most of his time in Damascus, until his death, as a scholar and teacher of the Sufi thought of Ibn al-'Arabi (1165–1240), "al-Shaykh al-Akbar" ("the greatest master") and his "akbari" branch of Sufism. From several stays in the major centers of Islamic scholarship in the Arab world, not least Mecca, 'Abd al-Qadir was familiar with the latest trends in hadith studies as outlined above. He promoted openness to the principles of rationalist causality as Western science used it because he argued that all causality came in its essence from God and was with God. 'Abd al-Qadir's disciples in Damascus, among them members of the leading scholarly families and future luminaries of religious life of the city, studied the Qur'an and hadith in light of akbari thought and modern rationalism. 'Abd al-Qadir considered the Sufi pursuit of realizing the unification with the divine being – to become one with God within *wahdat al-wujud* ("The Unity of Being") – as only attainable by the very few inductees of the *akbari* way. It was left to 'Abd al-Qadir's disciples and their descendants in the early twentieth century to translate the rationalist strand of his teachings into a popular anti-elitist approach. A group of middle ranking *'ulama'* with ties to members of 'Abd al-Qadir's circle were at odds with the orthodox leaning Islamization and centralization policies of the Ottoman Sultan Abdülhamit II, who channeled his Islamization policy through old established families in the capitals of the Arab provinces. He also supported their economic interests at the expense of the families of these middle ranking *'ulama.'* In addition, Abdülhamit's reliance on the Rifa'i Sufi order to propagate his Islamization policy disagreed with the rationalist attitude of the descendants of the 'Abd al-Qadir circle, who formed the core of the nascent Salafi trend in Syria. When the centralization policy of Abdülhamit II and the Young Turk rulers started to fuel ethnic antagonism, the socio-economic and theological contestations found a new outlet in Arab cultural nationalist trends among the early Salafis (not to be confused with modern day Salafists), which they shared with the young Arab graduates of Ottoman state schools. Last but not least, the loss of state patronage under Abdülhamit II drove Salafis to turn to the populace for support. According to this line of argumentation, a popularization of the Salafi message ensued, combined with a vernacularization of the related teachings, creating a new basis for a popularized activist Arabic language. Even if this storyline over-simplifies intricate local power relationships, it nevertheless provides localized intellectual background and a trajectory of cultural continuity that help explain in broad terms the veritable groundswell of Arab nationalism as a popular movement in the wake of the dissolution of the Ottoman Empire at the end of World War I. It also provides context for the question about the relationship between Arab nationalism, secularism and religion that is covered below.[18]

At the end of the day, an inquiry into the cultural roots and structural nature of Arab nationalism needs to distinguish between the intellectual history of modernity in the Arab-Muslim world, which is the genealogy of modern thought, and the evolution of institutional structures, means and media, language and terminology, or, broadly speaking, the representative forms of modernity – nationalism being one. Many of these representations unquestionably were adopted from the West – never as direct emulation, but instead in a complex and creative process of adaptation, building on the centuries-old cultural legacy of the Arab-Muslim world. The latter provided a cultural framework that greatly facilitated the swift adoption and forced a thorough adaptation of European models and structures under the condition of European hegemony in an encounter based on openness to reform that derived from changing patterns of social interaction and worldviews that preceded Napoleon's disembarking at Alexandria by decades if not centuries.[19]

How secular is Arab nationalism?

The culture of Arab Nationalism is situated in an Islamic culture, not only in terms of the Sufi-Salafi genealogy. Arab nationalist acts – such as the formulation of its ideological doctrines, debates about its political and cultural roles, political acts that are motivated by it, and representative actions that have it as a reference point – happen in an Islamic context shaped by religious practices, languages and narrative structures of the majority population. Arab nationalists, regardless of their actual creeds or sectarian backgrounds, have to respond to this broader cultural environment, to its imaginary patterns and structure of meanings.[20] For example, historical consciousness finds expression in religious pride of the achievements of the Arabs as founders of a new civilization. Such historicism and myth-making are crucial for societies and communities to locate themselves within the flow of time, particularly in reaction to crises and challenges such as the demise of the Ottoman Empire.[21] To historicize the events of early Islamic history means to assign them a place on the trajectory of secular time, to mark them as past and gone. The Prophet becomes a role model, a *Great Man in History*. In that, historicism differs from the anthropocentric approach to the Prophet of Neo-Sufism, the adherents of which seek the presence of Muhammad as a spiritual union. The present day radical Salafists and Jihadists, to whom modern day media often refer, aspire to a concrete reconstruction of the original and pure community of the Prophet and his followers. Thus they are much closer to the secularizing historicism of the *islamiyyat* literature in 1930s Egypt, which the intellectual Muhammad Husayn Haykal spearheaded in his 1935 book *Hayat Muhammad* (*The Life of Muhammad*), than to the mystic evocation of the Prophet in Neo-Sufism. Haykal introduced an image of the Prophet that put the man and his model life over its spiritual meaning, rejecting the miraculous content of the conventional biographical (*sira*) literature as superfluous to an understanding of the genius of Muhammad.[22]

The question about the relationship between the religious and the secular has played an important role in the debate about the nature of Arab nationalism. In this, it is an over-simplification to consider pan-Islamic and pan-Arab trends as merely two sides of the same medal, as mid-twentieth-century scholars argued. Rather, the relationship between the two has been one of "complex interaction."[23]

Many nationalists may well have argued for a strict separation between the sphere of the nation and the sphere of religion, but

> [i]n practice, nationalist, as well as Islamic discourses have moved between and combined these principles in relation to the problems and situations in hand. Few Islamists have followed the logic of Islamic community as against the nation, and few nationalists have not accorded religion a place of honour in the attributes of the nation.[24]

Radically secular voices like that of the Syrian intellectual Sadiq Jalal al-'Azm stand out and have received a great deal of attention, especially in the West. Al-'Azm's relentless criticism of the lack of a separation between religion and state, his sober analysis of socio-political reasons for the Arab defeat in the war against Israel in 1967, and his attack on the prevalence of anti-Semitic stereotypes in Arab nationalist thought of the time are the product of a particular intellectual and scholarly setting in Beirut and the circles around the American University in the late 1960s. They reflect a society that was more open and pluralist than at any time after that – even if al-'Azm's criticism brought him into serious conflict with conservative authorities in Lebanon. Still, the likes of al-'Azm should not merely be considered the exception to the rule of religiously dominated thinking among the people of the modern Arab world. Leftist secularism, secular Arab nationalism, Islamic cultural identification and Islamic social mobilization present a spectrum of possibilities in modern Arab societies that a growing young educated population of men and women could and still can choose from.[25]

Arabs, and Muslims for that matter, are certainly not alone in fomenting *hybridity* in the formation of modern identities, putting a certain "Islamicness" next to their Arabness in the usage of slogans, symbols, and a shared narratology of origin and direction of the community. Islamicness and Arabness are not substantial, but they are acquired as an easily accessible framework providing orientation, often as an aspect of state education, which, as a secular institution in the modern nation state, is hardly a zone free of religious references and contents.[26] The nineteenth and twentieth centuries belonged to a "world time" of "moral education" where state schooling became a breeding ground for such trends in many parts of the world. The "desacralization" of spaces and functions (the school, the teacher, the state, the monarchy, the judge) did not result in a full secularization of minds. One should not "underestimate the sacred."[27]

In theory, Arab nationalism as a historicizing and thus secularizing concept is running up against deep-seated religious convictions and prominent cultural markers based on religious practices. In reality, the conflict is constantly being mediated, such as, for example, in attempts to come up with syntheses that maintain the sacred aura while holding on to a very worldly agenda. The outcome can be quite convoluted, as can be seen, for example, in the rhetoric of Michel 'Aflaq, one of the "founding fathers" of the secular Ba'th party.

In 1943, 'Aflaq (1910–1989) gave a speech commemorating the "Arab Prophet" on the steps of the Syrian University in Damascus.[28] At the time, his organization was still an exclusive club of inductees, which mainly consisted of university students that had gathered around the three founding fathers of the party, Zaki Arsuzi (1899–1968), Salah al-Din al-Bitar (1912–1980), and 'Aflaq. Bitar and 'Aflaq had been students in Paris in the 1920s and teachers of secondary education in the 1930s in Damascus where they developed a vision of a socialist and pan-Arab nationalist party as an elitist, radical and activist community, officially secular but imbued with strangely spiritual views of the nation, and an ambivalent relationship with Islamic civilization as the glue that held together the society that surrounded them. The origins of the party date to 1941, and 'Aflaq was its general secretary in various forms for much of the rest of his life. At the end of the day, however, he and Bitar found themselves sidelined by civilian and military factions in the party, split between Iraq and Syria.

Arsuzi had acted as the intellectual–spiritual leader of the group after he took up exile in Damascus in the wake of Turkey's annexation of his birthplace, the Sanjak of Alexandretta in 1939. Even if Arsuzi was a declared atheist, the secretive nature of the gatherings with his Damascene disciples and the reverence they had for him reminds one of the mystic-spiritual pre-disposition of Sufi circles. This, but also, possibly, the Sufi roots of Damascene intellectual life, may have had an influence on the leaders of the Ba'th, as the surprisingly mystical tone of some passages in 'Aflaq's commemoration of the Prophet suggests.[29] Religious references have certainly been a mainstay of most nationalisms worldwide since the nineteenth century – Arab nationalism is no exception in that sense. 'Aflaq's speech nevertheless sticks out in the way that the Syrian nationalist leader used hardly comprehensible allusions and figurative speech instead of providing a compelling historicist account. For 'Aflaq, the Prophet was not a hero of the past, not a mere point of orientation, but a living presence:

> The Islamic movement as represented in the life of the noble Prophet is not only a historical event for the Arabs, ... but it constitutes an immediate connection to the unbound life of the Arabs [...] Until now, people looked at the life of the Prophet from the outside, like an awesome picture existing for our admiration and adoration. It is on us, however, to look at it from the inside to bring it to life. Every Arab today can live the life of the Arab Prophet. [...] Muhammad was every Arab, so today every Arab has to be Muhammad.[30]

The speech holds a prominent place in a scholarly debate about the compatibility between Islam and secularism in Arab nationalism and Ba'thism in particular. In 1988, Kanan Makiya (then still publishing under the pseudonym Samir Khalil) referred to the speech in an inquiry about "National Identity in Islam" that forms part of his book *Republic of Fear*. The book has been heavily criticized for comparing Hitler's and Stalin's totalitarianism with Saddam Hussein's rule in Iraq.[31] In a more sophisticated argument, Khalil-Makiya interpreted 'Aflaq's speech as an expression of his view that Arab nationalism was unique among other nationalisms, because it had not been formed in reflection of and distinction from European nationalisms, but had its own specific cultural spark in the origins of Islam. For Makiya, 'Aflaq's positioning of the Prophet Muhammad indeed constituted a "pseudo-mystical reading of the Islamic experience" turning Arab nationalism into a form of faith, equal to Islam itself. In a similar vein, the eminent Iraq historian Hanna Batatu argued that 'Aflaq had intended to create a realm of emotional references evoked by familiar religious topoi rather than a systematic doctrine.[32] Indeed, 'Aflaq hardly presented arguments and evidence in the speech, but talked from a position of conviction instead, moving around the figure of the Prophet in circles in a quasi mystical way: The dynamic of the occasion and the activity of giving the speech were more important than the contents of the speech itself. Context and concurrence provided legitimacy.[33]

It is difficult to reconstruct the immediate impact of a speech such as 'Aflaq's, which was edited, printed and re-printed several times after the fact. When the text became canonical, it was severed from its original context and re-inserted into new ones, only to provide the party exegetes of Ba'thist thought food for doctrinal deliberations. The writings of founding fathers and near-mythical leaders like 'Aflaq became fetishes for party members to foster allegiance and identification, rather than objects of deep analytical engagement.[34]

There are fewer obstacles to the contextualization of the speech-giving act of a less prominent figure. It provides an insight into the dynamics of making sense of concurring convictions – at a particular place and moment in time such as, in the following example, Baghdad in 1940, when the city became the center of gravity of extreme Arab nationalist activities during the early years of World War II. In August 1940, the Baghdad nationalist daily *al-Istiqlal* published a speech by Kamil Shabib, a member of the so-called *Golden Square* of *Four Officers*, entitled "The Constitution of Muhammad and the Desired Strength" ("Dustur Muhammad wa'l-quwa al-manshuda").[35] Shabib was a leading staff officer in the Iraqi army at the time, but more importantly, he belonged to a group of junior officers who were the driving force behind informal military rule in Iraq that started with the first Arab military coup in 1936 and ended in a short-lived military alliance with Germany in 1941 and eventually in the Iraqi defeat in a war against Britain. Shabib was hanged in 1942 as a conspirator.

The strong Islamic undercurrent in Shabib's speech stands out in the generally secular tone of the Arab nationalist discourse in most leading Iraqi newspapers at the time, even if the major topics of his speech were familiar: the current weakness of the Arab nation as a consequence of the lack of unity, or the vanguard role of the youth in strengthening the society, and so forth. However, he focused in his terminology on the Islamic umma, which was in his own definition the Arab Muslim nation that had given in to indulgence. Instead of the Arab nation as a secular historical entity returning to the glory of the past, he demanded a restoration of the unity of the umma as a continuous obligation through "Muhammad's constitution."[36]

Shabib's speech was part of a fundraising event on the occasion of the "Festival of the Air Force," which was broadcast over Iraqi radio. He framed a call on Iraqis to donate money as a religious duty. The purpose was the creation of an Iraqi program of national aircraft manufacturing, which was supposed to strengthen the entire Arab Islamic umma. The centerpiece of the speech was, however, not about arms and current military affairs. Like many historically minded Arab nationalists of the time, he pointed to the heroism of the early Muslim warriors as examples of military prowess. Shabib's terminology is remarkable, however. In reference to the nation he used the word "umma" instead of "watan" as other Arab nationalist writers would have done at the time. He did not even put the epithet "Arab" next to it. When he singled out the achievements of the early generations of Islam, he spoke of them as "salaf" ("forefathers") instead of "ajdad" ("elders"), which was a common, more secular term. By the late 1930s, *salaf* and *salafiyya* were identified already with somewhat radical Islamist notions of revival.[37]

The nation, according to Shabib, believed in the constitution of its leader and prophet. The Prophet had made religion perfect, brought to his people the grace of his Lord, had accepted for them Islam as a religion that prescribed to serve God alone, who had no associates. Apparently, Shabib saw the unity of God as parallel to the unity of the fatherland, and no divisions of the latter should be tolerated. In addition, infidels should not be allowed to rule, and neither should be "dhimmis" (members of protected religious minorities) as long as they were "not of our kind." Shabib thus seemed to distinguish the Christians and Jews who were native to the Arab lands from those who had colonized them. The term he used for those colonizers was unusual, again: "a'ajim," the "non-Arab speakers," who according to a popular historical narrative at the time had started to undermine Arab predominance under Abbasid rule when increasing numbers of ethnic Persians and Turks served the Islamic state. According to the same narrative, this entry of foreign elements had initiated a period of decadence and decline in the world of Islam.[38] Shabib's terminology thus established several layers of foreignness to explain Arab weakness that needed to be remedied: Religious and ethnic difference, as well as modern imperialist confrontation. He cried out:

> Enough indulgence, we shall fear God! [...] The preservation of unity befits us because we are the people of *tawhid* [the declaration that there is only one God], so that we guard the unity in all things: one Lord, one *dustur*, one *qibla* [direction of prayer], one history, one *umma*, one highest goal, one fatherland.[39]

Shabib's usage of the term *dustur* (modern standard Arabic for *constitution*) is unusual, if not original. Etymology traces the word to ancient Persian, where it designated the Zoroastrian priesthood and, in a broad sense, someone with authority and power. Among a variety of usages in medieval Arabic, the one that comes closest to the contemporary meaning is related to the rules and regulations of urban guilds and corporations. The usage designating an abstract set of fundamental laws is modern, even though it is hard to establish a date when it was first applied. Tunisia's first constitution, the first in an Arab land, dates to 1861, but under the name "Law of the Tunisian State" ("Qanun al-Dawla al-Tunisiyya"). Other early Arab constitutional documents were called "Basic Law," such as Egypt's "al-La'iha al-Asasiyya" of 1882, and Iraq's 1925 "Organic Law" ("al-Qanun al-Asasi"). The Ottoman Constitution of 1876, revoked by Sultan Abdülhamit II in 1878, bore the same name. However, when the Young Turks forced the Ottoman Sultan's hand in the revolution of 1908 to re-institute the 1876 constitution, all of Cairo celebrated "'Id al-Dustur," "the Festival of the Constitution," invoking Ottoman brotherhood, and the Tunisian anti-colonial opposition founded "The Free Tunisian Constitutional Party" in 1920 in reference to the 1861 constitution, calling it "al-Hizb al-Hurr al-Dusturi." Still, the usage of the word in "Constitution of Muhammad" in 1940 seems to be without precursor.[40]

Is there an echo of *tariqa Muhammadiyya* ("the path of Muhammad") in this terminology? There is no information available about the prevalence of the concept in Baghdadi Sufi circles in the interwar period, or about Sufi or Islamic reformist influences in Iraqi military circles.[41] Moreover, Shabib left open what the actual contents of the "constitution of Muhammad" were supposed to be. In his mind, it probably stood for a certain Islamic ethos that was to guide the modern Arab nation state, an ethics of unity and a morality based on the re-creation of the spirit of the first generation of Muslims. In light of the ideas that floated around in nationalist discourse at the time, about the need to integrate and streamline Arab society, Shabib added a sharp Islamic edge to the imagery of a disciplined society, in which the term *tawhid* took on an eerily totalitarian dimension.

Islam as a means to foster social discipline, the streamlining of society within the confines of the modern nation state, the *tawhid* of a nation, the image of which is blurred between markers of shared faith and common ethnicity – Shabib's speech arguably reflected a pool of complementary elements in an identity-building tool box that none of the practitioners of socio-political interaction considered contradictory.[42]

It is fruitful to weigh these arguments in the light of postcolonial theory and Talal Asad's arguments about the incompatibility of nationalism and Islamism. According to Asad, the essential difference between the pre-modern state and the modern nation state is one of worldviews. Religious transcendence determined the world order of the pre-modern state as an image of eternity, or in other words, as the reflection of the will of a higher being. In contrast, the modern nation state is a product of secularization where society is a secular and *true* space, or an essence in and of itself that is an immediate reflection of reality through the senses. Society thus can be shaped and formed by man; it has problems that can be solved to set it right. In addition, secularism as a doctrine postulates that all communities are naturally secular, whereas religion is merely a *false consciousness*, the liberation from which is thus an emancipation of society. Charles Taylor calls this frame of mind "exclusive humanism." In Asad's view, secular nationalists assume that man has full responsibility and accountability and therefore directs his allegiance and loyalty deliberately towards the nation as a worldly community. In that, myths, images, or historical narratives remind or convince the human being of the necessity of his or her allegiance, while – realistically speaking – political structures of power and hegemony in the modern state coerce him or her to declare allegiance.[43]

Asad postulates that, in contrast, Islamists do not consider the story of the Muslim community as one of a nation's rise. Instead they believe that it "articulate[s] a Qur'anic world view." Whereas Arab nationalism "is inconceivable without its history, the Islamic umma presupposes only the Qur'an and the sunna." When nationalists and Islamists collaborated in the past, they did so, according to Asad, because they shared enemies, such as imperialism or Zionism, and in spite of essential differences. Both refer to the prophet and his lifetime in legitimating discourses, for example, but nationalist imagery of the prophet as the foundational spiritual hero of the Arab nation is clearly distinct from the Islamic image of the prophet as a timeless model of perfect conduct. For Asad, the apparent overlap between nationalism and Islamism is a product of the fact that both use the modern nation state as a reference point. Islamist movements, however, only vie to take it over because they are in a competition with secular nationalists in the public sphere who claim the state as their realm.[44]

It comes as a surprise in the light of Asad's dialectics that a nationalist Iraqi officer of the early 1940s employed concepts that derived from Islamist discourse even though conventional readings of Arab nationalism and the Iraqi army as its arm would suggest otherwise. The argument in this book is that Asad's distinctions do not matter on a practical and situational level where language is used as a legitimating tool appealing to the dispositions of the audience. Asad himself puts into question – in a different context, but still in a seemingly self-contradictory manner – if a strict division is tenable between religion and the state that relegates the former entirely to the sphere of the private, as secularists would claim it. He argues that privatized religion shapes individuals in their upbringing or education and determines the individual's responsiveness in public discourse. For Asad, "de-privatized" religion re-entered the public sphere of the modern Middle Eastern state forcefully in the 1970s again after it had been confined to the private sphere for decades. It is arguable, however, that this confinement had never been complete, and religion had only been concealed underneath a layer of hegemonic secular discourse under authoritarian conditions of military rule since the 1950s. Instead, it always belonged to the "social imaginary" of cultural understandings shared by a given people.[45]

How popular is Arab nationalism?

The intellectual and political leaders of the Arab nation preferred to mitigate the haze and blur of public discourse, however. The myths, stories, images, and ideas they produced were supposed to form a wholesome master narrative, elite thinkers and writers would provide interpretations where needed, and together they would be disseminated for absorption by the "masses."[46] It is a common criticism of the scholarship on Arab nationalism of the past half century that it considered the movement as rooted in intellectual idealism, and thus as a product of a hermetic exchange of ideas "among a small circle of cultural producers" – an elitist project, which posited non-elites merely as passive receivers. The dominant narrative also considered Arab nationalism in the Middle East as the exclusive and original representative of nationalist ideology in the Arab lands, and thus it negated the possibility of alternative nationalisms in the region. In the same vein, the evolution from Arabism as a cultural movement to Arab nationalism as a political ideology has been considered as smooth and uninterrupted, thus excluding alternative and divergent developments.[47] To what extent the populace actually bought into the identity markers that were laid out for them is a question that is difficult for the historian to answer because the elites themselves produced the commonly used and easily accessible primary sources. At best, they contain *echoes of dissidence*. It turns out that imposed secularist worldviews clashed specifically with the heritage of religious practice and the belief of the "common people."

This section – *How popular is Arab nationalism?* – addresses two overlapping issues therefore: first, the *popularity* of Arab nationalism that can be measured by the trickle-down effect and impact of nationalist doctrine and imagery handed down from above; second, *populist* manifestations of Arab nationalism that have the potential to disrupt master narratives and invert power relationships in times of change and crisis. In addition, the question arises to what extent the state- and city-centered approach to the study of nationalism in the Arab world has actually forestalled the recognition of an even larger diversity of nationalisms in the Middle East.

Studies that cover the popularity of Arab nationalism are few and far between. They can be found on the pages of works of anthropology and the social sciences, which use interviews and modern media as working material. They indicate that narrative topoi of Arab nationalism showed a remarkable persistence as identity markers for the "common people" even at times when the political rhetoric of the Arab leadership lost its appeal. For the consumers of media, cultural notions of Arabism rooted in the shared linguistic heritage play a central role and are essentially compatible with a pronounced Islamic identity.[48]

Textual studies that look back further into the twentieth and nineteenth centuries hardly present reflections of popular attitudes in their sources. The question of orality versus textuality and of vernacular language versus high language has always been at the center of a debate about the compatibility of elite visions and popular visions of cultural identity. The industrialization of script as a medium played a crucial role in this competition. Print, it has been argued, significantly altered the epistemological nature of the Arabic language. Before print, written Arabic text was a vehicle for individual teaching where the act of pronouncing the word was, due to the lack of vowels in Arabic script, already an act of interpretation in an individual process of transmission of knowledge between master and disciple. Certainly, this image of pre-modern Arabic literacy limits the gaze to the elite circles of Islamic jurisprudence, as if no other literary realm had existed. In fact, as has been referenced above, there was a vibrant proto-bourgeois literary culture in Egypt and the Fertile Crescent in the eighteenth century already, based on the large-scale manufacturing of manuscripts that presented daily life sensibilities and a simple language attuned to the needs of a rising commercial class.[49]

There is no doubt, however, that the arrival of the printing press in the Arab world, and particularly in Egypt facilitated and accelerated the standardization of language beyond the scholarly circles of the '*ulama*.' This standardization responded to the needs of the centralized state to make itself heard and understood by the masses, and to the desire of the members of a growing educated class to make themselves heard by their peers. An abstraction of the meaning of words as manifest in the reproducibility of movable letters was the necessary consequence. The exact meaning of words was no longer in the individual speech act of the master to be emulated by the disciple. The exact meaning was instead in the printed shape of the word as it existed in innumerable copies. The meaning was therefore supposed to be the same for every member of the newly emerging national society who consumed public media, or at least this is what government agents assumed, and so did the elite intellectuals of the bourgeoisie that ran, financed, and consumed the products of the new publishing industry, especially the newspapers and magazines that appeared in increasing print runs in Cairo, turning the city into the Arab intellectual hub during the last quarter of the nineteenth century. Editors and popular writers, like the Lebanese-born Christian Jurji Zaydan, who will be introduced in detail below, played a central role in the dissemination of political agendas, intellectual concepts, and the topoi of popular narratives, as well as of a modern standard version of Arabic that became the vehicle of middle-class communication. The bourgeoisie takes on a central role in this image of a top-down dissemination of modern thought.[50]

In recent years, studies of Arab nationalism have moved into different directions, however, as for example in inquiries into the role of popular culture in shaping national identity discourses. Colloquial Arabic occupied, for instance, a much more prominent place in Egyptian media at the turn of the twentieth century than previously assumed. The argument is that oral communication should not be underestimated in its importance in the transmission and popularization of concepts, ideas, and terms. However, it is probably an exaggeration that colloquial Arabic was, in fact, far more influential and important as an identity marker than *fusha* standard Arabic. In fact, the levels of language between dialect and standard versions are merely different registers available to the speaker, either an orator, or an actor on stage, or on a gramophone recording. Vaudeville plays performed in Cairo in the early 1900s used all registers to underline different modes in the plot, between earnestness and respectability and comedy. Certain situations demanded serene *fusha* poetry, whereas others called for the immediacy of the jocular colloquial. The available scale of linguistic registers merely reflected the availability of identity markers between local pride and trans-local cultural allegiance to an Arab realm. To what extent one or the other took pride of place in a person's self-perception certainly depended on class adherence and was hardly ever exclusive.[51] Above all, it is significant that Arabic was and remains both the medium and the object of nationalist deliberation. In its different registers and its oral and written varieties it represents the cracks and fissures of high and low, pan- and local identities, while it remains the single most important unifying cultural brace in the Arab world.

It is yet another question if, and to what extent the popularity of nationalist politics and ideology, as well as popular culture in as much as it fomented national identity, yielded populist nationalist politics, or, in other words, how bourgeois elites interacted with or used the populace in the realm of national politics, and finally, how the populace defined an agenda of its own. Most of the time, these politics were an expression of the struggle over hegemony where changing elites in Arab societies were generally successful in establishing their control over the public sphere and the dominant nationalist narratives. It became, however, increasingly necessary for elites in the course of the twentieth century to use popular appeal, and consequently a populist agenda to build rapport with the emerging mass societies. In times of crisis, populism could also be a means in itself to challenge existing power structures. It is therefore wrong to postulate that the nationalist elites, including lower and upper levels of the bourgeoisie, merely impregnated an amorphous mass with the nationalist seed, as the conventional history-of-ideas and elite-politics approach to Arab nationalism would postulate. Instead, particular historical situations provided openings for grass-roots actors and bottom-up community organizers to develop distinctive forms of political action that were accompanied by the formation of entire subsets of stories and imagery to create loyalty and allegiance in a very circumstantial way and in varying registers of speech and language. Only in rare moments these anti-hegemonic forms of nationalism come to the fore. A primary example in the literature is the period of Arab rule in Syria after the breakdown of Ottoman rule in the wake of the defeat in World War I, the Egyptian revolution of 1919, the Iraqi Revolt in 1920 or the anarchy of the years and months leading up to the Egyptian revolution in 1952.[52] The culture of Tahrir Square in the 2011 Arab Revolutions probably constitutes the most recent example. But even if populist grass-roots movements triggered these events, later regimes were generally successful integrating them into their hegemonic narratives, as is evident in some of the examples below.

* * *

The following chapters highlight the variety and diversity of manifestations of nationalist culture along concrete case studies. They are informed to various degrees by the trends of Arab nationalism research outlined in this introduction, but they also add further dimensions. All chapters are self-contained, which means that they were not chosen to address any of the above topics specifically and exclusively. Instead, they constitute discrete narrative entities offering a range of perspectives on the question of to what extent Arab nationalism as a system of cultural references frames or is framed itself in the political sphere of Arab societies of the twentieth century, either within discrete local frameworks or in transgression of localities. The chapters address issues of the national, regional and transnational formulation and dissemination of nationalist narratives – in other words, the politics of these narratives. They also address the struggle for control over who gets to define cultural hegemony, and the interaction between ruling elites, aspiring elites and the populace in the public realm.

The first chapter introduces biography as a narrative device to illustrate how life stories and nationalist myth-making intersect. The trials and tribulations of the nationalist poet Fu'ad al-Khatib provide a vehicle to set the stage for the rest of the book in as much as they embody central elements of the historiography of Arab nationalism.

Throughout the book, zooming in on individuals will be a recurring method to illustrate broader trends in Arab nationalism and its cultural manifestations. Case studies will place such trends firmly in thematic, local, and conceptual contexts that highlight distinct aspects of the culture of Arab nationalism. The first set (Chapters 3 to 5) in the sequence of studies is driven by questions about geographies and spatial boundaries. Chapter 3 covers the entire Arab cultural realm in the context of literary imagination and collective historical memory. The case study looks at literature and poetry and the way they act as loci for the creation of national myths, realms of memory, and collective identity. The cases under review are the evolution of Salah al-Din, or Saladin, as a Great Man of the Arabs, and Islamic Spain or *al-Andalus* as a mythical location in pan-Arab historical consciousness. The second case study (Chapter 4) focuses on the gelling of historical identity within the borders of clearly defined political boundaries, between Arabness and peculiar national identity: "Of Kings and Cavemen" presents museums and memorials as institutions that anchor nationalist narratives in the public sphere of societies. The focus is on the history of the creation of the Museum of Egyptian Civilization in Cairo around the period of World War II. "Damascus Transfers" (Chapter 5) focuses on exchange and competition between several Arab political state entities and their respective politico-historical legacy. It looks at festival and performance as aspects of the public representation of nationalism and how it could be undermined, choosing state funerals for close inquiry. Not only burials, but also the movement of bodies and re-burials play a central role in examples that involve Iraq, Syria, and Algeria.

The second set of studies (Chapters 6 and 7) leaves the realm of spatial identification and moves to representations of institution and ideology within specific and prominent sub-topics of Arab nationalism research. "Nearly Victorious" (Chapter 6) covers the material culture of Arab militarism and presents the institutionalized commemoration of the armies of Egypt and Syria in military museums and war Panoramas. Last but not least, Chapter 7 returns to ideology, not as an inquiry into the genealogy of ideas, the consistency of thought, or the practical implications of concepts and policies or their failure. Rather, the case study inquires how Arabs received fascism and Nazism, related to them, or used them to develop political and societal epistemologies vis-à-vis two lead ideologies of the twentieth century that stand for its moral cataclysm. As such, fascism and Nazism are cultural benchmarks in the Arab world as much as in the West. They gain shape, however, in the broader discursive context of the atrocities of World War II, Arab perceptions of the Holocaust, and the creation of the State of Israel, which is why the chapter locates them within the topical complex of the relationship between Arabs and Jews.

Needless to say, this sample of issues and case studies is not exhaustive. It offers a framework for possible further inquiries. It shifts the focus from primary actors on the world stage to second row politicians and intellectuals whose fame hardly transgressed regional boundaries. The availability of sources for this book nevertheless commanded an approach that gave a great deal of weight to bourgeois perspectives. Where possible, this perspective has been questioned and mitigated. The challenge remains to continue to look for ways to give a voice to the previously unheard in the diverse public spheres and vibrant cultures of the Arab lands. Future studies will hopefully choose to integrate such margins and peripheries – both geographically and socially – in broad conceptual reassessments of Arab nationalism as a fragmentary and heterogeneous, but essential reference system that remains available to Arabs to explain the world.[53]

2 The trials and tribulations of the poet Fu'ad al-Khatib

A biographical essay on the origins of Arab nationalism

One way to understand the evolution of Arab nationalism in the twentieth century is to break it down through the prism of individual life stories. Nationalists endorse a collective national narrative, but each individual has to make sense of its stories and their interpretations as they are offered by teachers, writers, or in the media. In addition, the individual has to make sense of political, economic and violent shifts that challenge the hegemonic narrative. Hegemony is therefore never absolute, and always in competition with other forms of individual identity, such as gender, local and ethnic, familiar, and sexual identities. In contrast, a mere "history of ideas" of nationalism tries to find consistence and coherence, where there is, in fact, only incoherence and volatility as the individual strives to make sense of the world. The life stories of not so well-known personalities tell more about general patterns of perception and attempts at making sense of one's life therefore than the biographies of the truly exceptional and famous people, who have to worry about a public legacy. Biography is therefore a good way to tell the story of Arab nationalism in this book, not as the emergence, success and failure of a political ideology, but as a story of high hopes and deep disappointments, and of shared experiences and common practice.[1]

This chapter's exploration of the origins and evolution of Arab nationalism uses the life story of Fu'ad al-Khatib (1880–1957), a poet, revolutionary, politician, diplomat, and a very stubborn man, to highlight some of the breaks and fissures of Arab society and its political culture in the first half of the twentieth century. Fu'ad al-Khatib moved in a nationalist universe that was only gaining shape in the years around World War I. The war functioned like an hourglass, releasing the pressure of a variety of cultural and political forces that had been clogging up before 1914, but were now set free in a confused and still amorphous fashion.[2] During this time, an Arab activist could still be a universalist: a politician, a teacher and intellectual, a civil servant, and an acclaimed poet at the same time. That was before a class of functionaries, professional demagogues, and military men started to dominate nationalist politics in the Arab lands in the 1930s, and before this class took control of the Arab states in the post-World War II revolutions. Fu'ad al-Khatib, who came of age just before the collapse of the Ottoman Empire, was just such a man, one who witnessed and commented on the transformations that were going on at the time. He was also a tragic figure. His career as an Arab nationalist was a failure because he remained a cultural nationalist throughout his life; he did not join a party or did not align with any of the professional groups that came to dominate the public sphere in the emerging Arab nation states. Al-Khatib refused to accept the political realities of state formation in the Middle East and remained a romantic adherent of a pan-Arab idea, while his generational fellows used the opportunities that the new postwar state system offered to claim their slices of the cake. His was the wrong cultural capital: He was neither an officer of the Arab Revolt, like the powerful Sherifian Officers who had fought with Prince Faysal, and who al-Khatib all knew personally, nor was he an acclaimed urban notable, like the Damascene bourgeois elite, the members of the Egyptian Wafd party, or the likes of Rashid 'Ali al-Kailani in Iraq, who belonged to an urban aristocracy of inherited religious authority. Nor was he young enough to become an extremist ideologue like the *Young Effendiyya* intellectuals who started to challenge the old generation of nationalists in the 1930s and laid the foundations for nationalist or socialist activism ushering in the post-World War II revolutions. Nor was he able to preserve his fame as a nationalist poet beyond the interwar period. He spent his last years as ambassador for Saudi Arabia in Afghanistan, and when he died and his body was transferred back to his birth country, Lebanon, few seem to have taken notice.[3]

Certainly, al-Khatib's recollections, and the selective presentation of documents and quotes in the biography that his own daughter Ihsan published, offer only a limited perspective on his life.[4] Other than that, there is but scant information about him in archival collections and memoirs. Al-Khatib's poetry survives in a *Diwan* edited by his son, and in a recent edition of the poetry he wrote during the time of the Arab Revolt, published in Jordan to commemorate the heroism of the Hashemite dynasty.[5] The anecdotal structure of the biography reflects Ihsan al-Khatib's personal memory and the conversations she had with relatives. In addition, the account rests on Fu'ad al-Khatib's poetic work and its evolution over time. Like many well-known Arabic poets, he rarely composed poetry as stand-alone pieces of art, but most often as commissions, or in reaction to events or experiences. There is, therefore, a quasi-autobiographical account in the chronological sequence of Fu'ad al-Khatib's *qasidas*. The biography remains a construct, though. Ihsan al-Khatib wrote and edited it decades after her father's death to create his image as the stubborn but steady and faithful man. In that, Fu'ad al-Khatib's poetry is a remarkable monument for the rise of a radical vision of Arab national identity among a rising generation of ethnically Arab intellectuals in confrontation with the competing imperial, Islamist, and ethnocentric narratives of the contested public spheres of the late Ottoman Empire and its successor states. Al-Khatib's biography thus becomes a focal lens for all major themes in the historiography of the emergence of Arab nationalism in quite a remarkable way, but this is certainly the image that the poet conveyed to his daughter, and the one that she tried to preserve as a family narrative. On the other hand, al-Khatib's contemporary poetry actually confirms that he belonged to an Arab nationalist vanguard during his youth. It is necessary, therefore, to analyze the biography and its material as part of the larger context of an Arab understanding of the history of Arab nationalism, within which the single narrative has to make sense.

Fu'ad al-Khatib was born into a rural notable family in the village of Shhim in the Lebanese Shuf mountains, south of Beirut. His grandfather, Shaykh Yusuf al-Khatib, was *qadi al-qudat*, chief judge, of Mount Lebanon. The family owned a document, a *firman* issued by the Ottoman Sultan, that recognized the family's service to the state. Shaykh Yusuf bought a house in the town of Bourj al-Barajneh (today a suburb of Beirut and location of a major Palestinian refugee camp) when his sons were drawn to Beirut for education because the city became a political and commercial hub for the prospering hinterland of Mount Lebanon after the establishment of the *mutasarrifiyya* government in 1861. Family life, though, continued to revolve around the Shhim property as Fu'ad's father Hassan became President of the District Court of Mount Lebanon, continuing the family tradition, but under modernized forms of Ottoman administration.[6]

A number of photographs in al-Khatib's biography give visual expression to the generational change that was going on in the poet's family between the late nineteenth and early twentieth centuries. The pictures, which are now apparently part of Ihsan al-Khatib's family archive, once adorned the Liwan, the representative reception area of Yusuf al-Khatib's house in Mount Lebanon.

The first (Figure 2.1) shows Shaykh Yusuf as a dignified old man, sitting on an elaborately carved wooden chair, with a white, well tended full beard, wearing a dark robe of glossy material over a white shirt, his left hand resting on a couple of books placed on a table covered with a dark cloth. The man in the picture is clearly aware of his position as a representative of an old order based on worldly and otherworldly powers, when he gazes at the beholder with a sharp and attentive, slightly distrustful look from his slim eyes set under a tall white forehead. The white *imama*, a turban wrapped around a *tarbush* hat, underlines his dignity, derived from Ottoman power as it was rooted in the sacred texts that his hand rests on. The other picture (Figure 2.2) belonged to Shaykh Hassan, the judge, and Fu'ad's father, eldest son of Shaykh Yusuf. The two photographs speak to each other in a conversation about subtle cultural transformations. Hassan had indeed inherited his father's dignity because he sat on the same chair, but the man with an enormous moustache wore a grey or light brown woolen suit instead of a robe. A clock chain, dangling from his waistcoat, indicated that its owner was in full control of his daily schedule. But the change of representation was not only in his attire, but also in the choice to include three of his children in the setting. Hassan's picture is different from his father's as it no longer frames the individual as the representative of an old and honorable institution – a backward connection to past and legacy. Rather than that, the family picture speaks to the future capacities of the lineage that Hassan as an individual had initiated, which is a radically different way of centering and justifying one's position in a much wider world, symbolized by European dress. In that regard, it is quite remarkable, too, that the children portrayed in the photography are not only Fu'ad al-Khatib's two brothers (the poet himself is not there) but also his sister in a shiny white dress.

Figure 2.1 Shaykh Yusuf al-Khatib, Fu'ad al-Khatib's grandfather.

The younger of the boys wears a suit with knickerbockers and a scarf decorated with flowers, the other, ca. 12-year-old boy's dress is an even less subtle reference to the fashions and obsessions of the day because he is depicted in military uniform. All three males wore a bare Tarbush on their heads, in stark contrast to Shaykh Yusuf's turban. Late Ottoman militarism and the desire to catch up with European power and culture were present in this image, but also a socio-political agenda that acquired increasing importance at the turn of the century. The paternalism that speaks out of the image reflected a re-fashioning of the public image of family relationships that had the nuclear family as the core of a healthy society and of masculinity at the center, and which became popular as an adoption from the nationalist bourgeois discourse of the European colonial powers, even in the representation of rulers such as Abdülhamit II in his aspirations to strengthen the idea of a pan-Islamic caliphate.[7]

Figure 2.2 Shaykh Hassan al-Khatib, Fu'ad al-Khatib's father, with three of his children.

Fu'ad al-Khatib lived in a period of even faster transformations than his fore-bears. Family bonds still determined his life when his father married him off to a cousin,[8] but he was also born into a generation of intellectuals in the Ottoman world, enjoying an education that opened a world of exchange across the traditional barriers of kin, locality and religious background. A revolution of learning took place in the Ottoman Empire in missionary schools and universities as in the Syrian Protestant College, later renamed American University of Beirut (AUB), and the Université St. Joseph, as well as in the Ottoman state schools, preparing the ground for various forms of political activism. It created a new middle class that combined commercial success with academic rigor to form self-confidence and class-consciousness, coming of age around and after World War I. Early scholarly works on Arab nationalism, such as George Antonius' foundational text *The Arab Awakening*,[9] gave a great deal of credit to apparent key institutions such as AUB in the dissemination of ideas of an Arab cultural revival at the turn of the century. It has become common sense among historians since that Ottoman state schools were equally important in the formation of a generation that was critical about Ottoman autocracy and developed a strong sensitivity for issues of ethnic privilege and prejudice in the empire. The majority of Ottoman subjects continued to look up to the caliphate as an embodiment of the necessary world order, however. Many of the old families of the Arab provincial cities had century-old arrangements with the Ottoman state that had kept them in powerful positions in their provinces. New forms of education, the bureaucratic overhaul of the Tanzimat era in the nineteenth century, and the autocratic rule of Abdül-hamit II did not change these power structures but simply meant that the lines of patronage came to be driven by new dynamics. The heads of notable households now started to send their sons to government schools to become administrators in the new bureaucracy that replaced mere succession along family lines in important provincial offices – old wine in new skins. In the context of the Young Turk revolution in 1908 and 1909, as well as the Young Turk coup d'état of 1913, conflicts arose between the families of the old order and the new Ottoman administration, because the prospect of parliamentary rule gave rise to new hopes and aspirations for greater autonomy among the representatives of local power in the Ottoman provinces – hopes that were often formulated in terms of Arab cultural distinctiveness, demands for decentralization and even in the language of ethnic confrontation between Arabs and Turks when the Young Turk administrators turned out to be quite authoritarian. A significant group among the Young Turks had in fact ethnic prejudices towards Arabs; at the same time, more and more literature of Islamic reform and about the renewal of the caliphate came out of Cairo under the umbrella of British colonial power and thus out of reach for the Ottoman censor. It had an undertone that gave Arabs preeminence in Islam as an ethnic group that had been suppressed supposedly for centuries under the Ottoman yoke. When the Ottoman Young Turks made efforts to break the power of local notable elites in the Arab provinces, replacing long-standing governors and people on tax farming positions with Young Turk newcomers or contenders from among the local families, to some, these actions smacked of "Turkification." After the confrontation had reached its height in the early 1910s, it ebbed down. The Young Turks were aware that they needed the loyalty of the Arab notability in the provinces, and the Arabs were aware that Ottoman rule and loyalty to the Ottoman state were guarantors of their positions, in the face of growing social unrest in the cities.[10]

Some young hot heads, as for example Fu'ad al-Khatib, were shaped by experiences that differed from those of the old urban elites in Ottoman Arab cities such as Damascus or Jerusalem. As students, they had their political coming of age moments at secondary schools and in universities where they joined secret societies for the furthering of Arab culture and self-determination. Hassan al-Khatib repeatedly tried to curb his son Fu'ad's political zeal, and even made his son's bride, his niece Munira, give two promises: She should convince him to stop smoking (chain smoking eventually killed him at the age of 77), and to give

up his Arabist politics, in order to keep him from ruining the very favorable relationship that the family had with the House of Osman. Fu'ad, an eccentric man
of slim stature, easily agitated but strong in his convictions, did not comply.[11]

Another group that developed extreme political convictions in the last years of
the Ottoman state were young army officers. In the long run they turned out to be
the more influential group. Their political radicalism stemmed from a high level
of frustration, which they built in the years preceding World War I. The officer
corps of the Ottoman army offered exceptional opportunities for social mobility.
Advancement through its ranks was merit based. Young boys from less well-
off neighborhoods of provincial cities such as Baghdad, or even from villages,
could profit from the expanding system of state education that could carry them
through primary and secondary schools to the provincial officer academies and
finally the Ottoman Staff College in Istanbul – a remarkable career, unheard of
only a generation earlier. The old families of the imperial cities endorsed civilian
state schools and administrative academies, but rejected military careers as un-
worthy. This way up was therefore open for the lower ranks of society. The sense
that the army was a merit-based institution, the experience of sky-rocketing
social mobility, the ethos of modernity in the military education, and consequently
the officers' self-esteem as a vanguard of new times came with high expectations and made the young men very sensitive to perceived injustice. In the period
leading up to the Young Turk revolution of 1908, the dwindling state budget led
to a situation where disgruntled officers, who had not been paid adequately, rose
up against Sultan Abdülhamit II, at first in the province of Macedonia where
the Ottoman army was deployed in humiliating campaigns against rebels. The
system of military advancement that was the Sultan's pride thus turned against
him. For Arab officers in the Ottoman army – among them many from the Iraqi
provinces – the discrepancy between their self-esteem on the one hand and the
lack of honorable engagement and waiting periods for promotion on the other,
gave rise to suspicions that Turkish soldiers were treated a lot more favorably
than they were. Resentment, combined with bonds of comradeship and contacts
with intellectuals of their own generation, motivated these soldiers to form their
own secret organizations. It is not clear to what extent the conspiratorial nature of these societies was actually taken seriously by Ottoman authorities, and
if the tales of persecution by the Ottoman state were to some extent a tool for
self-aggrandizement. Nevertheless, the young Arab officers built corps spirit that
formed the basis of networks, which later helped them form political elites in the
nascent nation states of the Middle East where some of these young soldiers took
the opportunity to claim a political role.[12]

In contrast to these military men, Fu'ad al-Khatib belonged to a civilian world.
When he entered the Syrian Protestant College in 1904, he found an institution
that offered exceptional leeway of political opinion and freedom of speech to its
members. An institution like the College indeed had the power to create networks
of radical and critical intellectuals who later on formed political parties, formulated ideologies and set the tone of nationalist literature with a remarkable longevity in the culture of nationalism in the Arab Middle East.[13] Take, for instance,

Fu'ad al-Khatib's career as a poet, who published his first articles and poems in the Beirut journal *al-Mufid*. Migration, then, turned al-Khatib into a pan-Arab poet. Due to differences with his father, who envisaged a medical career for his son and feared that his strong pro-Arab and anti-Ottoman convictions threatened his well-being, Fu'ad moved in with family members in Jaffa where he took up a teaching position at the Orthodox College and used his time to immerse himself in the intellectual and literary journals coming out of Cairo. Cairo was, at the time, the capital of an Arab *Republic of Letters*, where Egyptian authors and publishers mingled with Syrian and Lebanese colleagues who had escaped the restrictive press politics of the Hamidian regime in their places of origin. Their journals and books were read throughout the Arabic-speaking world. It was only natural then that Fu'ad al-Khatib followed his calling and set up residence in the Egyptian capital, which happened around the time of the Young Turk revolution. His biographer tells that once there, he submitted a poem to the renowned paper *al-Muqattam*, hoping that its editor Faris Nimr, one of the Syrian exiles, would publish it.[14]

The story that unfolded around the eventual publication of this poem, as Fu'ad al-Khatib told it to his daughter, puts his coming of age as a nationalist poet squarely into the context of debates about reconciliation between Arabs and Ottoman Turks in the immediate pre-World War I period. Al-Khatib performs in this story as one of the few steadfast Arabists maintaining a position of cultural confrontation. In his poem "Alam al-'Arab wa-amaluhum" ("Pains of the Arabs and their Hopes") al-Khatib put himself into the position of a caller who reminded the Arabs of their position in history. He spoke of the surprise about the awakening of the Arabs among the peoples of the East, and the concern it evoked in the Western world. In the past, fate had favored the Turks for some time, but now it reached out to the Arabs, who, however, were hardly ready to accept this positive development:

> What does one seek from a nation that, when it pronounced – the *dad* it said again and again that we are strangers [in the land]
>
> First Arabia has to be made strong – that object of desire, because there is glory and pride.[15]

The complex verses of the poem – stylistically, al-Khatib was rather a neoclassicist than a modernist[16] – lament the alienation of the Arabs from their roots, which al-Khatib located in the Arabian Peninsula where *those who pronounce the dad* resided. The *dad* is a letter of the Arabic alphabet that stands for a sound, which Arabs claim that only they pronounce. No wonder, al-Khatib seemed to say, that they felt estranged as long as they did not consider their roots. He probably pictured himself as a pre-Islamic, Jahili poet preserving the purity of the Arabic language to prepare it for the coming of Islam, which then would spread Arabic together with the religion throughout the continents like a force of nature. He evoked this image of the pre-Islamic and early Islamic period in an essay that came out around the same time. The Arabs had been weak and confused before the coming of Islam, he wrote, and careless about their language, spoiling it with incorrect and rough pronunciations. Only the regular fairs and markets were an occasion to practice and compete over the purity of the language, al-Khatib asserted. The coming of Islam, and the sending down of the purest of languages in the Qur'an, were therefore, in al-Khatib's reasoning, a taming of the Arabs through the taming of their language in a unified society. For al-Khatib, unification and purification had therefore been a condition for the spread of Islam and the Arabic language throughout the world, but emanating only from the purest Arabs.[17]

Al-Khatib did not promote a chauvinistic ethnocentric nationalism, however. In "Alam al-'Arab ...," he confirmed that the Arabs had welcomed the rule of the House of Osman initially, but he bemoaned that the Turks no longer did justice to them: "You [Arabs]: there is no fatherland among the Turks – for you, but still they are the lords of the land ..."[18] In a different poem, he opposed what he perceived as Turkification policy, but called for a brotherhood between Arabs and Turks instead.[19] Yet another poem, which had come out a little over three months before "Alam al-'Arab ..." in the Egyptian daily *al-Ahram*, expressed worries about frictions between ethnicities in the empire, but confirmed the strong links between them.[20] But these were reluctant affirmations, and al-Khatib had a hard time then finding a publisher for "Alam al-'Arab ..." Faris Nimr made clear that he ran a line of Ottoman patriotism in the wake of the revolutionary events in Istanbul; a ban on his journal in the Ottoman lands had just been lifted. Nimr told al-Khatib – as a fellow Lebanese countryman – that all this talk about Arabism was a confused fantasy.[21]

Finally, it was again the editor of *al-Ahram*, who agreed to a publication of the poem, but he inserted a commentary on the poem underlining that he disowned standpoints that could be read as defamations of Ottoman patriotism: He replaced the original headline with the words "Nafthat masdur." "Naftha" means literally "expectoration," and metaphorically the release of something that weighs heavy on one's mind, or of an accusation. "Naftha" is also used as an expression for a poet's works – the things he 'coughs up.' For "masdur," the dictionary gives "tubercular" as a possible translation.[22] But to the editor's surprise, and in spite of the disparaging headline, the poem was enthusiastically received and the highly respected and widely read *al-Mu'ayyad* magazine re-published a few lines, praising the author as an authentic Arab voice of the zealous youth. The commentator was concerned, though, that poems such as this were a sign for the loosening bonds between Arabs and Turks, on which the caliphate depended. In any case, the small uproar guaranteed Fu'ad al-Khatib access to Egypt's literary community as an aspiring and promising young poet.[23]

This coming of age story of a nationalist poet plays a key role in Fu'ad al-Khatib's biography, foreshadowing his participation in the Arab Revolt. There is context, however, that sheds a slightly different light on it and goes a long way to illustrate the truncations and manipulations of biographical writing. It is significant that Ihsan Fu'ad al-Khatib neither mentioned the first *al-Ahram* poem in the biography, nor the replacement of the headline of "Alam al-'Arab ..." Both were elements that added ambivalence to the story of Fu'ad al-Khatib's stance and standing in the circles in which he moved in Cairo at the time.

Fu'ad al-Khatib had to leave Egypt in order to find employment, shortly after publishing the first part of a collection of his poetry, a *Diwan*, in 1910. By consequence, he also expanded his nationalist itinerary, because he took up a teaching position at Gordon College in Khartoum in the Sudan. Founded in 1902, Gordon College was a colonial school the British used to shape a class of modern, well-educated functionaries to run the state under the British tutelage of the Anglo-Egyptian Condominium. Education, however, had the unintended side effect of producing a Young Effendiyya class in the Sudan that combined its elitist self-perception with nationalist demands. On top of that, enrollment at the college privileged the Arab population of the North Sudan at the expense of other ethnic groups. The College became a hotbed of nationalist activity in the interwar period, and many of its graduates ended up in leading positions in the post-World War II independent state. To hire a Syro-Lebanese teacher residing in Cairo for the teaching of Arabic and literature was therefore clearly a statement in favor of a pan-Arab vision of the cultural orientation of the Sudanese state.[24]

Fu'ad al-Khatib married during his stint in Khartoum and had a son. His wife opted to return to Lebanon for the birth of their second child, Fu'ad's later biographer Ihsan. The father followed shortly afterwards to see his newly born daughter, but also, as the biography insinuates, to feel out the extent of reconciliation that had happened between Arab activists and the Ottoman government. In the immediate years before World War I, Young Turk CUP government (Committee of Union and Progress) was looking for peace in the provinces and tolerated Arabist political activities asking for greater autonomy. Al-Khatib hoped to revive contacts of his student days, and had ample opportunity to do so because he had already made a name for himself as a nationalist poet and arrived in Beirut to an enthusiastic reception. War broke out in the meantime, though, and the Ottoman leadership turned wary of Arabist political activities again after initial Ottoman military success gave way to devastating defeats and loss of territory in Iraq and Palestine, which made the Ottoman leadership shift to a paranoid policy of oppression against the Arab population of Greater Syria, fearing subversive fifth column activities. The ensuing Ottoman war atrocities have gained an important place in the historiography of Arab nationalism, as well as in public memory of the war years in the Levante. The execution of Arab activists in Beirut and Damascus in 1915 and 1916, who were falsely accused of sedition, and the deportation of notable families of the major Syrian cities play a central role. Both events sent shock waves through the region because they affected members of some of the most prominent families of the Arab metropoles. In the wake of these developments, al-Khatib received a warning from a paternal cousin, who was a member of the Ottoman army stationed near his family home. The cousin advised Fu'ad to flee because his name had apparently come up on a blacklist of members of Arab secret societies, who were singled out for detention, if not summary execution. Al-Khatib left for Cairo immediately, and was therefore spared the fate of some of his friends in the nationalist societies who ended up on the gallows of Beirut and Damascus.[25]

Thus, the al-Khatib family story fit perfectly into the grand narrative of the rise of Arab nationalism. When Fu'ad al-Khatib left his wife and children in Mount Lebanon to escape persecution, he decided against continuing from Cairo to Khartoum, but instead joined Sharif Husayn and his Arab Revolt against the Ottoman Empire in the Hejaz. His family, however, was under threat of being deported by the Ottoman military authorities. Luckily, Fu'ad al-Khatib's service to Husayn in Mecca put him in a position to alleviate this danger. He was able to use Turkish hostages who had been captured at the beginning of the Revolt as leverage to guarantee that his family would remain untouched.[26] Notwithstanding the veracity or legendary nature of this account, it provides an important legitimating element in Fu'ad al-Khatib's biography, linking him to the martyrs of Beirut and Damascus, and the deportations. Even if the poet and his family were not affected by the atrocities themselves, it was important for the biographer to emphasize that the threat was constantly looming, in order to claim a small part in the general nationalist mythology of Arab nationalism.

Al-Khatib claimed, too, that he was the first Arab from outside the Hejaz to join the Arab Revolt. The biography does not offer any particular reasons for the step, so the reader is left to assume that it was due to his fervent nationalist convictions combined with the experiences in Mount Lebanon. At least, Fu'ad's decision to join predated that of many officers who would later fight alongside Prince Faysal, Husayn's son and military commander. For some, service to the revolt was the better option than a lengthy period as prisoners of war after their capture by the British. Some other Arab Ottoman war heroes, who went on to become influential Arab personalities after the war, remained loyal to the Empire until and even beyond its surrender in 1918. Meanwhile, Khatib developed a close rapport with the Sherif of Mecca and started to beat the drum of his fame in prose and poetry, taking over editorship of his newspaper *al-Qibla*. After the war, he became Husayn's Foreign Minister in the government of the Hejaz. Most of all, he became known as the "Poet of the Great Arab Revolt" whose poems were recited by school children throughout the Arab East.[27]

In other words, al-Khatib was Husayn's chief propagandist. His articles and poems of the time are full of praise for the Sharif – "[o]h son of the Prophet, you are today his heir" – and of incitement of "the Arabs" against "the Turks" – the "sons of Genghis [Khan]" – to fight them in the name of Islam.[28] Sharif Husayn's rebellion has remained the founding myth of Arab nationalism, standing for Arab revolutionary spirit and resilience against the Ottoman enemy, and representing – according to the mythology shaped during the *nahda*, the Arab literary renaissance period of the nineteenth and early twentieth centuries – the final wake-up call to the Arabs to throw off the Turkish yoke. Aside from the questions raised in the literature about the actual existence of an Arab-Turkish antagonism prior to World War I, the historical record does not support the image of Sharif Husayn as a nationalist leader rising up against his overlords for the sake of the Arab nation, either. Rather, Husayn started as a local leader who vied to turn his position as an Ottoman deputy in Mecca into a dynastic form of rule, antagonizing the Young Turk rulers in Istanbul who promoted an agenda of stronger centralization of the

Empire instead. World War I helped him to turn this aspiration into a broader regional power grab, and hotheads like al-Khatib facilitated the re-interpretation in the light of nationalist aspirations.[29]

Fu'ad al-Khatib fed on the credentials gained in the entourage of Sharif Husayn for the rest of his life, too. The time with the Arab Revolt was the core element of his nationalist life, and the foundation of his modest nationalist fame. It is no surprise that his family preserved stories, retold by the poet's daughter in the biography, emphasizing, probably even inflating, his influence on the Arab nationalist project. One story goes that one day during the days of the Arab Revolt, a representative of the Allied powers suggested to Sharif Husayn to flag the Arab boats leaving the coast for the Red Sea in order to distinguish them from Turkish vessels. When Husayn and al-Khatib discussed possible colors and shapes for this banner, the latter had a recollection of a reunion with nationalist friends in Beirut where they conferred about a flag to represent Arabism. Al-Khatib brought up the historical banners of grand Arab states: White for the Umayyads, black for the Abbasids, Green for the Fatimids. So why not compose the Arab flag from these colors, he suggested. The Sharif endorsed the idea, but added the color of the banner of the Quraysh, the lords of Mecca, based on the crimson color of the *'unnab*, or jujube fruit. The Arab flag then rose in white, black and green stripes combined with a red triangle, as a symbol that linked the present to a glorious past. Regardless of the veracity of this or other stories about the origins of the Arab flag, it remains one of the lasting symbols of Arab nationalism, a symbol of Arab unity because the colors and shapes persist until today, in various versions, in the national flags of Iraq, Syria, Jordan, the United Arab Emirates, Yemen, Sudan, Egypt, and post-Gaddafi Libya. The Palestinian Authority uses the original version, and even Polisario, the Western Sahara independence movement, puts the colors on its banner claiming sovereignty for the Sahrawi Arab Democratic Republic, and its independence from the Kingdom of Morocco.[30]

As much as the Arab Revolt created an inseparable link between Arab nationalism and the Hashemites, it was also the beginning of a lasting relationship between the family and Fu'ad al-Khatib, and on the long run between his family and Arabia. As a diplomat and senior political adviser, Fu'ad al-Khatib served Sharif Husayn himself, represented the government of the Hejaz in Damascus during Prince, later King, Faysal's rule over Syria, until al-Khatib left in the wake of the battle of Maysalun. He was again at the side of Sharif Husayn's oldest son 'Ali during his reign over the Kingdom of the Hejaz, and then of his younger brother, the Amir 'Abdallah of Transjordan, who would later become the first King of Jordan. He was also a friend of King Ghazi of Iraq because he had been his English teacher in the Hejaz. After he fell out with the Hashemites, King Ibn Sa'ud of Saudi Arabia remembered al-Khatib as a loyal spokesman of the Arab cause and honored him after World War II with a post as the first Ambassador of the Kingdom in Afghanistan, which is where Fu'ad al-Khatib died in 1957.[31]

It is hard to avoid the impression that al-Khatib's commitment to the Arab nationalist cause turned him into an uprooted man. He spent only limited periods of time in his home country Lebanon – usually when he had to gather his thoughts and strength in order to embark on a new political project, or after one of his frequent breaks with a political mentor, writing a great deal of poetry along the way. The periods when he pursued a political agenda were spent in countries other than his own, such as his early literary endeavors in Cairo, his appointment at Gordon College in Khartoum, where he helped instill young Sudanese Arabs with a sense of nationalist distinction; or during his service to the Arab Revolt and the Hashemite family in the Hejaz and Jordan, and later in his waning years in Afghanistan where he functioned as the grey eminence of Arabism among the diplomatic expatriate community. His life therefore went by as sort of an anti-career of Arab nationalism, where he lived the ideals of the pan-Arab Republic of Letters as a nationalist poet, and spent his efforts in the service of leaders, who embodied the pan-Arab cause for him. He also experienced many of the key events in the political history of Arab nationalism either firsthand or indirectly because he was familiar, or even friends, with their key actors. But he was barred from a real career such as that of the Arab nationalist Sharifian officers of Iraq, who abused their positions of power under the protection of King Faysal, and built an economic and socio-political powerbase through legislative and executive moves, land acquisition, and intermarriage with local elite families. Nor did he participate in the efforts of the Syrian and Lebanese urban and rural notability to perpetuate their control over patron client networks on their home turf in Damascus, Beirut, or Mount Lebanon and the Shouf Mountains, who turned from local Ottoman elites into bourgeois nationalists, using nationalist rhetoric, or the nationalist credentials they earned during World War I, to conceal their group interests. One might say that he did not understand the writing on the wall. According to the interpretation of his biographer, his sticking to the cause was in line with his character, because he was a stubborn, at times choleric, but fiercely loyal man, who was also easily offended. In the same vein, his shift to King Ibn Sa'ud, the arch enemy of the Hashemites, who had kicked King 'Ali Ibn Husayn from the thrown of the Hejaz, was due to his frustration about the performance of Sharif Husayn's family in the period between the World Wars. It seems that he acquiesced to this frustration and made peace during his time in Kabul before his death. The image of Fu'ad al-Khatib as a slightly tragic figure – moving from great expectations to dignified disappointment, seeking solace in neoclassical poetry – thus sets the stage for the following chapter on Arab nationalism as a culture of nostalgia.

3 Holding up the mirror

Imperialism and the poetics of cultural pan-Arabism

This chapter introduces literary topoi as points of reference in Arab nationalism and investigates their function in the process of building a manifest identity. The first example is the topos of the Great Man, embodied by the medieval Sultan and Muslim knight Salah al-Din al-Ayyubi, better known in the Western hemisphere as Saladin. A second, more elaborate, analysis covers the emergence and evolution of a multifaceted topos – al-Andalus, or medieval Muslim Spain – throughout the late nineteenth and twentieth centuries.

3.1 Saladin the Victor

National Saints, *Great Men*, and the rise of the individual[1]

The topos of the *Great Man* was initially a European concept of the Enlightenment. Instead of religious saints whose lives bore witness to direct divine intercession in the world and thus pointed to the hereafter, nationalism discovered earthly, secular superhuman beings, whose unique contribution to the glory and benefit of the nation was due to superior individual skills and authority. The transcendent presentness of the saint gave way to the historicist absence of the venerated dead who were brought to life in nationalist mythology. The life of a saint of the church provided an example that was not bound to a specific place in time. Great Men of the nation, however, were considered exclusive property of the community, marking its position in historical time. Great were only *men* because nationalism tended to relegate women largely to a passive nurturing role in society. A female realm of sainthood and veneration was lost to the masculine ideal of energetic activism and force. The Great Man was a product of historicism and its teleological view that the world was moving on a trajectory towards betterment, and the logic of this movement could only be grasped through history. There was a logic, a plan, divine or other, and Great Men had the capacity to shape and influence it. They merited veneration and commemoration in anniversaries, the naming of streets, the erection of monuments, or in plays and novels.

The Great Man entered the secular discourse of the Arab cultural revival movement *al-nahda* ("awakening") in the late nineteenth and early twentieth century through intellectual journals. Publicists such as Jurji Zaydan and Farah Antun were looking for the Great Men of the Arabs who had propelled Arab civilization to unprecedented heights. Arabic literature and popular culture started to use historical figures in increasing numbers with many of them largely unknown to an Arab public prior to 1900.[2] The literary foundations of this myth may have been in the *nahda* intellectuals' readings of such European works as Thomas Carlyle's 1846 work *On Heroes, Hero-worship and the Heroic in History*,[3] but it is also arguable that this *culte laïc*[4] was a response to the refutation of the traditional Islamic cult of saints by Islamic reformers and secularizing elites in the creation of a *civil religion* of nationalism.[5]

The assumption that history can be *made* is conditional for a history of Great Men. Observers of the French Revolution were the first to develop the notion that they were "witnessing history." A century earlier this statement would have seemed absurd when history was considered merely a set of lessons from the past. The experience of the changing pace of historical time, of being immersed in an accelerating current of uncontrollable events and transformations, was a foundational experience for people in the nineteenth and early twentieth centuries that pointed to the individualization of men because of the dissolution of inherited patterns of orientation, and the ensuing helplessness of the individual in emerging mass societies.[6] According to the Islamic Enlightenment paradigm, neo-imperialism and the expansion of the world market spread these trends across the globe in the course of the nineteenth century, where they coincided with and fired up parallel worldwide intellectual developments. There, as much as in Europe, new models of reasoning created an epistemological shift that put the individual into a radically different environment of self-location than was ever before experienced: Man was called upon rather to make history than simply abide by the course of nature; tradition did not provide a blueprint for the solution of present problems. History, however, offered material for stories that could be told and re-told time and again to help man to reflect on the present.

* * *

Saladin – in Arabic, Salah al-Din – is one of the central heroes of Arab history, with particular relevance in the countries of the Fertile Crescent.[7] There is an entire map of commemorative places stretching from the Cairo citadel, which is named after its founder Saladin, to an entire province in Iraq that bears his name because its capital, the town of Tikrit, is the Great Man's birth place. In 1991, the Syrian propaganda apparatus issued a poster that showed a painting of charging horsemen, juxtaposed with a photo of President Hafiz al-Assad, under the headline "Min Hittin ila Tishrin" ("From Hittin to Tishrin") drawing a line from Saladin's epic victory at Hittin (today in Israel) over the Crusaders in 1187 to the October (Arabic: Tishrin) War in 1973.[8] The hero's appropriation by the Syrian regime to propagate its struggle against Israel could hardly be clearer, although it is an open question to what extent the Syrian public was ready to lift Hafiz al-Assad, the aging dictator, to the level of the medieval knight and Sultan, whose larger-than-life bronze statue has become a landmark in Damascus' city center. On horseback, surrounded by some of his warriors triumphing over crusader leaders at their feet, he has adorned the entrance to Saladin's citadel, adjacent to the Suq al-Hamidiyye, since 1994.

Saladin's historical record, and his place in Arab historical consciousness as a Great Man, is more ambivalent and complex, though, than the rather crude instrumentalization in Syrian state official propaganda suggests. A case in point is the Saladin Mausoleum outside the walls of Damascus' Umayyad Mosque. Before the outbreak of the Syrian civil war in 2011, the vicinity to the grandiose monument of Arab-Muslim civilization used to put Saladin's grave on the itineraries of streams of visitors every year. The domed mausoleum is the only intact reminder of the medieval Madrasa al-'Aziziyya – one of the countless former religious academies in the city. Today, the tomb is a crossing point of several complementary visions of Saladin at the intersection of European and Middle Eastern nationalist narratives that underline the intricacies of public memory and ownership over heritage. The mausoleum contains two sarcophagi, the wooden Ayyubid original, and another one – a cenotaph – in Ottoman Rococo style that Abdülhamit II commissioned in 1878. In 1900, a gold-plated laurel was placed near Saladin's feet, commemorating that the German Emperor Wilhelm II had paid homage there during his visit to the Ottoman Empire in 1898. While in Damascus, Wilhelm made a fateful proclamation that he was the friend of all Muslims, endorsing Abdülhamit II's pan-Islamic claim. His words added a heavy symbolic weight to an alliance that led to the Ottoman Empire's entry into World War I at Germany's side in 1914, and eventually to the demise of Osman's dynasty. In 1915, a pendant copper lamp was placed above the Ottoman ceno-taph bearing the Kaiser's monogram and Sultan Mehmed V's seal, confirming the "brotherhood in arms." Wilhelm believed in his succession to the medi-eval German emperors, and hence the place embodied the mythical legacy of a chivalric and mutually respectful encounter between Muslims and Christians during the crusades. When T.E. Lawrence entered Damascus alongside Prince Faysal's Arab army in 1918, he removed the gold-plated wreath and donated it as a war-trophy to the newly founded Imperial War Museum in London. Lawrence was not the only one to contest German claims on the crusader legacy, though, in the face of the actual, physical submission of the Holy Land to European control; as a realm of memory, the tomb represented imperial contention for the French General Gouraud, too, who entered Damascus in 1920 after the defeat of the Syrian Arab army at Maysalun that sealed the French conquest of the country. Gouraud is said to have addressed the Sultan and medieval opponent of the Franks at his grave, using the words: "We are back."[9]

Saladin was consequently not only a hero of particular national identification, but also a dialogical figure: Arabs have used him since the late nineteenth century as a mirror to re- and deflect Orientalist stereotypes because he belonged to the repertory of European crusader mythology, too, representing Muslim chivalry. Already Abdülhamit II's commission of a renovation of the tomb and the place-ment of the new kenotaph in 1878 are evidence for the initiation of an Ottoman hero's cult, but only Wilhelm's homage to Saladin at his grave initiated a veritable revival of Arab remembrance of the Sultan and knight. Saladin did not play a dis-tinctive role in Arab or Ottoman literature until the second half of the nineteenth century. Neither were the Crusades a matter of great concern at the time. Even the term *al-hurub al-salibiyya* ("crusader wars" in Arabic) appeared in the mid-nineteenth century only when Christian translators of European historiography coined it. Namik Kemal, a leading Young Ottoman, published the first genuine Middle Eastern biography of Saladin in 1872 in Turkish in response to a Turkish translation of Joseph Francois Michaud's *Histoire des Croisades*. Kemal's work was a great success because it confirmed a rampant view that Europe's assault on the Ottoman Empire at the time was motivated by a general enmity towards Islam, allegedly just like during the Crusades. Sultan Abdülhamit II propagated this thesis in the pan-Islamic press. Wilhelm II's visit and his spontaneous remarks about Germany's friendship with the Muslims of the world offered an opportunity to Abdülhamit II and his contemporaries to fashion Saladin as a symbolic figure combining various strands of Muslim identity: the defender of the faith, the liberator of the Arab lands, and even Saladin as a Kurd – all images that had an impact on the Saladin reception for generations to come.[10]

Saladin's mausoleum is therefore not only a symbolic marker for the modern nationalist veneration of leadership and chivalry, but also a location of memory in a very concrete sense. The usage of the Mausoleum and its surroundings in the first decades of the twentieth century illustrates the transition from Ottomanism to Arab nationalism as lead ideologies and the handing down of a specific nationalist topos. Saladin had already been a Great Man and secular saint when the area next to the mausoleum became a small graveyard for *shuhada'* (martyrs) and thus a downscaled Panthéon.[11] Today, there is a line of five graves outside the Sultan's tomb. The grave closest to Saladin contains the remnants of Yasin al-Hashimi, a former Iraqi prime minister who died in 1937. The peculiar nature of his death and burial and their significance for pan-Arabism at the time will be the topic of a chapter below. The nationalist politician 'Abd al-Rahman al-Shahbandar was buried to al-Hashimi's right after his assassination in 1940. Shahbandar was a crucial figure of radical nationalism in interwar Syria, one of the political leaders of the Syrian uprising in the mid-twenties, and in banishment from Syria for most of the 1930s. Though never proven, there were rumors that the Syrian National Bloc party instigated his assassination. Its leaders belonged to the bourgeois elite nationalists that Shahbandar accused of collaboration with the French Mandate power.[12] Next to Shahbandar, to the far right, lie three Ottoman Turkish pilots, who died in a plane crash in March 1914. Their show flight from Istanbul to Cairo and Alexandria should have marked the entry of the Ottoman Empire and its army into the age of aviation, but it ended in disaster – almost a prophetic sign. One of the machines had a stop-over in Damascus to an enthusiastic reception. The death of three of the pilots who crashed in Palestine even made it to newspaper headlines in Egypt where people were in anticipation of their arrival. A successful completion of the show flight would have been a token for the unity of the Ottoman world, representing Ottoman command over the skies, and the capacities of the empire's technical vanguard to master its vast distances at breathtaking speed. The ultimate failure of the mission spoke a different language about Istanbul's true capacities, however.[13] Ahmad Shawqi (1868–1932) published a *marthiyya* or eulogic poem entitled "Fathi wa-Nuri" in reference to the first names of the pilots who had crashed near the Golan Heights. Shawqi, commonly known as the Egyptian "Prince of Poets," started as a panegyrist to the Egyptian ruling family and Ottoman patriot before World War I and later turned into an Arab nationalist poet.[14] From today's perspective the lines that Shawqi composed for the fliers sound like foreboding of the Empire's demise:

> [t]he lifespan of the eagles has become short – and this although they normally have a long lifespan / [...] / Ride the wings of the eagle, but do not feel

safe! – with him flutters Azrael / For every soul the hour is predestined, and who did not die – honorably in this hour, died in disgrace.

The image of the "eagle" is obviously a reference to the airplane and its pilots. It recurs several times throughout the poem, together with allusions to the sky as the martyrs' grave: "Who of the warriors who preceded you as martyrs – who of them had his grave in the firmament and lofty sky?"

The image works, however, in a different direction, too. A popular tradition in Cairo relates a huge stone relief of an eagle on the citadel to Saladin. The eagle, which is attached to a wall of the medieval structure facing west, probably dates to a later period than the Sultan's lifetime, though. It was probably moved to the current location during renovation work in the nineteenth century. This occasion, and its prominent position on the wall of Saladin's citadel may have given rise to the popular assumption that the eagle was the medieval Sultan's emblem. The "Eagle of Saladin" has since become a national symbol in Egypt, for instance as the official national emblem since 1958, adorning the national flag since 1974.[15] Shawqi's choice of the eagle metaphor in 1914 therefore alluded to the majesty of flight, but possibly also to the hero of the middle ages.[16]

Shawqi confirmed that Saladin was as much a favorite nostalgic reference to a better Islamic or Arab past for him as for many other poets[17] when he glorified the grave of the Ayyubid Sultan in the same poem as a mythical place giving shelter to the pilots:

> Damascus was in despair and its people – proceeded in sorrow with no words to describe / Grief walked with her and her gardens welted all out – between the brooks and the springs / In every plain there is groaning and wailing – on every rugged ground there is screaming and howling / As if all Umayyads announced the death – to the ruins of the Umayyad Mosque / [...] / The soldiers march with him [the deceased], but it is as if – in front, Gabriel marched with him, too / Until you [the pilots] come to lie in a place where there is the resting place – of someone who lied there before, and eminence is the occupant / The place is magnificent, but greater is the tomb of Yusuf above it – as if the dead man in it was a prophet.

For Shawqi, Damascus is an Elysium, receiving the fallen warriors. Their death even concerns the Umayyad Caliphs who personify the city's glorious past. Motifs of secular and religious sainthood fuse when Shawqi marks the burial place of the pilots as hallowed ground. Yusuf, which is Salah al-Din's birth name, lies in his grave like a prophet, and the presence of the arch angel Jibril (Jabra'il, Gabriel) in the funeral cortege is conspicuous because in Islamic tradition he is the "helper of the prophets," the conduit who brings the Qur'an to Muhammad. In the context of death, he also appears as the companion of the Prophet on his miraculous night journey and ascension to the heavens, which some Islamic traditions consider a symbol for the ascension of the dead soul to God for judgment.[18]

For Shawqi, Saladin was still a hero in a pan-Islamic universe, as the Saladin propaganda of the turn of the century suggested, even though his rather daring equation of Saladin with the Prophet already pointed to a secularization of the myth, which facilitated its nationalization. Almost 25 years later, the Baghdadi poet Kamal Ibrahim recalled an emotional visit to the grave of Yasin al-Hashimi, who had been buried next to Saladin's mausoleum a year earlier. In "A Flower Drifted over Yasin al-Hashimi's Grave," he interpreted the Iraqi Great Man's life as parallel to that of Saladin:

> With the humility of an adorer, in awe of death, and mournful contemplation / I stood between the tombs of two heroes: Yasin and Salah al-Din / Oh, what heroism, gathered in one place / [...] / In my imagination, alive is the one who is lowered into this grave, neighbor to Salah al-Din.[19]

The final stanza begins: "God's peace to you, oh audacious hero of Arabism / God's peace to you, oh burnished sword of Arabism." The "you" remains undefined, suggesting that in his imagination the author was so deeply touched by the presence of the two great dead men that they seemed to flow together into one heroic soul sacrificed for the sake of the Arab nation.

Saladin is also present in a different location that is exemplary for the religio-political set-up of the late Ottoman Empire and its ambiguity between local religious practice and the ideology of pan-Islam. The *mawsim* of Nabi Musa in Palestine is representative for the Ottoman state official appropriation of a local custom, which evolved into an enactment of Arab nationalist mythology during the twentieth century. Nabi Musa is a *maqam*, a saintly shrine a few miles east of Jerusalem, said to be the burial place of Moses. In the 1920s, Palestinian historians made efforts to date the foundation of the sanctuary back to Saladin in the twelfth century. Modern historians see the origins of the structure in the thirteenth century under the Mamluk Sultan Baybars only, however, and consider the Saladin chronology an invention. There is also no reliable evidence that the Ayyubid Sultan in fact established the shrine and the pilgrimage and festival around it, allegedly in order to strengthen the Muslim character of the Jerusalem region. Indeed, the *mawsim* celebration takes place each year in April, around Easter, giving rise to interpretations that the festival initially served to rally surrounding tribal communities to ready them for fending off Crusaders who were usually expected to arrive around that time. What is certain, however, is that the Ottoman government discovered the festival's potential in the late nineteenth century to display the regime's Islamic convictions against the infiltration of Western powers vying for influence in Jerusalem. The coincidence with the Easter celebrations helped to assert Islamic precedence in the Jerusalem region, and laid the foundations for the *mawsim*'s political character, which lasts until today. Photographic documentation between 1898 and 1917 documents the increasing presence of Ottoman military and Ottoman flags and emblems in the procession that led from Jerusalem's Damascus gate to the Nebi Musa shrine.[20]

When Ottoman rule vanished after World War I, the *mawsim* retained its bulwark symbolism of defense against foreign encroachment, but transitioned into the context of Arab nationalism. In the post-imperial world of more or less artificial nation states, Saladin took on a meaning as unifier of the scattered Arab lands (without reference to his Kurdish origin), just as he had unified the medieval Middle East against Christian rule. In the 1920s Saladin could be held up against British dominance and defiant Zionists in Palestine like a reflector of Western imperialism because he embodied all the civilized traits Western imperialists claimed for themselves, while the crusaders stood for all the greed and barbarity that Western Orientalism projected on the Arabs.[21] Consequently, Arab historians coined the term *isti'mar mubakkar* ("premature imperialism") for the Crusades.[22] The politically charged atmosphere of the festival triggered an early violent uprising of Arabs against Jews in Palestine in 1920 when the occurrence of the festival in the heated atmosphere of conflict around the future status of Palestine triggered an attack on Jews living in the old city of Jerusalem, which resulted in deaths and scores of injuries on both sides. The myth of Nebi Musa's origin thus took on a concrete nationalist meaning, and the chanting of Saladin's name in the procession became an act of militancy. The *mawsim* retained its dual character throughout the twentieth century, including the "folkloristic" elements of a *mawsim*, such as Sufi chanting, and the individual piety of a *ziyara* to a saint's tomb, as well as elements of a political rally even up until the 1990s when the name of Yassir Arafat was invoked next to that of Saladin as a liberator and a unifier.[23]

To add another dimension, there are also countless examples for a literary rendering of the Saladin myth in the twentieth century.[24] Arab authors of the *nahda* prepared the way for a twentieth-century Saladin revival when they participated in the invention of a tradition that presented Saladin as the vanguard of Arab liberation. Writers experimented with literary genres they found in European culture (novels, plays, essays), picked up European themes and filled them with Middle Eastern content, as in the case of Saladin – half-myth, half-historical figure – who they used as a mirror for European Orientalism. In nineteenth-century romantic literature such as Sir Walter Scott's *Talisman*, Saladin represented the opposite of the genre's stereotypes that viewed the Oriental as a lazy, cruel, and voluptuous squanderer.[25] Egyptian and Lebanese theater companies staged Saladin plays in the last quarter of the nineteenth century that were either translated from or based on works in European languages. An example is Nagib Sulaiman Haddad's *Riwayat Salah al-Din al-Ayyubi*. Haddad (1867–1899), a Maronite Christian residing in Egypt, was an influential translator of European drama. His *Salah al-Din*, first staged in Alexandria in 1895 and printed in 1898, may have been "inspired" by Scott's *Talisman*, but it is not a mere translation.[26] Even a cursory reading of both works reveals that the Egyptian author merely used themes from Scott's book, most importantly the topos of the immediate interaction between Salah al-Din and Richard the Lionheart, but constructed a new storyline to develop a new piece of art in elaborate Arabic prose and verse. In that, he and many other Arab writers did not differ from European playwrights who borrowed from

Greek tragedy to express the concerns of current days. Al-Haddad adopted some of the characters of Scott's play, but gave different names to some central figures. Some of the central elements of the plot in Scott's novel recur in Haddad, such as the motif that Saladin cured Richard the Lionheart from a disease as a doctor in disguise, but while he followed the basic narrative line, he changed the perspective awarding Saladin the central position from the beginning of the play, giving him most of the play's talking time in monologues and conversations with his friend 'Imad al-Din, who is not part of Scott's set of characters at all.[27] In Haddad, Saladin explains the inner motives of his actions, while Scott had rendered him a noble, but enigmatic figure. Instead of emulating Scott's novel, Haddad re-purposed it to appeal to pan-Islamic (and eventually Arab) pride. As a work of nascent English nationalism Scott's novel singles out King Richard as the prominent leader of the Crusade who prevails over his French and Austrian competitors. In Haddad, Saladin outwits them all. The trajectories of the narrative strategies in both works are therefore diametrically opposed.

When authors like Haddad and Shawqi discovered Saladin in the late nineteenth century, they were looking for a role model in the confrontation with European imperialist expansion and Western Orientalist arrogance. Earlier literary commemoration of the Crusades in the Arab world had had a different focus, such as for instance on Sultan Baibars I (1223–1277), who defeated King Louis the Saint in the seventh Crusade and played a central role in medieval Arabic folk tales.[28] Still in 1913, when the eminent historical novelist Jurji Zaydan wrote about Saladin, he did not emphasize his role as defender of the Muslim realm against the Crusades. Instead, he concentrated on his rise to power in Cairo and used only Muslim characters.[29]

Haddad's play focused on Saladin the reconciler between East and West, whereas Saladin's later role in the repertoire of Arab nationalist literature was a great deal more confrontational, as in the Battle of Hittin and the conquest of Jerusalem.[30] Farah Antun (1874–1922), an intellectual, journalist and author from Tripoli in today's Lebanon who resided in Cairo after 1897, brought out a play in 1914 entitled *Al-Sultan Salah al-Din wa-mamlakat Urushalim*, which covered Saladin's counter crusade between 1187 and 1189 and thus made Antun arguably the first to introduce Hittin and the re-conquest of Jerusalem as literary topoi in the Arab world.[31] The play had an impact both as a printed text and on stage in 1915 in Cairo, and in several other places in Syria and Palestine.[32] Like Shawqi, Farah Antun presented Saladin as a political hero, a liberator and a unifier under an Islamic (rather than an Arab) banner, but his work represents a shift towards a Middle Eastern Saladin reception that departed from the European enlightened and romanticizing Orientalist model towards an anti-imperialist discourse. Towards the end of the last scene, the Sultan exclaims: "Jerusalem ("Bayt al-Muqaddas") will remain ours forever, and our land will remain our land."[33] In an ambivalence that was typical for the late Ottoman Empire, Muslims (Shawqi) and Christians (Haddad, Zaydan, Antun) alike respected Saladin as a protector of the Islamic realm, belonging to which was an integral part of the various identity maps of late Ottoman citizens, regardless of their religious background.[34]

Antun, who was a staunch secularist, supported Ottomanism, but had misgivings about Abdülhamit II's pan-Islamic ideology because he feared that a promotion of Islamic piety alone might eventually undercut the unity of the Ottoman Empire. He also warned against separatist nationalist trends among the Arab citizens after the Young Turk revolution. Antun's intellectual biography is, however, an example for the malleability of late Arab-Ottoman identities. He observed the Young Turk coup from New York City where he had little success trying to build a career as an Arab exile publisher. After his return in 1909 he began to promote the characteristic prewar Egyptian nationalism.[35] Regardless of the motives that he and other authors entertained when they wrote Saladin into the canon of modern Arabic literature, the actions they described cover space between Cairo, Jerusalem, Northern Syria, and ultimately the tomb in Damascus. Saladin's liberation and unification of land therefore takes place on Arab territory. When Ottoman Muslims and Christians of Arab culture singled out Saladin as a role model, they created a potential that could be used at a later stage to turn this outstanding character into a unifying symbol of pan-Arab identity.

The reception of this literature went beyond mere elite circles. Theater in particular was a major means of political communication in the Arab world in the first half of the twentieth century. At the turn of the century, "Theater Fever" broke out in the Eastern Mediterranean countries, and in Beirut, Alexandria, and Cairo in particular.[36] Performances were often a spectacular mix: next to the play itself, there were musical performances, speeches, and poetry recitations. The audience reacted fiercely and emotionally, and sometimes even participated on stage. Translations and original plays abounded, as did the coverage of theater in the press. Newspapers and journals, new media of their own, played a central role in disseminating theater enthusiasm in the evolving public sphere of late Ottoman cities. In the early nineteenth century, reports of Middle Eastern travelers had first kindled interest in European-style modern theater – as opposed to the shadow plays of Middle Eastern popular culture or the reenactments of the Battle of Karbala as part of Shi'i Muharram rituals. Observers were fascinated by the possibilities for public commentary on social and political affairs that Western theater offered.[37]

In 1914, a play entitled *Salah al-Din Yusuf al-Ayyubi* was performed in Istanbul in Arabic on the occasion of the gathering of delegates for the Ottoman Parliament. Poets recited their works on the occasion, too, such as Faris al-Khuri, delegate for Damascus, and Shakib Arslan, delegate for the Hawran region south of Damascus. Poetry and theater were cultural performance as much as they were indeed vehicles to promote politics, but while the agents of culture were able to unite over matters of shared linguistic and historical heritage, their appearance on an Arabic stage in the Ottoman capital did not necessarily represent a political synthesis. The moment of Arab cultural representation in Istanbul in 1914 in fact reflected a compromise of Arab–Turkish cultural reconciliation that the Young Turk government was running before the outbreak of World War I, co-opting those who were willing to buy into an Ottoman centralized vision of the state while clamping down on those who were unwilling to comply. The synthesis lasted only for a short time. Arslan (1869–1946), for one, supported the pan-Islamic vision of a centralized Empire throughout the war as the CUP propagated it, whereas the Christian Faris al-Khuri (1877–1962) had to face allegations of subversive activities during Cemal Pasha's reign of terror in Damascus. After the war, he became a leading member of the bourgeois Arab nationalist Syrian National Bloc party, whereas Arslan remained true to the pan-Islamic Arab cultural nationalist hybrid that grew out of his Ottomanism, and that he cultivated during his self-imposed exile in Geneva, where he acted as the self-appointed representative of Arab-Muslim affairs to the League of Nations.[38]

There is no information whose play it was that was staged in Istanbul – maybe Haddad's *Salah al-Din* which had become one of the first literary success stories of the *nahda* period. Plays traveled from the Arab East to the Arab West together with the ensembles that put them on stage. Popular traveling theater companies had Haddad's piece in their repertoire, like Sulayman Qardahi's company, who was a Maronite from Alexandria and one of the crucial figures of early Arab theater. He introduced *Salah al-Din* on a tour of the Tunisian cities Sousse, Tunis and Sfax in 1908 and 1909, where he also staged Arabic translations of Shakespeare and other original Arabic plays. Theater was a popular, not an intellectual pastime during that period; Tunisian audiences could get quite rowdy, and plays received a lot of attention in the local press. The choice of plays therefore demanded a strong sense for the taste of broad sections of society. A healthy dose of musical theater was crucial for the success of a play like *Salah al-Din*, which remained part of the repertoire of Tunisian theater companies for years.[39]

The young Lebanese hothead Anis al-Nusuli was a theater enthusiast, too. Nusuli was a student at the American University of Beirut in the 1920s, a rising intellectual star, who would later gain some fame as the originator of the so-called *Nusuli Affair* and *Umayyad Riots* in Baghdad, which broke out in 1927 when Nusuli was a teacher in Iraq and published a book praising the Umayyads, which derided the Shi'i Imams in the eyes of Shi'i student protesters. In Lebanon, the Nusuli family was prominent in nationalist youth politics, including the formation of a Muslim Scout troop.[40] In the mid-1920s al-Nusuli published an article on modern theater in the Arab lands in an intellectual journal. He singled out Najib al-Haddad's work, still a quarter-century after his death, as a signpost in the development of taste among the "people of the nation," which speaks to the popularity and the impact of the author. As a young post-World War I Arab nationalist intellectual, Anis al-Nusuli could not help but criticize Haddad for his reliance on European translations. Had he focused more on models and stories from the East, his plays would have represented the "Arab psyche" ("al-nafsiyya al-'Arabiyya") and the "eastern mentality" ("al-'aqliyya al-sharqiyya") more accurately. Al-Nusuli argued for an Arab *littérature engagée* covering local and social affairs, rather than history. Theater, he argued, was best for the expression of emotions and for the imagination of the creative mind, but also to promote honor, patriotism (*wataniyya*), religion, and traditions – all values that human society esteemed most highly. Theater was social analysis for al-Nusuli; it should affect people in their lack of faith and their materialism and make them seek betterment for families, schools, religious denominations, in the workplace and the government.[41]

Al-Nusuli's mid-1920s article already displayed the typical authoritarian arrogance of interwar Arab nationalist intellectuals. Early Arabic theater had – in contrast – a subversive potential that was not so easily controlled. It provided space for interaction across communities of denomination or class, because amateurs could use it as much for self-expression as the trans-regional professional theater ensembles. The leftist inclinations of many Syrian theater activists (among them many secular Christians) had a great impact on the proliferation of leftist ideas in pre-World War I Egypt, for example. The theater as a public space empowered actors and audiences to enter into a subversive dialogue with a license to interpret, disassemble, add to, and improvise around the text. Unfortunately, the sources hardly provide information on the outcome of these processes, but the efforts that state authorities made to supervise and discipline theater audiences, or to censor plays, are testimony to the unruliness of audiences and actors alike.[42]

The effect of amateur theater is nicely displayed in a scene of Youssef Chahine's 1979 feature film *Alexandria ... Why?* Chahine (1926–2008), arguably the most important Egyptian, if not Arab, movie director of the twentieth century, used the scene to pay homage to the political meaning of drama bringing the stage and the screen together as two media that had had no equal during the first half of the twentieth century in their artistic immediacy. The autobiographical *Alexandria ... Why?* tells a story of adolescence in Egypt during the critical years of World War II, with Rommel's army approaching. The film is a variation on the interplay of the theater stage, the movie theater, radical politics, youthful dreams and desires.[43]

In the pivotal scene, Yahya, a high school student and Chahine's alter ego, directs a play that mocks and mimics the Nazis, arousing a great deal of anger and excitement among the audience, almost causing a riot. Chahine thus displayed the meaning of literature and drama in the cultural politics of nationalism at the time: the written word and the stage offered a politically engaged youth the opportunity to step into the limelight at a time when state and society were under the hegemony of a semi-colonial, bourgeois and capitalist elite. In hindsight, the film illustrated the desire of the youth at the time to establish realms of counter-hegemony using literary outlets, and the strong public response to these attempts. Beyond Chahine's own nostalgia, the film's prominent topic of generational clashes certainly transcended the confines of the epoch.

The cinematographic imagery and topical choices of Youssef Chahine's work belong to a "discourse of cultural representation"[44] that was characteristic for the Egyptian movie making industry after World War II, which had a wide impact throughout the Arab world due to the regional dominance of Cairo's studio system. Themes included anti-imperialism and depictions of the trials and tribulations of peasant life, and Chahine had a special fondness for the elements of song and dance that are so typical for Egyptian films. Questions of national identity were at the core of Chahine's work. In *Alexandria ... Why?* he portrayed the intellectual's inner conflict between his Egyptian belonging and the admiration for Western forms in theater, film, and literature. The West is endorsed yet rejected – in an ambivalence that has been characteristic for Middle Eastern intellectuals since the nineteenth century. *Alexandria... Why?*'s cosmopolitan setting, and the film's confusion of languages, images, gender identities and ethnicities, plays on this theme of national identity. Chahine was Egypt's most internationally acclaimed director – a status that offered him protection in spite of the postmodernism of his mature work and the political dissidence that it expressed. He was able to act out his marginal status as a Christian, a Catholic, an Alexandrine, not a Cairene, even including homo- and bisexual themes in his films, only after he initially worked successfully within the framework of the Egyptian film discourse.[45]

It does not come as a surprise therefore that an earlier work was Chahine's longest lasting success: The 1963 feature film *Al-Nasir Salah al-Din* (*Saladin the Victor*), which is a landmark of Arab nationalist image-making in spite of the rather crude depiction of Saladin. It was the first large-scale cinemascope production in Egypt, and attained large popularity in the entire Arab world. Frequent TV screenings prove its continuing popularity.[46] It has taken on the status of a "national allegory."[47]

Chahine picked the familiar topic of Saladin as an example of chivalry and pious justice, but interpreted it in the context of the 1948 Arab–Israeli war and the Palestinian expulsions from the future State of Israel. The title could be read as "al-Nasir," "the Victor," an attribute to Saladin. In a different reading, with an invisible colon between "al-Nasir" and "Salah al-Din," the hero embodied Egyptian president Gamal 'Abd al-Nasir. In the opening scenes, Chahine juxtaposed Saladin expressing deep concern about the people of Palestine under the yoke of foreign occupation, with images of streams of refugees, followed by a scene in a village being raided by marauding crusaders. The villagers gaze at the horizon expecting the arrival of Saladin, who they praise as "munqidh al-'Uruba," the "Savior of Arabism."[48] The allusions to Nasser, the dominant figure of Arab nationalism at the time, were quite obvious, as there are recurring quotes of Nasserite catch phrases in the film such as: "Religion is for God, the nation for all."[49]

Still, the film received praise at the time for not being blunt propaganda, but a subtle mirror for imperialist arrogance and the unjustified presence of the foreigner. Chahine contrasted the fanaticism and arrogance of the crusaders with images of religious tolerance residing in the Middle East. He chose 'Isa, an Arab Christian knight as one of the main characters of his plot, who commits to fight for Saladin for the sake of Arabism. Saladin thus embodied a whole range of Arab nationalist stereotypes that were representative for the discursive structures of Arab nationalism at the height of its political promise. He embodied ultimate justice and was a model of strength and reason, superior to the bloodthirsty, greedy, and treacherous crusader imperialists, but he also stood for the justification of Arab nationalist intransigence out of a defensive position: The Europeans had brought injustice, so that the Arabs had to fend them off courageously, even though they would prefer to live in peace. Moreover, Chahine, the Christian, acknowledged the importance of Islam as a backbone of moral superiority for the defenders, while he claimed a space at the same time for Christians paying homage to a vision of the Arab world as a multi-religious and tolerant environment. Last but not least, Chahine mitigated the image of the bloodthirsty crusader when he borrowed the motif of reconciliation between Saladin and Lionheart for his film, reaching back through the long line of Arab reception to Sir Walter Scott's *Talisman*. He thus delivered a film that presented the crusader topic from an Arab perspective, but avoided the temptation of the time to let his work deteriorate into a mere East-versus-West narrative.[50]

* * *

In the meantime, Saladin has turned into an omnipresent symbol of Arab nationalist prowess, in particular as a supposed forbearer of anti-Zionism. The image does not tolerate nuance or criticism, except maybe when Shiʻi religious authors point to Saladin's rather fanatic eradication of the Fatimid caliphs' Ismaʻili Shiʻism in Egypt.[51] The crudest abuse of the historical Saladin occurred in children's books presenting Iraq's Saddam Hussein as Saladin personified, and in newspaper editorials that equated the 1991 Gulf War as the coming of a new Hittin – coming full circle to Assad's propaganda at the beginning of the section.[52]

As a Great Man and a hero, Saladin was a reciprocal reference in Arab as well as European discourses in the nineteenth and early twentieth centuries. Western Orientalism discovered him as the noble foreigner who reflected the chivalric qualities of European civilization, celebrating qualities of respect and fair play. In a nationalist–imperialist context, it was important for writers in the West that Saladin belonged to a distant past when Orient and Occident were still on par, making the fact more easily acceptable that the crusaders had lost the battle for the Holy Land. In contrast, Arab cultural patriots and nationalists adopted the Saladin myth from Western sources precisely to re-purpose it as a mirror that Arabs could hold up to the Westerners to show them that they were still as barbarian as they had been during the crusader period.

Arguably, Arab nationalism is a particularly dialogical form of nationalism because of the importance that the defense against imperialism has played in its formation. Some images that have been constitutive for Arab identities were formulated precisely at the intersection between European and Arab Muslim cultures – such as that of Saladin, but also the nostalgic longing for *al-Andalus* that will be presented in the following section. They put emphasis on the historicity of the Arab-Muslim civilization in a diachronic juxtaposition with what has been and what is, what should be, and what might be. To historicize this past means to secularize it, as has been argued, but as such the act of secularization does not devalue the position of religion as an identity marker, because the historicized image of the Muslim past is compatible with a variety of religions, denominations, and local practices – or even the tastes of a multi-denominational urban theater audience. Only thus, a particular historical reference, such as to Saladin, or to *al-Andalus*, can attain universal validity across a vast cultural realm like the Arab lands.

3.2 From the glory of conquest to paradise lost

Al-Andalus in Arab historical consciousness

Historical narratives, and especially *Golden Age* myths, provide foundations for the creation of national identities and thus legitimacy for nation states. In the collective historical consciousness of Arab nationalists, the Crusades are one such topic. Another one is *al-Andalus*, or Moorish Spain.[1] A logic of competition between East and West, between the abode of Islam and that of Western Christianity – or what today's mainstream media in Europe and North America sometimes call "Judaeo-Christian culture" ignoring the long history of Jewish-Muslim cultural cohesion – binds together the two themes of *al-Andalus* on the one hand and Saladin and the Crusades on the other. This same logic was not lost on Ahmad Shawqi, the Egyptian poet, at the beginning of the twentieth century either, although he expressed it in a more subtle and artful manner. In 1913, he wrote a poem on the occasion of the fall of Edirne (ancient Adrianople) to Bulgarian troops during the first Balkan war, which he called "*Al-Andalus al-jadida*," "the New Andalus." The piece is remarkable in two ways. First, it is an example of Shawqi's Ottomanism at the time proving the thesis right that much of the topical repertoire of an Arab nationalist grand narrative was actually shaped in the context of the Ottoman discovery of Islamic unity as a political concept. Second, the title and the content of the poem provide evidence that the *al-Andalus* myth already belonged to this repertoire prior to World War I.

For Shawqi, Edirne was the new *al-Andalus* because of the role the city had played in the history of the Ottoman Empire, as its short-lived capital from 1413 until 1458 and as a burial place for a number of Ottoman Sultans, but most importantly as the vanguard of Ottoman-Muslim civilization on European soil. He saw the loss of Edirne to Bulgarian troops as part of the European encroachment of Ottoman lands evoking the memory of the Reconquista, and the Crusades. Edirne's fall repeated the fall of Granada, in the absence of a defender of the Muslim realm like Saladin.[2] Addressing a personified Edirne, Shawqi started the poem:

> Oh sister of *al-Andalus*, peace be with you / The caliphate has fallen from you, and so has Islam
> The crescent fell from the sky / ...
> Two wounds continue to bear down the two motherlands / ...

In a footnote, the editor of the poem explained that Edirne and *al-Andalus* were the "two wounds," and, in a rather crude differentiation between *Ottomanism* and *Arabism*, that the motherlands (or "two nations," as Shawqi chose the term "ummatan") were the Arabs and the Turks.

For Shawqi, the link between Edirne and *al-Andalus* was one of nostalgia for a period of Muslim glory, implying the ability to wrest lands from the hand of the Europeans during the periods of early Muslim conquests and the Ottoman expansion into the Balkans:

> Centuries have passed as in one night; fallen / have the states of the conquest as if it had been a dream
> [...][3]

A few stanzas down, in the same poem, Shawqi moved to another image of encounter between Muslims and Europeans. The stanza sets out with an address to "'Isa," meaning the Jesus of the Bible, not of the Qur'an. The verses introduced Jesus as the bearer of pains on behalf of the mortals, and as the one who returned dignity to slaves and cut their bonds, subsequently turning to the era of the Crusades while still addressing 'Isa:

> Uproar came under the government of Yusuf / and today it rises up for the second time in your ['Isa's] name
> [...]

Yusuf is again Saladin, but the reference to the crusaders is this time one of nostalgia: At the time, the struggle was pursued with dignity and common values of religion, but

> Today, gangs call out for the cross / for god and his spirit they are but offenders
> They mistake your cross for daggers and knives / all tools of injury and death
> Do you not see how they slaughtered their neighbors / between the houses as if they were sheep?[4]

Shawqi historicized the sequence of gain and loss according to periods of Arab, and subsequently Ottoman, dominance in Islam, without yet separating a golden era of Arab civilization during the Middle Ages from an era of perceived decline during the Ottoman period, as it became common later on in Arab nationalism. Shawqi also considered Western encroachment as continuous with the period of the Crusades. The new crusaders were, however, only scum who no longer knew of the mercy and humility of the Christian Jesus, who had died on the cross. They were far from the chivalric image of the Western warriors that nineteenth-century European novels painted.

A realm of memory

Much like the Saladin myth, Muslim Spain, or *al-Andalus*, is a crossing point of cultural references to a distant past for Arabs as well as for Europeans. It is a geographic name and a historic location, the Arabic reference to the present day *Comunidad Autónoma*, or "Autonomous Community" of Andalucía as a political subdivision of the Kingdom of Spain. It is also the name Arabs gave to the Iberian Peninsula during the period of Muslim rule (711–1492 CE). *Al-Andalus* is, however, also an imaginary space, a reference in collective memory in a great number of cultural contexts, ranging from references in Western poetry, opera and film, Arab literary and musical genres, to references in the so-called "War on Terror" of recent years. In the eyes of many, it is a symbol for magnificent and opulent culture, fine architectural achievements (the Alhambra, the Grand Mosque of Cordoba), lush gardens, and grand intellectual achievement (Ibn Rushd/ Averroes). The term *convivencia*, a synonym for a culture of fruitful coexistence and cooperation between Muslims, Christians, and Jews in medieval *al-Andalus*, has become a topos of nostalgic reference to the potentials of religious tolerance among promoters of dialogue between the three religions, with a dose of Orientalist imagination and kitsch thrown in for good measure.[5] In recent years, a festival culture has sprung up in Morocco, in particular, that celebrates the country's participation in a world culture of spirituality. During the performances at the festivals of Fez and Asilah, Moroccan–Andalusian music plays a central role in this creation of an official memorial space that helps to shape a hegemonic Moroccan Arab cultural discourse that is different from the pan-Islamic and radical voices that challenge the authority of the monarchy of the Maghreb country rooted in centuries of tradition.[6] Radical voices claim their share in the *al-Andalus* myth as well. After the 2004 terror attacks in Madrid, Spanish Prime Minister Aznar evoked historical memory of Spanish resistance against the Muslim conquest in 711, turning the country rhetorically into a battleground in the *Clash of Civilizations*, and presenting Arab and Muslim immigrants as an existential threat to the occident. Likewise, the Reconquista of Spain for Christian rule completed in 1492 remains a powerful symbol in Islamist propaganda calling for a roll back of Christian rule in order to achieve ultimate victory for fundamentalist Islam.[7]

Al-Andalus has diverse meanings as a powerful topos in a trans-local Arab identity, based on cultural memory. There are two trajectories in the exploration of cultural meaning in this inquiry: The *glory of conquest*, which is an analysis of the perseverance of a particular literary topos in modern Arabic literature (and beyond), and the *permanent exile* from the *lost paradise*, which looks at *al-Andalus* as a depository of nostalgic references reaching back to the glory days of Arab-Muslim civilization. *Nostalgia* takes on its literal meaning in this context, which is 'home-sickness': the longing for the deserted motherland. Its commemoration serves the identification of a shared cultural heritage, evoking two principle emotions: *pride* and *longing*, that were at the heart of an invention of a tradition.[8]

Conquest and *exile* thus frame a mythical period in Arab history – a classic Golden Age narrative. Inherent in this narrative is a theory of linear development of nations along a natural life cycle, from birth over adolescence to maturity, to decline and rebirth. The Arab *al-Andalus* story is just one of countless variants of this myth among the nations, such as, not least, the German romanticist longing for a *New Reich* in the nineteenth and twentieth centuries. According to the myth, decline is foreign induced, and rebirth is therefore a matter of necessity, towards a new Golden Age. This is not to say that Golden Age narratives are merely irrational constructs. Legions of historicist scholars have used their rigidly evaluated and interpreted primary sources to create singular and harmonized accounts of their nation's past. Nationalism as a worldview thus remains a paradox of modernity, in that it is founded on the desire for emotional allegiance, but requires a backbone of rationality in order to be distinct from religious forms of epistemology.[9]

Golden Age myths have played a central legitimating role in secular as well as religious discourses (including the range of positions between the two). Modern day Salafists relate back to the time of the prophet in the search for Islamic "authenticity," not only in order to reject Western hegemony, but also to fill ideological voids, especially since the post-1967 crisis of legitimacy of nationalist regimes. As a political ideology, Islamic doctrine has been transformed from a field of theological explanation of the world and jurisprudence to a system of norms and values in a social order, based on the legitimating power of the Golden Age of the Prophet's lifetime. In contrast, the *al-Andalus* myth has offered itself as a shared heritage for Arabs of all proveniences, whether religious or secular, due to the breadth of the motifs it entails, and due to the secular and historicist treatment that the myth underwent during the late nineteenth and twentieth centuries, as this section will show. Not only does *al-Andalus* offer identification as a historical Arab space, but it also represents the epitome of an Arabophonic realm of the Islamic Civilization.[10]

The Golden Age of *al-Andalus* played a significant role in the attempts by interwar Arab intellectuals to posit themselves vis-à-vis the perceived cultural superiority of the West. They used scholarly arguments to compensate for a feeling of being on the receiving end in a cultural pecking order of world history, induced by a century of colonization. A cross section from the Egyptian intellectual journals *al-Hilal* and *al-Risala* offers a wealth of examples for this myth-making process. In 1933, Ahmad Hassan al-Zayyat, the editor of the Cairene intellectual journal *al-Risala*, published an article about the global cultural impact of the Arabs. He praised *al-Andalus* as the abode of a superior civilization, tracing the origins of European science to Andalusian sources, which, to this day, is a commonplace of Arab nostalgic pride.[11] Muhammad 'Abdallah 'Inan did the same in an article about the history of the Arabs in Europe. 'Inan (1896–1986) was a prominent leftist liberal intellectual during the interwar period. He played a significant role in the popularization of Arab-Islamic historical narratives in Egypt.[12] 'Inan complained in *al-Hilal* that hardly anyone in Europe knew about the legacy of the Arab states in Spain and Italy. Spain in particular disregarded the Muslim period and had eradicated its memory, even though it was the most glorious period in its history. There were some historians in Spain and elsewhere in Europe, though, who, since the beginning of the nineteenth century, had freed themselves from this biased nationalist inclination when they came to appreciate the traces of Islamic culture in the West. In contrast, the contemporary "intellectual generation" in the Arab lands had lost touch with this past, complained 'Inan. They acknowledged its importance but only as if it was the history of a different nation. 'Inan bemoaned that Arab youth wanting to learn about their past had to depend on European writings. European nationalisms had dropped a heavy veil of oblivion and negligence over the Arab side of the story, however, as if it consisted of mere fantasy and tales.[13] This paradox situation commanded an Arab historian like 'Inan to remind his people of grandeur in order to revive a glorious memory that had been replaced by an inferiority complex vis-à-vis the Europeans. 'Inan was therefore convinced that he had to fill the gap of knowledge and provide sound historical information based on primary sources for the readers of the journals in which he wrote. Indeed, he filled many pages of *al-Hilal* and *al-Risala* with accounts about *al-Andalus*. Later he published his own political history of Muslim Spain in a monograph, primarily based on Arabic sources because he trusted them more than Christian ones, which, as he wrote, were more tinted with nationalist and religious extremism.[14] Like a typical historicist 'Inan remained faithful to the Golden Age narrative, combining his scholarly ethos with a nationalist agenda. He wrote in *al-Hilal* that "[t]he Islamic civilization in *al-Andalus* was the epitome of the genius of Islam, and the genius of this Arab nation, which carried its banner."[15] Likewise, the Alhambra in Granada was the "epitome of the glory of Islam and its state ..." and a "brilliant sanctuary for this Andalusian civilization that shed its brilliant light over Europe during the dark Middle Ages." The Alhambra was a "symbol for bygone glory."[16] 'Inan emphasized the Arabness of Andalusian civilization, but added an almost defiant claim on its Europeanness. The Andalusian legacy in Europe was apparently more important for him than the Andalusian legacy in contemporary Arab culture. The inclusive exclusiveness of the *al-Andalus* topos was therefore a typical example for the intellectual ambivalence of Arab scholars in the first half of the twentieth century, between attachment to the modernization project of the European Enlightenment and the desire to differ from European imperialist arrogance.

The examples on the following pages focus on the motifs of the *glory of conquest* and *paradise lost* as part of the legitimating Golden Age discourse of Arab nationalism, drawing from a variety of genres of literature including poetry, novel, autobiography, and travelogues with a short venture into film. According to their own chronological sequence, examples will start with loss and nostalgia and then turn to conquest. The choice of examples is certainly not exhaustive. In particular, it excludes one prominent field of the collective memory about Muslim Spain in the twentieth century, and that is Andalusian music, which has become an inseparable element of Arab popular culture from the Atlantic Ocean to Iraq – mostly as a shared reference for a vast variety of styles and forms in music and performance practice, as well as their social significance. However, music is, as a topic, a veritable ocean in its vastness, and exceeds the scope of this book.[17]

Paradise lost

In 1939, the Egyptian poet Hasan Kamil al-Sairafi (1908–1984) played to a popular romantic notion of paradise lost when he published his poem "Farewell to the Alhambra" in *al-Risala*. The first lines of the poem caught the moment when Abu 'Abdallah, the late Amir of Granada (known in the West as Boabdil) threw a last glance at the Alhambra, exclaiming in verse: "Who am I but Adam wandering about, crying – over his paradise in a state of misery / He sold the Garden but for disgrace – and I sold the Garden but for the lowering of my head." The poet thus drew a parallel between the biblical loss of the Garden of Eden, and the loss of Muslim Spain as an act of mere humiliation.[18] A more positive note was in a multivolume work that Shakib Arslan published starting in 1936 under the title *al-Hulal al-sundusiyya fi'l-akhbar wa'l-athar al-andalusiyya*, based on his experiences during a journey in Spain around 1930 when he stopped over on a trip to Morocco. He characterized the book in its subtitle as an "Andalusian encyclopedia, which encloses everything that came of this Lost Paradise." The title of the book – in translation the *Silk Clothes Among the Andalusian Stories and Monuments* – enhances the nostalgic atmosphere of the entire work as it alludes to a titling style in medieval and early modern Arabic literature that linked a poetic to a descriptive part of the title through internal rhyme. "The Silk Clothes …" – a phrase borrowed from several seventeenth- and eighteenth-century prose and poetic works about religion and history in the Arab West – was a hint that the book only covered the most select stories and places.[19]

The Arab West was a focal point in Shakib Arslan's Mediterranean network of personal and political relationships. He had a lasting influence on numerous Maghribi nationalists and religious reformers, in particular in Morocco.[20] *Al-Hulal al-sundusiyya* has nevertheless received little attention among his works. Three volumes appeared in Cairo between 1936 and 1939, of ten volumes that Arslan had envisaged altogether. Arslan started with a broad assessment of the reports of medieval Arab geographers on *al-Andalus*, moving on to a city by city description of Spain. In these chapters, he combined a travelogue with information about the Arab intellectuals that had emerged from these cities during the period of Muslim rule. The subsequent volumes that Arslan never completed should have extended the survey to other parts of *al-Andalus*, and added a history from the conquest to the Reconquista, as well as a history of the *Moriscos*, the formerly Muslim converts to Christianity.[21]

Arslan shared a peculiar approach to the travelogue genre with many contemporary Arab Muslim travelers in Spain, who evaluated the country in a nostalgic manner, with little regard to the post-Muslim period, not to mention the present. Here as elsewhere, the culture of nationalism is informed by a topography of the past: the topographer undertakes a journey to an imaginary land, not in a state of rational assessment, but in an emotive state of mind. As an historicist writer, Arslan takes his readers on a tour of collective imagination, beginning on the first page of volume 1 of *al-Hulal al-sundusiyya* where a black and white picture (Figure 3.2.1) presents Arslan sitting in front of the characteristic forest of columns that makes the Mezquita in Cordoba a monument of World Heritage today.[22]

صورة المؤلف أمام مسجد قرطبة:

Figure 3.2.1 Shakib Arslan in Cordoba.

Arslan reclines on a chaise covered with a throw rug in Persian style. Left of the chaise is a cushion, to the right is a small side table in Moroccan Oriental style, displayed with a conspicuously European-looking tea set. The floor of the foreground is covered with a large rug of indeterminate Oriental style, exceeding the frame of the image. Arslan is wearing a long black Arabian-Peninsula-style robe with what is probably a golden bordure. However, the robe and bordure are tightly wrapped around his body, not at all according to the usual look of this garment when worn in the Middle East. An undefined, probably colored cloth covers his right shoulder and barely reveals his right hand. He holds a book, the back of which rests on his lap stressing the image of the learned men of Spain's Muslim period. The turban on Arslan's head does not reflect any particular style, neither that of an *'alim* or *mufti* in the Arab lands. In sum, Arslan's posture, the clothes he is wearing, and the accessories form a quite eclectic ensemble. Altogether, they represent an undefined Oriental-ness: the turban, the robe, the leisure of a tea ceremony, but without care for the detail of a regional or national dress that people wear for clear distinction.

The backdrop is key to an interpretation of the image. The caption of the photo reads: "Image of the author in front of the Mosque of Cordoba." Arslan seems to be posing as an Arab inside the Mezquita. But should the wording then not be "inside the Mosque of Cordoba" ("fi dakhil ..." instead of "amama")? A closer look reveals that the background, while perfectly exact in terms of perspective and vanishing point, has a certain artificial flatness to it, as if painted. The lighting appears too uniform for such a large space, and there are no shadows on the floor. In addition, the floor is angled between the foreground and the background. A comparison of the perspectival ordering of the columns in the photo with a floor plan of the Mezquita reveals that the sight-line of the photo is impossible in the actual building. The axis of the gaze of the camera lens would have produced an unobstructed view through a straight line of arches, because they stand in line in the actual Mezquita and are not staggered. The astounding visual impression of being in the middle of a forest of columns only comes about when the onlooker's gaze protrudes the columns at an angle. In addition, the only place where the particular compo-sition of columns and arches immediately behind Arslan on the photo can be found is the entrance to the Capilla Villaviciosa near the old Mihrab of the Mosque, which would then have to appear in the background.[23] Evidently, the picture is make-believe, taken in a photo studio of the kind that is popular in many tourist locations where photographers offer to portray their customers in period costumes in front of a historical backdrop of their choice – either for fun, or to evoke a nostalgic identification with national history.

For Arslan, to place himself in an artificial Oriental setting meant that he, the Oriental, created his own Orientalist Arab–Andalusian imaginary. Most other existing photographs show Arslan in suit and tie as a respectable spokesperson of Arab modernity.[24] The fact that he submitted himself to the rules of the para-digmatic Western gaze when he staged himself as a stereotypical Arab was evidently not a mere hoax for Arslan the tourist, though. He chose the picture to introduce his voluminous homage to *al-Andalus* as the lost paradise of the Arabs. In addition, he chose to conceal the fake setting to his Arab readers. He probably assumed that most of his target audience would never have a chance to find out, but his choice also throws light on the entanglement between the authenticity of the place (Mezquita-Cordoba), its position in a historical narrative, and its central position in an identity-shaping imaginary. Arslan's *al-Andalus* was as rightfully claimed by Arabs as part of a common heritage as it was invented by European Orientalist poets and scholars. Its geographical distance and functional disentan-glement from contemporary Arab politics turned it into an ideal object of nos-talgic and largely inconsequential longing for most Arabs with a deep impact on their collective psyche as a shared point of reference.

The transportation revolution of the nineteenth and early twentieth centuries, and the related emergence of the tourism industry, nevertheless turned *al-Andalus* into a location that some in fact could reach, entering a complex realm of intertwined memory and cultural and political reality. They produced stories of *al-Andalus* that were meant to disentangle and simplify this relationship in the minds of people at home. It is a paradox, yet it also remains within the frame of the broader reasoning of this book, that only Europe's imperialist overpowering of the Arab world had made commonplace this travel back and forth between the realms and regions, at least for people of a certain class.

Arab travelers in Spain

After the fall of Granada in 1492, and the expulsion of the Moriscos from Spain in 1609, there were only few Muslims who set foot on the Iberian Peninsula. Knowledge of *al-Andalus* survived as historiography, such as that of the great historian of Muslim Spain Ahmad ibn Muhammad al-Maqqari (ca. 1577–1632), whose *Nafh al-tib min ghusn al-Andalus al-ratib* is one of the major Arabic sources on the country during the Muslim period because its author compiled a vast amount of information from texts that in many cases are no longer extant. Al-Maqqari wrote *Nafh al-tib* in Cairo in 1629, after he had left Morocco.[25]

Like many Muslim scholars throughout the ages, al-Maqqari was not bound to a specific place. Born in Tilimsan (Tlemcen in present day Algeria), he went to Morocco to study and gathered the material for *Nafh al-tib* while he was a student in Marrakesh. He became the Imam and Mufti of the Qarawiyyin mosque-university in Fes, but conflicts arose and he left for Egypt and undertook journeys to Mecca, Medina, Jerusalem, and Damascus.[26] The universality of the Arabic language as the idiom of Islam, as well as the universal validity of the four schools (*madhahib*, sing. *madhhab*) of Sunni Islam, made top scholars like him part of a trans-local community of traveling scholars-cum-jurists and administrators, who were in high demand at the courts and academies of their time – a very small elite community to be sure. Usually, they followed the travel patterns of the pilgrimage route during the yearly *hajj*, carrying with them their books, and stopping, sometimes for extended periods of time, sometimes for good, at scholarly centers along the way. This practice of long distance travel created a vast space of belonging that spanned the entire Muslim world. The presence of these scholars in the midst of eminent institutions such as the Qarawiyin in Fes, or minor madrasas and Sufi *zawiyas* along pilgrimage routes, was a manifestation of the bond that bound the umma of the Muslims together – even though this bond only materialized in the genealogies of literary works like *Nafh al-tib*. They show that *al-Andalus* remained a part of this umma, even if only as a legacy. Neo-Sufism, arguably, and definitely the mass media of the nineteenth and twentieth century then added an entirely new dimension and class basis to the dissemination of these shared identity markers.[27]

The Reconquista, in contrast, severed the physical bond between the Iberian Peninsula and the rest of the Muslim world. Travel by Muslims from Spain to the Arab lands became a one-way route of escape culminating in the expulsion of the Moriscos. Afterwards, Muslims who traveled to Spain traveled to enemy territory, and those who left written records of their journeys were initially either Moroccan or Ottoman Ambassadors.[28] Not long before the advent of French colonialism Moroccan Ambassador Abu'l-'Abbas Ahmad al-Kardudi went on such a mission in November 1885. Kardudi's report about the trip reveals less about his political business than about his impressions of the country. Kardudi spent some time visiting museums and monuments, as well as inspecting Arabic manuscripts in the National Library of Madrid. His Spanish hosts, who received him with warm hospitality, also gave him a tour of the major sites of Muslim Spain, including the Mezquita in Cordoba, the Alcazar in Seville, and the Alhambra in Granada. Al-Kardudi was, however, more impressed by modern military fortifications and maneuvers that were presented to him than by the reminders of the Muslim past. Only the Mezquita and the Alcazar invoked feelings of loss in him, but not in the sense that a once glorious civilization of his own had disappeared. In a more concrete sense, he found repugnant the maculation of the Grand Mosque of Cordoba through the presence of liturgical objects in a space that had once been filled with the sound of recitation of the Qur'an. Kardudi remained quite indifferent with regard to the "Westerners" whom he met, looked down upon them with pity, from a position of assumed superiority, but not with hostility or mistrust. As an emissary of a Muslim state, he did not consider his journey a visit to a realm of lost glory, but rather as a mission to alien territory. He considered the de-Islamization of Muslim monuments an outrage, but, different from many other travelers who came after him, he did not historicize this loss as part of a narrative of a competition between Christian and Muslim civilizations, in which the latter had lost ground since the period of the Reconquista. For him, the current margin between Islam and Christendom was rather a technical matter. Later visitors turned their longing for Spain's Muslim past into a powerful symbol for the perceived injustice of Europe's claim of superiority over the Muslim realm, and by extension Arab civilization.[29]

The nature of Muslim interest in Spain changed significantly in the late nineteenth century. As part of his Islamic revival propaganda, Ottoman Sultan Abdülhamit II sent a mission of historical inquiry to Spain in 1887 as a first step in the re-invention of the Iberian Peninsula as an Islamic realm of memory. The delegation included two North African scholars who were charged to produce a report about Arabic manuscripts in the various libraries of the country to complement a series of editions of Muslim manuscripts in Faris al-Shidyaq's publishing house *al-Jawa'ib* in Istanbul. Al-Shidyaq (1804–1887), of Maronite-Lebanese origin, was himself a traveler between cultures. He became a Protestant in his early twenties, spent years studying and as a publisher in Cairo, London, and Paris. He became a Muslim in Tunis in 1857, and moved to Istanbul in the same year at the invitation of the Sultan in order to embark on a very successful publishing career. His newspaper *al-Jawa'ib* appeared until 1884 and was the first international journalistic venture in Arabic. He was a representative of the pan-Islamic reform movement of the late nineteenth century under the auspices of the Sultan, and a forerunner of an Arabic revival. For his edition, he committed to critical standards by comparing various manuscripts, including those in European libraries. He knew about the contents of libraries in Paris, London, and Oxford, but missed information on Madrid, Sevilla, and Granada. Abdülhamit's mission was therefore probably a fruit of Shidyaq's intercessions.[30]

At the head of the 1887 delegation was Ibn al-Talamid al-Turkuzi al-Shinqiti. Born in Mauritania in the second decade of the nineteenth century, he had established himself as a scholar in Medina some time before he arrived in Istanbul in 1886 to take care of legal matters. Once there someone recommended him to Abdülhamit to take over the mission. Not long after his return from Spain he left Istanbul to settle in Cairo until his death in 1904. In Cairo, he may have been in touch as an al-Azhar teacher with the elite of reformers of the time, such as Muhammad 'Abduh and his circle, but he remained conservative in his convictions.[31]

Al-Shinqiti's companion and secretary on the trip was the young Tunisian 'Ali Ibn Salim al-Wardani (1861–1905). Born of a family of village grandees in the plains around Susa he belonged to the first cohort that attended the Saddiqi reform college in Tunis. He knew French and Ottoman Turkish, and became a close associate of the reformer Khayr al-Din al-Tunisi, who took him along to Istanbul in 1878 after having resigned from the Tunisian Grand Wazirate the previous year. Khayr al-Din recommended al-Wardani as a translator for the *al-Andalus* mission. After the completion of the journey, al-Wardani embarked on a career in the Tunisian administration before his premature death.[32]

Both travelers wrote separate, very dissimilar reports about their findings and their travel experiences. Shinqiti wrote poetry to exhibit how much he detested the involuntary contact with the Western world.[33] He complained about steamship travel, and compared it unfavorably to the qualities of camels and horses in the Arabian lands. Al-Shinqiti was no longer a young man and therefore unwilling to engage positively with what he encountered in Spain. In one poem, he expressed his longing for Medina while he had to endure the sound of church bells. His poetry was archaic in style, but it also contained remarks about the glorious past of *al-Andalus*, but, like al-Kardudi, he mostly lamented about the loss of *al-Andalus* for Islam and Muslim scholarship. His longing was not for the gardens of *al-Andalus*, but for the nights of the Arabian desert.[34]

When al-Shinqiti returned to Istanbul, a rather farcical scene unfolded when he refused to hand over his notes to his master Abdülhamit. He claimed that he wanted to get his remuneration first, which the Sultan refused, but it is likely that al-Shinqiti did not want to reveal that the actual author of the report was probably al-Wardani. Al-Shinqiti and al-Wardani apparently did not get along, the former being an old style 'alim, belonging to the stream of African '*ulama*' who set up residence in the Holy cities, whereas al-Wardani belonged to a new generation of students who had been raised in the spirit of reform. After his return to Tunis, al-Wardani published his notes about the Arabic manuscripts together with a travelogue. It appeared between 1888 and 1890 in a sequence of 28 articles in the Tunisian reformist journal *al-Hadira*. Al-Wardani encountered Spain as a follower of the reform school of Khayr al-Din al-Tunisi. He admired the architecture of the Islamic monuments, but he was equally interested in describing the mores of the Spanish population and the low quality of the country's educational system, which prevented the country from becoming modern and on a par with other European nations. He pointed to the ill influence of the clergy in particular. He had the opportunity to observe the stubbornness of Spanish churchmen when he tried to enter the Mezquita in Cordoba. When confronted by a priest who guarded the entrance, Wardani refused to take off his Tarbush because it marked his status. It took an intervention by the local bishop to convince the clergyman to give way. Aside from that, al-Wardani did not give much room to descriptions of the beauty of the Islamic monuments, but wrote about them quite matter-of-factly. There are some hints of patriotism in his report – to him, Spanish women were the most beautiful in Europe because of their mixed Arab and Spanish blood – but he added no historicizing romanticism about *al-Andalus*.[35] He nevertheless had a clear understanding that the remnants of Muslim culture that he encountered were in fact Arab. The rulers of medieval times were "Arab kings" for him, the monuments and their styles were distinctively Arab. The mores of the Spaniards were an Arab legacy.[36]

Only Ahmad Zaki's journey to Spain from late 1892 to early 1893 brought a true change of paradigm in the Arab reception of *al-Andalus*. Zaki (1866/7–1934) was an intellectual, literary figure, bibliophile, and Egyptian government official, as well as a confidant of Khedive Abbas II. He played a leading role in the publications of classical Arabic texts in Egypt. His cultural and literary activities earned him the nickname *Sheikh of Arabism* ("Shaykh al-'Uruba").[37] He was the first to publicize his travelogue in a grand framework, first in the Egyptian daily *al-Ahram*, and then as a widely read book. He was also the first to depart from the broad Muslim point of view, moving to an Arab–Egyptian one.

The actual destination of Zaki's journey was London, in order to attend the 9th Orientalist Congress. He traveled via Paris and spent some weeks there and also visited places in England, but dedicated almost three months to the Iberian Peninsula, underlining how important this part of the trip was for him. In the travelogue, Zaki addressed his readers not as co-religionists, but as "compatriots."[38] For Zaki, Egypt and *al-Andalus* were inseparably linked through civilization – different, yet under the same "religious and social principles."[39] He once referred to Iberia as the "second Arabian Peninsula." Egyptian students would profit greatly from a visit because of the double contact with modern civilization and the glorious "Moorish civilization" there.[40] He thus established a link between the two ages. His references to the past were no longer about Islam, but were rather ethnic and civilizational. Science was a lead topic of his thought, and Spain, in this context, represented the past glory of Arab science.

Khedive Abbas Hilmi II had encouraged and probably also financed his journey to the Orientalist Congress, and had entrusted him with the task to trace the vestiges of the Muslim presence in Spain from the time of Islamic rule to the present. Zaki therefore experienced, and reported about Spain through a prism, to the effect that he hardly took notice of the post-Reconquista achievements of Spanish culture.

There was something about Spain that reminded him of home. When he crossed the border, the smell of *al-Andalus* and the clearness of the skies were a welcome respite after the dark days of England and Paris.[41] Visiting monuments of Spain's heritage, such as cathedrals and museums, on his trip, he noticed only the remnants of an Arab past, but refused to take in the beauty of the monuments as a whole. Al-Maqqari's *Nafh al-tib* was his travel companion, yet Zaki's account established an original paradigm for the historical narrative that all following travelers used, and referred to, in their travelogues. He denounced the intolerance of the Christian rulers after the Reconquista, writing that Muslims had respected religion, law and property of the people after their initial conquest. After the fall of Granada, the Spaniards had introduced the horrors of the Inquisition and burned innumerable Arabic books. The modern Spaniards, who received him with great warmth and hospitality, retained many institutions but also numerous traits of the Arab character such as dignity, hospitality, and faithfulness, however.[42]

As for all other Arab travelers in this account, the climax of Zaki's experience in Spain was his visit to the Mezquita in Cordoba. It was a place that perplexed and confused people. Kardudi, for example, had been taken aback by the presence of liturgical objects in arguably the most magnificent interior of any Muslim prayer hall in the history of architecture. Zaki, however, remarked that he could not imagine any place of worship of whatever religion being a more perfect rendering of human religious humility. In contrast to his predecessors, who viewed the Mezquita as a Muslim space maculated by the Christian takeover, Zaki detached it from its mere function as a mosque and viewed it as Islam's contribution to world civilization. The fact that the Mosque had been turned into a cathedral was worth half a sentence to him only, and he remarked that it had not altered its general characteristic, and apparently, it also did not diminish his awe when he experienced his visit as an immediate encounter with the divine.[43] In other words, Zaki's impressions transcended the dichotomy of a Muslim past versus a Christian present within a realm of nostalgia and longing. His immersive identification was essentially different from the distant observer attitude of his predecessors.

There is confusion in Zaki's account as to how he used the terms Muslim and Arab. The latter occurs more often than the former, but he had no regard for the ethnic differentiation of Berbers among the Muslims who conquered Spain. Zaki separated strictly between Arabs and Spaniards, however, ignoring their intermingling during the time of Muslim rule in Spain in the same way as the European term Morisque or Moorish ignores it. For him as for later Arab travelers, Andalusian civilization was inseparable from his own Arab heritage, rather than being something peculiar in its own right. Zaki thus contributed to a nostalgic historicization of *al-Andalus* as an invented, but lost Arab homeland: When he had crossed from France into Spain, he wrote that he could not avert his mind from thinking about the glory days when the banners of Islam had flown over the land and the call of the Muezzin had risen to the sky. Ironically, he had been in Basque country then, which had never been under Muslim rule.[44]

Zaki's account left a deep impression among his contemporaries. It was praised in the press and published in various editions.[45] However, the most prominent and most influential visit to Spain was on all accounts that of Ahmad Shawqi, Egypt's "Prince of Poets." Shawqi had been court poet for Khedives Tawfiq (r. 1879–1892) and Abbas Hilmi II (r. 1892–1914). After the latter's forced abdication at the outbreak of World War I, and after publishing a poem criticizing the British stranglehold over his country, Shawqi was advised to seek exile in a neutral space. He opted for Spain but not out of nostalgic longing. Rather, Barcelona, where he spent the greater part of his exile from 1915 to 1919, was the major Mediterranean port of the country, and therefore offered quick access to a passage back home. *Al-Andalus* was not a prominent topic of Shawqi's panegyric poetry prior to his exile. A rare, if not the only occurrence is the Edirne poem quoted earlier. Before his Spanish exile, Shawqi was an Ottoman patriot, but the trip he undertook to Andalucía in late 1918 changed his vision of the country and his general intellectual trajectory. Today, Shawqi's work is considered crucial in bringing about the *al-Andalus* revival in Arab culture, not least because he was instrumental in the popularization of medieval Andalusian poetic forms for neoclassical poetry.[46]

Shawqi arrived in Barcelona with little intellectual baggage and few expectations, hoping for a swift return. On his request, his friend Ahmad Zaki sent him several books, among them his own *Safar ila'l-mu'tamar*, and a copy of al-Maqqari's *Nafh al-tib*. Initially, Shawqi seemed not taken with his new country, his poetry expressed longing for Egypt, but soon after, he started to copy and borrow rhyme schemes and meter from classical Andalusian poetry, thus foreshadowing a romantic reconstruction of an ancient, literary *al-Andalus*. This reconstruction reached its fulfillment in his long poem "al-Rihla ila'l-Andalus," which combines a reflection on his desire for Egypt with an account of his trip to Andalucía. He undertook the trip right after the armistice of Compiègne brought an end to World War I, when the end of his exile was within reach, and he decided to return via Southern Spain. As he explained in the introduction to his poem, he traveled in two modes: like a visitor who strolled from monument to monument in awe, but also with poets of medieval *al-Andalus* in his company. Shawqi tried to give shape to the fusion of the modern political identity of an exile with the inner longing of the self for a legitimating glorious past that occurred to him in sight of the remainders of Andalusian monuments. To formulate a new nationalist subjectivity that emerged in his verses he adopted the structures of a poem by the ninth-century Abbasid court poet al-Buhturi, in which the latter reflected on the sight of the ruins of the palace that belonged to the ancient Persian King Khosroe. Shawqi's *al-Andalus* poem thus marked his shift from panegyric poetry addressing the dynastic ruler to verses that spoke to the bourgeois individual, who identified with a broader national community grounded on a shared history.[47]

Shawqi's descriptions of the monuments he saw, in particular the Mezquita and the Alhambra, present the author in a dream-like state evoking the times of Andalusian splendor. In one verse, for example, he alluded to an adorned case in the famous prayer niche (*mihrab*) of the Mezquita that, according to legend, had once enshrined several pages of a Quran handwritten by the third Caliph

Uthman. Shawqi wrote: "The place of the book emits for you a perfume – of rose though it is empty, and you draw close to touch."[48] He went even further than Zaki in that he had no concern for the present day, or even the desecration of the places by Christians, but he re-invented them as vehicles for his imagination, informed by his readings on Islamic history and literature, invoking a deep melancholy over times past. The last verse of the poem (110) is a summary lesson, addressing Shawqi's fellow Egyptians: "If you have lost regard for the past – then you are lost to consolation."[49]

Shawqi's poems were crucial in triggering a broad interest in a distinctly "Arab" Andalusian past as living history. They became part of the repertoire of motifs that poets and novelists would use, and most importantly part of school curricula throughout the Arab world.[50] For Shawqi himself, they were a vehicle to express the pain of exile and the longing for a better place, either in a different location or in a different era. Next to "al-Rihla ila'l-Andalus," the same motif appeared in other Shawqi poems, such as "Saqr Quraysh," which is a variation on exile based on the life of 'Abd al-Rahman I "al-Dakhil," the founder of the emirate of Cordoba and the first Umayyad Amir of *al-Andalus*, written entirely in *muwashshahat* style, and in the poem "Andalusiyya," which he composed during his Spanish exile.[51] In that, Shawqi's references to *al-Andalus* arguably functioned in a way comparable to, though more subtle than, the self-orientalization of Arslan in front of the fake Mezquita interior. The stylizing of *al-Andalus* as a cradle of a superior Arab-Muslim civilization had its effect only because it placed this civilization into a European context, juxtaposing it, and thus implicitly acknowledging Europe as the world center with many peripheries. Thus, "the technique of finding one's identity in the uncovered traces of the past is used to combat the very Orientalism in which it originates." Still, the integration of Egyptian and Arab-Islamic heritage that emerged out of Shawqi's longing for a present Egypt and a past *al-Andalus* posited cultural self-assertion against the humiliation of colonial rule.[52]

The re-invention of *al-Andalus* as an Arab realm of memory was a means to create a chronological trajectory of eternity. Mustafa Farrukh (1901–1957), a young Lebanese artist, joined an exquisite line of predecessors when he traveled in Southern Spain in the late 1920s and published a travelogue in 1933. He described how he set out to ascend to the Alhambra immediately after he stepped off the train in Granada, exclaiming: "Off to the glorious Acropolis of the Arabs!"[53] During his studies in Rome and Paris he had certainly learned to appreciate the Acropolis as the vanishing point of Western civilization. It was the same for Farrukh, but Arab genius appeared in the architecture of the Alhambra. When he stood in awe gazing at the beauty of the Court of the Lions, he found that this was in fact "the *Ka'ba* of art, where man is lifted to the highest host, praising god for what he planted in the souls of this nation ("qawm") in terms of extraordinary talent and profound genius."[54] Earlier on in his book, he had written "I say to my compatriots ("abna' qawmi"): a nation that possesses such art, such a history full of considerable facts and famous deeds, is a nation that will not die."[55] Here, the young Arab nationalist enthusiast formulated more clearly what others had only implied: *al-Andalus*' glorious civilization offered historical depth to the Arabs ensuring at the same time that the nation had a bright future, if only its members cared to notice.

The title that Farrukh gave to his book points in the same direction: *A Journey to the Land of Lost Glory*. As seen, Shakib Arslan, one of the key figures of Arab nationalist thought and pan-Arab and -Muslim activism in the interwar period, published his book *al-Hulal al-sundusiyya* only a few years later and dedicated it to "paradise lost."[56] Arab authors had come a long way since the times of al-Kardudi and al-Shinqiti to develop a consciousness of a trajectory that simultaneously pointed to the past, turned this past into present heritage, and used it to build an expectation for the future. The term *al-Andalus* evoked visions of the harmony, wisdom, and beauty of paradisiac gardens, but it also offered a transcendent meaning of an elevated Arab state of mind. In religion, visions of paradise always imply loss and eviction, too. In turn, the notion of paradise lost implies the return to paradise, and the longing for paradise implies a promise of redemption and reinstallation into former grandeur.

Most Arabs had to replace the physical journey to Spain with a literary one. For some, however, the promise of redemption and return to the lost paradise has been more concrete than the poetic longing of the likes of Shawqi. In the early 1930s, Shakib Arslan and his Moroccan nationalist friend 'Abd al-Salam Bannouna, entertained the project to petition the Spanish government for a return of the Mezquita of Cordoba under Muslim control. It is remarkable in the context of Arslan's later liaison with fascist powers that he enlisted the support of Spanish socialists and communists in this endeavor, who were then coming into power. Apparently he trusted that their secularism and anti-clericalism would make them inclined, but he also hoped that an offer of Moroccan conciliation in North Africa and support for Spanish economic interests would work as incentives. In addition, he believed naïvely that the prospect of thousands of Muslims traveling to Cordoba to pray in the mosque would be regarded as positive for the local Spanish economy. At the end of the day, however, Arslan's vision rested on a romantic perception of Muslim–Christian *convivencia*, albeit under Spanish imperialist tutelage. In a way, the Mezquita project thus foreshadowed Arslan's later apologetic defense of Mussolini's invasion of Abyssinia.[57]

Another instance of nostalgia turned into action took place on a journey by the Egyptian publicist Muhammad Musa to Spain in 1948. As with his predecessors, he had gone to explore manuscripts at the Escorial and to dwell for some time in the land of the forefathers. He described his experiences in a familiar way, as a dream space that was somehow in-between ("huwa baina baina"), situated between east and west, past and present. Initially, his expectations were disappointed because the people he met after his arrival were not the people, and the faces were not the faces, that he had expected because Christianity ruled over everything. The only place that fulfilled his dream-space expectations was the Mezquita, which, for Musa, captured eternity, where Muslim, Jewish, and Christian scholars had debated and studied together in the one language of Arabic, and had learned and taught the one science, which was the Islamic science. The cathedral in the center of the Mezquita in all its giganticness did not even harm the spirit of the eternal Islamic monument. Musa's encounter with the presence of the Islamic past in the Mezquita moved him to pronounce the evening call to prayer from the top of the former minaret, and to prostrate to pray in the Mihrab. He used a low voice so that only those around him could hear. Musa was sure, though, that his companion, an Arabist from Cordoba, found this quite suspicious, but he nevertheless respected his passion and stood back together with everyone else who was watching.[58]

The rather innocent passion that carried Musa away has not always been considered as innocuous as in 1948. In 1932, the Tetouan nationalist Muhammad Daoud (1901–1984) had already had a rather aggressive encounter during a visit to the Mezquita. When priests insisted that he and his companions should remove their hats, the confrontation escalated and Daoud replied angrily that the Mezquita was in its essence a Muslim space, that the priests were the intruders, and that at some point Muslims would claim the mosque back and take revenge. Apparently, the priests were intimidated by this rant.[59]

In fact, Daoud hit the nail on the head as he invoked a fear that persists to this day among conservative Spanish Catholics. Since the early 2000s, Spanish Muslims have been asking for permission to pray in the Mezquita, advertising their request as a symbol of dialogue and unity between the different religions. Reactions from both the Spanish clergy and the Vatican have been negative, though, even to a renewed effort by the Spanish Islamic Board in 2006, taking advantage of the conciliatory atmosphere that reigned in the Vatican after the outcry that Pope Benedict XVI's Regensburg speech had created in the Islamic world, in reaction to his quotation from the anti-Muslim diatribes of a Byzantine emperor, which he delivered without mitigating comments. A further complication of the matter is, however, that most requests to open the Mezquita for Muslim prayer come from a side of the spectrum of Muslims in Spain that represents the community of converts to Islam. Muslim immigrants from North Africa have actually distanced themselves from the endeavor, fearing the possible backlash that the publicity of the demand could create. It is a phenomenon of the Spanish relationship with Islam in general and in Andalucía in particular that the Islamophilia of liberals and the promotion of a new *convivencia* by converts tends to have the opposite effect, rather than creating a more tolerant atmosphere towards Muslims. The broader Spanish public, and in particular its conservative sector has filtered the Mezquita debate through the lens of immigration policy and terror threats, thus adding fuel to a discourse that sees the growing presence of North African Muslims in Spain as a manifestation of a second conquest.[60]

An escalation of the debate took place in the spring of 2010, when members of a tour group organized by the *Muslim Youth of Austria* (*Muslimische Jugend Österreich*), who did not belong to the community of Muslim immigrants to Spain either, prostrated for prayer inside the building and were confronted by security guards. A scuffle ensued followed by injuries and arrests. Police accused one of the group members of having attacked them with a knife, but the spokesman of the Muslim Youth of Austria assured that the prayer had been spontaneous, and not a premeditated action with the intention to provoke. The young people had been naïve and quite shocked by the confrontation, he said. He nevertheless apologized to the Catholic Church in Spain for the inconsiderate action. When the case was finally brought to court in 2013, the Austrian Muslims were acquitted because of a lack of evidence for bad intent, much to the chagrin of conservative commentators who accused the Spanish justice of bias in favor of multiculturalism. It is a sign of a lack of moderation in public exchanges about this topic that as early as 2010, the Bishop of Cordoba had demanded that signs in the city pointing tourists to the Mezquita should no longer say "mosque-cathedral," but that the "mosque" part should be eliminated to prevent "confusion."[61]

The glory of conquest, or Transcultural intersections: Tariq Ibn Ziyad, King Roderick, and Florinda

As an Arab reference point, *al-Andalus* establishes a reverse chronological order. Eviction from paradise represents the end of the story and at the same time the beginning of a *permanent exile*, setting the ground for the current state of longing and nostalgia. To create the new *al-Andalus* – and for most except some fanatics and terrorists this can only be an imaginary one – Arabs are set to follow a reverse route back to the beginnings in the *glory of conquest*. Shawqi inserted this message of hope for restitution in his aforementioned Edirne poem, in the verse:

> Time poses to you a standpoint like the one that Tariq took: / desperation is in the back, and hope is before you
>   Patience and fearlessness were in him and they became / deadly [weapons], but even deadlier is not to have them[62]

This verse is a reference to a legendary speech that Tariq Ibn Ziyad gave after he led an Arab-Berber army across the straits of Gibraltar in 711, and before he defeated Roderic (Arabic *Ludhriq*), the last King of Visigoth Spain in the Battle of Guadalete. The speech belongs to the most prominent textual references of the early Islamic conquests. According to a widely accepted tradition, Tariq ordered the burning of the ships that the Muslim army had used to cross the straits, in order to show his soldiers that the decision for conquest and battle was irreversible and retreat was not an option. The original line, according to al-Maqqari, was

> Oh people, where is the escape? The sea is behind you, and the enemy before you, and by God you have nothing [left] but confidence and patience.[63]

Shawqi's verses therefore not only alluded to a popular historical account, but also to the motifs of patience and self-assertion as crucial virtues in the face of overwhelming enemy force.

The historical record of the Muslim conquest of Spain is complex. The first Arab accounts, which are extant, most prominently Ibn 'Abd al-Hakam's *Futuh Misr*, date to the ninth century.[64] There is, accordingly, considerable controversy as to the details of Tariq's biography and the actual circumstances of his conquest.

The success of his campaign seemed unlikely considering the relatively slow pace of his build-up after the landing in 711, and the potentially overwhelming size of the Visigoth army. Historians argue, however, that a deep schism ran through the Visigoth empire's elite at the time due to disagreements over the succession of King Roderic to his predecessor on the throne, Witiza.[65] The motif of weakness based on division on one side and strength built on unity on the other, as well as motifs of decadence and sectarian conflict as a cause of division, have been central to the modern reception of the Conquest of *al-Andalus* in the literature. The question notwithstanding if the story is myth or fact, Tariq Ibn Ziyad's speech after burning the ships is a mainstay of not only Arab, but generally Muslim belligerent rhetoric to this day.[66] It features almost identically in all modern Arab versions of the story of the conquest. As far as the origins of the topos are concerned, Ibn 'Abd al-Hakam (b. ca. 798/799, d. 871, Cairo [?]) does not refer to the burning of the ships, and neither does the eminent tenth-century Andalusian chronicler of the conquest, Ibn al-Qutiyya. The first mention of the event is probably in Abu 'Abdallah Muhammad al-Idrisi's twelfth-century geographical work *Kitab nuzhat al-mushtaq fi ikhtiraq al-afaq*. Fifteenth-century geographer al-Himyari added to this story that Tariq ordered the burning of the ships in order to impress his Arab seniors with the courage and determination of his mostly Berber army, which throws a peculiar light on the use or misuse of the story as a topos of Arab nationalism in the twentieth century.[67] The best-known version of Tariq's speech, including the famous quote, appeared in the seventeenth century in *Nafh al-tib*.

There are separate lines of transmission for the various motifs and elements of the story. Already the ninth-century Andalusian scholar Ibn Habib (b. ca. 796, d. Cordoba, 853) quoted the most famous line of the speech in his short account of Tariq's conquest, while he skipped the story of the crossing in its entirety. He wrote that on hearing that the Visigothic army was approaching, Tariq had assembled his "companions" ("ashabihi …"), incited them to Jihad and martyrdom, and then had spoken to them: "Ayna al-Mafarr …" Ibn Habib did include a story of looters, though, who grabbed the spoils of Ludhriq's riches after the battle and tried to escape across the straits, but their boat turned over in apparent divine punishment.[68] For this event to happen, the ships could obviously not have been burned, but even this early rendering of the story was a negative reference to defection from the army before completing the conquest – the very offense that Tariq tried to prevent when he ordered the burning. In contrast, Al-Idrisi's twelfth-century contemporary Ibn al-Kardabus briefly mentioned the burning of the ships, and added that Tariq only had told his soldiers before their march on Cordoba that it is either "Kill or die!"[69]

The origins of the topos may lie much earlier; Arab historians have argued that a Berber like Tariq would not have been capable of producing an Arabic speech as rhetorically refined as the one attributed to him, and alas, his Berber army would not have understood it anyway. According to one theory, both the traditions of the burning of the ships and the subsequent speech relate back to legends about the pre-Islamic conquest of Yemen by the Sassanian general Wahriz in the sixth century as al-Tabari related them in the tenth century.[70]

Tariq's speech is a central element of modern fictional renderings of the conquest of the *al-Andalus* story, regardless of its shrouded origins. It appeared, for example, in Fu'ad al-Khatib's 1931 play *Fath al-Andalus* ("The Conquest of *al-Andalus*"), which the poet published during his stay in 'Amman.[71] Al-Khatib's usage of rhyme and meter demanded certain adaptations of the original version of the speech, but there are also modifications owed to the author's Arab nationalist agenda. Al-Khatib sidestepped the problem of the Berber ethnicity of Tariq's soldiers by simply turning them into Arabs. The line: "Oh people, where is the escape?" became in al-Khatib's rendering: "Where, oh you, my people, is the escape?" and the term he used for "my people" is "qawmi" instead of the usual "al-nas."[72] The audience of al-Khatib's play would have interpreted this term unmistakably in a nationalist sense as "my nation," according to the usage that had become customary at the time, and this in spite of al-Khatib's rather archaic usage of language, in which he used "qawm" in various meanings, referring to people or nation, but also to group or kin. The specific adaptation of the widely known phrase from Tariq's speech would not have been lost on the audience of al-Khatib's play either. The speech is given at a crucial moment, right after Tariq and his army enter the scene, and right before the start of battle, the denouement of the entire piece. The line is therefore a rallying call, and al-Khatib put the answer that he deemed appropriate into the enthusiastic reply of Tariq's army on stage: "Here we are, we Arabs / we are the trimming swords."[73] "Qawmi" was therefore certainly not a Berber nation.

Fu'ad al-Khatib's son Riyad mentioned in the foreword to his father's Diwan that the play was performed in several Arab cities before the war.[74] One wonders nevertheless about the audience's response to the very complex and stylized language, and the declamatory characteristics of the dialogue. The play, set in the early eighth-century Maghreb, introduces a number of characters of early Islamic history, such as Tariq and Musa Ibn Nusair, governor of North Africa at the time, residing in Qairawan. Al-Khatib was clearly not an experienced dramatist; the plot lacks a common thread but consists of a series of building blocks that evoke various aspects of the historiographical and literary tradition of the Conquest story instead of weaving them together to create a single narrative line. This is why it seems odd at first glance that the poet assigned plenty of room in his play to non-Arab, Visigoth characters, some of whom even take positions as primary figures in his account, almost overshadowing Tariq's rather sketchy characterization, in spite of Fu'ad al-Khatib's Arab nationalist inclination and the role that the *al-Andalus* myth played as a signifier for nostalgic feelings of past Arab glory.

Two of the Visigoth characters are Count Julian, a noble man and vice regent of the North African enclave Sebta, modern day Spanish Ceuta, and his daughter Florinda. Count Julian plays an important role in the Arab historiographical tradition about the conquest of *al-Andalus* because he is said to have provided the ships for the passage of Tariq's army across the straits of Gibraltar. Among the earliest Arab chroniclers, only Ibn Habib did not know of Julian, even though he mentioned in his *Kitab al-ta'rikh* that Musa Ibn Nusair had sent Tariq to Tilimsan to gain allies along the coastline, find anchorages, and try to acquire ("... an yusiba ...") ships from the Christians ("al-Rum"), which could either mean for rent or purchase, or as booty.[75] Count Julian, however, makes an appearance in the chronicle of Ibn 'Abd al-Hakam, who was of almost the same age as Ibn Habib, but wrote in Egypt and was therefore exposed to many more lines of scholarly transmission than the relatively peripheral Ibn Habib. Ibn 'Abd al-Hakam's is probably the first extant record of a topos of abuse, treason and revenge in the story of the conquest of *al-Andalus* that has come to play a central role in various traditions. Count Julian, who is called Yulyan in Ibn 'Abd al-Hakam's account, plays a central role in this topos as headman of Sebta and vassal of King Roderic, or Ludhriq, who resided in Toledo. Yulyan had sent his daughter, who remains nameless in Ibn 'Abd al-Hakam's report, to Ludhriq for education. The King took advantage of the situation and raped her. When Yulyan learned of the assault, he said that he could not see another punishment but to send the Arabs upon his king. Yulyan then took the initiative and entered into an alliance with Tariq to provide him with transportation across the straits.[76]

A few examples suffice to show that there was a continuous chain of transmission of this topos in Arab historiography that arguably reached into the nineteenth and twentieth centuries. Both, the great twelfth-century Iraqi chronicler Ibn al-Athir in his *al-Kamil*, and the thirteenth-century encyclopedist and historian al-Nuwayri – the latter relying on the former – reported the story of the rape and the ensuing treason by Julian, adding that it had been a custom for Visigoth grandees to send their children to the Royal Palace for education and courtship.[77] Al-Maqqari's seventeenth-century account in *Nafh al-tib* included these aspects of the story, too. In the nineteenth century, *Nafh al-tib* was considered important enough to be among the new editions of Arabic classics that came out in Bulaq, Cairo. It already appeared in print in 1862 or 1863. It is therefore likely that it was among the works that had gained popularity among a literate growing urban middle class of the seventeenth- and eighteenth-century Arab East who were able to afford manuscripts.[78]

The first scene of al-Khatib's play, set in a North African location, maybe Tlemcen, contains an indirect recount of the rape story. Yulyan, in al-Khatib's wording "al-kunt" in reference to "Count," tells his friend Mughith, client of Caliph al-Walid and conqueror of Cordoba, about the letter he had received from his daughter Florinda, detailing the shameful incident.[79] In the broader context of the plot, Yulyan and Mughith's encounter serves to highlight Ludhriq's abuse as a typical manifestation of the baseness of the Goths, and eventually to justify the conquest as an act of deliverance. In contrast, the friendship between Yulyan, the Christian, and Mughith, the Muslim general, is a signifier of the benevolence and tolerance of the Muslims.[80]

In the context of the present inquiry, a small detail is of special significance, namely that al-Khatib called Count Julian's daughter by her first name Florinda. Neither had any of the Arab writers from Ibn 'Abd al-Hakam to al-Maqqari given her a name, nor does it come up in Arabic historical works of the nineteenth century, such as, for instance the Egyptian intellectual and statesman 'Ali Mubarak's 1892 translation of the French historian Louis-Amélie Sédillot's (1808–1875) mid-century *Histoire des Arabes*. Mubarak's translation of the passages that treat the conquest of *al-Andalus* in Sédillot's *Histoire* is an abridged, condensed and slightly rearranged, yet faithful version of the original. Most importantly, both versions merely include a reference to an "outrage" that was committed against Julian, but do not specify which kind of outrage. Sédillot could build on the fact that the Count Julian story was a well-known topos of European literature at the time, more on which below, but whether this was the case in the Egyptian reading public is questionable. It is arguable, however, that Sédillot's "le comte Julien" became "al-kunt Juliyan" in Mubarak's version, as a mere act of transcription. Ever since, "al-kunt" has been a standard epithet of the Julian character in twentieth-century Arabic renderings of the conquest story, including that of al-Khatib. In Mubarak, there is no trace of the name Florinda, though.[81]

The first Arabic rendering of the story in political activist drama, Mustafa Kamil's 1893 play *Fath al-Andalus*, did not contain the name either. Kamil only glanced over the rape story, introduced the Count as the Amir of Sebta, but did not give a name to his daughter.[82] Kamil, who was 19 years old when he wrote the play, is widely considered as the founder of the Egyptian nationalist movement. The fact that he chose the *al-Andalus* topic for the only play that he wrote is remarkable because Kamil's nationalism is often presented as Egypt-focused and skeptical of the pan-Arab cultural trends of the late Ottoman period. It appears therefore that Kamil's nationalism and his Egyptian identity construction were quite malleable over the span of his life and remained deeply rooted in Egypt's Arab-Muslim heritage. As for many other writers who came after him, the conquest of *al-Andalus* was a symbol of the victory of the superior over the inferior and corrupted culture, and a symbol for Muslim magnanimity: When Musa orders Tariq in the second act of the play to embark on the attack on Spain, he tells his general to act with clemency after victory as "… gentleness towards the defeated is the sharpest weapon of the truly faithful." Tariq, the Berber hero, replies that he was interested in nothing but the victory for Islam. What carried him was "Arab zeal and Muslim fervor."[83]

The Count Julian myth remains marginal in Kamil's play; he is more concerned about the plots and machinations that foreigners play to undermine Musa's and Tariq's plans to work for the glory and expansion of Islam – a less than subtle reference to the widespread opinion at Kamil's time that Europeans in Egypt and elsewhere in the Arab world undermined the sovereignty of Muslim rule. The rape and revenge plot is, however, central to another major work of Arabic historical fiction, namely Jurji Zaydan's historical novel of the same title, *Fath al-Andalus*, which first came out in 1903.

The influence of Zaydan as a historian, or popularizer of history in the Arab, if not broader Muslim world, can hardly be overstated. His novels continue to appear in countless new editions.[84] They have been translated into languages from as far as Indonesia. Reading Zaydan's novels has initiated many Arabic speakers to a popular historical consciousness. In addition, his historical novels paved the way for historicist thinking among the Egyptian-reading public – 21 appeared between 1891 and his death in 1914, instilling a sense of history's impact on the individual among their readers and popularizing perceptions about the characteristics of certain epochs of Egyptian and broader Arab history.[85]

As typical for Zaydan's approach to writing history, *Fath al-Andalus* combines historical accounts with fictional suspense stories, all based on meticulous research, expressed in numerous footnotes to increase the appearance of scholarly authority, and a bibliography of sources listed at the beginning of the book.[86] The author went a long way to uphold the impression that hardly anything in this novel was a matter of mere fiction, including its heroes. Yet at the same time, the novel arguably introduced the name Florinda for the first time in an Arabic text, and thus inducted it into the realm of Arab nationalist popular culture. Likewise, Florinda's father Julyan is "al-kunt" in Zaydan's novel, too. This and other elements of the plot suggest that Zaydan knew 'Ali Mubarak's translation of Sédillot's history.[87] One central element of Zaydan's story is, however, entirely absent from the tradition in the Arabic language historiography, which is the love story between Florinda and Alfons, the son of the former Visigoth King Witiza, who had been ousted by King Roderic, whom many Visigoth grandees therefore considered a usurper.[88]

Zaydan's style of writing and his technique of gathering material for his novels was highly innovative but also controversial of his time. He relied on both Arab tradition and Western scholarship, ranging from al-Maqqari's *Nafh al-tib*, over Reinhart Dozy's eminent works about Muslim Spain,[89] to London's Public Record Office. The usage of European Orientalist literature provoked criticism from Islamic reformer Rashid Rida, for example. Zaydan must have taken a great deal of inspiration from the European literary tradition, too, though, or indeed Spanish mythology as conferred by Romantic poetry, about the Muslim conquest of Spain, which is a source that he did not mention, but to which he usually took recourse in his writings.[90]

Zaydan's adaptation of European literary topoi was just one step in a complex process of cross-fertilization. He was certainly familiar with the Arabic tradition of the conquest of *al-Andalus*, but nevertheless he relied heavily, in his choice of characters, on a parallel European line of tradition that had developed independently from the Arab one throughout the Middle Ages until the twentieth century. Indeed, it has been argued that the story of the conquest of *al-Andalus*, and in particular the part of it that evolves around King Roderic, Count Julian, and his daughter Florinda, constitute a foundational myth and lead-topos of the literature of the modern Spanish nation, namely the myth of *La Cava* (who is Florinda) and her illicit relationship with King Roderic, the Spanish Rodrigo. The myth entails an archetypical story of seduction, sexual morality and the correlation between individual misbehavior and the larger dynamics of fate and providence.[91]

Early Christian sources of the Iberian Peninsula mention Count Julian but remain silent about details such as the rape and betrayal motif until the eleventh century, when chroniclers integrated it into several mythical stories about the origins of Muslim rule over Spain. The cross fertilization of Arab tradition and Hispanic-Christian mythology happened under the circumstances of the intellectual and linguistic coexistence of multilingual scholars in Muslim Spain, but it was not a story of *convivencia*. For Arab Muslim chroniclers, the conquest of *al-Andalus* was but one story in a long line of glorious conquests and triumphs over Christianity. The story of the rape of Count Julian's daughter fulfilled a narrative function vilifying the opponents and denigrating them as morally corrupt. For Christian authors of the Iberian Peninsula, Roderic and his act embodied the moral decadence of the Visigoth kingdom. As an explanation for the catastrophe of the Muslim conquest as punishment from God, Roderic's rape became one of the most persistent literary motifs of Christian Spanish literature. Spanish vernacular versions of the story first came up in the thirteenth century. In the course of the medieval period, the name Alacaba, which later turned into La Cava, was introduced for Julian's daughter, as an apparent adaptation of the Arabic name Hawwa' for Eve, as some argue. Authors transformed the outright condemnation of the protagonists for their moral corruption into a story of redemption, in which a defeated Roderic turned into an ascetic to pay for his sins after the battle of Guadalete. The name Florinda appeared for the first time in Miguel de la Luna's sixteenth-century book *La verdadera historia del rey don Rodrigo*.[92] The author, himself a Mozarab, claimed that his book was a mere translation of an Arabic source, but it was later revealed to be a forgery. The work was nevertheless of central importance for the further, Europe-wide reception of the myth. The name Florinda may have been Miguel de la Luna's brainchild.[93]

The Florinda–Roderic topos persisted in European literature until the twentieth century, undergoing a number of significant transformations. The interest of authors shifted from the motif of divine punishment, the vilification of La Cava as a whore seducing the king, to a tragic love story about the impossibility to withstand desire. Arabs and Berbers ceased to play a significant role, if a role at all, in these literary renderings. In Spain, La Cava became a popular topic for the composers of ballads and romanceros of the sixteenth and seventeenth centuries. Lope De Vega brought it to the stage at the turn of the seventeenth century in a little-known work entitled the *Last Goth of Spain* (*El postrer godo de España*). It also entered his epic poem *Jerusalen conquistada* (finished 1605), which celebrates Saladin, who learns humility from the story of the downfall of Roderic. In the seventeenth century, the La Cava–Florinda story became pan-European literary material. First, the English dramatist William Rowley used it for his play *All's Lost By Lust*, first performed in 1619 and published in 1633. The title says all about the morality tale the story had become. European writers turned the characters into prototypes driven by lust, treachery, and intrigue. Opera played a key role in popularizing the story. One of the artistically most outstanding versions is Georg Frederic Handel's early piece *Rodrigo*, first performed in Florence in 1707. The libretto of Handel's version by Francesco Silvani deviated widely from the historical kernel and thus initiated a new and subsequently influential version. Silvani was conscious to the taste of his time for historical drama and erotic themes and therefore transferred the plot to antiquity. It also lacked references to religious conflict; the Muslim conquest of Spain is therefore entirely absent.[94]

Thus, an almost unrecognizable version of the myth of the conquest of *al-Andalus* had entered the European canon of the arts. Jurji Zaydan probably took some inspiration from works by Walter Scott, Walter Savage Landor, and Robert Southey, who were all representatives of British Romantic literature. Their fascination for antiquity and the Middle Ages, combined with Orientalism, made the myth ideal raw material. Scott has been identified as an inspiration for Zaydan in other works. His epic poem the *Vision of Don Roderick* has little in common with Zaydan's novel, however, nor has Landor's *Count Julian*. Southey's epic poem *Roderic, the Last of the Goths* shares at least names such as Florinda and Alfons with Zaydan's novel, but his Roderic is a tragic hero, and his story begins only years after the battle of Guadalete.[95]

In the nineteenth century, the Marquis de Sade used the topos, and so did, in North America, Washington Irving and Thomas Holley Chivers.[96] German nationalist historicism motivated Felix Dahn, author of historical novels such as *Ein Kampf um Rom*, to publish a play on *König Roderich* in 1876. It appeared in the context of the *Kulturkampf,* which was a confrontation between Bismarck's authoritarian state and the Catholic Church, but the parallels to Zaydan's anti-Catholicism are probably due to sources they shared rather than familiarity. The European works of the nineteenth century share an anti-Islamic and anti-Arab prejudice, whereas the twentieth-century Spanish novelist and Islamophile Juan Goytisolo presented Count Julian's betrayal that facilitates the conquest of *al-Andalus* as a subversive and culturally fruitful act. In 1966, star tenor Placido Domingo received international acclaim for singing the title role in the Spanish–Argentine composer Alberto Ginastera's opera *Don Rodrigo* at the New York City Opera. Probably the latest rendering of the myth is the London musical production *La Cava* that came out in 2000, based on a 1977 novel by Dana Broccoli, wife of *James Bond* film producer Albert R. Broccoli. True to its genre, the motif of tragic love remains at the center of *La Cava's* script, with scarce Orientalist references, but none about religious conflict.[97]

The lines of transmission for the various motifs in Zaydan's novel remain unclear. Many elements are in Reinhart Dozy's historical account that Zaydan used, including the name "Florinda" in a brief footnote, but no reference to a son of the betrayed King Witiza called Alfons. In turn, al-Maqqari mentions that Witiza's sons held a grudge against Roderic, but he could nevertheless convince them to fight with him in the battle of Guadalete. The smoldering conflict had, however, weakened the Visigoth camp. In Zaydan's story, this internal conflict is a major theme, as Alfons is torn between the Arab camp fighting his nemesis and loyalty towards his kin. Alfons' aversion for Roderic finally prevails.[98] At the end of the day, Zaydan's novel remains a fictional account, in which several traditions that inspired him flowed together. He was thus able to turn the novel into a more compelling story than if he had relied slavishly on his sources. *Fath al-Andalus* then became the urtext of the modern day standard storyline of the conquest of *al-Andalus* in Arab popular culture. The novel, for instance, popularized a Europeanized spelling of the names of major non-Arab characters such as Roderic and Julian. Prior to Zaydan's novel, Arabic sources, including early historiography, used "Ludhriq" for Roderic and "Ilyan" or "Yulyan" for Julian.[99] Mustafa Kamil used the same spellings in his version, and only 'Ali Mubarak introduced "Rudiriq" and "Julian", adding the spelling in Latin script in parentheses, too, to make clear that his was a transcription. Zaydan then adopted "Rudirik," but kept the Arabic "Yulyan," while taking over the epithet "al-kunt" that Mubarak used.[100]

Next to the continuing success of Zaydan's novels, traces of his version of the story have become a mainstay of Arabic historical fiction and hero worship. Al-Khatib's *Fath al-Andalus* provides evidence, along with many other plays of the same title or with other *al-Andalus* references that were popular on stages throughout the Arab world in the interwar period.[101] Most Arabic renderings of the story concentrate on Tariq Ibn Ziyad as one of the great heroes of Islamic history, especially in books for adolescents. He is celebrated in a series of portraits of historical figures ("al-Najihun," "the Successful Ones"), published in Beirut, intended to be "a living school for the boys of the present and the men of the future." The 2000 edition (the 4th) of *Tariq Ibn Ziyad: Fatih al-Andalus* is basically an adaptation of Zaydan's novel, with all the characters – in his spelling – including Rudirik and Yulyan, as well as, of course, Florinda and Alfons. The book moves the focus to the Muslim and Arab characters of the story, though.[102] Other books referred to the story of La Cava-Florinda in passing, using Zaydan's nomenclature, and presented it as an oddity of the Arabic historical tradition that was nevertheless worth mentioning.[103]

The oddity of the tradition, along with the ambivalence of Zaydan's storyline is still a matter of concern for contemporary authors, especially Zaydan's religious pluralism and the role individuals and groups belonging to religious minorities play in his novel. In a critique published in 1994, the Jordanian author of children's books and literary critic Muhammad Bassam Mals (b. 1950) compared Zaydan's original *Fath al-Andalus* to an adaptation of the book for children published in Beirut in the late 1970s in order to find out about their respective value for Islamic education.[104] He felt it necessary to clarify that Zaydan's novel only offered an incomplete perspective on an event that was more than a love story, and more than a military adventure. It was, after all, the triumph of Islam over a superior enemy, the story of the unification of Arabs and Berbers that could only happen under the banner of Islam, and it was the realization of the Islamic goal of just government, not merely the striving for military success and booty. Mals took issue with what he considered Zaydan's decision to foreground personal convictions and emotions at the expense of Muslim religious fervor and *jihad*. Accordingly, Mals criticized the prominent role of non-Muslims in the story. He accused Zaydan of sowing the seeds of antagonism based on ethnicity when he mentioned the term "Arab" 49 times, "Berber" 11 times, but "Muslims" only 10 times in the novel. Zaydan's depiction of Jews was apparently so outlandish for Mals that he did not even believe he had to comment on such assertions in the novel that Arabs and Jews were cousins. He seemed to agree with Zaydan, however, when the latter, as Mals misunderstood his wording, referred to the Jews as "banu Isra'il" – "Israelites," or in Mals' reading "Israelis," thus confirming the identity of the plotting Jews in the novel with the citizens of contemporary Israel. In turn, Mals was quite pleased with the fact that the late seventies adaptation of the novel cut out the drinking that occurred in Zaydan's original, toned down Zaydan's depiction of Roderic's attack on Florinda that had exposed her bosom, and avoided the great novelist's original characterizations of the Jews. Mals was particularly incensed by Florinda's role in Zaydan's novel. Her story had no historical basis, but was a product of Zaydan's fantasy, he wrote. Her beauty and its effect on the men of the novel were in contradiction with Islamic principles. Particularly dangerous was her obvious practice of *shirk*, or *polytheism*. Even the children's adaptation did not eliminate scenes where she knelt in front of an effigy of the *Masih*, or Jesus Christ, or before an image of Mary, asking for protection. Finally, the author stopped short of blaming the victim, Florinda, for the attempted rape. For him, the way she addressed Roderic in one scene as merely his humble servant contradicted her bold and provocative resistance to him when he tried to rape her only moments later. Mals was, in contrast, much more content with the several leads in the novel that addressed vile characteristics of Jews, especially their greed and lust for money.[105]

Mals' dogmatic and at times irrational refutation of Zaydan's novel – blaming the Christian author for not having written like an orthodox Muslim – is characteristic for some Arab literary critics that have assessed the *Fath al-Andalus* and *Tariq Ibn Ziyad* literature from the perspective of an Arab nationalist or Muslim apologist. The attention they afford and the vehemence of their rejection should be taken as an acknowledgment of the persistent popularity of the story. The Saudi scholar 'Abd al-Halim 'Uways mistook the mythical element in the Tariq Ibn Ziyad story for ordinary historiography and then complained about its lack of logic and veracity. In a monograph focused on Tariq's order to burn the ships before the Battle of Guadalete, 'Uways lamented that this part of the great hero's story still could be found in school texts and popular books. While many other Arab authors before him had already contested its veracity, 'Uways added a scripturalist perspective of Islamic law. He reasoned that an event of this importance should have had an echo in the hadith traditions of the Companions of the Prophet that were still alive at the time. The silence of the literature did, however, not mean an implicit approval of the action by the forefathers, according to 'Uways. To the contrary, the Sunna made clear that suicidal actions – such as to cut off an escape route – were illegal, as much as the forbidding replacement cost of the ships. In addition, Islamic warriors of the time had not been in need of compulsion to go into battle.[106]

From a different vantage point, the Tariq myth also served opportunist authors to advertise the militarist doctrine of dictatorial regimes. They praised Tariq Ibn Ziyad for his virtue and manliness, but also rejected the Florinda story and the burning of the ships as tarnishing Tariq's reputation and the glory of the conquest. A Libyan author presented Tariq as a distinctly Berber hero, and thus as a model for unity with the Arab peoples under the banner of Colonel Qaddafi's rule. Literally, "[t]his Berber hero was a model of manliness and dedication ("jihad") for those who belong to the peoples of North Africa [of Arab descent] ..." In a dedication at the beginning of the book, he confirmed that he wanted to prove those wrong who belittle the illustrious people of Islam, and eradicate the history of Muslim heroism out of mistake or ignorance, … those who assign these mistakes as part of curricula, … those who believe that Count Julian ("al-kunt Yulyan") inspired the conquest of *al-Andalus* for his hatred of King Ludhriq who violated the honor of his daughter Florinda, … those who write the history of the heroes of Islam in the mind of the crusader Orientalists, in the manner that resembles the fables of the sources and stories of adventure and imagination.[107]

In a similar way, an Iraqi historian put the Tariq story into an ideological context, equating the spirit of early Muslim warriors with the determination of Iraqi soldiers fighting in the Iran–Iraq war. The account thus followed a particular Iraqi school of historians of the 1980s that succumbed to incentives and pressure to write in the service of the regime. The book was dedicated to "every decorated [?] field commander of the brave Iraqi army, to the offspring of this gigantic leader [Saddam Hussein], that they may follow on his path and his steps in keenness of resolution and strength of will." For the author, only Western sources could have contrived the phantasy story of Florinda. The Orientalists fell over each other to confirm this story in order to provide a tolerable reason for the Arab advance to "liberate" *al-Andalus*. They wanted to put the blame on "La Cava," which in their language meant "the evil woman."[108]

None of these arguments was very original. They were all quite out of sync with a proper distinction between mythical content and a rather narrow factual core of the conquest story, according to the history of its transmission. In the context of the argumentation of this chapter, however, it is remarkable to what extent the narrative line, developed by Jurji Zaydan and including the nomenclature of the main characters of the story, had become a component of the Arab storyline in the twentieth century, as if it naturally belonged to the tradition.

In a similar vein, a cartoon film *Fath al-Andalus*, produced in Saudi Arabia probably in the 1990s or 2000s, is a relatively free adaptation of Zaydan's novel.[109] It introduces Roderic (called Ludhriq) as a brute and primitive king of the Goths who abuses his servants and soldiers constantly. Count Julian features merely as "al-kunt." The film's adaptation of the story for children demands that Florinda's rape is skipped. Instead she escapes from the oppressive atmosphere in the palace, but is captured and imprisoned. Her father is in a rage about the abduction of his child and offers Tariq, who is welcome as a guest in Sebta, to help him cross the straits. The rest of the film is about the battle of Guadalete and the defeat of Roderic, the tyrant, including a long scene in which Tariq recites his speech about the burning ships. Florinda and her father drop out of the story, and the emphasis of the film shifts to the conquest as a Muslim endeavor, in contrast to Zaydan's and al-Khatib's version. The fighters are addressed as "al-muslimun" or "al-mujahidun," not as Arabs. Nevertheless, aptly pronounced classical Arabic remains the language of the film's heavy dialogues, providing evidence that the Conquest of *al-Andalus* story is still based on a popular Arab myth. Florinda and Count Julian remain a fixed part of the myth – familiar enough apparently that even children watching the film expect it to come up, including the epithet "al-kunt."[110]

The identification of these various lines of transmission must remain a matter of likelihood and informed guessing at the end of the day, but Zaydan's work certainly functioned like a focal lens of several traditions from various origins, bringing together motifs from Arabic and European historiography and literary history, thus highlighting the transnational background of this nationalist narrative. Zaydan introduced the Florinda–Roderic motif not only as an adoption, but as a radical adaptation of the European myth to the discursive context of the late Ottoman Empire. As a historicist, Zaydan used the material of the story to reconcile the growing Arab cultural awareness of his milieu with his own location as a Christian in a Muslim majority environment. When Zaydan depicted Visigoth Arian Christians as under pressure by the Roman Catholic episcopate that controlled King Roderic, Zaydan raised questions about the loyalty of a religious minority even to a dictatorial monarch. At the same time he highlighted the advantages of a morally superior Arab-Muslim ruler, yet also argued for a secular state when he propagated the division of church and state that had apparently existed under Arianism. The ambiguous, but not at all negative role of Jews in the novel is crucial in that regard. The positive depiction of Jewish resilience and the focus on Visigoth rather than Arab-Muslim characters such as Tariq Ibn Ziyad, who is ubiquitous in later treatments of the subject, mark this as a literary work of the *nahda*, or in other words, of proto-, if at all, nationalism. The main attack lines of later Arab nationalism were not there yet, including the emerging anti-Judaism of the post-World War I period.[111]

Epilogue: from permanent exile to *al-Andalus* al-jadida: the continuing presence of *al-Andalus* in the Arab mind

Al-Andalus retains a strong presence in Arab historical-cultural consciousness, not least in literature, and most of all because the *al-Andalus* myth lends itself to a wide array of metaphorical usages that illustrate the Arab predicament of the twentieth century, dominated by colonial confrontations and a perceived cultural competition with the Western world. Similar to the Crusades in the Levant and the heroic image of Saladin's chivalry, *al-Andalus* has become a literary *chronotope*, which is a place that is distant yet all too present in its locality and temporality, available to be used as a mirror for the present. While the Crusades offer a straightforward reference to past heroism in perceived moral superiority, the image of *al-Andalus* is more complex. It serves as a topos that offers nostalgic identification with a better life in a shared Arab national identity based on a common heritage of language and culture, but also a heritage of good governance and moral sovereign statehood. The popularity of the *al-Andalus* topic in novels and poetry is therefore anchored in the lasting affinity of Arabic literature for nationalism.[112]

The topos of paradise lost – rooted in the expulsion of the Muslim Arabs and Moriscos from *al-Andalus* – has been used since the interwar period to either foreshadow or mourn the loss of Arab territory to imperialist force. In 1939, for example, *al-Risala* published a letter to the editor by Muhammad Khalifa Sha'ban al-Tarablusi – from Gaza, but probably an exile from Tripoli in Libya – under the title "*al-Andalus* al-jadida" ("The New *al-Andalus*"). The author accused Muslim rulers of the world of passivity in the face of the Italian colonization of Libya, just as when the Muslim states had not reacted when *al-Andalus* was lost. Then, there had been no unity and no response, but only great grief and commemoration by poets and writers after the fact. Today, the Arabs were equally indifferent when monuments of Arabism and Islam were erased in Libya and Roman ones erected on their rubble. Maybe they waited to raise their voices until they could cry over the loss of Arabism and Islam in Tripoli.[113]

Around the time of the outbreak of the Palestine Revolt in 1936, the Egyptian press became concerned that Palestine might become a second *al-Andalus* and the Arab population might get expelled.[114] Yet still in 1937, Muhammad 'Abdallah 'Inan wrote in *al-Risala* about the common fate of the Spanish Jews and the Moriscos. He identified fissures, though, in the way the two fateful communities received their fair share of recognition. In the introduction to a serialized article about the last Morisco rebellion against Spanish rule in 1569, he made reference to the fact that the Spanish delegation to the Montreux Conference for the abolition of the capitulations in Egypt, which was going on when the article came out, had submitted a request that Sephardic Jews living in Egypt should be treated as Spanish protégés, and that therefore they should be granted the privilege of litigation before the mixed courts during a set period of transition until 1949, during which these courts, consisting of Egyptian and foreign judges, should remain active. A member of the Spanish delegation, which the Republican government had dispatched to Montreux, explained to the Press that these Jews belonged to the Spanish Jewish diaspora who had been persecuted by the Inquisition in the sixteenth century and dispersed into various countries. Republican Spain, now liberated from prejudice and fanatic inclinations, wanted to offer compensation to the descendants of this population group that had been wronged in an age of injustice, fanaticism and oppression.[115]

The request by the Republican government was in line with a trend of philo-Sephardism among Spanish liberals and leftists that went back to the late nineteenth century. Initially, the underlying assumption of this trend was that the mixing of Spanish and Jewish blood in *al-Andalus* had elevated the Jewish race, in contrast to its allegedly degenerate state in Northern Europe. The Spanish colonization of Morocco furthered philo-Sephardism because businessmen believed they could rely on the local Jewish population to work in their interest. The left-leaning government of the Second Spanish Republic, founded in 1931, revoked traditional anti-Jewish policies and offered easy naturalization to Moroccan Jews of Sephardic origin. Rumors spread among Sephardic communities worldwide that their restitution to Spanish citizenship was imminent, but they proved unfounded. Nevertheless, the Republican government intended to show goodwill through gestures such as the one at Montreux, built on the historical image of a Spanish Golden Age during the era of *convivencia* that had been followed only by decline after the expulsion of the Jews.[116]

Apparently, there was no room for the expelled Muslims or Moriscos in this selective narrative. Accordingly, the statement of the Spanish delegate stirred up sadness in 'Inan. After four centuries, Spain acknowledged its historical responsibility and condemned the Inquisition, but this was, as 'Inan noticed, only a small part of the wider truth, which was that Christian Spain also had annihilated what remained of the Muslim and Arab descendants who had ruled over the Peninsula for roughly eight centuries. The Jews, who prospered in the shade of the Muslim state, were victims of this barbaric policy, just as were the Muslims.[117]

Al-'Inan's complaint points to *al-Andalus* as an ambivalent metaphorical reference in the Arab–Jewish conflict. During the interwar years and until 1948, images of doom and being forsaken by one's friends and allies entered the Andalusian chronotope in addition to associations of interreligious harmony, while references to a shared Arab–Jewish fate of persecution and expulsion after the Reconquista ceased to make sense to the effect that today, the loss of *al-Andalus* remains a powerful symbol in verse and prose about the *nakba*, the catastrophe of the Palestinian expulsions in 1948.[118] Ultimately, *al-Andalus* is as successful as it is as a myth because of its malleability – as a symbol of Arab cultural superiority, of the power of Islam and Muslim generosity and tolerance, but also as a marker of the moral deficiency of the West. It has served as a token for inter-religious understanding, and for its ultimate failure.

The topos is most powerful, however, as a reference for nostalgic longing. A glance through a recent text book from Morocco confirms this. It offers elementary school fifth graders a mixture of stories and non-fictional texts that are clearly geared towards instilling a sense of modern citizen identity in the children. Patriotic texts about the homeland include a hymn about Morocco's independence struggle, a poem about Palestine ("Victory is coming"), stories on landscapes, on the economy and technology, texts about health, family, the Berber mountain resistance during the French conquest, about nature and the universe, and one about the Arctic. In a time – prior to the paradigmatic change of 9/11 and the Tahrir Revolution – that many would describe as a post-Arab nationalist period in the Arab lands, it is significant that the only two patriotic texts in the text book that are not Morocco-specific address Palestine and *al-Andalus*, forming the vestiges of a pan-Arab identity. Two texts of the Moroccan book introduce historical sites, one about Marrakesh, and the other one, which is the only one about a place outside of Morocco, the Alhambra in Granada. The author Ahmad Kan'an recounted his impressions from a visit to a friend in Granada – on quite familiar terms. After his arrival at the train station he could not wait to visit the Alhambra because it was the only trace of "monuments of our Islamic civilization." His friend agreed to an immediate visit, and they approached the site driving through a hilly forest landscape:

> From the beginning I felt like entering a different world. Trees of slim stature rose up in it to adorn the hills with Arab grandeur, and the pride of the noble Muslim knight. I was certain that I was, indeed, on soil that still longed for its inherited past,

Kanʻan wrote, setting the stage for yet another tour of the hallowed grounds in a dream-like fashion, reminiscent of Mustafa Farrukh's visit in the 1920s. On top of the page that contains Kanʻan's story is a watercolor with a rendition of the Alhambra on top of the hill, painted from a perspective of someone standing on the slopes of the Albaicin quarter opposite the castle. In the foreground of the picture there are several flat roof buildings with one pitched roof and a pyramid shaped roof, both with the characteristic green tiles that would be typical for Moroccan sacred architecture, but that are entirely absent from current Andalucía. While the story is set in contemporary times, it is therefore juxtaposed to an image that presents the Alhambra without any clear temporal markers, carefully integrating it into a familiar but imaginary Moroccan and Muslim environment. Accordingly, the watercolor avoids integrating the bell tower of a church that a photographic rendition, taken from the same spot, would have depicted in the foreground. Modern day Moroccans, like most Arabs, are taught to read the sights of modern day Andalucía, including the Alhambra and the Mezquita, like timeless representations of an Arab Golden Age.[119]

Both *al-Andalus* and the Saladin myth of the beginning of this chapter thus contain a myriad of points of identification at a crossroads of Christian-European and Muslim-Arab culture, as well as a multi-centered Jewish culture. The stories build on each other, reflect each other, and bounce off of each other. Only rarely do they conflate; always, however, are they broken characteristically through the prism of the twentieth-century imperialist entanglement.

4 Of Kings and Cavemen

Museums and nationalist museology in twentieth-century Egypt

The previous chapter focused on the virtual space of literature as a primary resort for the creation of a collective identity across an imaginary Arab space that encompassed the lands between the Atlantic Ocean and the Tigris River. This chapter sheds light on the creation of identity-making narratives in a single concrete location, Egypt, and a physical structure, the museum. Museology was new to Arab countries in the nineteenth century – a fact that did not prevent Arab intellectuals of the twentieth century from tracing the history of the modern museum back to Arab origins, and in particular – how could it be different? – to al-Andalus, the mythical treasure house of everything that was good in Arab civilization. In a 1943 article in al-Risala, *the author Muhammad 'Abd al-Ghanni Hasan acknowledged the role of Europeans in the creation of the museum, especially in Renaissance Italy, but he argued that the first collections that Europeans later turned into national property had been taken from the treasure houses of the Muslim kings of Granada to form the core of Arab collections in Spanish and other European museums. Collecting was therefore a habit that the Arabs first invented.[1] This assertion by an Arab intellectual – as much as it may have been a romantic invention – is quite pertinent to the following pages as it turned a European claim on originality on its head to showcase Arab cultural agency.*

The dawn of the Egyptian man

When the Museum of Egyptian Civilization opened its gates to Cairo's public in March 1949, a visitor who entered the first section of the museum's concourse encountered an impressive sight: a life-size likeness of a Paleolithic Neanderthal man with a staff in his hand, all naked except for a loincloth, exiting from his cave (Figure 4.1).

The Neanderthal was the only statue of this kind in the museum which otherwise used scaled dioramas, paintings, friezes, and maps to present the continuous development of Egyptian civilization throughout the ages from the caveman to the glorious dynasty of Mehmet Ali, the Ottoman military commander who had managed to carve an Empire and found a dynasty out of the prosperous Ottoman province in the first half of the nineteenth century. The irony may not have been

Figure 4.1 The caveman in the Museum of Egyptian Civilization.

lost on the visitors of the museum that the bewildered gaze of the caveman, as if incredulous to the wonders of Egyptian progress, stood in stark contrast to the distanced, ceremonial stature of the only other life-size statues at the end of the exhibition concourse in the halls that celebrated the reigning monarch Faruq and his father, the late King Fu'ad carved in stone.[2]

The guidebook that came out to accompany the opening of the museum explained that the modern species of man appeared towards the end of the Paleolithic era. "After this, man entered into a new period, which was all innovation, progress, and ascent. Without a doubt, the origins of our new civilization go back to this period called the Neolithic." These foundations for modern civilization and the origins of social and governmental life "… prepared the ground for political unity and the unified government in the early Pharaonic age."[3] The theme of unity and continuity loomed large in the official museum narrative. One of the principal authors of this narrative, Egyptian historian Shafiq Ghurbal (1894–1961), wrote in the official guidebook that "the museum is a unity, and its theme is: Egyptian civilization – as a unity, with its significance and greatness reaching through all its historical epochs."[4] According to this narrative, Egyptian history was a brace that connected the Stone Age with the present, and from the beginning, Egypt had been the vanguard.

Museums as institutions were certainly a Western import in the Middle East, but they nevertheless emerged in local contexts. Antiquities museums were founded in Cairo and Istanbul in the nineteenth century by Westerners for Western visitors, or catered to Europeanized elites. For the elites and visitors, the museums represented a supposedly global cultural community, albeit according to a unity of civilization as defined in Europe, functioning on a trajectory from the high cultures of early and ancient history via the Greeks and Romans and the Italian Renaissance to the dominant Western civilization of the day. The locals in Egypt or in the Ottoman provinces were not considered part of this civilization, other than the European tourists who started to flock to the Nile in the mid-nineteenth century. The locals adopted museums only in the twentieth century as projects of distinction and self-assertion. Instead of a world civilization with the nation states of Europe considered as its pinnacle, Egyptian museum makers were eager to define a separate civilization of their own, determining what was legitimately their own heritage of the past.[5]

In this context, the caveman played the role of the arch-Egyptian, at the origins of this glorious civilization, even if he was explicitly introduced as "Neanderthal Man," named after a valley in Germany.[6] In 1947, the leading intellectual journal *al-Hilal* introduced the caveman in anticipation of the opening of the museum as "the ancient Egyptian in the pre-historic age."[7] People were clearly fascinated by the caveman. Further articles in *al-Hilal* and *al-Risala*, another leading intellectual journal, gave him prominent space. He even inspired one author in *al-Hilal* to a broad reflection about the origins of man, asking if the force of nature in itself had brought about the slow emergence of man from his bestiality, if nature had served him or had been hostile to him.[8]

The caveman stood for an evolutionary image of history, placing Egypt at the center of a vision of civilization marked by a trajectory leading from the origin of the species towards modern man, who was capable of commanding nature and the members of his own species, as the dioramas of the museum's section about the modern period clearly pointed out, such as one on the Nile Barrages, one presenting a visit of King Fu'ad to the cotton spinning factories in al-Mahalla al-Kubra, or King Faruq laying the founding stone of a hydroelectric plant at the old Aswan dam.[9]

The Civilization Museum's version of Egyptian history echoed the secularist trends of leading Egyptian intellectuals of the 1920s such as Muhammad Husayn Haykal's and Salama Musa's Egyptianism and environmental determinism.

As positivists, Egyptian intellectuals perceived their country's uniqueness as based on the specific natural conditions of the Nile Valley, distinguishing the country and its population in a millennia-old history from other Arab lands, and thus undermining the primacy of the Arabo–Islamic heritage that had determined Egyptian historiography up until the nineteenth century.[10] The caveman symbolized Egyptian history as secular, historicist, scientistic and teleological, and thus represented a specific position in a contemporary contest over the meanings of history between secular intellectuals, liberally conservative Muslim thinkers, and Arab nationalists.[11] At the end of the day, however, a national project like the Civilization Museum had to reconcile all these positions.

In a metaphorical sense, the Neanderthal's emergence out of his cave depicted a coming of age moment, as if foreshadowing Stanley Kubrick's *2001* "Dawn of Man" film sequence. And a man he was: The exhibit at the Civilization Museum was somewhat daring in its stark nudity. The first available image (Figure 4.2),

Figure 4.2 The cavemen before the opening of the museum.

published in *al-Hilal*, shows the Neanderthal man in full nudity exposing his genitals.[12] A photo that appeared two years later in the same magazine showed the man, still naked, but from an angle so that his private parts remained hidden to the viewer (Figure 4.3).[13] Finally, the actual public exhibit as the museum catalogue recorded it had the loincloth added (Figure 4.1).

The exhibition thus opened the narrative of the museum in brute masculinity, as a token of the understanding of the museum makers that history was driven by male dominance and principles as they were prominently presented in the museum. War and conquest, hunting and seafaring, building, trading and politics of power, as well as science and technology dominated as male undertakings the visual representation of the Museum of Egyptian Civilization.

Figure 4.3 The cavemen before the opening of the museum from a different angle.

Figure 4.4 "Feast in the Harem."

The exception that confirmed the rule was an affresco mural of a "feast in the Harem" in the section that covered the Ottoman period (Figure 4.4). It delineated female space as sexualized in an Orientalist way. Other images in the section presented only public, external places as characteristic locations of Ottoman Cairo, such as a market place, or a combined public fountain and Quranic school (*sabil-kuttab*).[14]

The following pages will engage the Civilization Museum project as a crossing point of several lines of imperialist and nationalist imagination – some of them concurring, some of them in disagreement. It should be noted, though, that all these lines present different levels of power and elite opinion vying for hegemony in a late imperial discourse, involving an all-male Egyptian ruling elite, representatives of British, French, and Italian imperialism, as well as members of a new Arab–Egyptian elite of specialists. Grass-roots responses to this hegemonic discourse are hard to discern on the basis of the available sources, and must therefore be left to a different study.

Imperialist museology and elite nationalism

When the Civilization Museum opened in 1949, it already had a history. In early April 1939, King Faruq of Egypt presented a memorandum to a special committee, made up of members of the board of the Egyptian Royal Agricultural Society, who were tasked with the organization of the sixteenth Exhibition for Agriculture and Industry planned for 1941. The Society, founded in 1898 under the Egyptian Khedive Abbas II, was one of several institutions that represented Egypt's claim on modernity and development through science and engineering.[15] Faruq's memorandum, drafted by his private secretary Husayn Hasani, ordered that the committee should use the planned exhibition to set up a museum of Egyptian civilization.[16] Faruq had developed the idea during a visit to the Schweizerisches Landesmuseum in Zurich on a recent trip to Europe. Founded in 1898 as a national Swiss institution, the Landesmuseum displayed a synthesis of Swiss history and heritage in an easily understandable manner to great public appeal. At the time of Faruq's visit, it exhibited a meta-narrative along historical epochs, from pre-history to the present, in spite of the regional variations and strong self-confidence of the various Swiss cantons.[17] It must have been this harmonious and unified historical narrative that impressed the young Egyptian king so much.

Faruq's memorandum outlined the reasoning behind such a museum project in clear terms. Hasani, the author, had written that there was hardly any other nation in the world that equaled Egypt in terms of the longevity of its civilization, "from the dawn of history to the present." There was clear evidence for this fact in the museums that already existed in Egypt. However, they were scattered physically throughout the country, but also in terms of their specialized contents. To open a museum in order to record the continuous unfolding of Egyptian civilization would therefore be an immense service to Egyptian history and culture.

Hasani also suggested a program for the envisaged exhibition, both in terms of historical sequence and of the kinds of objects to be displayed.[18] The sequence ranged from Pre-History, the Pharaonic Age – including the Old, Middle and New Kingdoms, as well as the Persian conquest, the Ptolemies, the Roman period, and the "appearance" ("zuhur") of Christianity, to the Muslim conquest and consecutive Islamic states, the Turkish period, and finally the Napoleonic conquest, the "awakening" ("nahda") of Muhammad 'Ali Pasha the Great (Mehmet Ali), and to the contemporary period, altogether reflecting the historical program of a school of historiography that King Fu'ad, Faruq's father, had brought to life when the royal 'Abdin palace became a center for a new national, but paternalistic project of claiming Egyptian history for Egyptian historians. Shafiq Ghurbal, the aforementioned doyen of this national history, championed an effort to re-write Egypt's nineteenth-century past on the basis of a positivist historicism that he and many of his colleagues had imbibed as the first generation of Egyptian historians to be trained at Western, in particular British, universities.[19] The historicism of this generation paired the classical Hegelian sense of historical determinism – pointing towards the nation as the pinnacle of the development of human civilization – with a strong scientific rigor based on an almost blind trust in the truth of archival evidence. A major achievement of this generation of historians was the opening and organization of the Egyptian 'Abdin Archives that later transitioned into the Egyptian National Archives and document the administration of Egypt under the rule of Mehmet Ali's dynasty. This was no innocent effort, of course, as Ghurbal and his students published numerous volumes editing historical documents and translating them, following an agenda of securing a place for Egypt's recent dynasty among the praiseworthy in a historical succession of the country's rulers that incorporated admiration for the Pharaonic past as a national heritage with pride in the legacy of Islamic rule. According to this narrative, which follows the so-called "founders' paradigm," Mehmet Ali was the founder of a modern Egypt that restored the country to its appropriate place among the nations after centuries of decline and inertia under Ottoman rule.[20] More recent historiography has put the "founders' paradigm" in perspective and considers Mehmet Ali's rule and that of his immediate successors as a continuation of Ottoman practices rather than an immediate breakaway towards national independence, but a periodization of Egyptian history according to the Ghurbal school continued to dominate middle-class Egyptians' vision of their historical place in the world throughout the twentieth century.[21]

Most importantly, if the historical sequence of the Civilization Museum should promote a synthesis of Egyptian history with unmatched longevity for all Egyptians' collective imagination, it was certainly a top-down imposition emanating from the palace, as the narrative trajectory towards a culmination in Mehmet Ali's dynasty indicated. It was, however, also a populist and anti-imperialist project. The idea to create a fusion of the scattered museums on Egyptian soil represented an attempt to wrest control over the past of the country from the hands of foreigners who had commanded the Egyptian antiquities and museum business for more than a century. The goal of this fusion was to popularize an image of Egypt as the product of a millennia-old civilization, in which all Egyptians had a part. Like under the absolutist and autocratic rulers of the past, the dynasty was the focal point of the glory that emanated from the sequence of Egyptian history embedded in continuity. The new conditions of an emerging mass society and ever accelerating urbanization, not to mention the growth of a politicized middle class with nationalist aspirations, made clear, however, that the dynastic image needed a face-lift to render it legitimate in a civic society.

* * *

Museums became a crucial instrument for the practicing of civic-ness and the formation of citizenship in Europe during the modern period, and thus they became a token for modernity and liberalism. If art museums marked a nation's "political virtue and national identity," history or civilization museums played a similar role. They were presented as neutral vessels that store and exhibit objects, but were in fact ritualized spaces with a more or less concealed political and ideological function. Visitors were ready to participate in rituals such as following a particular tour to re-enact a narrative. For founders of museums, in our case rulers and state authorities, establishing a museum was a way of conveying messages of national pride and equality in the public sphere in the guise of an institution that the ethos of modernism considered a selfless liberal and humanist representation of civic engagement, and an outgrowth of a distanced scientific and objective mind. The museum made a cross identification between state and citizen possible: the former laid out what it meant to be civilized, the latter became part of the civilized realm via the ritual of the museum visit.[22]

Museums are 'go-to' places and thus they are essentially different from monuments. Museum visits constitute a break away from daily practices, whereas monuments are set up for constant public visibility, and thus become quasi invisible – a paradox that turns the public monument into a blind spot, part of the visual background noise, "impregnated against attention," in the words of Robert Musil – "[t]here is nothing in this world as invisible as a monument."[23] Museums are different. One decides to go there during an outing, for leisure, and one has certain expectations as to the benefits of the visit, be they educational or uplifting, or both, or maybe merely entertaining. One might even be taken there as part of an educational mission or a school curriculum, not only, but especially in an authoritarian state, with a particular agenda. It is therefore safe to assume that the museums discussed in this volume in fact had a public impact, even if impact studies and visitor statistics have not been available.

The historical roots of European museology are in the Renaissance period, when collections of valuable things, usually in the possession of men of power, were transformed from mere treasure houses into loci for the enactment of classification, understood as an attempt at an exact and systematic representation of nature, or more broadly speaking, the world. To exhibit meant to display taxonomy. The Medici Palace of fifteenth-century Florence is widely considered as the "first museum" of this kind, but it was not a museum in the modern sense. Taxonomies are historical and socially conditioned along lines of conventions of readability, and fifteenth-century conventions were not similar to the scientific systems that came up in the eighteenth and nineteenth centuries. The Medici collection represented patronage of the arts, and command over categories of taste and connoisseurship. Exhibits (in this case mostly art) were set up to impress, not to educate and elevate visitors. The Medici collection, like the *Kunstkammer* or *cabinet of curiosities* that became a mainstay of sixteenth- and seventeenth-century aristocratic palaces north of the Alps, should reflect the power and status of the family. The owner of the Kunstkammer claimed the authority to impose a program of classification and to direct the gaze of the visitors who shared in the owner's connoisseurship. The collections therefore confirmed difference and distinction.[24]

Early modern systems of classification as used by Renaissance collectors seem curious today. Modern forms of classification first came up during the period of the Enlightenment in the late seventeenth and eighteenth centuries. Instead of amazement and wonder, and classification along lines of similitude or individual association of things as in earlier times, taxonomies were now based on ever-finer differentiations that were based on measurement and signification. In the eighteenth century, scholars moved collections and classification efforts from the homes of private enthusiasts to institutions to promote exact science for the public benefit. Academies, learned societies, colleges and their collections and libraries became the basis for analytical comparison and experiment. Efforts at an ever more exact classification of things eventually produced precursors of the museum catalogue.[25]

The emergence of the modern museum coincided with the rise of nationalism during the French Revolution and the onset of imperialism as two of the crucial forces of European expansion in the nineteenth century. During the early French Republic and under Bonaparte's nation state, the museum became an instrument of social engineering, with the professional specialized curator as the engineer. Emperors and kings of European nation states of the nineteenth century inaugurated museums for the common benefit, and in order to underline the power of the state. The opening of the Louvre for public viewing and the enormous influx of objects triggered by confiscations of the royal household, by the secularization of ecclesiastical property, and by conquest, made it necessary to rethink the function of collections. As a consequence, inventories were drawn up. The ability of the new government (first republican, then imperial) to act as a connoisseur and collector as well as protector of art on behalf of the public was a means to increase legitimacy. The *civilizing mission* gave new rulers the opportunity to rewrite the history of mankind along the lines of reason and secularism, which were values that had to be taught to the public, calling for new curatorial and exhibiting techniques. The museum as a place for public instruction devised such means as written explanations that accompanied the artifacts. Catalogues were no longer inventories written for specialists, but actually explanatory devices for the visiting public. Historicism as a new worldview, based on the experience of the rupture of the revolution and the end of the dynastic cycle, promoted thinking in terms of a succession of eras and epochs. The concentration of a vast variety of objects in Paris prepared the ground for a diversification of museums, such as art and natural history museums. New laws gave objects protected status, isolating them from objects of daily life and use.[26]

The process of isolating objects from their context of utility, exhibited solely for scientific and analytical reasons, has been called *artification*, or the creation of an *artifact* as distinct from a *collectible*. In the first half of the nineteenth century, excavators dug up ancient objects from Egypt's soil to sell them in a private collectors' market for European aficionados. They sought to uncover a large amount of similar objects to spread them among collectors. When at the same time, curators of antiquities museums started to look for exceptional and unique pieces as artifacts without measuring their value in monetary terms, Egyptian workmen could hardly understand why Europeans would invest so much money and effort in digging out gigantic blocks of stone in the shape of statues or busts to transport them to, for instance, the British Museum in London.[27]

In contrast to the collectible, the artifact is "both an instrument (of pedagogy) and an end (to be appreciated) in itself ..."[28] For the archaeologist, the artifact is an object of study according to disciplinary – and disciplining – rules and practices that constitute the scholar's exclusive claim on handling it. In an inherent paradox (and again in contrast to the collectible), nobody was supposed to claim ownership of the artifact but human civilization. European intellectuals and scholars determined, however, what human civilization was. Thus, the question of ownership was resolved by the more or less implicit claim that only Western institutions could be appropriate custodians of the legacy of human civilization. In this context, collectors and curators justified the acquisition and removal of artifacts from Egypt to Western museums, which often amounted to mere theft, depicting Egyptians as too ignorant or as Muslim iconoclasts. In the East, archaeologists deemed it appropriate to acquire and remove artifacts for conservation in Western institutions at a time when the laws of their home countries already knew the term *national heritage* and banned the export of objects that were unearthed from the soil of European nations. In spite of all assertions by Western researchers and amateurs that the transfer of antiquities happened in the interest of conservation and on the basis of uninterested science it is therefore necessary to understand the artification of Egyptian objects as part of an agenda to establish

European imperialist hegemony.[29] The establishment of museums was thus an integral part of the colonial project, with the goal to "stag[e ...] Western science as universal knowledge." The civilizing mission of colonial powers, which was most pronounced in the case of France, imposed science as a marker of modernity. At the same time, however, the claim on the universality of science contradicted the paternalism of the colonial project. When Western scholars presented the idea of universal science to their counterparts in the East to justify their exploits, they also opened a window to the Easterners to develop indigenous agency based on the same universal principles.[30] The following excursus offers an example of this phenomenon.

Excursus I: ancient Egypt for the Egyptians

According to a conventional account, modern Egyptology started in 1798 when the French Scientific Mission arrived in Egypt – almost literally on Napoleon's coat tails. The Mission's internationally distributed publication *Déscription de l'Egypte*, the first volume of which came out in 1809, had a deep impact on conceptions of Egyptology as a modern science in Europe. The absence of Egyptians among the great archaeologists of the nineteenth century is therefore less due to an essential backwardness and hostility to modern science among Egyptians prior to the French conquest – a scholarly myth that has long been refuted[31] – than to clear-cut power relationships. Imperialist competition over the country used science as a surrogate battlefield and made it particularly difficult for Egyptians to insert themselves into the story of modern archaeology and art history in their country – in spite of the fact that native Egyptians began to develop a long-term historicist view of their country's history in the mid-to-late nineteenth century, already integrating ancient and pre-Islamic as well as medieval Egypt into a continuous storyline of the Egyptian nation.

There is no doubt that the systematic surveys of ancient Egyptian monuments in the *Déscription*, Champollion's decipherment of the hieroglyphics, and the development of modern excavation techniques in the course of the nineteenth century, were milestones of modern archaeology, philology, and art history. The Scientific Mission was, however, not the initiator of a long-lasting, distanced and a-political scholarly project, but it was driven by the worldview of the revolutionary French nation state and its civilizational ethos. In the following decades, intra-European rivalry cemented the link between Egyptology, colonial expansion and imperialist hegemony.[32]

The antiquities department of the British Museum opened to a small start in 1807, the first exclusively Egyptian museum opened in Turin in 1824, and the Egyptian collection of the Louvre was inaugurated in 1827. In Berlin, the *Neue Museum* opened in 1850. Geographical and Oriental Societies sprung up throughout Europe between the 1820s and the 1840s furthering research in Egyptology. Following this example, scholarly societies were founded in Alexandria in 1828 and the Egyptian Society in 1836 in Cairo. In general, these societies did not cater to Egyptians, however, but brought together Europeans residing in Egypt and offered library services to travelers. Native Egyptians participated later in the century only, with increased involvement of the Egyptian state in antiquities affairs, but they remained far from a majority.[33]

Nevertheless, Egyptians were anything but disinterested in questions of Egyptian heritage. 'Abd al-Rahman al-Jabarti (1753–1825/6), the famous chronicler of Ottoman Egypt, the French expedition and the beginnings of Mehmet Ali's rule, interacted closely with the members of the Scientific Mission, and Rifa'a Rafi' al-Tahtawi (1801–1873), the Egyptian translator and educationist, took courses on ancient history and languages while he officially accompanied Mehmet Ali's first student missions to Paris as an Imam from 1826 to 1831.[34] Mehmet Ali issued a decree in August 1835 that banned the despoliation of Egyptian ruins. Champollion himself had warned him that European greed for Egyptian antiquities and the local quarrying of recently uncovered monuments threatened to erode the country's antiquities. With full awareness of Western standards of heritage protection and display practices the ruler decreed that similar exhibitions should be set up in Cairo, but only for foreign travelers, who could benefit from the display, and not the local population. The decree had little effect and did not stop Mehmet Ali himself from authorizing the quarrying of ancient temples for building material, or to use Egyptian artifacts as diplomatic leverage. By the end of his rule, the project of a museum in Cairo had not come to fruition.[35]

The situation changed when Auguste Mariette (1821–1881) entered Egyptian government service and founded the Antiquities Service and the Egyptian Museum in 1858 on French Emperor Napoleon III's recommendation and gentle pressure. Mariette's loyalty was ambiguous, divided between his employer Khedive Isma'il, and his French fatherland that was in imperialist competition with other European powers. Mariette set up a temporary museum in Bulaq, then still on the outskirts of Cairo, but in his efforts to find a permanent location he looked for a place near the big Cairo hotels in Ezbekiyya. The museum catered so obviously to European visitors that Mariette felt it necessary to emphasize in an early catalogue of the collection that Khedive Isma'il intended to attract Egyptians to the collection, too. Mariette, however, made clear that they would have to be lured by an arrangement of the artifacts that was rather more pleasing to the eye than in accordance with the scholarly expectations of foreign visitors with regard to system and classification. He expected, though, that luring Egyptians would gradually afford them the ability to observe in a European manner. The new (and also current) Egyptian Museum finally opened in 1902 in a building of European neoclassicist design in Cairo's modern center (near today's Tahrir Square), becoming the most prominent representation of foreign hegemony in Cairo.[36]

It is worthwhile to compare museums in Egypt to those in colonial India that functioned outside the canon of the European classics, and were therefore not subject to a comparable competition over cultural hegemony. The Calcutta Indian Museum, in spite of being a namesake of the Egyptian Museum, exhibited natural history and geology only, as India's antiquities were not considered to be on a par with the legacy of European civilization. Still, the Indian Museum was a temple of classification and therefore represented British penetration and submission of Indian culture through a supposedly superior scientific understanding. The museum nevertheless attracted more than half a million visitors per year before World War I. Curators assumed that most visitors were illiterate, so they took little care to label exhibits correctly. Instead, like Mariette in the Egyptian case, they invested more energy in an illustrative organization of the exhibition to impress the natives visually rather than through text. It is remarkable that Indian elites considered the museum as too popular a place, therefore. In the long run, they would pick up principles of modern European science to distance themselves from both the Europeans and the lower classes of their own society. Similar trends existed in Egypt.[37]

Egyptian efforts to gain a foothold in the realm of exact science had started in 1869 when Khedive Isma'il founded a school of ancient languages in Bulaq. However, Mariette feared that competition by native scholars undermined the effort and the school ceased to function by 1874. In 1880, France institutionalized her dominance in Egyptian antiquities when the *Institut français d'archéologie orientale* (IFAO) was founded. Until 1936 all directors of the Antiquities Service came from the IFAO. The Franco-British Entente Cordiale of 1904 included a clause confirming that a Frenchman would head the Service. It remained part of the Ministry for Public Works until 1929, when it came under the purview of the Ministry of Education. This transfer represented a change of heart among Egyptian politicians and pointed to a new appreciation of the importance of Egypt's past for the education of youth – in line with the general changes in nationalist discourse. The Service came under the Ministry of Culture and National Guidance in 1958 only. But while Egyptian institutions were slow to adopt Pharaonic heritage, the usage of Pharaonic imagery for state representation was much older. Egyptian stamps and paper currency already depicted ancient Egyptian antiquities during the last decades of the nineteenth century. Even if Egyptians neither commissioned nor designed them, they used them on a daily basis. From the 1880s on, Egyptian rulers paid official visits to ruins during stately trips. Egyptian historians began to include ancient Egypt in their works in the late nineteenth century, but interest remained confined to elite circles.[38]

Nationalist discourse started to integrate the Pharaonic Age in historical references around the turn of the twentieth century. It prepared the terrain for a new museum discourse, too. Egyptian media, including through school textbooks, presented the link between ancient and modern Egypt as a continuum. Ahmad Lutfi al-Sayyid (1872–1963), a journalist, influential nationalist politician, and later Chancellor of the Egyptian University and Minister in the Egyptian government, was instrumental in introducing ancient Egypt as an integral part of Egyptian national heritage, appropriating it for a continuous national history.[39] Before World War I, he wrote in an article for his newspaper *al-Jarida*: "Our nation today does not exist independently from the nation of our past. The nation is a single unbroken, unbreakable whole. [...] Egypt's reality is both its past and its present."[40]

For early nationalist theoreticians like Lutfi al-Sayyid, ignorance of ancient Egypt, but also of the Arab monuments, was a matter of shame for Egyptians. In order to re-claim the past they said that Egyptians had to endorse the ideal of a science free of national inclinations. The Europeans promoted the ideal, but had failed to respect it too often, finding excuses for the extraction of artifacts and the exclusion of Egyptians from the Antiquities Service. An opportunity opened up to prove this point in 1922 when Howard Carter discovered Tutankhamen's tomb in the Valley of the Kings. A conflict between Carter and the Egyptian Antiquities Service over the regulation of access to the tomb and the distribution of the found objects culminated in a legal battle and a temporary withdrawal of Carter's license. The head of the Antiquities Service Pierre Lacau (1873–1963), a Frenchman, led the confrontation as a manifestation of the usual Anglo–French rivalry over Egyptian antiquities, but the Egyptian press took up the topic and turned it into an issue of Egyptian sovereignty. The context of the Egyptian revolution of 1919, independence, which Egypt achieved in parts in 1922, and the elections to the first independent Egyptian Parliament in 1924 fired the fervor of the journalists. They nevertheless cloaked the allegations against Carter in the language of universal science, claiming that he worked for his own fame and profit, and not for the advancement of scholarship.[41]

The task laid out for Egyptian Egyptologists was to acquire an expertise that put them on a par with European colleagues, and to popularize interest in the Egyptian past among the Egyptian people in order to turn Egyptianism into a crucial marker of identity – and all this without violating the rules of objectivity. Placing Egyptian nationals in leadership positions in Egypt's antiquities establishment was a crucial struggle in this regard, and one that was not crowned with success until the 1930s. Ahmad Kamal (b. 1851), the doyen of Egyptian Egyptology, who had been one of the students at Khedive Isma'il's school for ancient languages, never rose into a representative position, and when he died in 1923 he had no successor because a new generation of Egyptian Egyptologists was only just about to enter higher education at the time. King Fu'ad allowed for the opening of an Egyptian school of Egyptology in 1923 as a branch of the Higher Teachers College. It moved to the Egyptian University in 1925. In addition, he sent a small number of Egyptians abroad to be trained for work at the museum as assistant curators. They spent much of the 1920s in Europe for studies and returned in 1928 when Pharaonicism was at its height among Egyptian politicians and nationalists.[42]

Two questions were at stake in Egypt's museum landscape: not only who ruled over it, but also who was to profit from museums in Egypt – the tourists or the native population – and what the museums' objective was. The rifts separating various actors' positions in this debate did not in fact form a clear-cut divide between Europeans and Egyptians. The Egyptian specialists in the field of Egyptian antiquities, who rose to prominence in the 1930s, shared the exclusivist scientistic arrogance of their European colleagues towards outsiders of the profession as much as they despised European hegemony in the Museum landscape.

Salim Hassan (1887–1961), a member of the aforementioned student mission of the 1920s who entered service at the Egyptian Museum, had a rugged relationship with the leadership of the foreign run Antiquities Service. In 1912, Gaston Maspero (1846–1916), who was director-general of the Service at the time, refused to hire Hassan together with other students of a short-lived Egyptology school that Ahmad Kamal maintained at the *Teachers' College* before the war. Hassan finally entered the Antiquities Service as an apprentice in 1922, and benefited from the protection of several British, American and Austro-German Egyptologists. He left the Antiquities Service in 1928 to start a career at the Egyptian University and received a Doctor of Philosophy from the University of Vienna in 1935. Certainly, Hassan was grateful for the support that he had received from his European mentors, but this did not reduce his dismay for European dominance in the Antiquities Service.[43]

It seems that Hassan's personal nemesis at the museum was the British Egyptologist Reginald Engelbach, who had prevented Hassan from entering Tutankhamen's tomb at Thebes until Carter admitted him personally. By that time, Engelbach (1888–1946) was Chief Inspector of Antiquities in Upper Egypt. In 1924 he became Assistant Keeper, and in 1931 Chief Keeper of the Egyptian Museum. Engelbach studied engineering in London before he went to Egypt in 1909 to cure heart problems, but he never finished his degree. He had, however, some, if only informal training in Egyptology, owing his career to the patronage of the British Egyptologist Flinders Petrie (1853–1942), who revolutionized modern archaeology around the turn of the century. Both British and French colleagues greatly appreciated Engelbach's skills, but, as Stephen R.K. Glanville (1900–1956), himself a renowned British Egyptologist and Cambridge scholar, remarked in an obituary, his service "was recognized by his colleagues (if not by a much larger public who benefited from its results) ..."[44] Hassan and Engelbach competed over limited positions in the Egyptian Antiquities Service at a time when Egyptology had become a central topic among nationalists in Egypt (Glanville's "larger public") with regard to Egyptian identity and native sovereignty over the country's heritage. Hassan's moment seemed to have come when long-term Antiquities director Pierre Lacau was set to retire in 1936. The French considered this a crucial position for the safeguarding of their interests in the country. There was, however, no obvious heir, and the elderly Lacau, who had been celebrated in the Egyptian press for taking Egypt's position against Howard Carter in the Tutankhamen controversy more than a decade earlier, was now considered a representative of imperialist interests. The British High Commissioner Miles Lampson hoped to push Engelbach to succeed Lacau, but he also felt bound by the provisions of the 1904 Entente Cordiale and accepted the candidacy of the French Etienne Drioton (1889–1961). Egyptian circles, however, rooted for Salim Hassan, arguing in the press that his qualifications were superior, while the British and French embassies derided Hassan as mediocre, of bad faith, self-aggrandizing, even slightly mad, and a potential serious detriment to the Service. The Wafdist government at the time decided to placate foreign interests and accepted Drioton, feeling it necessary, though, to create a sub-director post for Hassan. Bad blood then cast a shadow over their future cooperation at the museum with Drioton and British High Commissioner Lampson trying to undermine Hassan's position and vice versa. Drioton's advantage was in his friendly relationship with King Faruq, which probably helped him remain in his position until 1952.[45]

Hassan had to aim lower than the director's chair in his ambition to reduce foreign influence in Egyptian antiquities, so he took on Engelbach, his immediate colleague at the museum. It seems that he was trying to curry favor with the King because the records of the Royal Diwan contain an entire folder documenting the campaign that Hassan led against Engelbach in 1937. A table of contents of the folder was signed by "Le Sous-Directeur Général du Service des Antiquités Egyptiennes," i.e. Selim Hassan himself.[46]

Hassan's choice of weapons in this confrontation was not only remarkable within the immediate context of the distribution of power in Egyptian Egyptology, but also in a more structural sense. He tried to defeat Europeans on the level of scientific aptitude, thus turning a major argument of cultural imperialism back at them. At first, Hassan had instructed three Egyptian curators at the museum, Mahmud Hamza, Muharram Kamal, and 'Abd al-Hadi Hamada, to prepare a report about missing objects and errors in the inventory of the museum. An interim report they provided mentioned that the initial order to produce the inventory had come from the Ministry of Education, but Hassan certainly used it to push his own nationalist anti-foreign agenda. On several pages, the three curators listed their grievances about erroneous or absent labeling, and about entirely arbitrary arrangements of objects as if merely thrown into exhibition cases. There were recurring remarks that the state of some of the documentation "makes one blush," that objects were scattered in hidden locations, without inventory numbers, and that there was a need for reorganization in a "scientific manner."[47] This attack targeted the very heart of the rationale of European hegemony over Egyptology, namely its agents' supposedly superior skills in scientific categorization of artifacts, and thus it was an assault on imperialism making use of the paradox of the civilizing mission: Europeans claimed that they needed to dominate what they considered to be lesser peoples for the benefit of human civilization, or in other words they claimed to rescue these peoples from themselves. Imagine the insult when Egyptians claimed that they commanded the rules of protecting human heritage better than sloppy European curators.

Hassan took the assault further and accused Engelbach of an obstructionist attitude in a memorandum that he sent to the palace. Though kept in Arabic, the content seems to indicate that the original addressee may have been Drioton, the Director General of the Antiquities Service. Hassan stated that he found the relationship between Egyptian and foreign employees as one of great mistrust. Egyptian colleagues complained that they had no chance to participate in the cataloguing of objects in the museum. Only when Hassan had confronted Engelbach, the latter had agreed to a reorganization of the work process that integrated Egyptians. Around the same time, press reports had come out alleging that golden objects had been stolen from the museum. In an initial inquiry, Hassan had found 26,000 of the 66,000 objects that were supposed to be in the museum unaccounted for, and therefore probably stolen or simply vanished. He wrote that Engelbach and other (read: foreign) museum employees did seem to obstruct a closer inventory, however. He therefore had turned to the three Egyptian curators to prepare the report about the rather depressing state of the museum. Otherwise, Hassan claimed, the Egyptian curators were not given any tasks at the museum:

> The reason for this is that Mister Engelbach does not want them to partic-ipate in useful work, and this is because of his aversion to Egyptians, and therefore it is his intention to restrict the useful work to the foreign col-leagues because he thinks that the Egyptians are useless for any work in the museum, and as long as this belief is fixed in his mind, the Egyptian curators will not be able to settle on any honorable task. This is how the foreign race remains in lead in this office, and this is all that Mr. Engelbach aims for.[48]

From here on, Hassan's complaints turned into humiliating *ad hominem* attacks. Engelbach was not even qualified as an archaeologist, but was only a survey engineer, he fired. The curator of the museum should no doubt be fluent in the ancient Egyptian language and be familiar with Egyptian monuments, neither of which was Engelbach. His Egyptian colleagues were, however, highly qualified; they would be the vanguard of Egyptology, had they only been given the chance to work without their hands tied by the likes of Engelbach. Hassan insinuated that Engelbach did not want the chaos in the museum to become apparent. He also believed that Engelbach would not accept any Egyptian authority above himself, which, Hassan emphasized, stood against the honor of independent Egypt. At this point, his argumentation began to waver between arguments of national honor, the rules of proper science, and attempts to discredit Engelbach personally:

> I am sorry to reiterate that it is impossible for Mr. Engelbach to work in the museum except when he is drunk. And he uses abusive language with the office boys that the pen refuses to note down.[49]

Finally, Hassan recommended that Engelbach should be removed from the museum until order would be restored under the guardianship of a competent employee with sufficient experience for the task to rectify a situation that was unheard of in any other museum of the world. Without a doubt, Hassan believed that he himself was this competent employee who would prove that only an Egyptian was capable of making up for the embarrassment that foreign curators had brought to the museum, driving home the point of Egyptian superior skills to take care of what he presented as the greatest national treasure.

The concern here is not if Hassan's attacks on Engelbach were justified or merely grounded on personal ambition and envy – there is in fact evidence that Engelbach defended his Egyptian colleagues on other occasions when their qualifications were put into question maliciously.[50] In any case, the attacks were not crowned with immediate success. Engelbach had to vacate his post in 1941 only to make way, not for Hassan, but for Mahmud Hamza, one of the three subordinate curators who had written the aforementioned interim report. Afterwards, Engelbach stayed on at the museum as a Technical Adviser until his death in 1946. This was, however, only shortly before most British employees left Egyptian museum service anyway. Earlier, in 1939, Drioton had already lashed back at Hassan after he felt secure enough because his contract at the Directorate of Antiquities had been renewed. He accused Hassan of financial irregularities and of taking part in antiquities trafficking schemes, which he had undertaken in part to put blame on the Europeans to accelerate their departure. He claimed that, after another inventory, only three or four artifacts turned up as "mislaid" since 1914, instead of the 26,000 objects that Hassan had reported in 1937. Nevertheless, Drioton did not show better manners than his Egyptian colleague when he emphasized that artifacts should not only be protected from international traffickers, but also "from Egyptian hands as well!!!" In a swirl of scandal and accusations that started in 1938 and ranged from embezzlement, selling antiquities illegally to Nazi Germany, to questionable moral conduct, Hassan was pushed out of office, to be rehabilitated after Nasser's revolution only.[51]

The tide turned after World War II. Not long after the opening of the Civilization Museum in 1949, the Palace ordered the Ministry of Education to replace plaques that adorned the façade of the Egyptian Museum inscribed with the names of mostly Western Egyptologists who once worked at the museum. As the inscriptions were in Latin, they were certainly utterly foreign ("ifranjiyya") and, according to the note to the ministry, not in accordance with the nationalism ("qawmiyya") of the country and the recognition of its national honor. Once more, the Palace tasked Shafiq Ghurbal, at the time deputy in the Ministry of Education, to find a way to remove the plaques and replace them with easily understandable Arabic, to "efface the symbol of colonialism from the façade of the Museum."[52] As a matter of fact, the Latin plaques are still on the façade today; they were not removed even after the July 1952 revolution when Egyptian antiquities moved under exclusive Egyptian control.

The Civilization Museum project

Thus, the question of dominance over Egypt's museum landscape was about to be settled by the time the Civilization Museum came into being. The latter, in turn, was to tackle the other question at stake, namely who the audience and recipient of a new museum narrative was supposed to be. The socio-political atmosphere of Egypt in the late 1930s has been described as a time of clashes between authoritarian forces, divergent generations of intellectuals and political activists taking recourse to increasingly radical political concepts, as well as a time of conservatism among members of the swelling ranks of the petty bourgeoisie. An Islamic turn ensued among publicists and intellectuals, at times the same ones who had championed secularism in the 1920s.[53] The political system of interwar Egypt rested on a triangular relationship between the British as the informal hegemon, the Wafd party that controlled the parliament, and the Palace, where first King Fu'ad (d. 1936) and then Faruq tried to extend royal powers, building on their executive prerogative. Outside the constitutional and imperialist framework, institutions such as al-Azhar University, the students of the Egyptian University, and the press and intellectual scene, played an increasingly important role in public life. The rivalry between the King and his entourage on one side and the Wafd on the other intensified in the late thirties. The party enjoyed stronger popularity than Faruq who belonged to a dynasty that many considered aloof. When attempts to expand the constitutional prerogative did not meet success, royal authority was to be expanded through representation and appeal to Islamic sentiments, but a campaign to make Faruq Caliph failed in 1939 because it was not well received among secular circles of the Egyptian political scene, as well as in other Arab lands. The King, however, and the conservative Islamic imagery, did appeal to members of the Young Effendiyya and to young Egyptian military officers who started to make forays into politics. Many of those who belonged to this group took on unmistakable authoritarian leanings if compared to the liberal outlook of the older generation of politicians and intellectuals.[54]

The palace thus tried to reassert its hegemony in the public sphere, wavering between an increased Islamic public representation of the monarchy and such projects as the Civilization Museum. The goal was a reconciliation between Egyptianist and Arabo–Islamic visions of the community, because the museum celebrated both elements as constitutive for Egyptian civilization, but it also culminated in a glorification of Mehmet Ali's dynasty. Above all, it was an effort to Egyptianize Egypt's museum landscape.

At the time, the Civilization Museum was a novelty in the landscape of Egyptian museums, which was split into two categories: First, the classic museums that were a legacy of more than a century of European hegemony over Egyptian antiquities, such as the world famous Egyptian Museum and the Museum for Arab Art in Cairo, and the Graeco-Roman Museum in Alexandria; and second, the 'practical' museums that had been founded since the enthronement of King Fu'ad (r. 1917 to 1936, until 1922 as Sultan). Before succeeding to the throne, Fu'ad had been involved in the creation of Egypt's first University in Cairo in 1908 and became a promoter of state sponsored cultural and scientific activities. The Agricultural Museum, the Museum of Irrigation, the Railway Museum, the Postal Museum, and the Museum of Education were all royal foundations of the 1920s and 1930s.[55]

The existence of the three museums in the first category reflected a division of the realm of the history of art and culture in Egypt along the lines of discrete scholarly disciplines – Egyptology, classical archaeology, and Islamic art history – that had evolved in European learned societies and later at universities during the eighteenth and nineteenth centuries. European researchers who visited Egypt, or tourists who toured the country, always considered the Egyptian Museum as the pinnacle of what Egypt stood for in their eyes, based on the nineteenth-century considerations among European scholars that ancient Egyptian culture had prepared the way for Greek antiquity, and thus, by extension, had paved the way for the rise of Europe.[56] The historical hierarchy that favored Pharaonic Egypt over all other epochs of the country's history is reflected in the museum's name that did not mark any chronology, even though the museum exclusively contained Egyptian antiquities up until the end of the Ptolemaic period.

The Egyptian Museum was founded in 1858 in a colonial context as part of a project to trace European roots. In contrast, the Europeans who founded the Museum for Arab Art in 1884 (today the Museum for Islamic Art) did not try to appropriate an ancient legacy. Instead the museum was a product of Orientalist fascination with the exotic and the foreign, and it was founded on a growing collectors' interest in Europe in Islamic artifacts. More practically, it was a byproduct of the efforts by European specialists in Egyptian service to safeguard Islamic artifacts from destruction in the wake of Khedivial modernization projects cutting down large swaths of old Cairo to make way for modern Haussman-style boulevards. In nineteenth-century Cairo, and until the end of the monarchy, the museology of ancient Egypt was the terrain of French specialists in Egyptian governmental service. The Greco Roman Museum (founded 1892) was a playing field for members of Alexandria's Italian community, and their vision of the Southern Mediterranean as being within Italy's cultural and imperial reach. It remained under Italian control until World War II. The first director of the Museum for Arab Art, Max Herz Pasha, was an Austro-Hungarian architect-turned art historian. The first Egyptian director, 'Ali Bahgat, who was appointed after World War I, was eventually replaced after his untimely death in 1924 with a Frenchman, Gaston Wiet. Wiet stayed until shortly before the Egyptian Revolution of 1952. The only exception to this rule of European hegemony over Egypt's great classical museums was the Coptic Museum, whose founder and first director in 1908, Marcus Simaika, was a Copt himself. It is arguable, however, that it nevertheless owed its existence to Biblical archaeology that became a popular discipline among the Western scholars in the nineteenth century who tried to prove the veracity of the Holy Scripture. Egypt's position in this endeavor emboldened Copts to carve out their own historical identity on Egyptian soil, separate from that of the Muslim majority.[57]

As mentioned above, King Faruq had drawn the inspiration for the Civilization Museum from a visit to the Schweizer Landesmuseum in 1939. Already his father, the late King Fu'ad, had tried to model his Agriculture Museum after an institution of the same name he had seen in Budapest. He even imported the Hungarian director of the museum, Alajos Peikert, to establish a similar one in Cairo. On January 26, 1931, at the inauguration of the museum, Fu'ad presented a declaration to "the Egyptian Nation." Agriculture, Fu'ad said, was the "basis for all economic and social life" in the country, and as this was a time of global recession, it was a "duty for the entire nation to do everything in one's power to promote and consolidate Egyptian agriculture." The museum should be a "stimulant" for farmers to improve their work, and should convey this message to a list of potential visitors, including farmers, merchants, manufacturers, "our brilliant youth," and the entire population of Egypt, rich and poor, urbanites and villagers, and also all foreign visitors.[58] The Agriculture Museum thus told a different story than Egypt's classic museums. Instead of an institution for neutral classification and the scientific organization of artifacts – and in Egypt the classical museums had not yet become a realm of popular education by the 1930s as they had in Europe – the Agriculture Museum was a vehicle for the spreading of community spirit, and for the dissemination of a sense of modernity as represented in technology and social responsibility, across the entire spectrum of the Egyptian population, putting a specific target on the younger generation. The Civilization Museum was supposed to tell a similar story, but in a more outright way.

All museums create narratives, including those in European capitals that reaffirmed white men as custodians of human civilization. They did so in the name of objective science, but portrayed hierarchies of power and race not as circumstantial but as facts of nature, as in ethnographic collections for example. Entire museum landscapes emerged in Western capitals during the nineteenth and early twentieth centuries, playing a decisive role in the recreation of coherent national narratives out of the diversification and scattering of disciplines that the initial specialization of collections and museums had brought about. The *Museumsinsel* in Berlin, or the National Mall in Washington DC are only two prominent examples for this process of anchoring a nation in the story of a linear evolution of human civilization. The inherent narrative structure of these places re-united scattered elements in a discourse that started with the primitive stages of civilization in anthropological and natural history collections and ended with the pinnacle of civilization in art or history museums. It is no coincidence that the cultures of colonized peoples were often depicted as part of the natural history collections.[59] The name Museum of Civilization is consequently a tautology, or to put it differently, it is simply a more honest label for an institution that usually employed a façade of scientific neutrality and service to humankind to hide that it was an instrument in the discursive imposition of hegemony. The Civilization Museum created a narrative like any other museum, but it did so without pretending to be merely a neutral transmitter, or simply a catalyst of knowledge that existed independently outside the museum itself or the scientistic discourse that it represented. The drafting of its peculiar narrative was a very concrete, conscious and painstaking process.[60]

Faruq's 1939 memorandum about the Civilization Museum drew upon a model that was quite distinct from the classic Egyptian museum of the turn of the century. Every section should contain miniature models of buildings and important monuments. There should be examples of clothing, of weapons, and explanations of military organization, as well as typical agricultural tools and tools of craftsmen, and models of means of transport, as well as maps and dioramas. All of this should represent every era, all layers of society, as well as, respectively, all ranks of the army.[61] First of all, this list of things to be exhibited stood for a vision of civilization that included architecture, agriculture, industry and engineering, crafts, transport, and, very centrally, the military, but not the arts, such as literature and music, or religious life. It also took civilizational unity for granted, disregarding competing visions among diverse communities, but this was arguably the whole point of the project. The industrial and military vision of unified national achievement was a clear legacy of Egyptian modernization projects of the nineteenth century.[62] Second, it is noteworthy that the artifact was not supposed to play a central role in the Civilization Museum, but could be replaced by models and copies. Unlike the classical museums, the isolated original with its exceptional value was of no interest to the initiators of the Civilization Museum project. Individual elements of the exhibit gained their importance from their significance in the context of a broader storyline. They became parts of a spectacle, a vision of museology that stood in contrast to the scientific museum as a storehouse for artifacts and a locus of categorization.

Modern museums of the late nineteenth century have been compared to fairs and exhibitions because they convey "cultural meanings and values" by way of a particular mind–body experience: their designated buildings or grounds circumscribe spaces that discipline the crowd to follow particular itineraries. Physical movement instills a particular meaning-making experience. A new trend in European museums, like in government-sponsored fairs and exhibitions, was to use them as instruments to channel culture for political purposes in the interest of social engineering projects to enhance the urban environment and for the moral and personal cultivation of the lower classes. In nineteenth-century London, museums, like libraries, parks, and department stores, were built for useful recreation and pastime, but also to facilitate the policing of crowds. Museum visits were supposed to raise the spirit of the lower classes in the presence of art or artifacts, and in their appreciation working people should learn to mimic bourgeois codes of behavior. Central courtyards, surrounded by galleries, structured the exhibition space to facilitate the free movement of large numbers of people without mutual obstruction but also to enhance the individual visibility of the visitor so that the members of the crowd would check on each other, forming a system of self-regulating public behavior. Museum architecture thus became strikingly similar to that of exhibition grounds and department stores with their galleries, lookouts, and elevated walkways.[63]

The classical museums of Egypt lagged behind this trend as they continued to be temples of classification, at the same time as curators began to divide collections of European museums into an illustrative section fit for exhibition to the public, and a part reserved for researchers.[64] Public education, it was assumed, required spectacle to command the attention of the crowds. The greatest spectacles of the era, though, were staged as the world exhibitions of the nineteenth and early twentieth century, where, to come full circle, sections on ancient Egypt played a central role in the creation of an imperial universe. The Great Exhibition in London of 1851 had an Egyptian court (in addition to a Moorish section), a decade before the Egyptian state took on the organization of its own pavilion in the 1862 Exposition in the same city, grouped with other pavilions in 'Oriental sections' of the fairground. The 'Oriental' scenes of these sections, such as the Cairo Street of the 1889 exhibition in Paris, were particularly popular.[65] Mariette's design for the Egyptian pavilion at the Paris exhibition of 1867 represented the Egypt of Khedive Isma'il in three pavilions on ancient, medieval, and modern Egypt. Thus, it anticipated to some extent the nature and function of the Civilization Museum. The modern pavilion even contained an exhibition about the Suez canal project, whereas the ancient Egypt pavilion combined elements of the classic museum and the exhibition because it was designed as a reproduction of the kiosk of Emperor Trajan at Philae, but also contained original artifacts such as a diorite statue of Pharaoh Chephren.[66] Together, the copy and the original constituted a spectacle for the senses that was in stark contrast to the way Chephren's statue is displayed as one of the centerpieces of Cairo's Egyptian Museum to this day. There, it is placed among other artifacts that are organized according to genre and epoch, but in the non-contextual environment of the Egyptian Museum's neoclassical architecture. There, the Chephren statue signifies a statement in the history of Egyptian art, but does not form part of a historical narrative. In contrast, the spectacle at the exhibition did not rely on the singular charisma of the original artifact, but on its significance within the historical narrative.

It was quite appropriate then in 1939 to plan to initiate the project of the Museum of Egyptian Civilization in the context of the sixteenth Exhibition for Agriculture and Industry to be held from mid-February to mid-April 1941.[67] Since the turn of the century, the Royal Agricultural Society had organized these exhibitions in order to show off Egypt's achievements, but also to entertain the urban masses. The first exhibition had taken place in 1897 on the initiative of Prince Husayn Kamil (r. as Sultan from 1914 to 1917), predating the foundation of the society by a year. The fifteenth exhibition had opened in February 1936 on the grounds of the Agricultural Society on the Cairo Gezira Island in the Nile, south of Zamalek. It was the largest to date, spanning over more than 60 acres, and, as a novelty, it took place in and around a number of newly constructed, highly representative buildings that the famed architect Mustafa Fahmi had erected for the Agricultural Society. The Paris-educated Fahmi (1886–1972) is considered Egypt's first modern architect. He directed the Public Works Ministry, Department of Architecture and Design in the 1920s and later became Palace architect. His style was an eclectic mix of neo-Islamic and modern elements, which was manifest in the Art-Deco design of the Agricultural Society.[68] The exhibition ground opened up behind two rectangular sandstone buildings, a Grand and a Small Serail that were arranged at an angle. Both Serails, which are still in existence, have a tower at one end, while the other end of the Grand Serail is connected to a large round exhibition pavilion. At the tip of the angle between the two Serails, a column stands high on top of a circular roof that once protected ticket booths controlling the entrance to the exhibition grounds, much like the access to a fairground or an amusement park. In 1936, the Grand Serail housed an agricultural exhibition. Companies presented their products and services on the grounds, but there were also attractions for entertainment, such as sports events or a narrow-gauge train that transported visitors across the premises. There is a photo in *al-Hilal*, part of a reportage, that shows the two royal princesses Fawziyya and Fa'iza on a visit to the exhibition grounds in February 1936, where they spent several hours touring the attractions. The image presented two neatly spruced up girls in identical dress with fancy hats, coats and white collars, looking rather unhappy. Fifteen-year-old Fawziyya, the older of the two, who later became the first wife of Mohammad Reza Shah Pahlavi and Queen of Iran, held the reins of a horse-drawn wagon. Another photo showed the façade of a pavilion of *Dar al-Hilal*, the publishing house that brought out the journal of the same name. The pavilion was located near the main entrance and contained a shop selling products of the publishing house and guides to the exhibition. In a peculiar resemblance to nineteenth- and twentieth-century world exhibitions in Paris or elsewhere, the front of the pavilion mimicked a Mosque façade, in a form of mere Orientalist representation, concealing that the building behind it had a very different function: Two tall minarets framed an arched entrance with a large disc on top with "Dar al-Hilal" written on it, supported by a half moon (in Arabic "hilal"). The façade is vaguely reminiscent of Bab Zuwayla, an old city gate of Fatimid Cairo with two minarets that its towers support forming part of the adjacent Mamluk-era Sultan al-Mu'ayyad Mosque. The public display of royalty – the appearance of female members of the royal family must have caused a small sensation[69] – alongside the use of Orientalist representation were part of the public spectacle of an exhibition that was supposed to exhibit Egypt to its own people as a modern country with an Oriental veneer. For *al-Hilal* the exhibition literally turned into "a big city that contained within it all facets of economic and social life." The exhibition was therefore not only a modern pastime for a growing urban middle class and the Young Effendiyya, that was likewise the target audience of publications such as *al-Hilal*. It was also a small-scale laboratory for social engineering like the grand world exhibitions or the popular museums of late nineteenth-century Europe or North America.[70] Precisely in this location, the Museum of Egyptian Civilization was set to gain shape.

* * *

When the committee that was charged to lay the foundations for the Civilization Museum convened for the first time in early May 1939 in the small Serail of the Agricultural Society, it brought together the entire museum establishment of the country, including old and respectable authorities of European hegemony over the museum landscape, but also Egyptian newcomers. Gaston Wiet, director of the Museum for Arab Art, and Achille Adriani, head of the Greco-Roman Museum in Alexandria, attended, but also the Egyptian directors of King Fu'ad's new museums, such as Labib 'Abdallah Hassan of the Railway Museum and the director of the newly founded War Museum, Captain 'Abd al-Rahman Zaki. His was the most outspokenly nationalist museum in the Cairo landscape. Etienne Drioton, the Director of the Antiquities Service, had excused himself, but attended most following meetings. The most enigmatic figure among the attendants was, however, Fu'ad 'Abd al-Malik, the director of the Cairo Wax Museum and true proponent of the exhibition as a spectacle.[71] It is a matter of informed guessing how Wiet – or Drioton, had he been there – may have felt in the presence of this man, who they probably considered at best a showman, if not a charlatan who had no place in the solemn world of museums.

Fu'ad 'Abd al-Malik was an artist and a businessman. He populated the grey area between showman and serious man of culture that an institution like a wax museum represented. Apparently, the rationale of his presence in the committee was that he could provide effigies for the exhibit. 'Abd al-Malik hoped that his participation would bring him the public recognition that was necessary to get Egyptian government support for his institution. The Cairo Wax Museum, which opened in the thirties in the center of the modern city, was a private enterprise and ran heavy losses, as a letter and memorandum that 'Abd al-Malik submitted to the museum committee in June 1939 made clear.[72] Apparently, he had admirers in the royal household who appreciated the spectacle of his museum. He wrote about support that he had received from Queen Nazli (King Fu'ad's wife) and Crown Prince Faruq (apparently before his ascension to the throne), from other Princes and Princesses, as well as Prime Ministers, Ministers, grandees, high officials, and also the ambassadors and tourists who frequented the museum. When Prince 'Umar Tusun, the President of the Agricultural Society, visited the museum one day and expressed his approval, 'Abd al-Malik dared to ask him if there was a possibility for cooperation with the Agricultural Society. Tusun actually brought this up with the board of the society, but the reply was that its projects had nothing to do with the wax museum. Neither did the Committee for Fine Arts of the Ministry of Education want to have any part in its activities. 'Abd al-Malik's presence on the premises of the Agricultural Society for the meeting suggests that the royal backing had not been without effect, though. In an introductory letter to Fu'ad Abaza, the Director General of the society, he insinuated that the display in his institution, consisting of models, images, and wax figures, largely corresponded with what King Faruq had in mind when he thought of the possible instructional value of the Civilization Museum. 'Abd al-Malik was probably right, because Faruq apparently wanted spectacle, not dry science.

The idea for the Cairo Wax Museum was an import from Paris. In the nineteenth century, the French capital had been a laboratory for the rise of modern urban mass entertainment that

> aimed to please this heterogeneous mass through the construction of shared visual experiences. [...] The visual representation of reality as a spectacle in late nineteenth-century Paris created a common culture and a sense of shared experiences through which people might begin to imagine themselves as participating in a metropolitan culture.[73]

A similar vision of museology speaks out from King Faruq's memorandum, but it aimed at the even grander goal of national integration.

When 'Abd al-Malik had left Egypt to study the fine arts in Europe about 40 years before the initiation of the Civilization Museum project, wax museums in London (*Madame Tussaud's*) and Paris (*Musée Grévin*) fascinated him, but also Munich's *Deutsches Museum* with its life-size dioramas of industrial environments.[74] When World War I broke out and the chief sculptor at the *Musée*

Grévin was called up for military service, 'Abd al-Malik's friend Mahmud Mukhtar was asked to fill in. Mukhtar, who later went on to become the leading Egyptian artist of his generation, asked 'Abd al-Malik to lend him a hand and gave him the chance to learn the trade. After returning to Egypt in 1919, 'Abd al-Malik set up a small gallery; in 1930 he rented the first floor of the same building to open an exhibition of wax figures.[75]

'Abd al-Malik's museum was probably the first of its kind in Cairo, if not the entire Middle East. In Europe, wax sculpting as a form of art went back to the Middle Ages. In a remarkable parallel to the genealogy of museums, wax figures served through the Renaissance Period as objects of admiration, awe and artistic value, while at the same time their major function was scientific: to serve as tools of anatomical instruction. In the nineteenth century, permanent collections of wax figures became a feature of traveling cabinets of curiosities on temporary fairgrounds, entertaining a broader populace. The growth of urban populations and urban entertainment later in the century made the establishment of permanent locations profitable. As opposed to the 'serious' public museums that opened at the same time, wax museums were private businesses for profit. Their owners had to struggle to be recognized as artists and not mere showmen of fairground spectacles. The life stories of the Swiss anatomist and wax artist Philippe Curtius (1737–1794) and his apprentice Marie Tussaud (1761–1850) are exemplary for this journey. Tussaud started a permanent exhibition in London in 1835. Curtius' wax cabinet in Paris (closed in 1847) found a worthy successor in the Musée Grévin that opened in 1882, co-founded by the illustrator Alfred Grévin and the journalist Arthur Meyer. At the time, dissecting dead bodies had been legalized, so wax models lost their scientific value and became mere means of entertainment and documentation of celebrity life, accompanying the rise of the tabloid press and predating the newsreel.[76] The Grévin's changing tableaus have been described as a "three-dimensional newspaper." But more than real-time actuality, the verisimilitude of the display fascinated visitors as a nearly perfect illusion that blurred the line between the representation and the actual. Wax museums framed reality like newspapers – or, for that matter, the writings of positivist historians of the day – that also claimed to be verisimilar reflections of reality. The depiction of a reality that visitors could recognize as their own – either reflecting current times or the national past as they learned it in school or in books and magazines, "... built social bonds among strangers, who now belonged to a community because they had visual evidence that such a community existed." Institutions such as the wax museum presented common knowledge as spectacle and therefore played an important role in popularizing nationalism.[77]

Like his European teachers and colleagues, 'Abd al-Malik struggled to balance his position between private entrepreneur in the entertainment business and serious museum director and artist. The museum, he wrote in his letter, was "essentially scholarly, with regard to Egypt's eternal history and its civilization from the Pharaonic period to the present." In the memorandum, he presented his work not as art, but as historical education, and therefore thought that the rebuke that he had received from the Ministry of Education was unfounded. For those who thought that his museum was merely a European-style folly he wrote that Egyptian artists and workers had built his exhibition to depict Egypt's history from the earliest times to the present in a scientific manner, and to provide evidence for the nobleness and honor of the Arabs, and, finally, to present the history of the royal family. He declared it his mission to prevent events of the nationalist revival falling into oblivion.[78] 'Abd al-Malik was obviously keen to address the various trends of nationalist identification that were floating around Egypt at the time, from Pharaonicism to Arab nationalism, to the version that saw Egypt's national valor represented in Mehmet Ali's dynasty (but not including the current local Effendiyya's turn towards Islamic piety: he was still a man of the Westernized elite).

Although private businesses, European wax museums had long been considered a manifestation of the nationalist spirit of the nineteenth and twentieth centuries.[79] 'Abd al-Malik complained that his museum, unlike profitable institutions like *Madame Tussaud's* in London or the *Grévin* in Paris, did not receive government funding. The Governments of Italy, Turkey, and America had founded similar museums because of their nationalist importance.[80] In this reference, 'Abd al-Malik lumped wax museums together with a number of new museum types that responded to demands for greater instructiveness and clarity than that which could be found in scholarly institutions like Egypt's classical museums. In Europe, technical museums like Munich's *Deutsches Museum* had already started to provide instructional material for students and apprentices in the nineteenth century, but later turned into institutions to inform the public of national achievements in science and engineering, much like the world fairs.[81] 'Abd al-Malik wrote that such national institutions served to "... cultivat[e] the uneducated for the common good, to turn the gazes of the people to the glory of the history of our eternal nation from the perspective of science, the arts, and war ..." In the common nationalist parlance of the time, the director of the Wax Museum added that the museum should "spread the spirit of audacity and courage for sacrifice, as well as loyalty towards the fatherland, which is so different from the propaganda [i.e. prejudice] among tourists coming to Egypt." 'Abd al-Malik hence envisaged a grandiose national museum for the Egyptians, and not for foreign tourists who confronted Egyptians with condescension. Ultimately, however, he hoped to use the occasion to secure some state funding to remain in business himself.[82]

While the directors of the classic museums in Egypt's museum landscape certainly looked down upon 'Abd al-Malik's grandiose designs, the King and other members of the royal family seem to have perceived them favorably, as the King's fascination by the Swiss National Museum suggests, with its way of contextualizing Swiss history and making it readable for the non-specialist through the reconstruction of entire interiors of historical Swiss buildings and a Hall of Arms representing past Swiss military exploits. There are nevertheless no traces of a major imprint that 'Abd al-Malik left on the Civilization Museum, even though he continued to participate in the meetings of various committees.[83] In contrast, the discussions were dominated by the grand names of the Egyptian museum business. However, they still had to abide by the parameters that the palace had set in terms of contextualization and the narrative line that the exhibits in the museum had to follow.

* * *

The creation of the *Museum of Egyptian Civilization* was thus a collective effort by the members of the Egyptian museum establishment, who sat on various committees to deliberate over the details of the museum displays and controlled their execution. However, as the museum was to tell a linear story, the plans had to be forced into the tight framework of a single chronological narrative of 7000 years of Egyptian civilization, which included the pre-historic and pharaonic, Greco-Roman, Arab and Ottoman, and modern periods. Shafiq Ghurbal, the frontline historian mentioned above, outlined this *leitmotif* for the first time in front of a gathering of distinguished museum officials at the Royal Agricultural Society later in May 1939. This meeting was even graced by the presence of Anastas Alfieri, the president of the Entomological Society.[84] In the following weeks, museum curators sent lists of available objects in their displays to the Agricultural Society. Progress was painfully slow, though. The plan was that an Egyptian Civilization exhibit for the planned 1941 run of the Agriculture and Industry Exhibition should form the core of a future full-scale museum. Some museum directors feared the cost of the endeavor, or the possible loss of objects from their own museums.[85] As shown, the King was not interested in originals, but in narrative, however. Drioton and his staff at the Egyptian Museum seemed to understand the King's vision best and suggested to divide a Pharaonic section into three thematic subsections about the life of the individual, the life of society, and artistic life in ancient Egypt. Interestingly, this sociological narrative smacked of the latest trends in museology and diverged markedly from the logic of the displays in the Egyptian Museum itself. However, their draft program also set ancient Egypt once again apart as an entity in itself, in disregard of Ghurbal's leitmotif of a linear progress of Egyptian civilization. In effect, Drioton thus laid claim once more to the primacy of ancient Egypt and his own authority over the way it was presented.[86] In stark contrast, 'Abd al-Rahman Zaki, the military officer and curator of the War Museum, presented a strictly nationalist plan for his contribution to the Civilization Museum section of the 1941 exhibition. Zaki (more on him in a following chapter) was a new voice in the concert of museum officials in the late 1930s, representing a nationalist turn. In an immediate response to Faruq's memorandum, Zaki wrote: "The Egyptian Army has a history that starts from the Pharaonic kingdoms and lasts into the twentieth century, and it is one of the oldest histories of any army." For him, the War Museum, which had opened the previous year, presented Egypt's "military spirit" ("al-jundiyya al-Misriyya") from the Pharaonic Age to the present in a more easily accessible display than the scholarly museums. It did not merely present objects, but illustrated them relying on images and models. It appears that Zaki was on top of the museum discourse that the palace had decided to endorse.[87]

The plans to inaugurate a provisional Civilization Museum at the 1941 Agriculture and Industry Exhibition came to naught, however. The documentation in the files breaks off in December 1939 and only restarts in 1942, in the midst of World War II. On March 18 of that year, with the threat of a German invasion of Egypt still looming, a re-constituted Committee of the Museum of Civilization assembled in the Agricultural Society. The president of the society, Prince Tusun, informed the present museum directors and scholars that the hiatus had been due to a budget freeze at the outbreak of war that had prompted a delay of the exhibition altogether.[88] A new momentum guided the efforts as is evident in a booklet that the Royal Agricultural Society printed to document the work of new subcommittees that were formed to give shape to the various chronological sections of the planned museum. The booklet became a blueprint for the museum display that gained shape over the following years.[89] Its chapters show that the museum project had evolved from a mere idea of putting together an improvised display to a vision of a full-scale museum. The museum was to occupy a substantial part of the buildings of the Royal Agricultural Society. The committees were no longer representing the various museums in Egypt, but were now organized according to Shafiq Ghurbal's epochs: the Prehistoric Age, the Pharaonic Age, the Greco-Roman period, and the Arab Age, which was a curious name for a period that started with the Muslim conquest of Egypt and ended with the demise of the medieval Mamluks. The Ottoman age had a separate committee. Another curious fact was the subdivision of the modern age into a subsection on the French expedition and one on the age of Mehmet Ali's dynasty. Not only foreigners, but also Shafiq Ghurbal argued that a separate section on the French expedition would respond to popular demand. It is not clear if "popular" meant the Egyptian educated upper-middle class who liked to identify with European civilization. Ghurbal certainly believed he had to underline the civilizational break that the arrival of the French meant in his historical narrative, paving the way for the dynasty. But special interests entered the Civilization Museum in other ways, too. Other than Ghurbal's 1939 leitmotif, the 1942 *blueprint* contained a section on the Copts. However, the respective subcommittee had difficulties fitting it into the chronological and teleological narrative of the Museum. In the 1939 leitmotif, the Arab-Muslim period followed directly on from the Greco-Roman period, and when the 1942 blueprint added the Copts to the program, it was not as the *Coptic period*, but as a separate *Coptic civilization*. As was obvious for everyone, this civilization was still alive and well, but the section was nevertheless tucked between two others that were chronologically defined. "Theoretically, the era of Coptic civilization starts in the first century of the Christian Era, but practically, it starts in the fourth century of the Christian Era," the committee members assessed in a somewhat confusing statement. In the display, posters should highlight important events that happened between the fourth century and the Muslim conquest, but Coptic art and photos of churches and monasteries should also be displayed. Unlike Pharaonic and Greco-Roman temples, they were still in use. The Coptic section of the blueprint thus represented a tension between inclusion and exclusion of the Coptic community in Egypt. It was presented as the missing link between ancient Egypt and the present, but the uncomfortable place it occupied in the deliberations served as proof that it took part in the national life of the twentieth century.[90] In contrast, communities such as Egypt's Nubians or the country's Jews were not granted space in this ethno-religious frame of thought.

Scaled dioramas and panoramic paintings, called "friezes," were to make up the greater part of the display. As shown, the museum eventually contained only a small number of life-size effigies, and none of 'Abd al-Malik's wax figures. The wax museum had a short and last appearance in the 1942 booklet, which contained a list of available wax figures of the Khedives, and one of the great Islamic reformer Muhammad 'Abduh. Only a few months later, the newly created Executive and Coordination Committees of the museum decided that only re-nowned and capable Egyptian artists should be commissioned for the preparation of the exhibition, in order to have "a representation of Egyptian art and a genu-ine Egyptian spirit in the museum."[91] The respectability of art, and its value to educate the masses in the civilizing ritual of the museum visit, thus trumped the appeal of the wax museum spectacle.

Excursus II: Egyptian civilization and the Empire in the Sudan

Another section that was new to the 1942 blueprint was the hall of the Egyptian Sudan. Shafiq Ghurbal had already voiced his vision in 1939 that Egypt's reach for the sources of the Nile in the nineteenth century deserved a separate exhibition, including the scientific and economic missions and the expansion of Egyptian rule in various parts of Africa that Khedive Isma'il had undertaken.[92]

Egypt's expansion into the Sudan was a prestige project of royal Egyptian power politics. Mehmet Ali made first forays into the Sudan in the 1820s to recruit slave soldiers for his New Model Army. Khedive Isma'il (r. 1863–1879) took on the project on a grand scale in the 1870s, mimicking European imperialism as he desired to join the rush for possessions in Africa in the guise of a civilizing mis-sion. Like its European counterparts, the Geographical Society that he founded in 1875 took a lead role in promoting colonial expansion in the guise of explora-tion. Foreigners, such as Germans, Italians, and Americans, even held prominent positions in the society, well into the twentieth century, and they also manned the scientific missions that accompanied Khedive Isma'il's Sudan adventures. When Ghurbal promoted a special Sudan section he confirmed that the state-sponsored nationalism that he stood for included an Egyptian African Empire as an impe-rialist hand-me-down. According to Ghurbal's vision, Egypt was an imperialist power next to European empires, and primarily next to Britain. As a matter of fact, Britain not only dominated Egypt, but also ruled over the Sudan as an in-dependent entity even if the Anglo–Egyptian condominium agreement of 1899 regulated that the two countries officially shared this responsibility. Egyptian achievements were hailed as a success in the Sudan section of the Civilization

Museum such as Gordon Pasha's expansion and governorship in the Sudan in the 1870s, which officially happened on behalf of the Khedive, but could only take place with the consent of the British government.[93]

Committee members did not, however, ignore the awkwardness of an Egyptian imperialist claim over the Sudan. In December 1939, the Executive Council discussed a request by Prince 'Umar Tusun during the last meeting before the temporary cessation of activities. Tusun had a deep interest in antiquities affairs in general, and specifically in the Civilization Museum and its Sudan section. He suggested avoiding the term "conquest" ("fath") in its context. In reply, the committee offered to use the term "retrieval" ("istirdad") instead. Tusun, however, still believed that "retrieval" had an element of "overpowering" ("istila'") in it and suggested two further alternatives: "Unification of Egypt and the Sudan" (tawhid), or "Return of the Nile Valley to its unity" ('awdat Wadi al-Nil ila wahdatihi).[94] Even if the discussion remained inconclusive at this point, the 1949 catalogue used terms such as "official integration into Egypt" ("dammaha rasmiyyan ila Misr"), "raising the Egyptian flag over ..." ("rafa'a al-'alam al-Misri 'ala"...), spoke of "scientific missions" and gave a prominent place to a diorama depicting the banning of the slave trade under the Khedivial dynasty to provide evidence for the civilizational impetus of Egypt's expansion – ignoring that Mehmet Ali's forays into the Sudan started as raids to extract slaves as soldiers for his new model army, and that the slave trade in fact continued roughly until the turn of the century.[95] A painting represented the Egyptian governor over the Sudan in ancient times delivering tributary payments to the Pharaoh, and another one a Nubian king paying tribute to the Mamluk Sultan al-Malik al-Nasir (r., with interruptions, 1293–1341) to underline the continuity of Egypt's rule over the Sudan.[96] Even if the Sudan Hall was part of the section in the museum that covered the Modern Period, it presented the country either as an object of Egypt's long-term imperial control, or, in one mural painting in particular, as an object of an anthropologist's gaze. The mural showed half-naked black Sudanese in front of straw huts harvesting their produce by hand – apparently on a similar stage of development as the cave men of the beginning of this chapter (Figure 4.5).

In addition, the Sudan section contained a painting depicting a traditional Sudanese Quranic school (*khalwa*). Modern institutions of learning such as Gordon College in Khartoum (a British foundation) were not mentioned.[97] There were, hence, various mechanisms of *othering* and *orientalizing* at work that juxtaposed a modernist, rational and reformed Egypt *with a history* on the one hand to a backward and *timeless* Sudan on the other.[98]

Mastery over the Sudan had served nineteenth-century Egyptian elites in delineating Egyptianness. The Sudan was a mirror, essential in building a self-perception as an independent, sovereign and powerful Egyptian nation, based on a racial hierarchy in a civilizing mission. The nationalist discourse of the interwar period popularized this notion. In 1947, then, the Institute of Sudan Studies was founded at Alexandria University bringing together Egyptians working in

Figure 4.5 A mural in the Sudan exhibition.

Egyptology, history, but also geography, and Africanists to promote the unity idea. Geographers made up the majority of the institute's directors in the following years – not because historians were not interested, but rather because of "an assumption that the Sudanese [had been] 'people without history' until Muhammad Ali's conquest[.]"[99] Geography and exploration demarcated the areas that were already highlighted, along with those that remained in shadow, waiting to become enlightened. Consequently, maps helped Egyptian nationalist scholars more than anything else in their effort to promote the concept of the "Unity of the Nile Valley" that became popular in the 1920s, insisting on Egyptian suzerainty to counter British designs to separate the Sudan from Egypt. Maps adorned the walls of the Sudan exhibition in the Civilization Museum, one depicting the empire in the age of Khedive Isma'il, one of Mehmet Ali's 1838–1839 journey to the Sudan, and finally one presenting all of the Nile Valley from the sources to the estuary.[100]

There is a report about the special visit of a Sudanese delegation to the Sudan section of the yet unopened Museum in 1947. It would be interesting to know how the members of this delegation reacted when they inevitably found out that they were treated by the museum as objects of an Egyptian narrative, and not as subjects of their own history, but unfortunately there is no according information. This confrontation of the colonized – probably elite members and maybe even graduates of Gordon College – with a version of their history and civilization neatly packaged and prepared by the dominant race, is starkly reminiscent of the visits by delegations of colonized peoples to the Oriental displays at the great European exhibitions.[101]

Was Egypt's hold over the Sudan indeed a form of colonialism? Like Prince Tusun, Shafiq Gurbal took issue with this formulation. In a book published during King Faruq's reign, Ghurbal discussed the benefits of Mehmet 'Ali's and his successors' southward expansions.[102] In an apparent refutation of what he considered narrow-minded criticism by foreign scholars, Ghurbal stated that Egypt at least brought the railway, telegraph, steamship travel, social statistics, and specialists to the Sudan. For Ghurbal, Egypt belonged to the advanced nations of the world at the time, in terms of agriculture and production, without having to fear a comparison with Russia, Hungary, Germany, and the industrial towns of England. As far as slavery in Egypt was concerned, it should be seen in light of what was going on in the Americas and the European colonies in Africa and Asia. Still, Ghurbal preferred to assess the Egyptian reach for the Sudan from a different vantage point than mere exploitation. When Mehmet Ali conquered the Sudan, he conquered neighboring Muslim territory, stated Ghurbal.

> This kind of conquest is not occupation or imperialism. Muslims do not own Muslim slaves. Conquest there is incorporation of a part of the Dar al-Islam into the Muslim Umma to enliven it and let it share in the greater Muslim life.

Besides, the Sudan had not been all that backward when the Egyptians arrived, added the historian. When al-Tahtawi spent years of exile there under Abbas I rule in Egypt (1848–1854), he encountered a thriving culture of Islamic scholarship and jurisprudence that even entailed women as patrons. Mehmet Ali's gift to the Sudan had therefore not been relief from ignorance. Instead he laid the foundation for modern unified statehood, connecting the Sudan with the greater Ottoman world, and the "present human life," i.e. modern civilization. Ghurbal thus argued along several intersecting lines: He emphasized Egypt's contribution to the technical and scientific development of the Sudan as in a civilizing mission, but played down its imperialist nature on the basis of a conservative reference to the Islamic community and traditional Islamic scholarship that some modernizing Islamic reformers of the late nineteenth century and the secularists of the twentieth century would have abhorred. In a nod to their agenda, though, he stressed the participation of women in Sudanese scholarly circles.[103]

Sudanese intellectuals were, in contrast, quite aware of the colonialist traits of Egypt's rule over the Sudan. The Agriculture and Industry Exhibition that opened alongside the Civilization Museum in 1949 welcomed a delegation of Sudanese journalists, who were introduced in the *al-Muqattam* newspaper as coming from the "South of the Valley" – explicitly not as visitors or as Sudanese, because they were indeed "at home, and not in a foreign country." This, however, did not prevent them from being treated with the same paternalism as that which they also encountered in the Civilization Museum, which the delegation probably visited, even if the sources do not confirm it. The Sudanese also listened to speeches about the fruits of the Egyptian revival in education, agriculture, and production and were continuously lectured, it seems, about the country's progress. As such, they were mere observers from a foreign place, in spite of all the rhetoric to the contrary.[104] On one occasion, though, the Sudanese fired back. When Haykal Basha, the President of the Egyptian Senate (*majlis al-shuyukh*) gave a feast honoring the delegation, the Sudanese journalist Bashir Muhammad Sa'id complained in a speech that many Egyptian leaders expressed in statements – easily available for the Sudanese in the press – that they wanted to exploit the Sudan and hold on to it. Sa'id voiced his and his colleagues' fear and disapproval of these messages that ran counter to their vision of the relationship between the Sudan and Egypt. Haykal Basha, who considered himself a Sudan specialist, had no choice but to assure the delegation that throughout his political life, he had never met an Egyptian leader or politician who had declared that Egypt wanted to rule the Sudan or had desired colonial control over it. Haykal rather blamed the controversy on half a century of rift between the Sudan and Egypt as the cause for the speaker's mistrust – a rift that was neither Egypt's nor the Sudan's fault but a result of the misdeeds of the imperialist power (i.e. Great Britain) who divided the people of the one country. When Egypt had striven to turn Egypt and the Sudan into one country under parliamentary rule with equal representation working together for success, and with ministers in the government from everywhere in the Nile Valley, the imperialist had rejected this, claiming that Egypt wanted imperialist control. As an alternative solution, he offered that the Sudan should be to Egypt what Scotland and Wales were to England: with their own parliaments and governments but under one crown ruling over the Nile Valley, because the separation was against God's and nature's will.[105] In light of the weakness of Egypt's parliamentary system during the postwar period, this offer certainly had a bitter taste for the Sudanese delegates. It is doubtful, moreover, that the appeal to divine provision and the familiar Nile Valley environmental determinism resonated at the end of the day with the young Sudanese nationalists among the journalist delegation.

Epilogue

Budgetary concerns, late submissions of artwork and a shift in the organizational hierarchy of the museum from the Agricultural Society to the Ministry of Public Education caused a number of delays to the opening of the Civilization Museum, and with it to that of the General Agriculture and Industry Exhibition.[106] There is no clear information in the documents about budgetary responsibility, but it is most likely that at first, the Agricultural Society had to shoulder the cost, probably with palace support in line with the late King Fu'ad's practice to sponsor the arts and sciences.[107] When the Education Ministry took over, funding structures were probably affected, too, even if the Grand Serail of the Agricultural Society was retained as the location.

The museum eventually opened on the morning of February 10, 1949, with a celebration in the presence of the King. Participants were happy that the opening coincided with Faruq's birthday on the following day, and they were certainly charmed by the visit of the two princesses Fawziyya and Fa'iza on the afternoon of the same day – a déjà-vu of the 1936 Exhibition visit mentioned above, again in identical clothing, only this time they were drowning in sumptuous mink coats.[108] The news of the opening even made it as far as North America, where the International Travel Section of the *New York Times* introduced the Museum of Egyptian Civilization as a "visual history book." According to the article, the new museum was a sign for the normalization of public life and resumption of tourist activity in Egypt after the Arab–Israeli war.[109]

If a journalist's reaction to the new museum is in any way representative of its public effect and appeal, a feature in the respectable *al-Muqattam* newspaper must have been quite to the liking of the museum makers. The author confirmed that the museum was more an "inventory of Egyptian life" ("sijill al-hayat al-Misri") than an illustration of facts; it was a museum of life rather than one of artifacts like the antiquities collections in Egypt. The purpose of the Civilization Museum was to educate, not to exhibit and exhaust historical circumstances, he wrote. Through the King's care the museum had emerged as one of a kind in the world, and all this by Egyptian hands, helping the Egyptian artist to reorient himself towards a nationalist direction, away from foreign cultures towards Egyptian culture. The journalist thus summarized the various aspects of the museum-making agenda, most of which had already appeared in Faruq's memorandum in 1939: the pedagogical approach, the demand for an integrative museum narrative, the Egyptianization of the museum landscape, the worshipping of the King, and the re-purposing of Egyptian museology in the direction of nationalism. As a side note, the only display that was mentioned in the article was, once more, the cave man.[110]

There is no immediate information about the initial public response to the museum. The fact, though, that it opened in concert with the 16th Agricultural and Industry Exhibition starting on March 1st, 1949, suggests that many people got a glimpse of it right away. Due to the expected large numbers of visitors to the Exhibition, it was planned to levy a separate entrance fee to the museum or to admit only a limited number of visitors at a given time in order to channel the masses.[111] The first two days of the Exhibition were reserved for visits by the royal family and invited guests, but afterwards the doors were open for the general public. Egyptian, Sudanese, and Palestine Railways offered percentages on tickets for Exhibition travelers, and so did airlines and hotels. Special bus lines brought visitors to the grounds, and there were designated parking lots. Signs for a broad public response to the Exhibition and the new museum were visible in warnings that visitors should be aware of forged tickets sold in front of the access gates. Finally the Exhibition was extended by five days to close on April 20 only. At its close, an estimated one and a half million visitors had attended the Exhibition, with complaints that at times it was so overcrowded that salesmen increased the prices for food and drink to the extent that people became agitated.[112]

* * *

As shown, the glorification of the Egyptian monarchy took center stage in the historical narrative of the Civilization Museum. In accordance with the theory and practice of late nineteenth- and early twentieth-century nationalist museology, the museum was designed to provide an integrated image of state sponsored Egyptian nationalism with a strong modernist and secular touch, a sense of civilizational unity, and a civilizing mission. The chronological organization of the display's itinerary, starting with the origins of the Egyptian man, culminated in a hall glorifying the royal family. There is a great deal of irony in the fact that the opening of the Civilization Museum happened at the same time as Israeli and Egyptian negotiators were trying to finalize an armistice agreement on the Greek island of Rhodes to end hostilities in the first Arab–Israeli war, which turned out to be the death knell of Egypt's *ancien régime*. When Faruq inaugurated the museum and opened the Exhibition in Cairo, a man called Gamal 'Abd al-Nasir was still holding out under an Israeli siege in the *Falluja Pocket*. When he rose to power in Egypt only three years later at the head of a group of conspiring *Free Officers*, however, only a part of the Civilization Museum became obsolete. The secular nationalist outlook of Nasser's regime after his final assumption of presidential power in 1954, violently marginalizing the petit bourgeois and working-class Islamism of the Muslim Brotherhood, built on the same image of Egypt's unique position at the intersection of what Nasser termed as three cultural circles: The Arab, the African, and the Islamic – a message that echoed Egyptian imperialism and its civilizing mission.[113]

* * *

In spite of the absence of data on numbers of visitors to the museum and their reactions over the years, it is possible to trace the existence of the museum throughout the second half of the twentieth century using travel guidebooks. There is information that the museum still contained its sections about the royal family in 1954, two years after the revolution.[114] The Guide Bleu of 1956, however, listed the sections of the museum from the stone age to the modern period, but mentioned that the Rotunda at one end of the Grand Serail exhibited a Coach and Car Museum, including a Ford motor car and several ceremonial vehicles. Before, the Rotunda had been most likely the location of the hall glorifying the achievements of Kings Fu'ad and Faruq.[115] A 1966 German guidebook still mentioned the Coach and Car Museum, but the *Guide Bleu* of 1971 already replaced it with the Gezira Museum of Fine Arts. The 1976 edition of the same guide finally pointed out that the Civilization Museum had a certain "charme désuet" (old fashioned charm). It no longer represented the cutting edge of museology, as it did when it was inaugurated.[116]

The narrative that the museum popularized has had a longer lifespan, though. The Egyptian middle class has continued to identify with the historical timeline it proposed.[117] A survey of recent Egyptian elementary school textbooks in reading and social studies suggests that the broad lines of the official standard narrative have not changed. The image of the Nile as the eternal life-giver of the country plays a central role in the texts, and so do the benefits of skills in technology and engineering for the economy, especially in agriculture. Moreover, the textbooks try to instill pride in the long history of the country as present in the monuments through the ages, and praise the military prowess of its soldiers as protectors. New is an emphasis on hospitality and honesty towards foreigners as an Egyptian trait because of the central importance of tourism for the country. A fifth grade Arabic reading lesson "[a]bout the good things of our country" explained that "Egypt was, and still is, a source of the good in its past and present, and it will remain in God's good grace, always ..." Her Nile was the artery of life; ancient Egyptian culture rose along its shores thousands of years ago. The river had been good to the generations of the past, and it continued to be good to them in the present and would do so in the future, God willing. Egypt's people in their different professions were just one of the faces of Egypt's goodness, the schoolbook said. The text then drew particular attention to Egypt's soldiers whose superior ability at war the world knew. But in addition, the sons of Egypt were active in all Arab lands as specialists, while people from Asia and Africa and the states of the world came to Egypt to profit from her knowledge. The text closed: "God protect Egypt ... and care for her sons, Muslims and Christians, in security and peace," and thus drew a line under an Egyptian ethos that was quite similar to the one that King Faruq had presented in his memorandum of 1939: a combination of historical depth, societal strength, superior technical skills, soldierly spirit, pride in the country but concern for the broader Arab nation, under the banner of unity among the religions. Two watercolors on opposite pages illustrated this image, one bringing together a hybrid figure morphing a female peasant and an Egyptian fertility goddess, leaning over spikes of wheat, with scientists, engineers, a physician, and students watching, and with a portrait of the important twentieth-century secular intellectual Taha Husayn towering over them, the second one depicting a farmer in the countryside, and a painter painting a portrait of an unveiled city woman, combined with soldiers preparing to go into battle during the 1973 October War, as well as Pharaoh and his wife in intimate company, reminiscent of a gold relief on the back of King Tut's throne in the Egyptian Museum. In this particular lesson, religion played only a very marginal role, which may have been due to the state's anti-Islamist backlash after the anti-terrorism battles of the 1990s.[118]

While this textbook only illustrates the broad brace of Egyptian history between ancient times and the present, a social studies textbook for the same grade level adopts the typical sequence of epochs in Egyptian history, presenting in a series of chapters "Personalities From Pharaonic History," "... From Islamic History," and "... From Modern History," ranging from Pharaoh Ahmose, Salah al-Din and the Mamluk Amir Saif al-Din al-Qutuz, victor over the Mongols, to Mehmet Ali and Nasser. King Faruq has no place in this narrative, but among Mehmet Ali's achievements that the textbook lists was – nota bene – the conquest of the Sudan, and its integration into Egypt, as well as, allegedly, the abolishment of the slave trade, which is more than a faint echo of the narrative that shaped the Civilization Museum.[119]

* * *

Today, the Civilization Museum is dilapidated. As of spring 2012 it was in a state of renovation. In the meantime, the Coach Museum has moved to the Cairo Citadel, and at least some of the pictures in the art museum were probably transferred to the Museum of Egyptian Art that is part of the new Cairo Opera complex, which now dominates the southern part of the Gezira Island, overshadowing the old Exhibition grounds. The Small Serail of the Agricultural Society hosts the National Center for Translation. The Art Deco facade of the Grand Serail remains an impressive sight, against all odds, and its tower still has "Museum of Egyptian Civilization" written on it in large fading letters, in both English and Arabic (Figure 4.6).

The museum will, however, never return to this site. Before the Tahrir Square revolution, the government of Husni Mubarak – more Pharaoh than King – was able to secure UNESCO support and funding for one of several grand museum designs that dwarf the late royal projects. In addition to the *Grand Egyptian Museum* that is set to open near the Giza Pyramids to replace the old one in central Cairo, the Egyptian government has now completed construction of a new Museum of Egyptian Civilization. In oblivion of the story told on these pages, UNESCO's webpage announces the museum as "[t]he first veritable museum of civilization in Egypt." The new Civilization Museum will be located near the ruins of Fustat, the core of Cairo's urban development in early Islamic times. Like the Grand Egyptian Museum, it will be far

Figure 4.6 The former Museum of Egyptian Civilization in 2012.

removed from the bustling city center. According to UNESCO, it is "[d]esigned as a major attraction for visitors to Egypt as well as an internationally recognized research and conservation centre," in a location that is convenient and safe for tourists. Six halls are planned, combining chronological with thematic approaches: "Dawn of Civilization, The Nile, Writing, State and Society, Material Culture, Beliefs and Thinking and the Gallery of Royal Mummies." The choice of themes within the sections remains unclear; it might well be inclusive in terms of chronology, but it is still revealing that the only two sections that have a clear chronological marker are the ones about ancient Egypt: Dawn of Civilization, and the Mummies. Once more, Westerners can come to Egypt to marvel at its "real," i.e. ancient identity, while proper classification and scientific preservation of artifacts remains assured. The museum world has returned full circle to the idea of a shared human world heritage according to the Western vision. The UNESCO seal of international cultural heritage served to provide international recognition and legitimacy to Mubarak, the new Pharaoh. It remains to be seen how a post-Mubarak Egypt will handle and negotiate national heritage.[120]

* * *

This chapter presented the museum as a medium of nationalism where stories become materially manifest. The special prominence of museums in the presentation of Egyptian culture to the world was behind the choice of the country study even if Egyptian nationalism plays a distinct, if not atypical role in the context of Arab nationalism. Egyptian nationalism is an *Arab* nationalism because of the central role that Arab references have played in Egyptians' efforts to define their place in the world. More importantly, however, the role of Egypt, and in particular that of Cairo as a cultural clearing house, a hub, and a pivot for the twentieth-century Arab world make the country a worthwhile object of inquiry, because its elites and burgeoning middle class – the very target audience of the Civilization Museum – led the way in the adoption and adaptation of modern media for popular dissemination and social engineering. The following chapter shifts the focus both eastward and westward, to Damascus as another political and cultural hub, and via the Syrian metropolis to its sister city Baghdad, and to Algiers, which for a time was the capital of Arab revolutionaries and the Third World decolonization movement.

5   Damascus transfers

Dead bodies and their translocal meanings

In this chapter, the action takes place largely in one location, but it also transcends geography in the wake of the physical movement of dead bodies. These movements within Syria or its capital Damascus, from other places in the Arab realm to Syria, or from Syria to other places mark out boundaries of pan-Arabism, rather in an idealistic and political sense than in a geographic sense, in a competition over the presence of dead bodies that sanctify the location, but whose trans-local significance makes local leaders jealously safeguard the bodies from competitors. In the context of the Great Man myth, to incorporate a body, to claim it successfully or unsuccessfully, or to give it up for another location are therefore highly symbolic acts. In a broader context, the chapter argues that the oft-cited dichotomy between secular and religious realms dissolves in the practice of festivals that constitute a form of nationalist expression.

Funerals, burials and re-burials are events at the intersection of secular and religious spheres. A funeral can never be an entirely secular event as it transcends the physical lifetime of the deceased, and as it constitutes an attempt to perpetuate his or her existence regardless of the social and political context of the event. A perpetuation in a secular ritual of memory is not all that different from a religious ceremony based on the expectation of an afterlife. Consequently, any nationalist or communist cult of the dead is essentially similar to one rooted in Islamic or Christian mystic spirituality and the veneration of saints. Likewise, the worshipping of relics of saints has always had a potential political element. Possessing a saintly relic, controlling access to it, and moving it around to circumscribe an area of influence has always been a matter of power. The covert transfer of the relics of Saint Mark to Venice in the ninth century is just the most prominent example for common practices of bodysnatching.

This chapter offers two examples for the transfer of bodies as a meaningful act in nationalism. In the post-Enlightenment European world of the secular nation state, state funerals of Great Men became an essential part of a *culte laïc* that manifested itself in festivals of public representation.[1] Funerals are thus part of the culture of nationalism. During the nineteenth century, governments of the French Third Republic excelled in using *republican funerals* to build a *civil religion*[2] around the Great Men – the heroes and modern day saints of the nation – as canonization no longer rewarded piety but service for the nation as its political, military, or intellectual leaders. The developing nations of the post-Ottoman Middle East, like Syria, Iraq, and Egypt were in need of similar rites because of the loss of the central symbol of the Ottoman caliphate and the painful inferiority complex that derived from colonial submission. Festivals like obsequies of Great Men were visible and public enough to compensate for the perceived inferiority. They were not *populist*, though, because they did not represent a grassroots initiative. Rather, they stood for *elite nationalism*. Hence, state funerals were meant to underline national consensus, but they also represented what the decision-makers wanted to see expressed in public festivities. Control of public sentiment, however, was not assured, and – as it happened in nineteenth-century Paris – state funerals often turned the streets of the capital into contested terrain between supporters and opponents of a particular vision of the state.[3]

Both cults of heroes and saints depend on locality and performance of memorization to gain meaning in national or religious discourse. Yearly festivals of memorization (such as *maulids* or *mausims*) and the *ziyarat* (visits) to the tomb of a saint or a hero (such as the patriotic pilgrimage to Atatürk's mausoleum *Anıtkabir*) constitute, ritualize and, thus, keep memory alive.[4] In that, most nationalisms rely on existing repertoires of ritualization and liturgy in their attempts to festivalize public space – as secular as the concept of nationalism may be. Secular nationalists in the Arab Middle East and elsewhere did not replace religious rituals, but rather appropriated, infiltrated and re-defined them. They did not intend to antagonize the customary heritage in order to maintain a semblance of popular legitimacy, or because they drew from the same heritage context. Religious festivals thus turned into hybrids of secular and religious elements under the conditions of the modern nation state, but they were structured along the lines of religious custom, which determined the available repertoire of rites.[5]

Funerals are festivals that take place at a particular moment and in a particular place, but they are commemorative festivals giving meaning and context to a biography that transcends the time and location of the ritual – either as part of a general redemption narrative as in the purely religious ceremony, or within a complex setting of intersecting local, trans-local, and transcendent idealistic narratives as in nationalism or class struggle. The movement of bodies, as well as re-burials, provides an opportunity for the community to re-constitute and re-orient itself. The re-burial re-interprets and re-contextualizes the commemoration of the deceased in a new time and locality; the movement of the body over significant distances opens up the locality to create new notions of space. The dead acquire trans-local meanings they might not have had before, as if notions of being in the right or the wrong place, far away or at home, transcended the moment of death. In that, the repatriation of bodies is a postcolonial phenomenon, or a phenomenon of decolonization related to the assumption that a body can only properly rest in its home-soil, but also that a nation only achieves completeness when all of its own are within its confines, as in the repatriation of the remains of dead soldiers. The transfer of a famous corpse "localizes part of the symbolic capital [it] contain[s] …" In post-Soviet European states the disappearance of the socialist imperial framework called for a reorientation in references of origin, ancestry and kin, triggering a wave of repatriations of corpses of Great Men. Similar challenges confronted the peoples of the post-Ottoman Arab world. Conflicts over the proper place to bury a Great Man therefore provided for a very physical and concrete connection between ancestry and soil, especially when the soil was "drenched with the blood" of previous wars. There is, hence, a double confirmation of ancestry through soil: It is a resting place, and it absorbs the essence of life of ancestors in its defense.[6] In the Arab lands, the intricate overlay of local identities with regional and pan-Arab nationalisms and the changing nature of their interplay provide for an intriguing context, in which definitions of *home* and *away* call for complex justifications. The following examples present some of these justifications in an Arab nationalist universe that spans a wide geography of Arab lands between Iraq and Algeria, focusing on the physical movement of dead bodies and the involved spatial symbolism, in the context of burials and re-burials.

Yasin, in Damascus

The first case is Yasin al-Hashimi's funeral in January 1937 in Damascus. In an earlier chapter, his resting place next to the mausoleum of Salah al-Din was introduced as a location where various aspects of the culture of Arab nationalism are condensed into one place. Hashimi's funerary rites and the events of the week that followed them mark his burial as a case study for several fault lines of interwar Arab nationalism. For a period of time, al-Hashimi's obsequies, his lying in state in Damascus, the eulogies, and the coverage of the events in the press of several Arab countries created a meaningful pan-Arab community – a community, however, that had different meanings for its diverse participants.

Al-Hashimi was born in 1884 in Baghdad into a family of modest means. The claim on descent from the Prophet's tribe that the last name entailed was quite questionable and al-Hashimi received status only as a high-ranking Ottoman staff officer and a military hero of World War I. Al-Hashimi presided over Prince Faysal's War Council during the latter's rule in Damascus, and when Faysal became king of Iraq in 1921, al-Hashimi joined him once more as a very ambitious politician, mistrusted by his contenders for political power. He held two premierships, from 1924–25 and from 1935–36.[7]

Al-Hashimi was opportunistic and ruthless, but a highly skilled politician. In 1937, eulogies praised Yasin al-Hashimi as a gifted manager of state finances, who stabilized Iraq's budget in the 1920s and 1930s, but he had also backed legislation that drastically favored large landholders and, thus, his personal economic interests. Al-Hashimi promoted the economic welfare of the ruling class he belonged to because he believed it was the primary condition for the preservation of law and order or, in other words, social discipline in the country. When political infighting and the tribal pressure that he was able to exploit brought al-Hashimi to power in March 1935, he intended, as an admirer of Kemal Atatürk, to form a regime that was more authoritarian, militaristic, and nationalist – if also more efficient – than its predecessors. Al-Hashimi worked towards the creation of a single state party and curtailed the freedom of the press. The state clamped down on the leftist opposition and instituted military conscription. The government also drafted a new labor law (which never went into effect) that would have banned child labor and allowed the creation of unions, albeit under almost insurmountable restrictions. Oil royalties allowed al-Hashimi to focus on economic development and the improvement of infrastructure. However, he gave a clear priority to military needs. To quell smoldering tribal unrest in the south, he banned Shiʻi Muharram processions. A cornerstone of his regime's disciplinary strategy was the creation of the Futuwwa youth organization.[8] When the Palestine Revolt broke out in 1936, it propelled Yasin al-Hashimi – as the head of what Arab nationalists in other countries regarded as the only truly independent and nationalist Arab government – into a position as leader of pan-Arab solidarity with the Palestinian rebels, although he himself was reluctant to take on this role.[9]

Dissatisfaction with al-Hashimi's autocratic style and perceived arrogance fueled the domestic opposition to his rule that led to his downfall in the military coup of October 1936 followed by exile in Beirut and his premature death of heart failure only three months later.[10] Staged by the Iraqi chief of staff Bakr Sidqi, a Kurd, and supported by the left-leaning *al-Ahali* group, the coup also opposed the Arab nationalist mainstream of the Iraqi political elite.[11]

In the mid-1930s, Yasin al-Hashimi – the war hero, the staunch opponent of British influence in Iraq, the promoter of Palestinian resistance – was an icon of Arab nationalism, inside and outside Iraq, and a point of reference for pan-Arab nationalists of many different provenances.[12] His death turned him into a public hero. The funeral in January 1937, its symbolic itineraries, and its speeches illustrate how Arab leaders used the deceased's charisma to turn pan-Arabism into something to be physically experienced by the people in the streets of Damascus and by the youth groups that escorted the coffin. First-rank politicians used shared pan-Arab feelings to popularize their own claim to leadership.

Al-Hashimi died in Beirut on 21 January 1937, in the presence of his brother Taha al-Hashimi.[13] Telegrams went out announcing the death to important Arab leaders and organizations, including Amir ʻAbdallah of Transjordan, the Mufti of Jerusalem Amin al-Husayni, the Syrian National Bloc party, and the Egyptian government. One telegram asked for permission from King Ghazi of Iraq to transfer the body to Baghdad. Lebanese dignitaries who came to offer their condolences suggested a burial in Damascus instead.[14] The family decided that doctors of the American University of Beirut (AUB) should embalm the body. The Syrian government had already started to plan for a burial next to Saladin's mausoleum when notice arrived from Iraq that the body would be admitted to Baghdad. However, the Iraqi government would not allow the deceased's brother, Taha, to participate. In spite of concerns about the sincerity of the Iraqi government, the family accepted this proposal. The coffin was to be brought from Beirut to Damascus and then – after a funeral ceremony – to Baghdad.[15]

Yasin al-Hashimi's death was understood as an event that concerned the entire Arab nation. The list of those who received immediate notice via telegram included the top elites of the newly founded Arab nation states. Newspapers in Palestine remembered al-Hashimi's uncompromising support of the Palestine Revolt and announced that Palestinian delegations would travel to Damascus to participate in the obsequies. "All of Palestine" would hold prayers for the deceased in the mosques, and church bells would ring.[16] *Al-Difa'* bemoaned the tragedy of al-Hashimi's death – "in Beirut, and not in Baghdad. In Syria, and not in Iraq ..." – as a harbinger of bad times for the Arabs and the Palestinians in particular.[17] A eulogistic poem printed in the same newspaper a few days later praised him as "... the singular hero / al-Hashimi / The genius ..."[18] In Egypt, *al-Ahram* agreed that al-Hashimi's passing away was a calamity for the Arab nation.[19] Even the Egyptian Islamist journal *al-Fath* noted that rarely had an Arab leader achieved esteem among the people similar to that of Yasin al-Hashimi, both in life and in death: "The telegraph lines between Egypt, Syria and Iraq trembled from carrying messages of deep sadness."[20] There was very little echo of the loss in al-Hashimi's home country of Iraq, however. In Syria, *al-Qabas* was stunned by Iraq's unfaithfulness to its hero while dignitaries from all over the Arab world gathered in Damascus, the "Great Capital of the Arabs," to bid farewell, and *al-Akhbar* wrote: "Cain! ... What have you done to your brother?"[21] There was clearly a sense of competition over who the better "Arabs" were and where they were located. In spite of the pan-Arab rhetoric that was au courant at the time, borders separated Syria and Iraq. Even if they had been drawn after World War I by the colonial powers France and Great Britain to the dismay of Arab nationalists, in the eyes of former Ottoman notables they confirmed the coherence of provincial elites and the local patriotism of the respective capitals and major cities. In Syria, the old elites endorsed Arab nationalism to safeguard their inherited control over Syrian society, without offering room for any change in patterns of social stratification. Urban notables transformed themselves into a national bourgeoisie, maintaining their paternalistic hegemony over society through existing patron–client networks. In Iraq, former Ottoman officers such as al-Hashimi had allied with old urban and tribal elites to form a new class of landowners who used the Iraqi state to further their interests in spite of their pan-Arab convictions. In the later 1920s and in the 1930s young professionals, intellectuals, and students of modern institutions of learning—the Young Effendiyya—used their growing influence in the nascent public sphere of both states to challenge the dominance of the elite.[22] Under these circumstances, the notables-turned-bourgeois nationalists in the Syrian government used Yasin al-Hashimi's funeral in an existing competition over regional leadership and ideological hegemony.

Yasin al-Hashimi's death and funeral, as well as his actual burial in Damascus on 28 January, were "timed" in a peculiar way. The year 1936 witnessed a number of seminal events in Arab politics, including the Iraqi coup, the Anglo–Egyptian treaty, and the Palestine Revolt; there was great nervousness throughout the Arab world. Moreover, Syria had its own issues. Two months before al-Hashimi's death, a new government of the National Bloc entered office after the country's first free elections under French Mandate rule. In the fall of 1936, the *Bloc*, largely under the command of the bourgeois nationalists, negotiated a treaty with the *Popular Front* government in Paris. If ratified, it would have given Syria a considerable degree of autonomy, comparable to the 1930 Anglo–Iraqi treaty. In December, after the *Bloc* delegation's return to Damascus and its landslide victory in the November elections, the Syrian parliament ratified the treaty, anticipating that the French *National Assembly* would follow suit. This, however, never happened because the *Popular Front* fell soon afterward.

Thus 1937 began with great excitement in Syria. The recently founded paramilitary youth organization and strike force of the National Bloc, the *Iron Shirts*, commanded the streets of Damascus, celebrating imminent independence from France.[23] However, only a few days after al-Hashimi's funeral on 22 January, Turkey won a concession from the *League of Nations* in a territorial dispute over the Sanjak of Alexandretta (Iskenderun), which led to an outbreak of violent protests and large-scale demonstrations against the passivity of the National Bloc with regard to maintaining the territorial integrity of the Syrian state. The students' unrest brought the government to the brink of collapse. The irony is that al-Hashimi's funeral marked the climax of the National Bloc's popularity, and his burial on January 28 took place when it had reached a low point. Within a few days, the Sanjak affair had led to the evaporation of the credibility won during the funeral.[24]

The strong efforts that the Damascene government put into the obsequies on January 22 were obviously not entirely altruistic, though all reports on Yasin's funeral processions in both Beirut and Damascus agree that there was great enthusiasm and participation in great numbers. The procession of Yasin's coffin from Beirut to Damascus and the funeral on January 22 combined several layers of symbolism, including Arab nationalist references to Saladin and tributes to the battle of Maysalun. The strong presence of the Iron Shirts represented modern urban politics. Yasin's cortège made two symbolic stops on its way to Damascus, paying homage to the heroes of Faysal's days: one at the site of the battle of Maysalun of 1920 (more on which in the following chapter), and the other at the tomb of Yusuf al-'Azma, the commander of the Syrian irregular army during this battle. The National Bloc sent a delegation of Yasin's old comrades from World War I.[25] In Damascus, thousands of people gathered around the National Garden to receive the body.[26] Troops of Iron Shirts and Boy Scouts lined up around the new building of the *Tajhiz* school,[27] joined by students of the Syrian University and the secondary schools. Police squadrons prepared to salute the deceased. Government representatives including Prime Minister Jamil Mardam, the Saudi consul, the British vice consul, representatives of the Christian patriarchs, and the president of the Jewish community, as well as other dignitaries, prepared to greet Yasin's coffin shortly before it arrived around one o'clock. A policeman and an Iron Shirt on motorcycles headed the cortège that moved along the Barada River into town past Iron Shirts, Boy Scouts, and students standing in formation. Police marched with swords drawn, some with bayonets pointing downwards. Christian

Orthodox and Kurdish Boy Scout troops as well as representatives of the League for National Action participated. Carriers with wreaths marched in front of the truck with the bier, Taha al-Hashimi walked behind it, surrounded by state representatives. Large crowds followed the procession. *Al-Qabas* reported that the city had not seen so many people in the streets. The procession crossed Victoria Bridge, then continued on Hijaz Street[28] and al-Nasr Street to the entrance of Suq al-Hamidiyya. Iron Shirts flanked the Suq all the way to the Umayyad Mosque. In spite of the short distance, the procession took more than one and a half hours. At the Mosque, Iron Shirts carried the bier through the courtyard into the prayer hall, placing it in front of the Shrine of Imam Yahya. After prayer, Prime Minister Jamil Mardam gave a speech, and then the Iron Shirts, followed by the mourners, carried the bier into Imam Husayn, the Prophet's grandson's shrine in the eastern wall of the courtyard where they placed the coffin to lay in state with a guard of honor of policemen and Iron Shirts until a National Bloc delegation would bring the body to Baghdad the next day.[29]

The leaders of the National Bloc used the craze about Yasin al-Hashimi to underline their control over the city in a very physical sense. The Bloc's youth movement and paramilitary wing played a significant part in the choreography of the funeral, and its leader Fakhri al-Barudi, a high Bloc functionary, had a central role in its organization. The itinerary of the procession linked the nationalist claim of the party, which gained a youthful appearance through the Shirts, to Arab tradition and the roots of the Bloc leaders in the city. From Lebanon, via Maysalun to the new city of Damascus, past the Hijaz railway station, and then through the Ottoman Suq towards the heart of the old town, the Umayyad Mosque, and back into the origins of Islam in Imam Husayn's shrine – a journey worth a millennium of history.

Jamil Mardam's eulogy in the Umayyad Mosque used language that established the link between soil, heroism and self-sacrifice that is common for a nationalist cult of the dead. The speech was, however, also a primary example for the ambiguity of Arab nationalism between local and regional power politics and the ideals of pan-Arabism. Mardam emphasized that Yasin, the hero of Arabism, hailed from a country that had left the course of Arabism, while Syria continued to hold up its beacon. He continued: "Damascus [...] wanted that her earth that is moist with the blood of martyrs enclosed his body, too, and she wanted to build him a grandiose mausoleum at the side of [...] Salah al-Din."[30] This lash against a competing Arab government was intended to make the nationalist light of the Damascus government shine even brighter, but the addressees of this legitimacy-building measure were local. Like in a French republican funeral, the Damascene powerful used the occasion of a hero's death to build hegemony over a heterogeneous society. The presence of representatives of both the modern state and traditional dignitaries of all religious communities, including the Jews, in the cortèges and communal prayers, gave support to this endeavor. The representatives of the modern age were dominant, however, especially the disciplining forces of the police and paramilitary brigades and the organized youth of the Boy Scouts, including a Kurdish troop. The associations and individuals that had commissioned wreaths for Yasin's coffin included the Chambers of Agriculture, Industry, and Commerce; the Telegraph and Post Directorate, the Nationalist Youth, the League of National Action, the Iraqi students of the Syrian University, the Tajhiz college, a women's cultural society ("Jam'iyyat dawhat al-adab al-nisa'iyya"), the Jewish community in Damascus, leaders of neighboring Arab countries, as well as many other individuals and organizations.[31] However, not a single wreath from the Iraqi government was mentioned in the papers. All groups had to fit into two ambivalent sets of nationalism: The first one was Syrian, the second was pan-Arab, represented most strongly by the Palestinian delegation.

To the National Bloc's embarrassment, things turned out differently than expected. At some point, the Iraqi government decided to deny entry to all Syrian delegations so that the family eventually found it safer to bury Yasin al-Hashimi next to Saladin, as had been suggested earlier.[32] The nationalist press in Damascus criticized that rivalry and petty infighting between Iraqi and Syrian governments were a disservice to the pan-Arab idea.[33] Obviously, people noticed the paradox of the pan-Arab symbolism of al-Hashimi's funeral on the one hand, and the way the Syrian dignitaries tried to use his credentials to gain leverage as a local elite, on the other. The symbolic itineraries of the funeral, and its speeches represent how political leaders exploited shared pan-Arab feelings to popularize their own claim on leadership. They used the deceased's charisma to turn pan-Arabism into something to be physically experienced by the people in the streets of Damascus and the youth groups that escorted the coffin. The funeral stood for the government's power over the public discourse and marked the symbolic climax of the legitimacy of the Syrian National Bloc. The Syrian state elites tried to give evidence for their capacity to stage a solemn national festivity, celebrating themselves and showing off to the French Mandate power and the Arab brother countries.[34]

Against all intentions, the lying in state of Yasin's body in Imam Husayn's shrine stretched over an entire week. The site was peculiar as it marked the place where once the Imam's severed head had lain for a while after the Battle of Karbala in 680AD. Today, the shrine has become a prominent part of Shi'i pilgrimage itineraries. Yasin, however, belonged to the Sunni elite of the Iraqi state. It would be a mistake, though, to project on the past today's exaggerated sectarian meanings attached to particular sites of worship. In its present location and state, the shrine is a re-invention of the nineteenth century, when the collapse of a wall in the eastern part of the courtyard of the Umayyad Mosque laid it open, and it is not clear if it was then considered a site of primarily Shi'i worship.[35] Contemporary newspapers do not tell why this particular shrine was chosen for Yasin's lying in state, but they also do not consider it unusual. There is no information as to whether it had been used for this purpose before, but it certainly became the center of a pilgrimage of sorts in the presence of Yasin's body. The newspapers were full of reports about delegations, including the Palestinian, visiting Yasin's coffin, carefully watched over by the guard of honor. Delegations came from all over Syria and filled the shrine with flowers and wreaths. *Al-Ayyam* mentions the members of women's societies that came to pay homage to Yasin.[36] Najib al-Rayyis, the editor of the newspaper *al-Qabas*, made an attempt to give meaning to the association of al-Hashimi with Husayn. He wrote that the fatherland stood under the dome of the Umayyad Mosque:

> at the side of the Mausoleum of Husayn Ibn-'Ali, Iraq's first ill-treated martyr, bemoaning the death of Iraq's second ill-treated martyr! What similarity is harder to bear than the one between the two dead men, and what is unhappier than the end of their stories. Both men's lifeless bodies were carried to Damascus, Iraq and the Iraqis forsook them.[37]

In this attack on the Iraqi government, al-Raiyis secularized the image of Imam Husayn at the same time as he sanctified Yasin al-Hashimi. They met halfway in the grey zone of a civil religion.

In spite of this and similar efforts, Yasin's funeral occurred at a turning point for the nationalist reputation of the Damascene elites. When the League of Nations document calling for a French–Turkish accord over Alexandretta became public only two days after Yasin's death, the Syrian government came to the brink of collapse. The accord would have set up a separate administration of the Sanjak of Alexandretta under the French Mandate but with Turkish involvement. Turkish claims on the Sanjak had been a major matter of conflict between Syria and Turkey for a long time. The announcement that Turkey had won a concession on this territorial issue led to a fierce outbreak of violent protests and large-scale demonstrations, which brought crowds of unruly students into the streets during the week that followed al-Hashimi's funeral, shouting slogans such as "Let us die for the fatherland! This is all a French plot, down with Atatürk, the Sanjak is Syrian ..."[38] The National Bloc tried desperately to recreate the serene atmosphere of the funeral, but the hegemony over the civic space was lost again to contenders in the public sphere. The irony is that the funeral of Yasin al-Hashimi on January 22 marked the climax of National Bloc standing, but his actual burial on January 28 took place when it had reached a low point as a consequence of the Sanjak affair.[39]

Subaltern pressure had forced the National Bloc to take a tough stance on independence in 1936 already and to lead a general strike to push the French government into treaty negotiations.[40] In January 1937, there was also unrest among the poor sections of Syrian and Lebanese society. Bread prices were soaring because of a devaluation of the franc, there were strikes because employers were unwilling to adjust salaries, and taxi drivers refused to work in several Syrian and Lebanese towns because of the high price of gasoline.[41] People started to call for a general strike against the new government, which they nicknamed, according to French sources, the "gouvernement de la vie chère."[42]

Two kinds of demonstrations therefore took place in late January 1937, on the one hand a classic republican funeral challenged, on the other, by a student-led outburst of popular nationalist sentiment in response to the Sanjak affair. The urban topography of Damascus provided a stage for this clash between the old elite and the students, who adopted the populist demands of workers and shopkeepers into their agenda. The presence of al-Hashimi's body in the city was supposed to transcend the local power base of the urban notables, who used the funeral of the Arab hero to create the semblance of pan-Arab leadership in order to increase their political legitimacy in the eyes of the younger generation. A prime target of these efforts was the League of National Action, founded in 1933, which represented a new generation of Syrian nationalists, made up largely of students from the university and secondary schools – a group that rejected the Bloc's paternalistic hegemony over Syrian politics and was difficult for the old elite to control.[43] When the Alexandretta protests filled the streets with angry student demonstrators, the National Bloc lost its hegemony over the civic space of the city to contenders in the public sphere of the young Syrian polity, highlighting the uneasy coexistence of two generations of nationalist activists, as well as populist forces, which was characteristic of Arab nationalism in its formative phase during the interwar period.[44]

The protests hence combined political with social and economic grievances. The days between January 25 and 28 saw student strikes and riots, shop keepers closing down their stalls in protest against the government, and attempts by the Bloc to regain control over the streets and alleys of the city, sending Iron Shirts and so-called "zgourts" (roughs of low-class origin) out into the streets to intimidate the protestors. Protests were not only about Alexandretta. Students attacked Christian missionary schools and roughed up their teachers, challenging the paternalistic structures dominating state and society symbolized by institutions of learning that were reserved for the privileged. Slogans were directed as much against the Syrian government as against Turkey or France, and expressed concerns about the dire economic situation, for which the Bloc government did not seem to care or, at least, had no answer.[45]

Attempts by politicians to calm the crowds were to no avail because the Bloc's paternalistic claim to leadership was seriously shattered. There was a stark contrast between Yasin's funeral procession as a show of government authority and the regime's inability to present strength during the demonstrations leading up to January 28. The week had started with an increase of the popular credentials of the Bloc government, but ended with a populist assault on the same government. When they buried Yasin in the afternoon of January 28 (still two days before the end of the wave of street protests), they also buried their dreams of unchallengeable leadership. Several members of government and some diplomats attended the burial, alongside a number of Damascene and Arab dignitaries, but no large crowds.[46] No paper printed the news on the front page. Shukri al-Quwwatli, the Minister of Defense and Finance, and some paramilitary youth entered al-Husayn's shrine to carry the coffin to Saladin's mausoleum, where they took out Yasin's body and lowered it into a freshly dug grave.

The interrupted movement of Yasin al-Hashimi's body stands out as an example of the intricacies of Arab identity in the interwar period. Yasin, the Iraqi, was a pan-Arab leader, but why did dying in Beirut mean that he died in exile, on foreign soil? The bourgeois nationalists of Syria, in contrast, argued that a burial in Damascus was a homecoming of sorts for Yasin, because of Iraq's hostility.

The motives of their presumptuous efforts to organize a funeral in the streets of their city were entirely local, however. The shallowness of their pan-Arab commitment came back to haunt them in the Alexandretta crisis, which in turn developed its own dynamics in combination with local grievances.

The dignitaries who were the architects and choreographers of Yasin's earthly afterlife in Damascus certainly carefully selected the locations of the lying in state and of the tomb, according to their potentials for shaping meaning. There are no documents to reconstruct their rationale, though, but the places retained an inspiring character. A year after Yasin's burial the Iraqi government that had banned his body's entry into the country had fallen and the late Prime Minister had been rehabilitated. In a turn of events, it became fashionable again for Iraqis to celebrate the former leader, as Kamal Ibrahim's, the Baghdadi poet's visit in 1937 and his inspired poem "A Flower Drifted over Yasin al-Hashimi's Grave" has illustrated in an earlier chapter.

'Abd al-Qadir, between Algiers and Damascus

Both in secular and religious contexts, it is meaningful where one is buried and with whom. In Islam and Christianity, to be buried next to a saint has been a privilege over the centuries for either the most virtuous and venerated, or the most powerful and wealthy in the community. In the world of Islam, urban and rural landscapes are dotted with tombs of saints distinguishable by a domed structure, a *turba*, sheltering a sarcophagus with the saint's body. Often, mosques, madrasa-academies, or *zawiyas* (Sufi lodges) are attached. Next to the large coffins of the saints, the domes often contain smaller graves of lesser or later followers of the holy men or women. One such place in Damascus is the shrine of Muhyi al-Din Ibn al-'Arabi in the Muhyi al-Din quarter on the slopes of Mount Qasyun, adjacent to the mosque that bears the name of the medieval mystic. Ibn al-'Arabi is one of the most revered figures in the history of Islam and his works belong to the most influential Sufi teachings. He was born in Murcia in Muslim Spain in 1165 and died in Damascus in 1240 after a life of teaching, writing, and traveling throughout the lands of Islam. The *turba* above his grave initially belonged to the family of the Damascene judge Muhyi al-Din Ibn al-Zaki, but was reconstructed and expanded by the Ottoman Sultan Selim I in the wake of the conquest of Egypt in 1517. He also added the Mosque and a Sufi lodge.[47]

Today, Muhyi al-Din Ibn al-'Arabi's sarcophagus is enshrined in a glass box. The inside of the *turba* is decorated in a contemporary style with crystal chandeliers and brightly illuminated by white and green neon tubes. Another grave, which is the one of concern to this chapter, is located next to that of the Sufi master. It is smaller and made of stone, without much decoration. The sarcophagus was made for the Amir 'Abd al-Qadir al-Jaza'iri (1808–1883), who is one of the eminent figures of nineteenth-century Middle Eastern history, and whose prominent role in Damascene reformist circles has been laid out in an earlier chapter.

'Abd al-Qadir was the offspring of a family of Sufi shaykhs of the *Qadiriyya* branch that had its center in Guetna, near Mascara in Western Algeria. In the wake of the French conquest of 1830 and the subsequent colonization of Algeria the young Sufi sheikh took over the leadership of a resistance movement of tribes from his father. His war against French expansion was initially so successful that he forced the invaders to recognize his sovereignty over great parts of Western Algeria until he was eventually captured and banished in 1847. After a few years of detainment in France, he was released in 1852 to settle in the Arab East. After some years in Bursa in today's Turkey 'Abd al-Qadir moved to Damascus in 1855, where he spent the rest of his life with a French government stipend. He returned to the earlier vocation of his family and led a life in the context of Sufi mysticism, becoming a renowned religious figure in the city, an accomplished poet and a writer on Islamic mysticism and scholarship. 'Abd al-Qadir became an urban notable, too, with a great deal of local authority and a local power base built on the number of followers that he was able to gather when his presence became a point of attraction for Algerian exiles who left the abode of French colonial rule to go east.

He received worldwide renown when he protected the Damascene Christian population during the massacres that happened in the context of the civil war in Mount Lebanon of 1860. 'Abd al-Qadir, who befriended a number of foreign diplomats in the city, took in a large number of Christians while their quarters were ransacked, and sent out his own armed men to guide people from their houses to safety.[48] As a consequence, he had a career as an icon, too: Nineteenth-century romantics from Europe to North America praised 'Abd al-Qadir's bravery as a chivalric Muslim leader against the French onslaught in Algeria in stories, poems and Orientalist paintings. In the twentieth century, the Algerian national resistance to French colonization appropriated his legacy, too. Nationalists referred to his leadership and the creation of his sovereign state in Eastern Algeria when they argued that an Algerian national consciousness had existed prior to the French invasion of the country. The French argued the opposite in order to justify their 'tutelage' over Algeria.[49]

When 'Abd al-Qadir died in 1883, his burial next to his mystical forbear Ibn al-'Arabi followed the Algerian's own wish. His family was well established among the big families of Damascus at the time. The Algerian community in Damascus continued to expand in the second half of the 1880s when economic problems in Algeria added an additional motivation for migrating east to the existing political and religious ones. The Ottoman authorities granted land to farmers and exempted them from military service to encourage them to settle and naturalize. Earlier on, Algerians had remained under French consular protection in Syria, which was a status the French tried to maintain in order to keep the community as a foot in the door in Ottoman lands. 'Abd al-Qadir's declared loyalty to France after his release from detention, and his financial dependence on the stipend, encouraged a stance in which, paradoxically, Algerians who had left Algeria, supposedly to escape French oppression, received a higher status as French protégés by an imperial decree of 1865 than that which their fellow countrymen enjoyed in Algeria as *indigènes*. Accordingly, the local population regarded the Algerians initially as suspicious foreigners, in particular after the 1860 massacres. Sooner or later local political and religious leaders came to realize, however, that 'Abd al-Qadir's actions on behalf of the Christians had helped to preserve a positive image of Islam worldwide, and they propagated respect for the Algerians among their clients. In the course of the late nineteenth and early twentieth centuries, the Algerians melted more and more into Ottoman society. By 1885, 433 Algerians were registered with the French consulate as protégés, by 1907 the number had shrunk to 79. On the eve of World War I, ca. 8500 Algerians lived in Syria, of whom ca. 3500 were distributed between Damascus, Beirut and Aleppo. The rest were village dwellers, and only ca. 600 more were living in the rest of the Ottoman Empire. Many were farmers, but there was also a considerable number who worked in all sorts of urban professions, including officers in the Ottoman army. 'Abd al-Qadir's family was split into some members who retained French protection under a government stipend, and others who had Ottomanized. The official head of the family by 1907, Amir Mehmed Pasha, was an Ottoman general who lived in Istanbul. His brother Amir 'Ali Pasha, the actual strong man of the family in Damascus, had made a fortune as an absentee landlord. Amir Khaled, son of the late Amir Hashim, another of 'Abd al-Qadir's sons, attended the French military academy of Saint-Cyr to become a *Sipahi* officer in World War I. He turned into a leading figure of the anti-colonial movement in interwar Algeria. Like him, all Algerians in Syria retained a strong group identity in Damascus based on the memory of 'Abd al-Qadir, and their shared living space in the Suwayqa neighborhood.[50] The prominence of the immediate descendants of 'Abd al-Qadir continued into the interwar period and beyond, when they played a distinctive role in local urban politics. When the Ottoman administrators withdrew from Damascus at the end of World War I in the face of advancing Arab and British troops in 1918, they entrusted 'Abd al-Qadir's grandson Sa'id al-Jaza'iri with the government over the city. He played a lead role again as a Damascene leader during the 1925 Syrian Revolt.[51]

* * *

In the spring of 1966, Houari Boumedienne, chairman of the Algerian Revolutionary Council and head of state, sent a letter to Syrian President Nur al-Din al-Atasi asking for a return of the remains of 'Abd al-Qadir, so that he could be interred, according to Boumedienne, alongside the graves of martyrs of the Algerian revolution, as a witness for future generations.[52] Only a little earlier, on February 23, 1966, Ba'thist officers of the Syrian army had staged a coup removing a government dominated by rival party members. They successfully challenged the old guard of pan-Arab party leaders on behalf of a younger generation of civilian radical socialist Ba'thists who were disillusioned with the prospects of creating a pan-Arab state. Politically, the alienation between the generations rested on divergent opinions about Arab unity. In 1961, so-called Syrian separatists ended the experiment of the United Arab Republic of Egypt and Syria

(UAR), which Nasser had ruled since 1958 with a heavy hand. The separatist regime had its foundations in the Syrian bourgeoisie and among anti-Nasserites, and was again removed in a coup in 1963, which brought Nasserites and Ba'thist Unionists to the forefront of the Syrian government, including the ageing founders of the Ba'th party Salah al-Din al-Bitar as Prime Minister and Michel 'Aflaq as the general secretary of the party's National Command. Initially, they managed to start a new round of fruitless union talks with Nasser, but were unable to prevent the rise of so-called *qutriyyun* ("Regionalists") and members of the Military Committee into influential positions in the Ba'th party. *Qutriyyun*, such as Nur al-Din al-Atasi, promoted the primacy of the well-being of the existing states (such as Syria or Iraq) over the pursuit of a national union of all Arabs in one state. The same kind of pragmatism permeated the ranks of Syrian military officers who had been in forced exile in Cairo during the time of the UAR. Many of them belonged to the *'Alawite* sect, such as Salah Jadid and Hafiz al-Assad. The February 23 coup of 1966 thus affirmed a development that had already dominated the national congresses of the Ba'th party, namely a movement towards the preference of socialism over unionism, and the growing strength of officers in the party leadership. As a consequence, the 1966 coup led to the ouster of Bitar and 'Aflaq from positions of political influence. Both went into exile soon thereafter, whereas al-Atasi became the new president of the state, Hafiz al-Assad Minister of Defense, and Salah Jadid deputy leader of the regional leadership of the Ba'th and the actual strong man behind the scene.[53]

In spite of their political dominance, the new party leadership, and the officers in particular, had an image problem. They had to fend off allegations that they were heretics, extreme socialists and atheists, or promoters of sectarianism, and opposed to unionism. The popular hostility was based in part on class differences between the traditional Sunni bourgeois leadership of the cities and the new elites, many of whom were of rural origin, not to mention the prejudice against Alawites who had lived as outcasts in Sunni majority territory for centuries. A first taste of future confrontations with radical Islamists had occurred in 1964 already when Muslim dignitaries incited street protests against Ba'thist secularism, culminating in a bloody standoff between Ba'thist security forces and young radicals who occupied the Sultan Mosque in Hama for nearly a month. In 1965, less than a year later, a violent army crackdown preempted similar events in Damascus' Umayyad Mosque.[54]

Boumedienne, the Algerian, was in a comparable situation. In June 1965 he headed a military junta that overthrew his increasingly autocratic predecessor Ahmed Ben Bella, Algeria's first president after independence in 1962. Boumedienne took over as head of government and chairman of the newly formed Council of the Revolution, still having to establish his credentials as a nationalist leader against the populist image of Ben Bella who was one of the most symbolic figures of the Algerian revolution and war of independence from 1954 to 1962. Likewise, the new powerful men in Syria had to counter an image of being separatists who had done away with Arab nationalist icons like 'Aflaq and Bitar and their partisans, such as the popular president Amin al-Hafiz.[55]

When al-Atasi then answered positively in the spring of 1966 to Boumedienne's request for 'Abd al-Qadir's remains, both men had certainly in mind that they could use the transfer of the body of the iconic leader to stage a festival that would celebrate their, or their own clique's, legitimacy as representatives of a great nation – once more in the spirit of a republican funeral to be celebrated once in Damascus and then again in Algiers. In effect, the Syrian Ba'thists and the FLN (Algerian Liberation Front) were rather unequal partners because the former had just risen to power from years of petty infighting between various factions of Ba'thists and other political groupings in Syria, whereas the FLN was preparing for the fourth anniversary of Algerian independence. Worldwide, the success of the FLN in getting rid of France was seen as an unprecedented achievement of the decolonization movement, in spite of the incredible sacrifices and the blood-shed of the Algerian War on both sides. The repatriation and re-burial of 'Abd al-Qadir's remains were supposed to crown the anniversary celebrations on July 5, 1966. Other than the new Ba'thist leadership, the Algerians had nothing to fear in terms of their strong pan-Arab credentials. They had gained them during the war, not least through the support of Nasser's Egypt. Consequently, they could use 'Abd al-Qadir flexibly as a proponent of a particular Algerian and a broader Arab nationalism. Nor did they have to shy away from the religious symbolism and the feelings that the transfer of a Sufi sheikh and saintly figure such as that of the Sunni 'Abd al-Qadir could evoke. Since the 1930s, the religious reformists of the *Association of Algerian Muslims Scholars* (*Association des oulémas musulmans algériens, AUMA*) under the leadership of Abdelhamid Ben Badis (1889–1940) had been formulating an ideological–spiritual framework for Algerian Muslim resistance against French rule, but even more importantly against French cultural dominance in the country, under the slogan: "Islam is my religion, Algeria my country, and Arabic my language." Arguably, the combination between a Salafist form of piety and a strong cultural affiliation with the Arab world weighed heav-ier in a process of Algerian identity formation than the socialism of the political leadership of the independence movement that Messali Hadj (1898–1974) and his *Parti du peuple algérien* (*PPA*) stood for before the FLN outflanked them at the beginning of the Algerian war. The religious connotations that a re-burial of 'Abd al-Qadir might evoke therefore entailed no risk for the FLN leadership, as his Sufi heritage had long been re-contextualized: "The official, national Islam of the new Algeria had not eliminated the sainthood but had re-enabled it in new forms, producing new kinds of venerated ancestors."[56]

The Syrian Ba'thists were in a more difficult situation. They were isolated after a split with Nasser had occurred in 1963 already when the Ba'thist National Guard militia violently suppressed a Nasserite coup attempt in Syria. The Egyptian President attacked the Syrian leadership as irreligious heretics in his international radio propaganda – a dangerous allegation for a party that was led by 'Alawis, Christians and Isma'ilis in top positions.[57] In addition, Syria was surrounded by hostile Arab neighbors: Iraq under the rule of 'Abd al-Rahman 'Arif was in Nasser's camp, whereas the Arab monarchies of Jordan and Saudi Arabia were the central foe of Ba'thist doctrine. The Syrian newspapers of the weeks leading up to the ceremonies of the transfer of 'Abd al-Qadir's body were full of attacks against these "reactionary regimes" and their mingling with the imperialists, mostly the United States. The farewell celebrations for 'Abd al-Qadir in Damascus were therefore framed as an encounter between the Ba'th and the Algerian Liberation Front strengthening the position of the "progressive forces" in the Arab world, and as a historical landmark in their march to Arab unity. In mere lip service, the Syrian party organ *al-Ba'th* included Nasser's Egypt on this *Axis of Progressivism*, but in fact, the Syrians tried to distinguish themselves as the true seekers of Arab unity. An alignment with the heroes of the Algerian Revolution made it easier to present Syrian antagonism towards the monarchies in a light of progressivism versus reaction instead of the regionalism and separatism they were accused of. It also helped to play down dependence on Nasser. To use a Great Man and leader such as 'Abd al-Qadir was a welcome opportunity to link the Ba'thist leadership to the image of a widely venerated hero. There was therefore a curious resemblance in the motives for the usage of a dead man's body to seek legitimacy between 1966 and similar efforts the bourgeois nationalists had undertaken in 1937 around the funeral of Yasin al-Hashimi.[58]

* * *

As seen above, the events unfolding in the context of Yasin al-Hashimi's funeral in 1937 reveal a great deal about dissidence, diversion, and resistance against elite attempts to build hegemony over national narratives and urban space. For the 1966 events around 'Abd al-Qadir's farewell in Damascus, traces of resistance are much harder to discern due to a scarcity of primary material as it is common for times of military dictatorship.[59]

Yet, there are echoes of dissidence or at least of the potential for dissent with the hegemonic narrative on the pages of the party newspaper *al-Ba'th*, where the party leadership tried to forestall criticism. In his public reply to Boumedienne, al-Atasi had hastened to announce that the tomb of 'Abd al-Qadir, even as a *cenotaph*, would be retained in Damascus, as a reminder to future generations. Against the grain, this statement could be read as an assurance that the location in the vicinity of Muhyi al-Din would remain unaltered against concerns that the removal of 'Abd al-Qadir's remains was an unacceptable ingression into the Damascene landscape of public piety.[60]

Hasty preparations started in Damascus as soon as it became known that an Algerian delegation would arrive by the end of June to receive the remains of 'Abd al-Qadir. It was announced that sports teams – including the Algerian national soccer team – and artists would land on June 27, followed a couple of days later by a delegation of FLN leaders and military men headed by Abdelaziz Bouteflika, Algeria's Foreign Minister.[61] The Syrian leadership formed a committee to prepare an appropriate nationalist celebration for the occasion. Next to representatives of various ministries, the committee also contained an odd member, Lady Amal al-Jaza'iri, as a representative of the family. The Ba'thists apparently found it necessary to avoid the impression of simply sidestepping one of the most prestigious families of old Damascus. The same article that announced the formation of the committee also mentioned that the oldest living descendent of 'Abd al-Qadir, the Amir Sa'id al-Jaza'iri, had announced the republication of a commentary on the Qur'an that his grandfather had written. The book would come out to mark the occasion.[62] The author of the article did not care to relate this book announcement to the rest of the article, so that it stood out awkwardly as a reference to 'Abd al-Qadir's religious and intellectual achievements in the midst of a plethora of articles in the official newspaper that celebrated him as a military leader, an arch revolutionary, a "pioneer" of Arabism whom the "people of Algeria had elected" to be their leader.[63]

The artists of the Algerian delegation gave their first show in the theater of the Damascus exhibition grounds on June 30, staging a play titled "132 years," in reference to the duration of the French presence in Algeria. The director of the artists' delegation greeted the audience as "brothers and offspring of the Banu Umayya ...," repaying his hosts in terms of praise for historical heroism.[64] On the same day, the Algerian national soccer team and the Syrian army team played a match at the Damascus stadium. As was appropriate for the occasion, the teams tied. The article in *al-Ba'th* reported that crowds watched the game on site and even more in front of the television screens.[65] While it is hard to discern how seriously Syrians took *al-Ba'th*'s propaganda, or how many actually read the paper, it is most probable that they took an international soccer game quite seriously, thus unwittingly participating in the 'Abd al-Qadir festivities.

Certainly the people took seriously, too, that the Prophet's birthday (*maulid al-nabi*) fell on July 1 in 1966 (12 Rabi' al-Auwal 1386 A.H.), the day after the match and the theater play. Even the Ba'thists could not ignore this coincidence, as this was the first *maulid* with the new government in power. Hence there was a discernible risk that the nationalist celebration of the transfer of 'Abd al-Qadir, coinciding with a traditional religious holiday, might be interpreted as nothing but the abduction of a local saint. Consequently, the leadership could not allow the *maulid* to be overshadowed by the celebrations of Algerian–Syrian brotherhood. It is therefore a matter of some speculation if the arrival of the Algerian political delegation was postponed without further explanation to July 1, in order to give the Ba'thist leadership enough room to prove itself as worthy representatives of public piety.[66] This way, President Atasi could attend a major celebration to honor the Prophet's birthday in the Umayyad Mosque at noon of June 30, the day before the *maulid*. Had the Algerian delegation arrived as originally planned in the afternoon of the same day, it might have interfered with the President's schedule.

The reports about the *maulid* celebrations stand apart from the general master narrative of the paper during these days, which focused centrally on anticipation of the 'Abd al-Qadir event. The party tried to seize the moment. There was a sizable military presence in the central celebration in the Umayyad Mosque, and party strongman Salah Jadid attended alongside representatives of state religion, such as the Minister of Religious Endowments and the General Mufti of the state. The Minister was clearly a man of the Ba'th and confirmed in a speech after prayer and Qur'an recitation that the prophet was the "messenger of unity, strength and progress," and it was only natural to celebrate him in an age of revolution. He was a pioneer (ra'id) of Arab nationalism (*qawmiyya*). "We Arabs are your army and your people, oh messenger of God."[67] The prophet was thus integrated into a vision of military nationalist prowess and socialist progressivism. To some extent this was also an endorsement of religion as a matter of civilization and a means for moral guidance, but not without strong skepticism about the parts of it that were outside the control of a Ba'thist hegemonic discourse. An op-ed piece in *al-Ba'th* made this quite clear.

The author wrote that Muslims in all nations saw Muhammad, the Arab prophet, as a prophet and a messenger, and Islam as a religion, and the Qur'an as a light in their lives ... But the Arabs, and no other Muslims but them, were much more invested in this than anybody else, because the gracious Arab Prophet was for "us" not just a Prophet and messenger, but also a nationalist leader ("za'im qawmi") like no other in old or recent Arab history. Islam was not only a heavenly religion, but also the spirit of the Arab nation and its civilization, and its long experience ... The Qur'an was not only a heavenly book, but also a sanctuary of nationalism, which, among other things guarded the Arabic language ... The life of the prophet was not only a clarification (tarjuman) of Islam [for "us"], but it was the highest living and pure example of manliness, sacrifice, and independence, and for the scientific, positivist and populist ("sha'bi") thought. Muhammad was with the Arabs a nation ... in its realistic presentness ("waqi'iyya") and populist humanity ("insaniyya sha'biyya").[68]

It is worth quoting these statements at length because they provide an example for the legitimizing discourse of Ba'thist ideology, trying to appropriate tradition in the form of religion as an identity marker for most Syrians, but interpreting it in light of the nationalist doctrine, using familiar topoi of a leadership cult such as "manliness, sacrifice, and independence." Socialist jargon, such as references to science and positivism, completed the image of typical twentieth-century syncretism at work in this rhetoric. 'Abd al-Qadir fit well into this syncretic image of a modern Arab identity. It allowed for religious references, but rejected the relative autonomy that traditional Islamic authorities had maintained over the centuries: For the Ba'th this syncretism defined their stance towards Islam. However, imperialism and its allies among the reactionaries, capitalists and feudalists said something different, continued the author of the op-ed piece:

> [As] If a geography teacher stood up and told his students that the earth is spherical, and revolves around itself and around the sun, and some greenhorn, misled by an imposter of Islam, challenged him that this was apostasy... Science ('ilm) has become apostasy for the reactionaries, and superstition is for them belief and religion. Imperialism knew that it had an enemy in the scientific mind among the Arabs, ... superstition and belief in it are the enemy of the mind, and therefore imperialism tried to preserve it

and to destroy the roots of the mind, and science, and healthy knowledge. The reactionaries are agents of imperialism, knowingly or unknowingly, and want to make superstition our religion, and our progress a superstitious progress. …They want to lead us back to the age of decline.

The Arabs would teach them a better lesson, the article concluded.[69]

There is a rich argumentation in this excerpt. It takes on imperialism as the protector of reactionary religious leaders, and launches what sounds like a reformist-Salafi attack on superstitious practices in Islam such as those of Sufi orders and traditional Islamic elites. Colonial governments, in particular the French, indeed instrumentalized Sufis as their agents in order to keep indigenous populations docile.[70] The term "reactionary" evokes the hostility between Ba'thists and the Arab monarchies, but in combination with "superstition" and "imperialism" the terminology points to a local context in which the party leaders were trying to streamline popular religion, penetrating the realm of the Sufi saint when they laid their hands on 'Abd al-Qadir. Even if there is a certain degree of speculation in this reading of the op-ed piece, there is certainly an echo of dissidence in the author's tirade against traditional religious authorities, who had retained a prominent position in Damascene religious hierarchies and a great deal of mobilizing force in popular quarters throughout the Mandate period, at times in alliance with the burgeoning Muslim Brothers. The tirade against superstitious practices was therefore also an attack on the Syrian '*ulama*' and the Muslim Brotherhood as major contenders for urban popular support, conflating Islamic activism with traditionalism and a perceived mystic irrationalism.[71]

The party newspaper established an explicit link between the Prophet's birthday and the festivities around 'Abd al-Qadir and the Algerians, too, as if the *maulid* celebrations were now re-fashioned as a run up to their arrival. In a further op-ed piece, *al-Ba'th* presented the Prophet as the "greatest of all revolutionaries," using terminology that had characterized the Ba'thists and their Algerian comrades in previous issues. The author of the piece wrote that Damascus received the Algerian revolutionaries in the spirit of commemoration of Muhammad, who was "entirely free from exploitation, injustice, and distinctions of class, tribe, and race …" The revolutionaries met in revolutionary Damascus to march hand in hand towards development in order to return the means of production to their rightful owners, drawing many lessons from the *sira* (biography) of the first Arab revolutionary.[72] The hybridity of this comment is drawn from similar sources as the syncretism of the previous example.

To what extent did this language matter? It represented one of several ways that the regime used to communicate with the people, to explain its actions in the realm of religious customs and traditions where the Ba'thists walked on thin ice, but which they could not ignore if they wanted to maintain some legitimacy in the eyes of the population, especially in the face of allegations that they were a-religious or, worse, heretics. To achieve this purpose, the propaganda apparatus of the party bombarded the people with messages, and those who did not digest the convoluted interpretations of op-ed articles could hardly avoid the public spectacle: How bad could the new government really be if its leaders observed the *maulid*? If they organized international soccer matches? And if they honored Great Men from the Arab past?

The events that were part of the 'Abd al-Qadir celebrations dominated the public space of Damascus during the days of late June and early July in 1966. On the day of the *maulid* itself, the Futuwwa paramilitary youth organization of the party put on a great show in the municipal stadium together with the National Guard party militia, with marching exercises, speeches, weapons and close combat exercises. Girl scouts paraded a large image of 'Abd al-Qadir through the stadium.[73] The Algerian delegation visited the Golan Heights front line with Israel, and Bouteflika laid down a wreath at Quneitra's Martyr's Cemetery. Muhammad Istanbuli, a member of the Algerian arts and sports delegation, recited a poem for the soldiers at the frontline, denouncing all betrayers of Arab unity as hypocrites, and declaring that Algeria was madly in love with Damascus. An actress of the Algerian theater troop gave her jewelry to one of the border officers, apparently in a spontaneous act of support and admiration.[74]

The handover of 'Abd al-Qadir's remains took place in the late afternoon of July 3, in time to send the Algerian delegation home for the anniversary celebrations of Algerian independence on July 5. *Al-Ba'th* printed a call to the working people to come out to Muhyi al-Din Square in large numbers where the mosque complex with the *turba* was located, and where the cortège with the coffin was supposed to start.[75] Thus, a relatively small square in a popular quarter, far from the commercial and administrative center of the Syrian capital, took part for a moment in an event that was of concern for the entire Arab nation, as its organizers wanted to make everyone believe. It raised the interest of the international Third World community, too, as proven by a photo essay that appeared in the Paris-based journal *Jeune Afrique*. One picture presents the inside of Muhyi al-Din Ibn al-'Arabi's *turba* with a group of men, who, according to the caption, recite the "Fatiha" in front of a coffin, probably made of wood, which contained the remains of 'Abd al-Qadir ready for travel. The caption also indicates that the descendants of the Amir were among them (Figure 5.1).[76]

One of the men, with a Fez or Tarbush on his head, is identifiable as the elderly Amir Sa'id al-Jaza'iri. Next to him, adorned with the characteristic turban and beard of an imam, as well as a suit, tie and sunglasses, stands Abu'l-Faraj al-Khatib, the director of the Umayyad Mosque who delivered the Friday sermons there. He was not a man of the regime, but belonged to an established reformist '*ulama*' family of the city.[77] The glaring absence of military uniforms on the picture is remarkable because *al-Ba'th* reported that otherwise, soldiers played the lead role on Muhyi al-Din Square. Even though some details about the course of the ceremony are missing, one might assume that the family members carried the coffin out of the *turba* and then handed it over to soldiers who lifted it on a gun carriage and saluted the dead body. By then, the coffin was wrapped in a "Syrian revolutionary flag" that was not on the coffin when the family members said their prayers in the *turba*. The coffin was then paraded in a cortège through

Figure 5.1 Praying over 'Abd al-Qadir's coffin inside Ibn al-'Arabi's *turba* in Damascus.

the streets down towards Port Sa'id Square (formerly Victoria Bridge) in the central part of town, accompanied by soldiers and military police, wreath carriers, and the Algerian and Syrian officials alongside the family members and religious functionaries, followed by workers and peasants with many people standing along the way and watching. On Port Said Square, the coffin was lifted onto a podium from where it was to be handed over officially to Abdelaziz Bouteflika.[78]

The different stages of the coffin's procession out of Muhyi al-Din's *turba* and through the streets of Damascus contained a wealth of symbols in that it passed through several layers of transition. Why, after all, would it not have been possible to simply hold the entire handing-over ceremony on Muhyi al-Din Square? The obvious answer is that a modern central town square offered a better stage for the ceremony than the narrow and crowded alleys of a popular quarter. But the difference between the organically integrated presence of the Saint in the middle of Muhyi al-Din's quarter and the representative openness and stately atmosphere of Port Said Square is symbolic in itself. According to the choreography of the event, it was the family who had the authority to uproot and extract the body from its customary place, and pass it into the hands of the military, which then had to extract it from the intestines of the popular environment – and reactionary superstition – to pass him on to the clarity of the stately space. Symbolically, this extraction stripped 'Abd al-Qadir of his saintly nature, and once prepared in such a way, he could be passed on to the revolutionary and nationalist brothers. This happened after both al-Atasi and Bouteflika gave speeches and performed a flag ceremony spreading an Algerian flag in a second layer over the Syrian flag that already covered the coffin. After that, the coffin was taken by car to the airport, handed over to Algerian officers who brought it on board the airplane for departure the following morning.[79]

There is a small but significant phrase in the report about the handover of 'Abd al-Qadir's remains, mentioned casually as if unimportant: "When ['Abd al-Qadir] left Muhyi al-Din square, slaughter animals were slaughtered, and military units of the Syrian army took the lead in cheering his remains."[80] The question arises why the Ba'th performed a traditional ritual sacrifice, certainly followed by a public feeding of the poor of the quarter. As a practice, the slaughtering was reminiscent of customs of popular religion, such as during major holidays like the *'id al-adha* and during festivals of saints. To slaughter an animal and provide food to the poor is usually a charitable deed, which brings merit to a pious and wealthy Muslim. The Ba'th therefore may have wanted to please the crowds in this situation, to pay respect to the people of the quarter, maybe even to preempt protest. The fact that soldiers took the lead hailing the saint may have had the comparable purpose to preempt the singing of popular songs or chanting to mourn the departure of a deceased. However, the single sentence on which these speculations are based is, once more, only a faint echo of dissidence or the potential for it.

Al-Ba'th's report awarded a lot more attention to the speeches that al-Atasi and Bouteflika held in front of the crowds on Port Said Square. There is only one element that is worthy of note in Atasi's otherwise quite uninspiring speech. He started with an appeal to all "Arab brothers": "… when our Arab forefathers (ajdad) left their Arab Peninsula, they were messengers of a revolution, and carriers of a message, in fact carrying the banner of freedom …" The term that he used for messengers was "rusul" which he invoked again at the very end of his speech: "Innana rusul al-thawra", "Indeed, we are the Messengers of the Revolution."[81] A quote from his speech was printed in large letters on the front page of the same newspaper, underlining the fact that this terminology was important for al-Atasi and those that disseminated it in the paper: "Nahnu rusul thawra … hadafuna tahqiq al-wahda al-'Arabiyya," "We are messengers of a revolution … our goal is to realize Arab unity." "Rusul" is the plural of "rasul," which stands for *messenger* or *prophet* and is usually, but not exclusively used as an epithet for the prophet Muhammad. Al-Atasi's usage was not coincidental a couple of days after the *maulid*. Earlier on, *al-Ba'th* had evoked the Prophet as "Muhammad al-tha'ir," "Muhammad the revolutionary," hence the evocation of "rusul al-thawra," "messengers of the revolution," was certainly not an unintended parallel. On the contrary, the appropriation of religious heritage for secular goals was part of the message that was supposed to stick in the minds of the listeners, observers and readers.

Abdelaziz Bouteflika's speech on the podium, next to 'Abd al-Qadir's coffin draped in flags,[82] was richer in content. In one place he used almost exactly the same words as Jamil Mardam had at Yasin's bier, 30 years earlier, when he praised that Syria's "pure earth was rich with [the remains of] the most gracious of the sons of the Arab nation [...] penetrating deeply into history, towards Salah al-Din al-Ayyubi, and towards 'Abd al-Qadir." 'Abd al-Qadir's choice of Syria as an abode had therefore not been incidental when the Arab world had still been united. Even if Bouteflika did not mention that 'Abd al-Qadir had come to Damascus for religious reasons, his speech was nevertheless replete with deliberations about the role of religion in national liberation. His rhetoric was quite spontaneous in this regard, mixing formulaic speech about Arab unity with hints and references to religion that he did not fully elaborate on. After all, Bouteflika was only 29 years old at the time. One passage of the speech constitutes a characteristic attempt to reconcile Islam with nationalism and socialism. Bouteflika, however, did not try to reduce Islam to its historical and civilizational contribution to Arabism, as the Syrian op-ed pieces tried to do. Instead he acknowledged the role Islam had played and continued to play in the mobilization of the people to act on behalf of their desire to promote social improvement: "We confirm that religion was in your times, 'Abd al-Qadir, the most important incentive in the struggle against imperialism." He continued that Algeria proclaimed that religion was not at all incompatible with the expectations of the masses that were deprived of well-being and social justice. If religion was merely a tool for regression, why would the poor and deprived adhere to it, asked Bouteflika, postulating that the collective will of the masses was necessarily rational. If Islam did inhibit thinking, he said, the years of decline, that is, the years after the Golden Age of Islam in the middle ages, were the natural state of things, there would not have been an Islamic civilization at all. The climax of this passage was Bouteflika's assertion that

> [i]f religion was a mere tool to silence true talent, it would be limited to a few dervishes who utter empty formulas in exchange for money, and who would be in the way of the people. This is why Algeria uses scientific method on the way to socialism.

This last remark left room for the principles of the Salafi scholars that had played such an important role in the grounding of the new Algerian state in reformist Islam.[83]

There were, hence, two different visions of the relative roles of religion in building a nationalist identity that became manifest in the context of the festivities around the transfer of 'Abd al-Qadir's remains from Damascus to Algeria in July 1966. In contrast to the Algerians, the Syrian Ba'thists were uncomfortable with the saintly aura of 'Abd al-Qadir and made efforts to depict the Algerian leader in a staunchly secular nationalist light. His ambiguous position in the traditional fabric of the city and its lineages of religious and political authority shines through in another newspaper report that is an ill fit among the affirmatively secular nationalist articles of *al-Ba'th*. On June 28, a few days before the handover of 'Abd al-Qadir's body, the tomb in Muhyi al-Din's mausoleum had already been opened in preparation for the transfer. A short article in *al-Ba'th* related that a sidepiece of the grave of the "Arab hero and revolutionary" had been removed in the presence of official representatives and Amir Sa'id al-Jaza'iri. Amir Sa'id reported of the event that they had found the head of 'Abd al-Qadir covered in flesh on more than one side, that his white hair had been visible, and that the skeleton of his honorable body had been complete in spite of 86 years having passed since his death. There is a certain echo of the hagiographic topos of a saint's body's immunity against decay in these lines, underlining 'Abd al-Qadir's aura as a man of God. The author of the article confirmed this image recounting a family tradition that Amir Sa'id passed on to him. Amir Muhyi al-Din al-Jaza'iri, a nephew of 'Abd al-Qadir and father to 'Izz al-Din al-Jaza'iri, who in turn was a martyr of the Great Syrian Revolt of 1926, had told him that during the Ottoman period, in 1892, which was 12 years after 'Abd al-Qadir's death, the authorities had wanted to bury a Wali in a tomb next to the latter's tomb. 'Ali, one of 'Abd al-Qadir's ten sons (and therefore a cousin to Muhyi al-Din al-Jaza'iri) had witnessed and related that during construction, a side of 'Abd al-Qadir's tomb had collapsed, exposing the shrouded body, which had been intact "as if alive."[84] The story confirms several kinds of authority that held sway in traditional Damascene life: the authority of the saint through his miraculous physical presence, the authority of the notable family that protects and passes on knowledge, like in the *isnad* of a *hadith*, and finally the blessing that emanates from the pious ancestor and continues to sit within the family. This blessing, in turn, legitimates the position of the family in the urban social fabric. All these were elements of a social hierarchy that Ba'thists had committed to bring down by ideological conviction – not least because it contradicted the acquired authority of the army officers with minority status.

A year later already, the Ba'thists seemed more certain about their secular public image, as the toned-down *maulid* celebrations of 1967 suggest. In a remarkable contrast to the 1966 festivities, no regime figures except the Minister of Religious Endowments attended the central ceremony in the Umayyad Mosque. Shaykh Muhammad Rashid al-Khatib, a further leading preacher of the Umayyad Mosque, spoke in the presence of the State Mufti. The context for this *maulid* was certainly peculiar as it followed two weeks after Syria's devastating defeat in the Six-Day-War, which dealt a serious blow to the legitimacy of the military government. The absence of the state leadership, passing on the opportunity to present engagement in trying times seems conspicuous, but it should be seen in the context of a turn to more assertive attempts by the Ba'th to control religious institutions and marginalize them in the public sphere.[85]

The Algerian vision of the role of religion was, in contrast, more flexible; it allowed for some ambivalence between secular socialist and nationalist principles on the one hand and the human desire to maintain a role for the spiritual and transcendental in the promotion of collective redemption towards a better, social and nationalist future on the other. However, this was only true within the confines of an officially sanctioned rational reformed Islam that the state could oversee. Bouteflika's speech attacked the corrupting effect of what he described as the dervishes' mumblings instead of referring to 'Abd al-Qadir's mystic past. Accordingly, the remains of the great leader were brought back to Algeria, but not quite to his home soil, which would have been in Mascara, but to Algiers, where he was interred in the martyrs' cemetery as a saint of national liberation – having come a long way from Muhyi al-Din's side.[86] It might have brought some solace to 'Abd al-Qadir that at least his grandson Sa'id accompanied him on this final journey to shake hands with Houari Boumedienne after he had received the delegation and helped carry the coffin out of the plane.[87]

* * *

In summary, the two nationalist funerals of this chapter illustrate how the semiotics of elite nationalism rub against populist and popular dynamics of street politics, and how they intersect with religion in the public sphere. In the communication between Arab elites and their populaces, there was no clear separation between Islam and nationalism, and between the realms of the religious and the secular, because elites used an understandable and inherited frame of reference in the politics of representation to be able to reach the people. In 1937, they did so out of their own convictions; in 1966, under the Ba'th, they did so to legitimate their own move from the margins of society to the very center, though uncomfortably. Ultimately, the goal of urban public festivals such as state funerals was to cover ground in the city – to lay claims to the various layers of its heritage. The final purpose for the nationalists was to develop a hegemonic and increasingly static discourse. The more the twentieth century progressed, the narrower the room for dissidence to challenge the hegemonic discourse and give expression to social grievances became. The public violence of the 1937 protests against the government thus stood in stark contrast to the faint echoes of dissidence in 1966 when the Ba'thists went to great lengths to mute and preempt it. Their arguing with tradition, however, hardly anticipated the descent of nationalist discourse into vulgarity that followed the consolidation of personalized dictatorships in the 1970s.

6 Nearly victorious

The art of staging Arab military prowess

The military as an object of societal veneration, and militarism as a form of nationalist representation are subjects of this chapter. It investigates the staging of militarism in memorials, museums and commemorative ceremonies. The chapter returns to these forms of nationalist representation to argue that the rise of the importance of the military in Middle Eastern societies, and the accompanying rise of militarism, added to the increasing vulgarity of Arab nationalist discourses in the last quarter of the twentieth century.

Army officers occupy a paramount role in the history of Middle Eastern politics and society in the late nineteenth and twentieth centuries – from the Urabi Revolt in Egypt in 1881 and 1882, the military involvement in the Committee of Union and Progress (CUP) and the crucial role of Ottoman officers in overthrowing the Ottoman Sultan Abdulhamid II in the Young Turk Revolution of 1908 and 1909, to the pioneering nationalist associations of Arab officers during the years of CUP rule and World War I and their entry into politics in the interwar period, starting in interwar Iraq. When military rule became the standard in Arab lands from Algeria to Iraq in the second half of the twentieth century, officers built on a long established military ethos, which nationalist politicians and intellectuals had promoted since the 1920s. The imagery of a militarized society was a mainstay among right-wing ideologues and their propagators in schoolbooks and the media where they presented ideas about the necessity to strengthen the state and society against the imperialist onslaught. Even old elites and the nationalist bourgeoisie shared in this "au-courant" imagery to boost nationalist credentials. A new generation of military men grew up and imbibed this spirit of soldierly elitism in the military institutions that the newly founded Arab states established. Junior officers took their civilian elders by surprise when they dared to take over power themselves, in a first attempt in Iraq in 1936, and then for good in the late 1940s in Syria, in Egypt and Iraq in the 1950s, and in Algeria and Libya in the 1960s, with the Sudan to follow in the late 1980s.[1]

The prominence of high-ranking soldiers in Arab governments was, however, indirectly proportional to their success on the battlefield, as the military outcomes of Arab wars in the second half of the twentieth century prove, ending in crushing defeats or uneasy stalemates. The perceived need of military leaders to focus on the preservation of domestic power and the control over the means of coercion, and an obsession with controlling and continuously militarizing socio-political discourses go a long way to explain practical underachievement. Military representations in the army's self-staging and self-fashioning efforts therefore do not merely belong to the accidentals of military politics in Arab states, but to their core.[2]

* * *

Since its inception, the Cairo War Museum has been celebrating the achievements of Egyptian soldiery in the wave of nationalist museum foundations in the 1930s. The predecessor of the current war museum opened to the public in 1937 in two ground level rooms of the War and Navy Ministry. In late 1938 it moved to a temporary building in Garden City near the Qasr al-Nil bridge. After the British army vacated the Cairo Citadel in 1947, the government refurbished the female and family quarters of Mehmet Ali's palace complex (the *haramlik*, est. 1827) as a permanent location for the museum. It opened officially in November 1949.[3]

Fu'ad I, the father of Egyptian nationalist museology, had already started a small military collection inside 'Abdin Palace after World War I, but in contrast to the King's projects, the War Museum was not a palace initiative, but driven by Egyptian military officers, following the growth of their self-esteem as protectors of national pride and self-assertion. Chief promoter of the museum was an officer in the War Ministry who went on to become the pioneer Egyptian military historian 'Abd al-Rahman Zaki (1904–1980). Zaki presented a first draft for the creation of a military museum in a memorandum to the War Ministry in 1929. In spite of a positive response from the Office of Military Works, the project did not go further, allegedly due to British resistance to the idea.[4] What Zaki did receive, however, was financial support for a journey through European military museums to look for inspiration as it was common practice in the Egyptian museum business during the 1930s. In the summer of 1931, he visited museums in various European capitals, including a prime location: London's Imperial War Museum (IWM).[5]

At its creation during World War I, the IWM represented a new model of military museum. Earlier institutions such as the Tower of London or the Berlin *Zeughaus*, all of which Zaki knew, occupied an awkward position in museology. Their origins go back to the early modern period, but in spite of their museum-like exhibitory qualities they are not considered part of the scientific enlightenment project of the modern museum of the nineteenth century. Their original dual function was as storage places for surplus arms during peacetime, and for the presentation of war booty, celebrating the exploits of a monarch or a particular general. They stopped being warehouses when the nature of wars and weaponry changed at the beginning of the modern period, but kept their function of presenting military prowess and to glorify deeds on the battlefield. In the nineteenth century, the fact started to dawn on people that war was no longer a dynastic endeavor but an affair that concerned and affected the entire nation, but it took the catastrophe of World War I for this perception to sink in. The IWM stands for this transition. At first, it grew out of the desire to celebrate the deeds of the British army during World War I by exhibiting examples of the growing amount of captured military equipment. The "democratizing effect" of the indiscriminate death of hundreds of thousands of soldiers regardless of rank and social origin then made it impossible for a country in shock and mourning to accept a war museum as a celebratory institution. After 1918, the display of war trophies was integrated into a narrative that presented the war as a civilizational breaking point, after which no further such carnage was thinkable – an inherent contradiction that has never been resolved. Quite fittingly, the IWM moved in 1936 from temporary locations to the former Bethlem lunatic asylum (better known as Bedlam) where many shell shock victims of World War I had been treated. In contrast, the Cairo War Museum moved into the most civilian of all places, Mehmet Ali's former family quarters.[6]

A war museum existed in Ottoman Istanbul, too, where the Imperial Armory in the former Hagia Irene church became a private museum of arms and antiquities for the Sultan in the mid-nineteenth century. The museum went through several stages of reorganization until it opened for the public in 1910 under the auspices of Young Turk officers, who transformed the Istanbul museum from a mere location for the glorification of the military exploits of the Sultan to a place where they could propagate a particular militarized image of the state. As a "museum with a narrative," it even predated the IWM, and the curators introduced battle paintings, dioramas and nostalgic performances of Janissary bands to popularize the efforts of the Ottoman military in the later years of World War I. The "democratization of war" found expression in exhibits celebrating rank and file military heroes.[7]

Likewise, 'Abd al-Rahman Zaki had a vision of an Egyptian military museum that transcended a mere exhibit of the glory of the ruling dynasty and its army: it should fulfill a civic function, namely to refine the military spirit among civilians and strengthen their bond with the military people. His sketches are full of references to European models, but without even the slightest recognition of the Ottoman precursor. In 1936, he presented a memorandum to the King suggesting that the monarch should emulate the museums that he, Zaki, had visited in Europe. Foreshadowing the debates about the Museum of Egyptian Civilization, he envisaged a museum that contained objects gathered from the classical museums and embedded in the broad context of the longevity of Egyptian military prowess – from King Tut's chariot to the bombs of modern aerial warfare.[8]

The marriage between the desire for recognition of current military strength and the reliance on a historicist perception of modern Egyptian identity was quite en vogue, as previous chapters have shown. A writer for *al-Risala* magazine undertook an "[e]xcursion ("jawla") between artifacts of the past and of the present" in the museum shortly before its opening and published his findings in an article titled: "Journalistic Investigation: 50 centuries in the War Museum." For *al-Risala*'s reporter, who claimed that he frequently mingled with officers in their clubs, the museum would certainly raise the nationalist spirit among the youth when it confronted them with the grand memories of the deeds of Thutmosis and Ramses, Salah al-Din, and Ibrahim Pasha because "commemoration quenches the thirst of the believers!"[9]

Over the decades, the museum has been evidence for the continuity of the historicist vision of Egyptian identity. The cover page of a 1958, post-Revolution edition of the museum guide placed a sketch of a Pharaonic archer in characteristic profile pose in front of a schematic silhouette of an Islamic city with a domed Mosque with two minarets in the far distance, probably depicting the Muhammad 'Ali Mosque on the citadel. The archer's gaze is directed towards a missile, shaped like a German V2 rocket, that is taking off in the middle-ground.[10] Like the museum exhibit, the guidebook thus layered various periods of Egyptian history, one on top of the other, with the purpose of forming a cohesive whole. The "founders' paradigm" and its focus on the military achievements of the Khedivial dynasty still made up a great part of the post-revolution exhibition. A section about the first Arab–Israeli war and a "Liberation Hall" celebrating the Free Officer Revolution was a mere attachment whereas modifications to the old narrative of Egypt's military legacy remained hidden between the covers of the guidebook. An interpretive essay largely avoided positive references to Mehmet Ali or his dynasty. It endorsed his military expansions but bemoaned that afterwards, Egypt had fallen into a "shameful period" bound by imperialism. Only the army had held onto its glory and had liberated Egypt in the Revolution.[11]

The *Vulgarity* of monuments

Today, the Cairo National War Museum is still an altar for the modern Egyptian army. Every arm of the service has its own dedicated room, from the navy to the paratroops to the signal troops. It is also a place full of contradictions. Its exhibition is a mix of life size dioramas of historical events and settings, models of military installations and weaponry, and plaques, graphs, and paintings explaining and highlighting Egyptian military achievements, alongside the obligatory mannequins dressed in the uniforms of the various ages. Since the 1993 re-opening of the museum that followed a thorough makeover, these materials have been interspersed with paintings by North Korean artists that were made according to the wishes and plans of the Egyptian authorities. When this author visited the museum on January 24, 2011, Husni Mubarak was still hallowed in a personal cult, when his seemingly unchallengeable sovereignty over the Egyptian state was still intact. Only a day later, on the 25th, large-scale demonstrations broke out when masses of people flooded onto Tahrir Square to demand the overthrow of the regime, which would eventually lead to the old man's downfall. On January 24, the centerpiece of the Mubarak cult was a monumental oil painting greeting the visitor from a wall in the museum's grand entrance hall, facing the access door. The painting, which had hung there since the

1993 re-opening, created a super- and subtext for the narrative structure of the place. The iconography of the Korean-made picture put Husni Mubarak at the center of a tale of historical continuity in Egyptian military prowess and present generous leadership (Figure 6.1).[12] The technical quality of the picture's execution is as stunning as the naïveté of the symbolism and the crudeness of the propagandistic composition are off-putting. It is a typical example of modern North Korean illusionary painting (more on which below). Mubarak, in black suit and tie with his jacket open, is taking a step forward towards the onlooker, whose perspective is that of crowds of people from all walks of life cheering Mubarak while he proceeds on his way, surrounded by officers and generals. The people who cheer Mubarak include an engineer in a suit with a blueprint sketch of a project rolled up in his hands, a group of *fellahin* (peasants) from the countryside in their traditional *gallabeyas*, middle-class Egyptian women, both veiled and unveiled, simple soldiers, a little girl in a neat dress with her nanny, and a towering bearded man of religion in a white robe and a white cap. A red carpet is visible half way in the background marking the official course of the delegation, but the President has veered off in order to mingle with the people. Further back, there are Egyptian flags and a banner that reads "Allahu Akbar, al-Nasr li'l[lah]" (last part cut off: God is Great, Victory is to God). Doves in various colors, many of them white, populate the foreground; combined with the yellow, pink and blue balloons that rise to the sky in the background, they give the picture a candy sweet tone of kitschy pacifism. It is an armed pacifism, though, because in the far background, above a rendering of the pyramid-shaped tomb of Anwar Sadat in Cairo, there are sketches, like a writing in the sky, of the decisive battles that Egypt fought in its long history: A battle in ancient Egypt

Figure 6.1 The tableau of the entrance hall to the Cairo War Museum in January 2011.

with an archer, probably Pharaoh, who speeds in his chariot in front of a scenery including the pylon and obelisks of an ancient temple, next to the Sphinx and Pyramids, followed on a chronological line from left to right by a storming front of medieval Muslim horsemen, galloping in front of the Cairo citadel with its ramparts that Salah al-Din had erected, culminating in a group of modern-day soldiers emerging from the trenches waving an Egyptian flag and celebrating victory. A caption under the painting explains the sequence (in disregard of geography) in golden letters in both English and Arabic: "The Egypt of Honor, the Egypt of Authenticity and of History, the Egypt of Qadesh, of Hittin, and of October 73."[13] Altogether, the painting conveys a rather simple message that military prowess had preserved Egypt throughout the history of its civilization, that this history was preserved by the modern army, but that the ultimate guarantor of Egypt's "authenticity" ("asala") was Mubarak, who stood in for the people, with the ultimate goal of peace. After all, Mubarak is the only one wearing civilian clothing among the army officers in the picture.

What might a revolution do to a museum's grand narrative? And how quickly do changes take effect? From a different vantage point: Would the absence of changes in the grand narrative reflect the absence of meaningful changes in a post-revolutionary socio-political system? The last statement is proven right by the course that the events in Egypt have taken since 2011.

The author paid a second visit to the War Museum in mid-April 2012, more than a year after the revolutionary events on Tahrir Square, with their ambivalent results becoming apparent. The autocrat and his personalized regime had gone, only to be replaced with the rule of a military oligarchy, as it already seemed at the time. It was not likely that the War Museum would adjust its entire Mubarak-centered narrative within a matter of a year, and so it did not come as a surprise that paintings of Mubarak as sitting president prevailed in a hall celebrating the 1952 Free Officer coup, and that Mubarak was still hailed as the commander of the air force in the 1973 Arab–Israeli war. The most crucial change had already taken place, though: The grand tableau greeting the visitor in the entrance hall had been touched up and revised. At first, in a temporary solution, a pole with an Egyptian flag was put in front of Mubarak's representation to alleviate the embarrassment of the course of history.[14] By April 2012, however, a permanent solution had been found and Mubarak, no longer at the center of the spider's web, had been painted over and replaced by a man in uniform, Field Marshal Muhammad 'Abd al-Ghanni al-Gamasy (1921–2003, see Figure 6.2), Chief of Military Operations in 1973 and thus one of the engineers of the Egyptian breach of the Israeli defense line along the eastern shore of the Suez Canal – a military coup de main that is known among Egyptians as al-'ubur ("the Crossing"). Gamasy was later a major negotiator in the preparation for the Camp David Accords, but withdrew from public service in the early eighties, apparently no longer in agreement with the state leadership.[15] His background as a son of the army, his independent mind, and his association with Egypt's greatest military achievement in modern history made him arguably a perfect choice to replace Mubarak, along with the fact that he was sure to have dropped dangerous ambitions – because he

Figure 6.2 The same tableau in April 2012.

was dead, after all. However, this change on the entrance tableau also gave the grand narrative of the museum an entirely new direction. Mubarak's civilianness had balanced the heavy weight of the military uniforms on the picture. Mubarak embodied the benevolent ruler who did not forget his institutional roots, but also functioned as a bridge between the populace and a military that people perceived as a formidable but aloof institution. It was a bold move to touch up the painting in a quasi Stalinist manner. All of a sudden, there was Gamasy blending into a phalanx of officers that people hailed as saviors, and no longer the single ruler and his entourage. The same picture, slightly changed, told a radically different story of who held the reins in the new–old Egyptian polity.

A monumental personality cult such as that displayed on the Mubarak tableau was quite atypical for the Egyptian regime, but rather reminiscent of the style of fellow Arab dictators like Hafiz al-Assad and Saddam Hussein. The personality cult is, however, a characteristic element of the monumental North Korean illusionary propaganda paintings that companies like the Mansudae Art Studio and the Paekho Trading Corporation manufacture and trade for export. During the 1980s and 1990s, North Korean artists were active in all of Iraq, Egypt, and Syria to produce monumental sites for the commemoration of military achievements. The signature art form of the Korean painters is the Panorama, an otherwise nearly extinct genre of mass entertainment that was very popular in the nineteenth and early twentieth centuries, but afterwards only survived as a totalitarian propagandistic vehicle in socialist states. Only recently has it undergone a small-scale revival in European cities.[16]

Egypt had long-standing relations with the North Korean People's Republic both as fellow socialist countries and in terms of military cooperation. There are reports that North Korean pilots flew for Egypt in the October War. Economic relations, especially in the arms trade, survived the end of the socialist era in Egypt. Mubarak visited North Korea several times throughout the eighties and in 1990.[17] On one such visit in the early eighties, Mubarak was shown a Panorama painting about the Korean War, probably *Operations for the Liberation of Taejon*, which was finished in Pyongyang in 1974. Apparently, he was so taken by the experience that he asked North Korean leader Kim Il Song to have one prepared for Cairo depicting the Egyptian assault on the eastern shore of the Suez Canal that opened the October War (*al-'ubur*). It is likely that Mubarak's request was motivated by a Panorama race, too, that was going on between Middle Eastern autocrats – to the benefit of the Paekho Trading Corporation. Mubarak probably tried to catch up with Saddam Hussein in Iraq, who had opened his panorama about the Battle of Qadisiyya (fought in 636 near Baghdad) in 1980. Hafiz al-Assad's October War Panorama opened in Damascus in 1998 only.[18] This section analyzes the Cairo and Damascus Panoramas.[19]

The Panorama as a genre of monumental painting emerged in the nineteenth century as a radically new art form that combined a high degree of artistic faculty with a successful business model. Panoramas were large naturalistic paintings covering huge canvases attached to circular scaffolds depicting landscapes or urban scenes, often related to religious and historical themes or, predominantly from the late nineteenth century, battle scenes. Spectators stood in the center of the circle, normally on an elevated platform, surrounded by a painting that enclosed one hundred percent of their sight. Indirect lighting from an invisible source illuminated the canvas, so that daylight seemed to emanate from the painting itself, enhancing the illusionary effect. Panoramic painting had precursors in illusionary landscape frescoes of Roman villas or Renaissance palaces. Later, the monumental paintings in the vaults and domes of Baroque churches – seemingly opening up to heavenly spheres – reminded onlookers of their minuscule status in the cosmos. In contrast, the horizon of the Panorama painting was lowered to give the impression to the spectator that he or she was in control of the gaze and able to grasp his or her environment in its entirety, no longer enmeshed with the elements, but juxtaposed and superior. Initially patented in England in 1787 for military reconnaissance training and strategic planning, businessmen soon discovered the Panorama for entertainment purposes that attracted large crowds to round wooden sheds of itinerant showmen in fairgrounds, or later in the nineteenth century, to the huge permanent brick and mortar structures that were a mainstay of European and North American cities. During the heyday of nationalism, international Panorama companies exhibited canvasses of militaristic and religious nature in more or less frequently changing displays, including titles such as the *Battle of Algiers* in Paris in 1833, the *Battle of Gettysburg* in North America after the Civil War, or the *Battle of Sedan* after the Franco–Prussian War of 1870 to 1871, as well as the Crucifixion Panoramas of Altötting, Bavaria, and St-Anne de Beaupré near Québec City.[20]

The Panorama has often been presented as a precursor to cinema as the dominant illusionary medium of its age, when the exhibition of a newly produced canvas was as impatiently anticipated as the opening of a new blockbuster movie today. The Panorama is a product of the industrial capitalist age, when the division of time in work and leisure created a demand for entertainment, which entrepreneurs exploited to market means to fill these hours. During their heyday, Panorama painters maintained workshops employing scores of workers who helped paint the pictures, installed them in Panorama rotundas, and set up the *Faux Terrain*, which is the area connecting the spectator platform with the canvas, filled with three dimensional objects and set up on natural looking ground, thus creating a smooth transition to the perspectival scenes depicted on the canvas. With the arrival of cinema, panoramas went out of business as a capitalist venture, however. It is no coincidence that the new technology of photography and cinema go back to Louis Daguerre, who invented the large-scale Diorama theater, which was a sibling of the Panorama in that it used a black box with frontal vision on the canvas to create an illusionary, cinema-like effect rather than the total vision of a 360 degree view.[21] When the Panorama was already a dying art form in Western Europe due to its lost business momentum, it was at the same time about to pick up a new career in the Soviet Union, where dozens of new propagandistic battle Panoramas and Dioramas were created between the end of World War I and the fall of the Soviet Empire. Other than in the West, Soviet Panorama Art was state sponsored and carried out by Panorama Brigades and the State Center for Panorama and Diorama Art.[22] Hence the association of socialist dictatorial regimes with Panorama art, which was later transferred via North Korea to the Middle East.

As a sub-genre of illusionary art, the Panorama is a totalitarian art form par excellence. Its makers strive to create "illusion spaces" that offer deep "immersion" into a visual field by way of a dissolution of the "subject–object" juxtaposition that normally constitutes the position of the viewer vis-à-vis an art object.[23] The onlooker is overwhelmed to the extent that he or she is put in a position of a perceived unmediated reception of the work of art: as if it was a form of reality. Early critics of the panorama bemoaned the ambivalent effect of complete visual immersion while, at the same time, the scenery was mute and immobile. On the other hand, functionaries of the politics of culture in France and Britain realized that the images had a potential to impress and educate the masses – a fact that explains the dominance of military themes and battle scenes in late nineteenth-century Panoramic art. Western Panoramas were private enterprises, so the selection of topics and themes rested on a reciprocal understanding of what the nationalist public expected, and what pleased the paternalistic state. Prior to World War I, heads of state would give endorsement to battle scenes by visiting the opening of the exhibition, thus enhancing business. Panorama entrepreneurs tried to outdo each other in the realism of their shows (which came to include sensory effects of sound and smell in the course of time). Still, they had to reconcile the patriotic spirits of the audience with the limits of taste, because an overly realistic depiction of the excessive violence and gore of war might have put off the audience and would have had an adverse effect on ticket sales.

Panoramas fixed the onlooker at the center with the illusion of total vision and complete oversight. In battle scenes, viewers could easily switch between the panoramic perspective of the horizon and the soldier's perspective that drew the viewer into the dynamic energy of the detailed foreground, creating identification between viewer and soldier. The paintings were thoroughly crafted, and only full immersion and verisimilitude made the onlooker forget that he or she was looking at a stylized visual program, which presented a narrative that was under the control of its maker. The unframed image left nothing to the critical imagination of the beholder.[24]

Despite these totalitarian aspects, Panorama art was first of all a genre of the entertainment industry at the turn of the twentieth century. Its makers had no control over the behavior of the visitor, who had the option to dislike and openly ridicule the scenes. It has been argued, therefore, that the Panorama had a democratizing function in European capitalist societies because the market mechanisms of demand and supply guaranteed access for all layers of society, who thus shared an equal vantage point (even if they accessed the Panorama building at different times for different ticket prices). In authoritarian systems like the Soviet Union, and later China, North Korea, Iraq, Syria, and Egypt, Panorama art became a mere instrument of propaganda based on the exclusion of potentials of dissidence. In these cases, the Panorama dropped the democratizing function of shared access and point of view, and foregrounded the totalitarian function of complete immersion that fixes the individual together with all others at the center of a clearly defined and controlled space with no escape and no potential for falling out of the frame.[25]

* * *

The October War Panoramas in Cairo and Damascus were state-sponsored projects, too. Plaques at the entrances commemorate their openings as the result of friendly exchanges between Mubarak, or respectively Assad and the Korean leader Kim Il Sung. Both institutions are located outside the city centers, far away from tourist attractions or popular boulevards where accidental passers-by seeking entertainment would drop in to see the show. Unlike the occasional pleasure of a movie, a visit to a theater, a centrally located museum or an exhibition, the visit to the Panorama requires organization and takes place as a planned family excursion, or in the context of an outing for school children, students, or other associations. During the author's personal visits to both Panoramas only few foreign visitors were among the audience, even though shows in European languages were available. Visits certainly take place as part of a school curriculum, but even families frequent the place during leisure hours in a spirit of receptiveness for nationalist elevation, as this is how the Panoramas are advertised. Indeed, the Panoramas put on a great show of dramatic battle scenes and sound and light.[26]

Both Panoramas depict the October War of 1973, when Syria and Egypt attacked territories that Israel had occupied in 1967 on the Golan Heights and in the Sinai Peninsula. Both countries maintain that they came out of the war victoriously, if not militarily, then politically. For the Syrian regime, the war ended in a crushing defeat. Still, it made clear that the Israeli army was not as invincible as had been assumed after the Arab debacle in the Six Day War. According to this reading, the war was a harbinger of the expected ultimate victory for Syria.[27] In Egypt, the war stands for regained military prowess, too, but it also produced a more tangible outcome, despite defeat: The ultimate return of the Sinai Peninsula in the Camp David Agreement.[28]

It is safe to say that a majority of Syrians and Egyptians would subscribe to these narratives, regardless of their opinions about Assad or Mubarak and their cliques. In both countries, specific battles stand symbolically for the whole of the achievements of the October war. The paradox of this war, its course, and the differing interpretations of its outcome are condensed in the Panorama structures that turn into fetishes of Syrian and Egyptian Arab nationalism, and the visit to the fetish becomes a ritual to ban the evil spirits of a century of Arab humiliations. They are victory monuments without victories.

The structures in Damascus and Cairo are quite similar in their basic set up. The Panorama itself consists of a multistory round building that is reminiscent of a medieval fortress. Both Panoramas are surrounded by gardens and exhibition grounds where heavy weaponry and other military exhibits that were used in the October war are on display, both of Syrian or Egyptian army provenance and booty that was claimed from the Israeli army during the war. The Damascus display boasts of two Israeli airplane wrecks. The veneration of late Syrian leader Hafiz al-Assad is a central theme of the Damascene Panorama whereas the Cairo Panorama praises the collective military leadership, presenting Husni Mubarak, who commanded the Egyptian air force at the time, as the "Hero of the First Strike" against Israeli positions, but without giving him an all too prominent role.

The visit to the Cairo Panorama happens in several stages. First, the audience proceeds through an entrance hall that contains various maps, reliefs and models that highlight aspects of the war, then it watches two consecutive shows, one a computerized diorama presenting the first strike of the air force, the other a film about the years preceding the war. The centerpiece, the actual Panorama painting, is on the top floor of the building. A rotating platform provides comfortable seating to the visitors who can view the entire Panorama while they move around all of 360 degrees in about twenty minutes. Audio commentary, patriotic songs and sound effects enliven the experience.

The Cairo painting compresses the first few hours of the Egyptian attack on the Eastern shore of the Suez Canal into one single moment that condensates a plethora of events and actions into one single moment frozen in time. The Panoramic effect of total perception therefore transcends the mere sphere of the visual and extends to an eerie experience of synchronicity: various steps and elements of Egyptian strategy that followed one another, overlapped each other, or took place in a quasi-chaotic string of events are neatly laid out next to each other on different sections of the canvas: the initial bombardment by the Egyptian artillery and the interception of enemy aircraft with batteries of Soviet missiles stationed on the Western shore. The crossing of the canal with inflatable boats, the storming of the Israeli Bar Lev line, the transportation of military equipment via floating bridges, and – in the foreground and in most detail – the taking of the city of al-Qantara al-Sharqiyya all seem to happen simultaneously but in perfect harmony, which is a perspective that is impressive in its verisimilitude, but impossible to have in real life. The Panorama nevertheless fixes the onlooker into an inescapable position confronting him or her with this narrative. The inherent narrative of the painting has its climax in a group of soldiers praising God and praying in front of graffiti of "Allahu Akbar" scribbled on a random wall in the conquered city. One of the soldiers is kneeling on the ground, letting the Sinai sand run through his fingers in a moment of contemplation of glory in an otherwise dynamic scene. Egyptian soldiers storm forward, confused Israeli soldiers try to hold them back or withdraw confronted with superior force. Israeli soldiers are killed and wounded in their backward movement, while only very few Egyptian soldiers die, and if they do, mostly in a forward movement, assaulting. A further scene that stands out is the planting of an Egyptian flag on top of a dune reminiscent of an iconic World War II photograph and the Marines monument near Arlington Cemetery of Washington DC – a noteworthy reference in a North Korean, anti-Israeli painting. On top, there is an inescapable irony in the fact that the Panorama painters' choice of perspective places the onlooker in the center of the Israeli strongholds, with Egyptians attacking from all sides, with the implication that the patriotic visitor is actually fixed in the position of the vanquished and panicking enemy soldiers.[29]

This implicit irony went unnoticed when Egyptian newspapers discussed the Panorama as a work of art and patriotism after it opened in October 1989. Referring to the duration of one complete ambulation of the visitors' platform, a journalist indulged in the show's delusory effect and wrote that these were

> [t]he 17 greatest minutes of rare human joy in Egypt's history: you can relive them here. You will forget the destruction of the sixth dynasty, the treason that broke al-'Urabi, and the bitter taste of the defeat of the June emergency.[30]

Computers were set up in the entrance hall to research the names of the fallen (Arabic *shuhada'*, "martyrs") with no regard to rank, or distinction between "Girgis and Ahmad," that is Christians and Muslims. In full loyalty to the regime and the agenda behind the Panorama, the author added that "[i]t is a piece of work that millions will witness: the truthful citizens, and the honorable. As far as thieves and Islamists are concerned: they will abstain."[31] The journalist thus made it quite clear that a visit to the museum was an act of patriotism and support for the political status quo by goodwill citizens in a period where it was under threat by a nascent Islamist insurgency.

Another reporter described the experience of full immersion:

> Today, you can live through the Battle of October in a matter of 60 minutes [including all elements of the show], on a plane of 22,000 square meters,

you witness the theater of operations in Sinai and above the Canal in all its smoke and fire and weapons and crossing and storming and prisoners and fighting ... and heroism and sacrifice ... indeed: the full picture of what went on 16 years ago as if it happened today. – The image, the story, and the bloodshed: the Panorama of the Ramadan War brings them all together ... and time and place flow together in it. [...] you feel that you are in the middle of Sinai ... the Sinai of October 73 ... It is truly the Sinai with all its details before the moment of the crossing and the storming – all things condensed into one panoramic picture, as if it displayed the "reality of things": "Innaha al-ma'raka bi'l-fi'l ..." – "Indeed, it is the battle in reality ..."[32]

Hardly could the illusionary effect of verisimilitude have been captured more pointedly.

All articles shared great pride in the technical achievements of the Panorama, the largest of its kind in the world.[33] The fact that it took Korean artists to produce this shrine of Arab nationalism was a source of embarrassment, though. Egyptian artist and critic 'Izz al-Din Najib (born 1940) wrote in October 1989 that he had choked when he first went to see the Panorama, because the presentation of the Crossing had been executed by Koreans, not Egyptians. When he left the exhibition, though, his feelings had been entirely different, in awe and pride about the military miracle, and the skill and achievement of the art. The Korean artists, he continued, had come as close as possible to the Egyptian soldierly spirit. The work depicted the climax of the battle in a mythical atmosphere "... and embraces you within itself until you forget to think about styles or schools of art which have become our single concern." Full immersion created a patriotic sensation that trumped the artist's concerns about the awkward involvement of Koreans, a people who were as remote for him as could be from Egyptians' usual allegiances and sympathies. The mentioning but subsequent denial of the concern was probably as far as public criticism in Egypt's authoritarian-dominated press of the late 1980s could go. To cultivate the goodwill of the regime, he had to attribute any criticism of the vulgarity of the Panorama's realism to the alleged decadence of the critics. An artist colleague next to him, apparently himself a veteran of the Crossing, who normally refuted realism, had nevertheless been deeply impressed by the show. Najib derogated those contemporary Egyptian artists who were all professors at fine arts colleges but unwilling to work for the community – and at the same time incapable of realistic painting anyway.[34]

Needless to say that no visitor of the opening of the Panorama noticed the elephant in the room – none except one: a Soviet correspondent who pointed to the belligerence of the Panorama narrative and asked Mubarak if it was a warning to Egypt's enemies. Slightly annoyed, Mubarak answered that the display only presented details about the past. Egypt, he added, was not a threat to anyone, but only defended itself – unlike the Soviet Union, he implied. Indeed, the Panorama displayed a remarkable belligerence for a country that was officially at peace with its neighbor, including a humiliating depiction of the cowardice and helplessness of Israeli soldiers. It took a lot of self-delusion for even the most ardent nationalists to ignore how far this image was from reality. But then, the Panorama continues to be an instrument of collective delusion, and visiting it has been a ritual of defiant self-assertion. In his opening speech, Husni Mubarak said that "[t]he Panorama is something that lifts the head of every compatriot." The paradox of the Panorama is that the verisimilitude of representation that it displays stands in stark contrast to the manipulative potentials of its technology. This inherent contradiction reflects the tendency of Arab states in the last quarter of the twentieth century to submit to the pragmatism of international politics for the sake of power preservation, while continuing to use nationalist rhetoric and to focus on national strength and militarism to lull internal opposition.[35]

Information about the origins of the Damascus Panorama is scarce. Syrian newspapers delivered only monolithic praise, as could be expected from the press in Syria's secret service state under Assad rule. Their nearly complete silence about the Korean origins of the Panorama speaks volumes, though. Apparently, the Syrian propaganda machine did not take any chances with regard to the discrepancy between the crude Arab nationalism and belligerent militarism of the monument and the fact that Syrians needed Korean assistance to build it. Articles referred to the Panorama building as a grandiose work of Syrian–Arab architecture, but kept silent about the origin of the oil paintings.[36] This, even though the Korean connection of the monument is in the face of every visitor: not only the commemorative plaque at the entrance celebrates it. The last stop of the Panorama tour is in a Hall of Glory, hailing the late Hafiz al-Assad. One end of the hall is adorned with a monumental painting celebrating the man in the midst of his people – a variation on the theme of the Mubarak painting in the Cairo War Museum – and vitrines contain letters of allegiance to the leader written in blood by ordinary Syrians. A large photo-like tableau is attached to the opposite wall above the exit showing Assad shaking hands with Kim Il Sung.[37]

The narrative structure of the Damascus Panorama finds expression in two monumental paintings – one a Diorama depicting the Syrian assault on Jabal al-Shaykh (Mount Hermon), a temporarily successful attack by Syrian crack units on an Israeli reconnaissance station; the second, a full-scale Panorama detailing the battle for the Syrian border town of Quneitra, which Syrian troops held for a short period at the beginning of the 1973 war. The town has become a centerpiece of Syrian Ba'thist commemoration of the war since the authorities left it in a dilapidated state after Israeli troops vacated the place as scorched earth in a negotiated settlement of mid-1974. As in the Egyptian counterpart, the paintings impress by the minute detail of the foreground and the vastness of perspective in the background. They compress a long and complex sequence of events into one frozen moment.

The newspaper reports that appeared around the time of the opening of the Damascus Panorama in 1999 and in the following years were dull and repetitive, mostly reiterating descriptions and technical details of the Panorama exhibition. Paradoxes recur such as the misnomer of the 1973 war as the "Tishrin War of Liberation," as the war did not result in the liberation of the Golan for Syria, and the simultaneous acknowledgement that Israel was not defeated, but only saved through American help.[38] The Syrian writer Iskandar Luqa, a man of the regime, used a critique of a 2004 exhibition about World War I in the Berlin German Historical Museum to reflect on the commemoration of war and the usefulness of military exhibitions in general.[39] His deliberations in the *al-Thawra* newspaper displayed the characteristic ambiguity between belligerence and military prowess as presented in the Panorama on the one hand and a message of peacefulness on the other, attributing Arab military action only to Israeli aggressiveness. Luqa wrote in his rather opaque article that exhibitions such as the one in Berlin not only presented war as an occasion to exhibit strength, but made people think twice today in light of the blood and destruction before they started a war simply to press a political point. *Al-Thawra's* reader could understand this as an implicit justification for Syria's ongoing indecision in the Golan and Palestine issues, in spite of the war rhetoric. In a typical paradoxical turn, Luqa proposed that similar exhibitions about wars, coups and revolutions like the Damascus Panorama could offer instructional benefit to Syrians, too. He ignored that the Berlin exhibition probably presented a more complex image of total war and its effects than a mere celebration of heroism as in the Panorama.[40]

As previously argued, newspaper articles can easily be ignored, but visitors such as pupils and students, or subaltern functionaries cannot avoid organized outings to the Panorama where the authorities expose them to visual propaganda.[41] The Panorama museums embed the monumental paintings in a rich context of objects in the adjacent exhibition rooms that offer such visitors an intriguing narrative of national military glory. In Damascus, they contain marginal references that integrate the 1973 events in a broader litany of Syrian–Arab nationalism about a nearly victorious army receiving legitimacy through association with broader historical narratives by mere juxtaposition. Once more, a set of Korean-made oil paintings in a round hall on the lowest level of the Panorama building exhibits the familiar paradox between belligerence and peacefulness. A large canvas showing Assad in the midst of his generals during the October War dominates the room from the far end opposite the entrance to the building. Along the circular walls of the hall further canvasses present scenes in history where – according to the tour guide – victorious Syrian and Arab rulers made peace and ended wars. They are, on a side note, a primary example for the blending of pan-Arab and Syria-specific themes into a particular Syrian–Arab nationalism. The first picture displays the unification of Syria in the third millennium BCE, after the battle of Ebla and the signing of what is presented as the first peace treaty in the history of mankind. The second painting depicts Queen Zenobia of Palmyra consulting her senate. The third painting shows Caliph al-Walid Ibn 'Abd al-Malik flanked by Musa Ibn Nusair and Tariq Ibn Ziyad, returning from the conquest of al-Andalus. Members of the Visigoth royal family prostrate before the Caliph. According to *Tishrin*, historians confirmed that this was "the culmination of Arab glory in the year 715." The last painting is of Salah al-Din, with vanquished Franks in front of him, and the Dome of the Rock in the background, "which is and will remain a symbol for the Arabness of Jerusalem and Palestine," again according to *Tishrin*.[42] The choice of these themes combines pan-Arabism with Syrian nationalism, balancing the ambiguity between the nationalist doctrines of the Ba'thist regime with the very local nature of their power base and course of political action. In concert with the October War Panorama, the message is as simple as it is clear: The 1973 war, fought for Syria as much as for Palestine, was just the extension of a historical vocation reaching back into millennia of history.

The Panorama images display a lack of life in empty heroism that is reminiscent of the monstrosity of colossal monuments such as those commissioned by another dictator: Iraq's Saddam Hussein. The vulgarity of these monuments is in the unmediated nature of their message: the directness and literality of the symbols used, which offer little room for interpretation. There is no need for "imaginative assimilation" or "critical explication." The monuments lack all depth. The two Victory Arches that have guarded the access to Baghdad's parade ground since 1989 are prominent examples for such vulgar displays. The arches consist of two crossed swords each held by monumental forearms, said to have been modeled on those of Saddam Hussein. The technique of direct casting creates a verisimilitude that is supposed to represent the omnipresent but unique and authentic authority of the dictator, but the duplication thwarts the effect. In the same way, the Panorama painters of both Damascus and Cairo are said to have used real soldiers and veterans as models for their images and spent extended periods of time in the respective locations. Nevertheless, the attention to individual detail did not mitigate the fact that in terms of technique, style, narrative structure of the composition, and perspective, the paintings in both cities are eerily similar. They lack all the individual intersubjective appeal of works of art. In general, repetitiveness is a mainstay of monumental art in Syria and Iraq (less so in Egypt) to the extent that one wonders why leaders resort to a propaganda strategy that undercuts their claim on representing unique authenticity. According to one interpretation, repetition sedates people into accepting a mythology of leadership in societies where the wars and revolutions of the twentieth century caused a rapid if not abrupt dismantling of traditional leadership structures. In such times of crisis, people were ready to cling to any framework that provided orientation, even if it was as constructed and overblown as in Saddam Hussein's Iraq, where the leader felt that he was not only in control of the present, but also of the past. For example, Saddam Hussein announced in 1979 that he was a descendant of 'Ali, the son in law of the Prophet and arch-*imam* of Shi'i Islam. To press the point, he rode a white stallion during the consecration of the Victory Arches in reference to the preferred horse of Imam Hussein, the son of Imam 'Ali and arch-martyr of Shi'ism.[43]

From today's perspective, it is obvious that Hussein's efforts had no lasting success, and that he failed particularly in his efforts to claim the mythology of a hostile Shi'i community for himself, which he also submitted to the most extreme forms of violence. The entire argument about the receptiveness of a population under totalitarian control is, however, based on a simplistic model of society and the different forms of agency within it. As forceful as authoritarian visions of the community and the things that bind it together may be (such as shared memories of war, or myths of an origin in a distant past), they always compete with remnants of patterns of identification from earlier, possibly more liberal periods (the present volume presents several examples of such patterns of identification). The constant repetition of a highly incredulous narrative therefore produces merely a lulling effect and evokes phlegm as a coping strategy.[44] It is important to note, then, that the public display of allegiance to, say, Hafiz al-Assad and his personality cult as embodied in the omnipresence of crudely executed monuments, did not equal actual allegiance. The Assad cult was not a means to convince people of contents, but rather to force them into compliance by obligatory participation. The cult "clutters public space with monotonous slogans and empty gestures, which tire the minds and bodies of producers and consumers alike."[45] The Panorama is thus only one prominent stop on a seemingly lifelong procession from one site in the Assad cult to the next. They stake out the realm of licit movement in the public sphere – under the leader's watchful eye. In this context, citizenship is defined in submission to the cult, and not as participation.[46]

Contents are, however, not entirely unimportant, as there are potentials to subvert the message: Nominally Arab nationalist regimes like those of the Ba'thists in Iraq and Syria cannot entirely disown the inherited elements of the Arab nationalist narrative that produced familiar stories and became part of a shared imagery during the first half of the twentieth century. This is why the propaganda of these regimes wavers between absurd references such as Saddam Hussein's descent from 'Ali on the one hand, and appeals to well-known ("culturally resonant") images of national pride on the other that evoke emotional reactions, producing an "Ambiguity of Domination." The combination of incredulous claims with references to widely accepted nationalist topoi (such as the rallying cry of anti-Zionism) makes the incredulous more easily digestible.[47] The following pages introduce such a well-known and "resonant" nationalist narrative, which Assad tried to appropriate.

Maysalun and the cult of the dead

A statue of the Syrian military commander Yusuf al-'Azma adorns a central square in Damascus of the same name. A missile of the Syrian army, Iranian engineered but Syrian made, is named *Maysalun*, after the site where in 1920, al-'Azma led irregular forces into battle against the French. Many streets and places in Syria bear these names.[48]

Al-'Azma was born in Damascus in 1883 into a wealthy landholding family – a rare social background among the comrades and fellow students he met at military academies who often stemmed from the middle or humble ranks of society due to the low regard that notables had for armed service. Al-'Azma rose through the ranks of the Ottoman army to become a decorated staff officer during World War I. He served the Ottoman state faithfully until the end of the war, unlike some of his peers who were members of Arab Secret Societies before the war and joined the Arab Revolt under Sharif Husayn. When the Ottomans surrendered in 1918 al-'Azma chose to join Faysal's Syrian Arab government from 1918 to 1920 as Minister of Defense. In the face of French troops marching on Damascus in July 1920 to impose their Mandate authority, al-'Azma put together an irregular army and was killed fighting superior forces on the hills near Maysalun next to the road between Damascus and Beirut, on the slopes of the Anti-Lebanon.[49]

The battle and the Arab commander feature prominently on one of the reliefs adorning the façades of two wings that flank the Damascus Panorama building. To the left of the entrance an onlooker sees a frieze presenting the "accomplishments of the reforms under the leadership of President Hafiz al-Assad," depicting the late leader in the midst of persons and objects symbolizing social, agricultural and scientific development.[50] The relief on the right side depicts the battle scene of Maysalun with Yusuf al-'Azma towering in the center, easily recognizable by his iconic moustache, his uniform and the helmet with a neck guard that have been familiar for generations of Syrians in publications and on monuments promoting al-'Azma as a central figure of local nationalism, with reverberations throughout the Arab world.[51] On the relief, soldiers of his irregular army surround him, adorned with peasant kuffiyah headscarves, manning a *Maxim* machine gun. Yussuf al-'Azma has his left arm stretched out directing his men towards a hopeless but heroic assault (Figure 6.3). The imagery comes full circle in a large bronze statue that dominates the small square and garden in front of the Panorama. It presents Hafiz al-Assad in military uniform, from his waist up

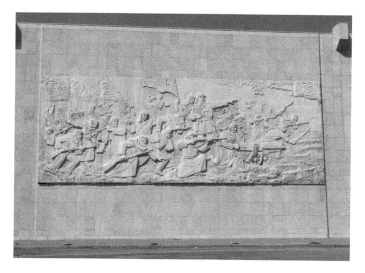

Figure 6.3 The Maysalun frieze on the Damascus Panorama building.

Figure 6.4 Hafiz al-Assad cast in bronze, with the Maysalun frieze in the background.

with a beret on his head (another iconic image). He, too, has his hand stretched out pointing forward, mirroring al-'Azma's gesture (Figure 6.4).

This symbolic association-by-juxtaposition of Assad with the war hero and martyr constitutes a more or less subtle effort to profit from the legitimating power of Syria's Arab nationalist past, where an explicit equation of al-'Azma with Assad would have been too pretentious and a potential source of ridicule. Even today, in times of civil war, Maysalun and Yusuf al-'Azma live on as components of the regime's self-legitimizing Syrian–Arab nationalist propaganda. A 2013 article in *Tishrin* celebrated him as the one who first cleared the way on the long road to the expulsion of the French from Syria, and as a righteous man who followed the course once taken steadfastly. This reference to al-'Azma was meant to confirm that President Bashar al-Assad was right to maintain a steady hand in the face of what regime propaganda upheld as foreign attacks by alleged imperialists and Islamist extremists after 2011.[52]

Maysalun is the culmination of a complex chapter in the history of Arab nationalism. It constitutes a key moment in the collective memory of the family of Fu'ad al-Khatib, too. Fu'ad 's daughter Ihsan recalled in her memoirs that demonstrations took place in Damascus around the time of Faysal's departure from his capital in the face of advancing French troops. People chanted songs, such as:

> I sacrifice my soul for you, oh fatherland – you who cannot be sold for a price / I don't shy away from protecting you against hardships – forever, unless I get wrapped in the shroud / I will defend you with my very heart – the

blood of the Arabs flows through it / I will defend with the essence of my heart – to restore with it the Arabs to good condition.

Others clamored: "To death, to death, for the fatherland!" while one of Ihsan's uncles sobbed: "What a shame, oh Faisal! May God give that you return!" The al-Khatib residence was a focal point for political and cultural actors in Faysal's Syria, and Ihsan remembered Yusuf al-'Azma from visits he had paid to her father. He had asked her to dance and sing: "Faysal, oh Faysal, oh Ghazi's father – Oh you father of the knights on the day of the competition!" Later, Fu'ad Al-Khatib used to say that al-'Azma had foreseen his fate, and that he had told him in their last encounter: "I am on my way to meet death!"[53]

In hindsight, Ihsan's memories present the last days in Damascus before the debacle of Maysalun as a period of doom, but heroism in conscious sacrifice. So far, her account thus confirmed a myth, purported by later Syrian propaganda as we have seen, that Maysalun was a last stance on behalf of Arab nationalism against the foreign onslaught. Since its occurrence, various powerful groups in Syrian politics and society have interpreted the battle as a constituent moment of national identity, according to their own specific convictions. The actual affair was a lot more complex, however. The events took place at a moment when inherited patron–client communities in the urban context of Damascus were clashing with the supra-regional aspirations of a clique of Hejazi aristocrats – like Faysal – and nationalist-minded ex-Ottoman officers of mostly Iraqi origin. The mobilization for the battle of Maysalun in July 1920 was therefore a much more ambivalent act and not just a unified move for the sake of the nation under the leadership of al-'Azma. In fact, the last stance against the French followed on from a popular uprising against the Arab government of Faysal, who had acceded to French demands to dissolve his Arab army and the General Syrian Congress, which demanded Syrian independence. Notables of the city had been mobilizing their urban clients against what they considered an alien leadership, consisting of Peninsular Arabs and former Ottoman officers, who they saw as culturally inferior. When Faysal surrendered to the French because he believed that resistance was futile, al-'Azma refused to follow suit.[54]

Even Ihsan al-Khatib's memory takes account of the ambivalences of the time. She tells a story that unwittingly puts her father in an ambiguous light of collaboration in the battle's aftermath, if not of cowardice from a perspective of the nationalist ideal of relentless readiness for self-sacrifice. According to Ihsan, Fu'ad al-Khatib received a request from Prime Minister 'Ala' al-Din al-Durubi who had taken over the government after the French entered Damascus. Durubi asked al-Khatib to join a government delegation, which included himself, that would set out to calm down unrest among tribes and revolutionaries who opposed French rule in the Hawran region south of Damascus. This happened circa a month after Maysalun, and after the final departure of Faysal into exile. Apparently, people were angry that the king had betrayed the cause, and the delegation had been commissioned to assure the compatriots that he would continue his struggle from Europe and seek support for the Syrian–Arab state. In any case, al-Khatib's entire family was of utmost distress fearing for the life of the father, and finally they convinced him to abstain from joining the delegation. In the context of al-'Azma's nationalist martyrdom story that Ihsan related, the abstention could not be read as an honorable act, even if it was life-saving. The Prime Minister and one other member of the delegation were ambushed and shot dead during their mission. For al-Khatib, this was enough reason to burn the bridges once more and leave the country and head for the Hejaz where he felt more welcome.[55]

Maysalun and the death of Yusuf al-'Azma have taken on a variety of meanings since Syrian elites started to exploit them for their particular goals soon after the battle took place in 1920. The tomb of Yusuf al-'Azma in Maysalun is still a commemorative site today. It is well maintained and has been renovated several times, but it retains the basic shape that it already had in the 1930s.[56] The tomb is located in a grove shaded by trees. It consists of a stone sarcophagus with a triangular roof-shaped cover on top that is adorned on one side with a relief of *Dhu al-Fiqar*, the legendary two-pronged sword of the Prophet Muhammad. The sarcophagus stands on a platform with steps leading up on one side. On the other side, a flat column made of concrete that narrows towards the top and is painted in the colors of the Syrian flag carries a massive concrete roof supported by a stepped beam. The entire roof structure looks somewhat like the tail unit of an old-fashioned passenger airplane. Today, the Syrian military claims the space during yearly celebrations of Maysalun Day when a delegation of officers honors al-'Azma in a military ceremony. It is questionable, though, that the tomb sees many other visitors due to its remote location. It is an odd structure in an odd place for a grave, without religious references except one to Islamic history in *Dhu al-Fiqar*. The grave is not even part of a war cemetery, as there are no further tombs of fallen Maysalun fighters around, even though it constitutes a site of memory in a cult of the dead.

Commemoration of the fallen is an integral part of human social life; in a "convergence of politics and religion" commemorative rites serve to give meaning to individual sacrifice for the community's "survival, liberation, victory, or even redemption."[57] There is an international repertory of rites and architectural forms to commemorate the dead, which originated in nineteenth-century Europe and made its way across the globe in the footsteps of colonialism. A signature structure of this kind is the Tomb of the Unknown Soldier, which originated in post-World War I Britain, but can now be found in places such as Baghdad, Damascus (a structure that opened in 1994 and has a certain semblance to the Panorama), Cairo, and Algiers, among many others. European commemoration of the fallen took a sharp turn after the French Revolution from the veneration of war heroes and fallen military leaders to the inclusion of the common soldier in the commemoration after the introduction of mass conscription. Accordingly, the service of the individual soldier came to be sanctified as service to the national community, and the cult of the dead was no longer an aristocratic privilege. The inscription of names of fallen soldiers on monuments, regardless of their rank, was supposed to individualize what appeared as the meaningless undiscriminating slaughter of thousands of soldiers on the battlefields of Europe and North

America in the nineteenth and twentieth centuries, the most prominent example being the Vietnam War Memorial in Washington DC. There are, however, also small memorials in small town squares or churches throughout Germany, Britain, and France. Commissioned by the communities themselves, the monuments combine the mourning of individual loss, and the commemoration of the void the fallen had left, with attempts to contextualize their death within broader categories such as "nation" or "freedom," or even "class struggle."[58]

It is beyond the scope of this chapter to inquire how Middle Eastern societies found or did not find answers to the tension between the imposed forms of commemoration of war and perceived heroism on the one hand, and the need to cope with individual loss and mourning in the Arab countries after the massive deaths during the Middle Eastern Wars of the twentieth century on the other. During the war with Iran in the 1980s, the Iraqi Ba'th party banned collective ceremonies and the burial of the war's martyrs in war cemeteries in order to guarantee that the commemoration happened on an easily controllable small scale. Early in the war, however, the government had already commissioned a monumental Martyrs' Monument that is surprisingly void of specific Ba'thist propaganda. It is for this particular reason that it remains a somber commemorative site for the fallen of Iraq that is popular to this day. It contains a wall of the martyrs' names that are carved in stone regardless of rank and origin, reminiscent of the Vietnam memorial on the Mall in Washington, DC.[59]

The central war memorials in Cairo and Damascus – the Panoramas, the Unknown Soldier monuments – hardly respond to the needs of individualized commemoration. The computerized database of Egyptian deaths in the October War Panorama is no longer extant, and only the *Martyrs' Hall* of the Cairo War Museum displays photos of the fallen of the various wars that Egypt has fought since 1948. Other than the Martyrs' Monument of Baghdad, Cairo's Martyrs' Hall lists only officers, with the exception of a section on Operation Desert Storm of 1991, which has rank and file soldiers, too.[60]

The Arabic word for martyr, *shahid*, as it is used for a "fallen" soldier is ambivalent in the context of the semantics of the Arabic language (including the derivative usage of the term in, for instance, Turkish or Farsi) and the history of its usage for political purposes and social mobilization – it "defies easy categorization." Modern usage ranged between the tendency in late Ottoman times to apply the term to any sort of unnatural death, the nationalist notions of self-sacrifice on behalf of the community reminiscent of European models, and its omnipresence in more recent times in discourses of Islamic militancy including suicide attacks. All of these usages occur as efforts for finding justification for forms of violence and death that had been unknown prior to the late nineteenth century.[61] In that, the *shahid* of war memorials is quite compatible with a Western image of national sacrifice, despite the heavily religious connotations that dominate the semantic field of the term. Still, the tomb of Yusuf al-'Azma takes a rather ambiguous position in the categorization of monuments of war. As a burial place of a war hero it reminds of a pre-French Revolution commemoration style. However, al-'Azma's tomb was born out of an ambiguous dynamic in the formation of the

Syrian nation: a popular and indeed populist uprising among an urban society dominated by notables, but on the brink of becoming a national mass society. The tomb, therefore, has offered a range of possibilities for appropriation and interpretation since its inception, reflecting the political orientation of hegemonic elites at various times and how they related to the populace.

During the interwar period, the nationalist bourgeoisie of the National Bloc party claimed the memory of Maysalun and Yusuf al-'Azma for itself. As seen, the Bloc represented the established notable families of Syria's major cities who tried to maintain their inherited control over urban clientele politics. Its members endorsed a moderately nationalist and anti-colonial political agenda after the suppression of the Great Syrian Revolt in the mid-1920s had dealt a serious blow to the popular and broadly based national independence movement.[62] Al-'Azma had shared the social background of the notables and consequently, the Bloc members commemorated him as an individual hero and Ottoman officer, as a martyr who had died for the sake of the nation, but as if he had fought all by himself. The collective of the fighters and their general sacrifice did not play a role, as Najib al-Rayyis, the editor of the National Bloc organ *al-Qabas* confirmed in 1930:

> [W]e laid down a hero who did not know how to win, but only how to die. It is no shame for the weak, if they do not know how to win, that they know how to die. In the history of war, only force knows to win, and the powerful knows the meaning of victory, whereas the brave but weak knows the meaning of honorable death.

In this version, al-'Azma was the lone and lost hero who fell like an ancient warrior in a classical tragedy. The foot soldiers who had died at the hero's side did not receive recognition.[63]

The ideals of heroism and self-sacrifice, which were so central for the imagery of Arab nationalism, remained at the center of the Maysalun commemorations. There were, however, also voices that spoke a more inclusive language. In 1930, Jamil Mardam Bey, a high National Bloc functionary tried to make sense of individual death for the sake of the community:

> Yusuf al-'Azma's sacrifice did not deliver the country, and everybody who presumes that it is within his capacities to lift that weight will no doubt be disappointed, because the sacrifice of the individual is small in comparison to the sacrifice of the community. The benefit is in the combining of efforts and energy, in every individual's standing up for its duty.[64]

Mardam Bey's populist reference may have been lip service by a member of the elite bourgeoisie, but apparently he deemed it necessary to add a note that resonated with members of the popular classes and their veterans of the battle.

In the following years, the Maysalun commemoration became a fixed part of the Syrian calendar of nationalist festivities, resembling Remembrance Day in

European nations. *Al-Qabas'* front page of Maysalun Day, July 24, 1936, showed a large image of Yusuf al-'Azma. At the bottom of the page was an image of a French war cemetery at Verdun with the caption that "[v]eterans who participated in the World War go there, and families from many countries visit the graves of relatives and friends." The juxtaposition of this photograph with that of al-'Azma established an unmistakable parallel, even without any text on the page that made this link explicit. In addition, al-'Azma's fighters were now deemed deserving of a place in the commemoration, too, even if only as the "small martyrs" ("al-shuhada' al-qala'il") who died with him, but would be nothing without him, as one article said.[65]

The years around 1936 and 1937 were a period of heightened nationalist activities throughout the Arab world, and the Syrian Bloc made large efforts to consolidate its grip on power in the face of mounting resistance from a younger generation of nationalists against the bourgeoisie's hegemony. Accordingly, the Bloc's own Iron Shirts youth militia started to make a strong appearance on *yawm maysalun*, giving the celebration a military outlook.[66] By 1937, the entire ceremony, "the first in the era of freedom and independence" after the signing of a (yet inconclusive) treaty of independence with France, had become quite stately. There was a flag ceremony, Bloc members participated in their official function as ministers, and nationalist hymns were sung. A list of participating individuals and organizations printed in the papers shows that the event started to reach beyond the circles of the nationalist bourgeoisie. Next to representatives of the forces of tradition, there was a long list of associations that attended, including a veterans' society, the League of National Action presenting the young and more radical nationalists, the Communist Party, and even representatives of a society of Syrian Arabs living in Argentina.[67]

A year later, Maysalun Day had turned into a full-fledged national unity event when even Khalid Bakdash, the leader of the Syrian Communist Party, gave a speech at the grave of al-'Azma. The invitation for Bakdash to speak reflected the Communist leader's line of accommodation with the National Bloc. He used the opportunity to compare the struggle of the Syrians with the struggle of the French for the realization of the ideals of the French revolution, and the struggle of French workers against the capitalists.[68]

By the late 1930s, al-'Azma had turned from the lone hero into "al-shahid al-awwal," or "al-batal al-awwal," the "arch martyr," or "arch hero," who initiated a long and increasingly inclusive line of martyrs and heroes who sacrificed themselves for the nation. According to the rules of *honorable cooperation*[69] with the French authorities that the National Bloc maintained, this message did not even call for confrontation. During the 1937 celebrations, Mardam Bey instead called for reconciliation with the old adversaries of Maysalun.[70]

This stance, however, radically changed again within a couple of decades after a rather violent secession from French colonial control in the course of World War II and its aftermath, as well as after the subsequent years of turmoil that brought about a series of military coups. In 1957, Shukri al-Quwatli, who had been Interior Minister and Minister of Finance of the 1937 cabinet, was now President of Syria, but in spite of the continuity in personnel, the Maysalun rhetoric had undergone a transformation. In his speech at the tomb of Yusuf al-'Azma – read in absentia – Maysalun was no longer the first of a series of continuing battles, but it was the harbinger of national independence. France had ceased to be a necessary ally, but had used "perfidy and lie" in the battle, whereas "innocence and righteousness" had been on the Syrian side. Al-'Azma was no longer the *arch martyr*, but just one of "all the martyrs who fell on the fields of honor, in all places of this fatherland. [T]hey redeemed the fatherland with their blood, and they offered their soul for the sake of freedom and honor ..." – a language that belonged to a fully developed nationalist cult of the dead. As a novelty, women participated in the 1957 celebration, and to underline the inclusive nature of the event, a member of the Women's Union gave an address.[71]

When the Ba'th party took over the state in the coup of 1963, an even starker transformation in the commemoration of the battle of Maysalun ensued, especially after 1966 when a further radicalization of Ba'thist politics followed the coup that brought an 'Alawi officer faction alongside radical socialists in the party's wings to the front, and a very populist tone onto the pages of the party newspaper *al-Ba'th*. Having crushed the last remnants of bourgeois nationalist influence in Syrian politics and ousted the old and familiar civilian leadership of the Ba'th, the new leaders were in need of the nationalist credentials that the heritage of the anti-imperialist struggle had to offer. The military commemoration aspect of Maysalun Day offered an opportunity – only three weeks after the 'Abd al-Qadir celebrations – to link up with a less ambiguous legacy of Syrian–Arab nationalism, and the 1966 celebrations were therefore primarily a military affair with top ranks of the army in attendance. Television and film crews were present, and jet planes flew in formation over the site. In Defense Minister Hafiz al-Assad's speech – once more read in absentia – the battle of Maysalun became popularized. He introduced the martyrs as members of the popular classes of society, reflecting the populist discourse of the regime: "All layers of society rushed into battle: Military and civilian, men and women, the elderly and children, workers and peasants, students and functionaries." And further:

> the remembrance should urge all to adhere to the struggle and to carry the nationalist message further, which is the message of the grand Ba'th party, toward the realization of the goals of the Arab nation in its unity, freedom, and its socialism.

In Assad's mind, the torch of nationalism had been passed to the party, who had in fact wrung it from the hands of previous generations of nationalists.[72] This collective message had no exclusive place for al-'Azma's heroism anymore. A different author wrote in an *al-Ba'th* feature about Maysalun Day that al-'Azma was merely "... an example in his martyrdom for the Arab soldier ... to receive the bullet with his chest and say: I may die so that the fatherland can live."[73]

During the following decade, the remembrance of Maysalun became a military routine. In most years, even on the 50th anniversary in 1970, short, standardized notes mentioned that the commemoration had taken place under the patronage of President al-Assad, in attendance of a number of top-brass military functionaries, but with only little echo on the popular level. One name, however, appears frequently in the context of the cultural contextualization of Maysalun: Jean Aliksan, who is a Syrian writer and critic, born in 1935 and – as far as can be told from a distance – an important functionary in the Ba'thist cultural apparatus.[74] The signature story of Aliksan's contributions is about a peasant woman named Zaynab Mustafa al-Ghazawi from the village Maliha in the Ghuta plain South of Damascus. The Ghuta plain was a major recruiting ground for the popular committees that organized the irregular troops who fought in Maysalun under the command of Yusuf al-'Azma. Zaynab was one of three women who participated in the fight. The first available trace of this story is in an article that Aliksan published in 1960.[75] He related the same story again in 1968 and 1975.[76] In the Maysalun feature of 1968, Aliksan proposed that the history of Syria's national battles should be written anew from a perspective of the people and the revolutionary workers and not by people who had never carried a gun, as an old veteran of Maysalun he had interviewed had complained. Simple people fought but remained unremembered such as Zaynab, the old man said. Subsequently, Aliksan was able to track her down in the Shaghur quarter of Damascus. Zaynab told him how she had forced her brothers at gunpoint to let her participate in the battle, and how she had marched to the battlefield wearing the clothes of her deceased husband. According to Aliksan, 4000 peasant fighters from the countryside and villages of Damascus' hinterland had been among the 5000 Syrian fighters in Maysalun – 1100 of them fell.

The participation of women had indeed been a sign for a strong populist element in al-'Azma's irregular forces and for the liminality of the anarchic situation in Damascus on the eve of the battle.[77] Half a century later, the same story fit, however, neatly into the populist ideology of radical Ba'thism and its vision of society, in the way Aliksan re-interpreted the battle. The way it was appropriated had changed dramatically from the 1920s to the Ba'thist period – from the image of the heroic death of the lone hero to the mostly nameless, but equally heroic death for the sake of a combined class- and nationalist struggle. Aliksan foregrounded the important role workers-cum-warriors had played in Maysalun, and underscored their exemplary humility. Most workers who he had tried to interview about their crucial contributions to national battles actually preferred not to talk about them. They said they had simply done their duty, and added: "Too bad we did not achieve the honor of martyrdom!"[78]

* * *

In the 2000s, the military apparatuses of Middle Eastern states appeared like hermetically closed blocs forming impermeable military-industrial complexes, most of all in states like Algeria, Egypt, and Syria, as well as Iraq before the end of the Ba'thist era in 2003. The old imagery of the invincible Arab warrior had already collapsed in the 1967 war. By then, officers were no longer the convincing proponents of social revolution. The pragmatism and increasing professionalism in the armed forces came along with the military elite's deep encroachment of the state-run economic sector. The consequences are visible today in how the Egyptian army "handled" the revolution of 2011, or the symbiosis of Syrian military and economic elite interests that provide much of the glue that holds the Assad regime together to this day.[79]

But even the most monolithic hegemon cannot do without some legitimacy in the eyes of the public, in particular as the army derives much of the dominance it holds in Middle Eastern societies from real or perceived outside threats, which justify the maintenance of large conscription armies. Since the beginning of the age of nationalism in the Middle Eastern and North African world around the turn of the twentieth century, soldiers and their military prowess have been considered guarantors for the sovereignty of states embodying societal modernity, which in turn was a guarantor for the states' staying power. The many crises of the twentieth century, in particular after the end of World War II, created a variety of situations that put this prowess into question. Many nationalists considered it vital – either for the creation of a pan-Arab state, or the survival of the individual nation states – to *stage Arab military prowess* as a surrogate for actual military success.

This chapter has told a number of stories and has introduced several sites where such efforts became manifest in museums, monuments, and commemorative sites, as well as the festivals that tried to breathe life into them. None of these sites and festivals, though, seems to have been capable of popularizing a notion of shared service to the country, and even less so of giving meaning to a shared suffering on behalf of the survival and well-being of the community. The commemoration in places like the Panoramas in Cairo and Damascus evokes victory where wars were actually lost. The totalizing medium of the Panorama does not leave room for the ambivalence of a memorial that helps the mourning of loved ones. The personality cult in these and other institutions stifles all potential for the foregrounding of grass-roots perspectives. Yet all these institutions represent efforts to communicate with the populace – even if they attest to a failure of communication. The evolution of a specific ritual of military commemoration – Maysalun Day in Syria – over several decades in the twentieth century shows how different actors used it as a stage to underline their own position vis-à-vis society. Maysalun Day started out exclusively as an affair of the bourgeois elite, but became more inclusive – peaking in the mid-1950s when governments allowed representatives of diverse social actors to participate. The festival moved back to exclusiveness when the Ba'thist army appropriated the memory of Maysalun again for itself after the mid-1960s, turning the commemorative festival into an annual routine. Articles about the participation of a peasant woman in the battle were but a faint echo of the once populist dimension of the fight. Chances were missed to plant the army centrally as a carrier of an inclusive foundational myth of the nation.

Most of all, neither commemorative sites and practices, nor shared months and years of compulsory military service brought about the cohesion that was so hard to come by in societies under authoritarian rule. The creation of Pretorian guards to protect the inner corps of clique-based regimes in Iraq, Syria, and other places made the idea obsolete that militarizing a society could create cohesion, as the crushing of the Shi'i uprising in Iraq in 1991 by Saddam Hussein's Republican Guard or the onslaught of the Syrian civil war since 2011 have shown.

7 Arab nationalism, fascism, and the Jews

The final chapter takes on ideology as a central theme in a critique of Arab nationalism, approaching it from a perspective of contention, discursive contexts, and lines of transnational influence. Context and phenomenology are more important in this approach than typology and doctrine. In light of the extremes of twentieth-century European nationalisms, Arab nationalism continues to be evaluated for its racist content and – in concrete terms – for its stance towards fascism. Arab–Jewish relations play a central role in what often turns out to be a highly politicized blame game. Racialized imagery, often with anti-Semitic content, and reflexes of demonization have thus helped to shape the dark side of the culture of Arab nationalism.

Fu'ad al-Khatib was an Arab nationalist; he knew many of the Arab luminaries of his time, and he was for an extended period of his life a close adviser to the Amir of Transjordan. It is only natural that he became embroiled in the Palestine conflict, and his stubborn character made it likely that he would be fierce in taking the Palestinian side, if only to antagonize his more moderate master on the throne. Khatib's statements are therefore exemplary for an entire and particularly problematic set of issues related to the cultural manifestations of Arab nationalism, with reference to broad ideological orientations and considerations about the compatibility of worldviews as part of cultural history. What is at stake is how Arab nationalists related to Jews, and by extension, in the context of the twentieth century, how they related to fascism, Nazism, and the Holocaust. In the perception of Western literature and Arab historiography, politics, and demagoguery, these topics have been inseparable. By way of introduction, some extracts from Fu'ad al-Khatib's biography will provide a useful frame of reference to illustrate some points for closer analysis in the rest of the chapter.

As typical for Arab nationalists from the 1930s on, the Palestine conflict was the lens, the trigger, and the measuring bar for the way al-Khatib related to Jews. Palestine represented a new cause for him at a time when his Amman years turned out to be a low point after the enthusiasm of World War I, the Arab Revolt, and his involvement in the affairs of the Damascus and Hejaz kingdoms. The Palestine Revolt's *mujahidun* were an embodiment of the combination of nationalist and religious zeal that he endorsed, carrying "the Qur'an in one hand

and a rifle in the other," as he used to say. According to the biography, al-Khatib even opened his Amman house as a conduit for arms deliveries from Iraq to the Palestine rebels. Moreover, the Palestine Revolt led al-Khatib, like many others in the Arab world at the time, to give up differentiation and the century old benevolent, though usually condescending, attitude towards Jews.[1] Ihsan al-Khatib quoted her father as saying to her several times that

> [i]f the Jews had a right in Palestine because they once ruled it in the past for a while, [then] why should the Arabs not have a right in Spanish Andalusia, which they ruled for much longer than the Jews ruled Palestine? ... The greed for power is becoming dangerous among them ...Today, you find a Jew who is not a Zionist, but after a while all Jews will become Zionist.

Next to the ethnic antagonism that characterizes this statement, the *al-Andalus* reference is a remarkable variation on the topos of comparing a looming loss of Palestine with the fall of Granada. Here, Fu'ad al-Khatib used the perceived absurdity of an Arab claim to *al-Andalus*, in spite of Arab identification with it, to highlight what he perceived as an even greater absurdity: the Jewish claim to Palestine. Fu'ad's voice, however, also speaks to the increasing unwillingness among Arabs, not only in Palestine, to distinguish between Zionists and Jews – due to the radicalization of the conflict and an Arab misreading of Palestinian-Jewish society, but also due to Zionist propaganda that depicted the movement as representing all of world Jewry.[2]

The al-Khatib family had a relationship with a key personality of the thematic complex of relations between Arabs and Jews, too. Amin al-Husayni, the Grand Mufti of Jerusalem during the Mandate period, who is notorious for his active exile in Nazi Germany during World War II, was a house guest of the al-Khatib family in Amman, and Fu'ad apparently admired him because he had restored his believe in Arabism. Like many Arab nationalists, al-Khatib observed the rise of Nazism in Germany with curiosity and ambivalence. He dreamed of a strong role for Arabs in world politics, if they could manage to unite behind a leader.[3] Appeals to the need for charismatic leadership in the Arab world were often connected with a cult of youthfulness and the image of a young generation waiting for takeover to clear away anything that was old-fashioned. Uniformed paramilitary youth movements became a constant presence on the streets of major cities, using a form of public representation that raised concerns among foreign observers that the Arab lands were moving towards an endorsement of fascism. In this context, another acquaintance of the al-Khatib family, young King Ghazi I of Iraq (1912–1939), who followed Faysal I on the throne after his premature death in 1933, symbolized for many, in Iraq and beyond, the rise of a new generation. The young king was, on the other hand, derided by sober-minded observers for his erratic behavior, such as using a private radio station to broadcast nationalist propaganda, and for his detachment from the diverse constituencies of Iraqi society. When Ghazi, who liked to dress in military uniform and surrounded himself with young hot-headed officers, died in a car crash in April 1939, rumors abounded in anti-British nationalist circles that his vehicle had been tampered with and he had been murdered. Ihsan al-Khatib, who wrote that she had been an avid listener of Ghazi's radio broadcasts, reported that everyone at the school where she worked in Amman was deeply shocked at hearing the news of Ghazi's death, and that the school closed for three days of mourning. The latter may have been rather due to the family connection between the Transjordanian princely household with the King of Iraq than to public demand, but for Fu'ad al-Khatib and his family, the relationship was a personal one going back to his time in the service of the Kingdom of the Hejaz. Ihsan tells that she and her father were in a state of immense nervous irritability after Ghazi's death. Once, she said, she cried out: "It is the Jews who killed him!" and Fu'ad replied: "Away with them! They are even too contemptible to be the murderers of Ghazi!" (Amir 'Abdallah in turn wondered: "What will Shaykh Fu'ad say about Ghazi? Could any more be said about him than that he was a drunkard, a troublemaker, and a reckless person?") The immediate nature of Ihsan and Fu'ad al-Khatib's exclamations and Ihsan's concrete memories about the location of her and her father's nervous breakdown (in the family residence) make it likely that the quotes are authentic. It is impossible to determine, though, if they were representative of al-Khatib's stance in the late 1930s or just spontaneous outbursts in the heat of the moment.[4]

There is also a brief hint in the poet's biography at another theme of Arab–Nazi relations that plays a central role in the historiography: radio propaganda. After falling out with Amir 'Abdullah, al-Khatib left Transjordan towards Lebanon where he took up residence in South Beirut around the time of the French surrender to Germany in World War II. Al-Khatib decided to keep his distance from representatives of Vichy France who approached him. One day, a radio journalist suggested that he should recite poetry critical of Amir 'Abdullah, the English and their allies. Al-Khatib's reply was: "In clear terms, you want me to be the Yunus al-Bahri of Beirut, isn't it?" Yunus Bahri is infamous for his role as the Arabic speaker of Nazi German radio propaganda in the war, with its fierce anti-Semitic content. Apparently, al-Khatib did not approve of such activities because he rejected the French advances strongly. He would not even do it for a fortune, because he had "honor, and a history" that would not allow for this kind of involvement. Instead, al-Khatib chose to partake in a British organized poetry contest to counter German propaganda, over *Al-Quds* radio. Al-Khatib was to head a committee to select the best three poems from submissions covering the topics "Arab Unity" and "World Peace." The latter probably took place during Rommel's North African campaign, but after the British had secured the Arab East from the Nazi threat winning the wars in Iraq and against Vichy France in Syria.[5]

The information to hand is far too scarce to draw conclusions about al-Khatib's actual stance towards Nazism and fascism in general. Rather, it is likely that he took a position between admiration for the image of strength and efficient leadership on the one hand, and skepticism about the expansionist language and actions of the newly arising European powers on the other. At the end of the day, al-Khatib opted against the fascist Axis camp, including Vichy France, and for Great

Britain, once it resolved to withstand German advances in the Mediterranean. However, al-Khatib did not shy away from anti-Jewish remarks that bordered on anti-Semitism. In his play *Fath al-Andalus*, he depicted the Jews as deceiving and plotting, using bribery and infiltration to bring about the downfall of the Goths. The stereotypical rendering of the Jewish characters could, however, also be read as a metaphor for Zionist infiltration of the British administration in Palestine. In contrast, al-Khatib also gave credit to the Jews of *al-Andalus* for throwing in their lot with the Arabs in exchange for protection. Whatever this ambivalence, he still used crude anti-Semitic imagery to characterize the Jews as anti-Gothic conspirators.[6]

Jews and Arabs: cracks and fissures

How representative were Fu'ad al-Khatib's statements for other Arab national-ists? Today, this question has become paradigmatic in defining scholarly and political approaches to key areas of Middle Eastern history. It has shaped studies of the historical and ideological roots of Arab nationalism, the Arab–Israeli con-flict, and the emergence and perseverance of authoritarian regimes in the modern Middle East. The ways that politicians, intellectuals, political movements, and the Arab public related to Nazism and Nazi anti-Semitism have been used to contest the legitimacy of twentieth-century Arab political movements across the ideological spectrum. Historians have been ruminating about the involvement of individuals such as Amin al-Husayni in the crimes of Adolf Hitler, Heinrich Himmler, and Adolf Eichmann; the roots of Arab nationalist doctrine in German *Volk* ideas; the mimicry of Nazism in organizations such as the Iraqi Futuwwa and Antun Sa'ada's Syrian Social Nationalist Party (SSNP); and Arab public sympathies for Nazi anti-Semitism dating from the 1930s or even earlier.[7] Until recently, European and Anglo-American research on these topics – often based on a history of ideas approach – tended to take for granted the natural affinity of Arabs towards Nazism. More recent works have contextualized authoritarian and totalitarian trends in the Arab world within a broad political spectrum, choosing subaltern perspectives and privileging the analysis of local voices in the press over colonial archives and the voices of grand theoreticians.[8] Nevertheless, cur-rent debates on the Arab-Israeli conflict, about Muslims in Western societies, and the perceived *Clash of Civilizations* between the democratic West and the world of Islam have connected Islamic fundamentalism, Muslim states, and Islamist terrorism to fascism and Nazism, pointing to alleged structural commonalities between Islam and Nazism as such, summarized under the term *Islamofascism*.[9]

There are three sub-topics that serve to highlight the overall problematic that is at stake in this chapter: Arab perceptions and reactions to the news of the Jewish Holocaust, before and after 1948, are key to understanding the relationship between Arabs and Jews in the second half of the twentieth century in general, including the currently widespread usage of anti-Semitic language; Arab imme-diate encounters with Fascism and Nazism (in occupied lands, as POWs, as exiles in Germany) provide historical background for, and in fact a corrective against, the alleged natural affinity between Arabs and Nazism; and, finally, it is a matter of debate if there was actual adoption and adaptation of fascist ideology in the Modern Middle East, and to what extent we can talk of *Arab fascism* as a reality. While all these topics have to be part of an exploration of the dimensions of fascist trends in the Middle East, they are not necessarily interconnected: Positive views of Nazi state- and society organization in the late 1930s did not automatically entail an adoption of Nazi anti-Semitism, for instance.

There is also a chronological dimension of the differentiation work that needs to be done. Promoters of the Islamofascism paradigm often ignore, deliberately or not, the foundation of the State of Israel and the first Arab Israeli war as a paradigmatic change in an Arab *Geschichtsbewusstsein*, or collective assessment and resulting awareness of history (in a more precise translation: the *historical consciousness*) related to Jews, the Holocaust, and the Nazi state. To ignore an all-important marker of historical consciousness – the Holocaust for Jews and the Nakba for the Palestinians – represents an epistemological disconnect that fuels populist and pseudo-scientific debates conflating the rules of public opinion-making with the historical record. This happens mutually and deliberately between the two parties in the Middle East conflict.

A differentiated approach, therefore, needs to be based on a distinction between pre- and post-1948 assessments because the occurrences of pro-totalitarian, pro-fascist, and pro-Nazi trends and representations in the interwar Middle East require a different explanation than the examples of near-totalitarian state control and the widespread occurrences of anti-Semitic propaganda in the Arab Middle East since the end of the World War II.[10] Studies on anti-Semitism and Holocaust denial in the Middle East paint a rather gloomy picture of the reception of Nazi ideology and anti-Semitism in the post-World War II period. Yet, before 1948, the position that Arabs took vis-à-vis the Holocaust was more often than not one of empathy. Even more, there was a remarkable absence of racism and anti-Semitism in the Arab press of the pre-World War II period, and a high degree of critical engagement with all forms of fascism and totalitarianism.[11] Research that follows this line of argument highlights the sometimes very critical perceptions that Arabs had of National Socialism and fascism. Thus, this literature counters the widespread assumption that Arabs had a general affinity towards Nazism, which ignores the strength of socialist and communist, even explicitly anti-fascist, movements in the Middle East.[12] Work on Iraq paints a vivid picture of political pluralism during the interwar period, with particular regard to social democracy. Even staunch Arab nationalists were highly eclectic in their perception and adaptation of European thought. The Iraqi Communist Party stood firmly against anti-Semitism and was wary of fascist trends among right-wing parties. Researchers have recorded the dissonance of voices that emerged from Syria and Palestine.[13] Admiration for totalitarian state-organization coincided with a deep skepticism about anything that came from the West. A critical discourse about fascism and Nazism took place in Egyptian intellectual journals that were authoritative as shapers of intellectual standpoints throughout the Arabic speaking world. Intellectuals like the Egyptian Salama Musa transited from supporters of Nazism and fascism in the early 1930s to fierce opponents under the impression of the Abyssinian war. Even the founder of the Muslim Brotherhood Hassan al-Banna took a remarkably outspoken stance against Nazism. At the same time there were also many instances of support for Nazism in the 1930s, such as in the movement and party Young Egypt.[14]

It remains astonishing, however, how easily Arabs, including intellectuals and political leaders, moved almost seamlessly from the critical stance of the prewar years to one of sympathy for Nazi racist politics that has been a mainstay of Arab public discourse since the end of World War II.[15] Examples of this about-face are 'Abbas Mahmud al-'Aqqad (1889–1964), who turned from a leading liberal and anti-Hitlerian intellectual of the interwar period into a propagator of anti-Semitic imagery and conspiracy theories in the Arab world, founded on his disappointment after World War II; or Niqula al-Haddad (1870–1954), a Christian Lebanese who emigrated to Cairo in the early twentieth century and became a well-known writer and Arab nationalist in the 1920s and a fierce propagator of anti-Semitic language when he worked for the magazine *al-Risala* from 1947 to 1949, even adopting a strategy to "Islamize" anti-Semitism.[16]

How was it possible that the language of Nazi anti-Semitism was so quickly adopted after World War II? Arabs were avid consumers of news media in the 1930s, and they were well aware of what was going on in Europe during the 1930s and the World War, as analysis of the Arab press has shown. Anti-Semitic topoi and imagery were also known in the Arab world and some had adopted them in the propagandistic confrontations of the violent second half of the 1930s during the Palestine Revolt.[17] The propaganda speeches that Amin al-Husayni broadcast from his Berlin exile certainly received attention, even if, in their fierceness, they probably sounded quite alien to many listeners in the Arab world during a time when the Palestine conflict lay dormant because of the war. A poll, sponsored by Allied administrative authorities, about radio usage among Arabs in the Eastern Mediterranean recorded around 1943 that the German and Italian propaganda stations were by far the least popular, and least trusted, even if the pollsters were uncertain to what extent "reticence under war conditions" might have influenced the tally.[18]

The paradigmatic change of the war of 1948, however, opened the doors to a repertory of images that could be used to denigrate and vilify the opponent, which arguably happened in a psychological sense to overcome the collective trauma of defeat and humiliation at the hands of the Zionists. Conspiracy theories came in handy for that. A shift occurred towards allegations that the State of Israel was abusing the Holocaust for its national interest. Holocaust denial is, in contrast, a more recent phenomenon, whereas the usage of anti-Semitic stereotypes, based to a large extent on the *Protocols of the Elders of Zion*, gained in popularity immediately after 1948.[19]

The usage of anti-Semitic language and imagery thus underwent a transformation that followed a sequence of deep shifts in the Middle East conflict. Between the end of World War II and 1948, there was a period of ambiguity. Fu'ad al-Khatib wrote a defiant poem in late 1947, where he derided Arab leaders because of their reluctance to come to the rescue of the Arab brothers in Palestine. Criticizing people's half-hearted commitment to Arabism he said:

> Oh you calamities, blow as violently as you like / I am 'Palestine' and I have not been defeated
>
> Empires poured their rabble / slowly into me, but where is the vow, where the protection?
>
> On my account, Arabness was before [the time of] the herdsmen[20] / after [the time of] Prophethood, and until the bones will be called to rise.[21]

To interpret the "rabble"-quote as an adoption of European anti-Semitic imagery may be a stretch, but other authors showed a similar ambiguity. For example, the Egyptian intellectual Ahmad Hasan al-Zayyat (1885–1968), who showed some sympathy for fascist social order before the war while being a fierce opponent of Nazi racism, became an embittered hater of the Jewish state in the course of 1948 and took on anti-Semitic inclinations in his journal *al-Risala*, founded in 1933 and a bulwark of liberalism before the war. During the war of 1948, *al-Risala* would serialize the first complete translation of the *Protocols of the Elders of Zion* into Arabic.[22]

Already in January 1947, long before the outbreak of hostilities in Palestine after the November vote by the United Nations in favor of the partition of the country, al-Zayyat wrote an ambivalent commentary entitled "God have mercy upon Adolf Hitler." This commentary has been used in the literature as evidence for the almost inexplicable shift towards anti-Semitism that even first-rate intellectuals like al-Zayyat undertook, even before 1948, in spite of their knowledge of the Holocaust. Selective quotes from the article, when taken out of context, seem to display clear anti-Semitic stereotypes and pro-Nazi standpoints, such as an attack that capitalism was a creature of "the Jews and their agents among the parasites that live on the blood of society just like mosquitoes and lice who live on the blood of people," or the statement that there would be no Palestine problem, had Hitler been the judge at Nuremberg.[23] A close reading of the text in its entirety reveals, however, that it is a cynical piece, which attacks French and British imperialism rather than the Jews. Zayyat put the anti-Semitic remarks into Hitler's mouth without directly endorsing them himself. He started the article with a verse from an unidentified poem saying: "Many a day I cried, but once – I entered into another day, I cried over the former," which is a sarcastic comment about a possible change of mind in his perception of Hitlerism, meaning that he might have stood up against Nazi Germany before and during the war, but things had been better then still than they were today. The actual article opened with a fictitious scene in which Hitler – "may God let rain come down [to irrigate] his grave if he had a grave" – sat in a tavern in Munich pondering over the Treaty of Versailles, complaining that his people were deprived and hungry in spite of their abilities, and that other people who were sly and cunning were instead rich and satisfied. "In a revelatory moment [...] it dawned on him" that "the capital" was the reason, and that the Jews "spelled out the meaning of the capital ..."

Al- Zayyat inserted the anti-Semitic remarks about the "mosquitoes and lice" in this context, continuing, in Hitler's imagination, that if the

> heads of the money ("ru'us al-amwal") were cut off, the tongues that lie and the hands that steal would be cut off, too ... And upon this, the venerable [meaning Hitler] spoke the death sentence over Weizmann, Renault [standing in for France], and Churchill!

"Ru'us al-amwal" is wordplay on *ra's al-mal*, the Arabic word for *capital*, which is an etymological translation derived from *caput* (Latin "head") as the root of the word capitalism, *mal* meaning *money*, or *sum*. Capitalism is *ra'smaliyya* in Arabic.

These lines present Hitler as a rather simple-minded demagogue who used the Jews as a scapegoat to blame them for the injustice of the Treaty of Versailles. Zayyat continued that if God had wanted peace on earth and harmony among the people, Roosevelt and Stalin had not nullified the sentence that Hitler had spoken. But for reasons of God's will, he judged that the judge should be hanged and the criminal set free, wrote Zayyat. If it had been "divine predestination that Hitler be the judge at Nuremberg, there would be no Palestine problem, no problem in the Sudan, no tragedy in North Africa, and no massacre in Indochina."

Zayyat's text was certainly political satire, but on the basis of his unquestionable knowledge of the Holocaust, his cynicism was cruel and in very bad taste. But it does not reflect an unmistakable endorsement of Nazi anti-Semitism. Rather, it is an expression of disappointment and disillusionment with the dishonesty of Britain and France in light of the Palestine conflict first of all, but also with the continuity of imperialist politics in other parts of the world, in spite of the loyalty that intellectuals like Zayyat had displayed towards Western liberal ideas. Sarcasm seemed to be an appropriate answer for him, even if it was interspersed with vile anti-Semitic stereotypes. In the second half of the article, al-Zayyat put the blame for oppression and injustice in the Arab lands squarely on the British and the French who displayed colonial arrogance despite their near defeat in the war. At the end of the article he wrote:

> I wish I knew when the veil of deception will be lifted from the hearts of [France and Britain], so they will know that they have not been victorious, and their Nazi opponents have not been defeated; on the contrary, human consciousness has been victorious, and it will not be tricked; instead, the imperialist mind has been defeated, and it will not be possible to defend it from now on.

When al-Zayyat thus used his own voice, and no longer sarcastically spoke through Hitler, he did not refer to the Jews or resort to anti-Semitic language any longer. For him, Hitler's sentence, which al-Zayyat referred to as having been nullified by Stalin and Roosevelt, had been over Zionism and French and British imperialism, and arguably not about Jews as a racial category. It did not take much, though, to cross this fine line of distinction.[24]

After the catastrophe of 1948, there was only little room for the kind of ambiguity that al-Zayyat displayed, though. Open anti-Semitism entered a secular discourse of Arab nationalism in the 1950s and 1960s along with a thorough reception of the *Protocols of the Elders of Zion* in a blunt and immediate adoption of European stereotypes in Arabic translation. At the end of the day, the debate about the Holocaust among Arab intellectuals was a debate about the European Enlightenment, too, as an ideal to which they subscribed. The fact that even eminent Arab intellectuals such as al-Zayyat or al-'Aqqad, both beacons of rationality during the interwar period, turned towards anti-Semitism after 1948 is evidence of the depth of paradigmatic change brought about by the first Arab–Israeli war. The more that Western intellectual idols like Jean Paul Sartre identified the Holocaust as a breaking point of European civilization, the more difficult it became for Arab intellectuals to reconcile their admiration for postwar social revolutionary thought and critique in the 1950s and 1960s with their nationalist, anti-imperialist, and anti-Zionist convictions. During this period, secular, leftist and liberal intellectuals often found themselves on the receiving end of a paternalistic relationship with Western thought. Strategies such as equating Nazism with Zionism, contesting the numbers of Jews killed by the Nazis, or negating the Holocaust altogether were not only a perfidious denial of established facts for propagandistic purposes, but also the provocative behavior of subalterns challenging the supposed moral and intellectual superiority of the superego. Nevertheless, intellectuals took a wide range of positions in their reflections about Jews, Zionists, Israel, and the Holocaust, between hatred and denial on the one hand and empathy and acknowledgment, paired with rejection of the politicization of the topic and the ineptitude of European colleagues to negotiate historical responsibilities vis-à-vis Jews and Palestinian Arabs, on the other. Proponents of such differentiation were a minority, though.[25]

After 1967, however, the growing Islamization of the political discourse in the Arab lands also affected anti-Semitic themes in attacks on Israel and the Western world. References to selective and de-contextualized readings of anti-Jewish passages of the Qur'an and the broader Islamic textual tradition were a novelty in their systematic and widespread usage as, for instance, in the Hamas Charta of 1988, which combined them with topoi borrowed from the *Protocols*. It is important to note, though, that this "Islamized anti-Semitism" built on Western stereotypes, to which selected quotes from the Islamic tradition were attached. There is, in contrast, no Islamic tradition of anti-Semitic readings of the Qur'an that predated World War II. It is therefore incorrect to speak of a specific autochthonous Islamic anti-Semitism, which in itself would motivate Muslims to oppose the State of Israel, as proponents of the Islamofascism paradigm would claim.[26]

Arabs and Nazis: wartime encounters

The record of Arab-German encounters during the Nazi period is not as clear-cut as is often suggested, either. Direct encounters between Arabs and Nazi Germany's World War II military machinery and its extermination politics were rare. They were grouped into immediate military encounters on the battlefield or under occupation, Arab experiences in the Holocaust, which mostly happened to Prisoners of War, and Arab exile life in Nazi Germany, which had its roots in the interwar period.

Encounters of the first category were largely confined to two battlefields in Arab lands, which saw the deployment of German troops in Iraq and Syria in 1941 and in North Africa. In the former case, the presence of German troops was small in numbers (some fighter planes and a delegation) and short-lived, less than two months. The anti-Jewish pogrom that took place in Baghdad at the beginning of June 1941 in the aftermath of the British-Iraqi war and the departure of the pro-German Iraqi government has often been attributed to Nazi influence. Recent studies, however, give more weight to local and socio-economic factors that explain the outbreak of uncontrolled violence.[27]

On the other hand, only little information is available about the nature of encounters between German, or respectively Axis soldiers and the local population of North Africa during the African Campaign. A myth of chivalry and clean warfare in empty desert spaces still surrounds the military actions between fall 1940 and spring 1943. Studies focus mostly on the atrocities that German troops committed against the local Jewish population in Tunisia, but major atrocities were also committed against the Muslim population, in Libya in particular.[28] Among Arab Jews, those of Tunisia suffered most under German occupation. Luckily, most survived forced labor and deportation to local camps. There is archival evidence for German plans of an extension of the Holocaust to the Jews of Arab lands, in anticipation of a victory over British forces in North Africa and the Middle East. Directives for a deployment of *SS* and *SD* (*Sicherheitsdienst* or Security Service) troops existed to undertake "executive measures against the civilian population" in Egypt and elsewhere. These "measures" were to be similar to those the *SS Einsatzgruppen* (Special Operation Units, or Mobile Killing Units) were carrying out in the Soviet Union, where death squads made up of policemen and SD personnel roamed the countryside in the wake of the German army's advance, systematically murdering Jews and members of other targeted communities. The plans for the Middle East were never carried out, and neither were planned transfers of Tunisian Jews to European death camps due to the Axis defeat in North Africa. There is also no evidence for assumptions in the literature that Arabs were ready to collaborate in a planned Middle Eastern Holocaust comparable to the collaboration of local populations in the European theater. In fact, German efforts to recruit Arab exiles as volunteers for a special army unit called *Deutsch-Arabische Lehrabteilung* (German-Arab Training Division) had little success. The *Wehrmacht* established the *Lehrabteilung* in Greece following the fiasco of German involvement in Iraq. They were to serve as support troops and propagandists to win over the Arab population should Germany succeed in occupying the Fertile Crescent. Results were disappointing, too, when the *Lehrabteilung* was deployed to Tunisia in early 1943 to conscript local volunteers. There were, however, local guards who watched over Tunisian Jews in internment camps. Camps with similar personnel existed in territories under Vichy rule, but many Muslims also protected Jewish neighbors. The *SS* and *Wehrmacht* had greater recruitment success among Muslims in the Balkans and among the peoples of the Soviet Union, many of them POWs, but it is question-able if this was due to ideological commitment. Rather, anti-Soviet feelings and the prospect to escape the dire, if not deadly conditions of German POW camps provided motivations. The lack of enthusiasm among Arabs, and Berbers in par-ticular, stands in sharp contrast to the loyal service of North African Muslim soldiers, including Algerian conscripts and Moroccan *Goumiers*, in the Free French army during the Allied invasions of Italy in 1943 and France in 1944.[29]

One should also note that violent abuse and death in the Nazi system of terror belonged to the experiences of the Arabs with Nazi Germany, although num-bers were comparatively small. Research in German archives has brought to light that Arabs of diverse backgrounds wound up in concentration camps during this period after they had committed crimes as *Fremdarbeiter* (foreign workers) or as POWs. They became entangled in the Nazi penal system because they had refused to perform their forced labor duties, had tried to escape from labor or prison camps, or had been involved in forgery, trafficking, or rape. After their convictions, they made their way from jail to jail, being finally, and sometimes terminally, relocated to a concentration camp.[30]

In contrast to German–Arab encounters at the front line, the presence of Arab nationalists in Nazi Germany before and during World War II has been com-paratively well documented. However, the case of Amin al-Husayni, the Mufti of Jerusalem, in particular, and to some extent that of the former Iraqi Prime Minister of the '41-government Rashid 'Ali al-Kailani overshadow the more am-bivalent cases of Arab exiles who lived through the war in Germany in much less prominent, and sometimes precarious positions. Al-Husseini and al-Kailani attracted a great deal of attention from German diplomatic and propaganda circles. In a competition over resources and institutional support, al-Husseini proved to be more cunning and ruthless as an opportunist and offered himself up for exploitation as an anti-Semitic propagandist on Arabic shortwave radio, and as a figurehead for Heinrich Himmler's plans to form Muslim SS-battalions in Yugoslavia.[31] The Mufti's use of Nazi anti-Semitic language in his propaganda speeches to the Arab world and in particular his efforts to prevent the emigration of Jewish children and adults from Bulgaria, Rumania, and Hungary to Palestine in 1943 in order to avoid deportation into extermination camps are crimes against humanity.[32]

The Mufti's relationship with Adolf Eichmann has been a source of major con-troversy since the end of World War II. Amin al-Husayni's alleged close associa-tion with the ultimate architect of bureaucratized mass murder has been used as evidence of his own culpability for the Holocaust. Eichmann and the Mufti both denied that they ever had a close exchange, but remarks by the German's former aid Dieter Wisliceny suggested that several meetings between them took place. The issue remains unresolved due to inconclusive evidence. In her book about the Eichmann trial in Jerusalem, Hannah Arendt doubted that the rumors about a Mufti–Eichmann link were true. It should be noted, though, that the book has since been criticized as too easily accepting the Nazi bureaucrat's attempts to present himself as merely an administrator. Immediately after the war, Simon Wiesenthal claimed that al-Husseini visited Auschwitz and Majdanek, approving of the unspeakable atrocities committed in those places, and that he was friends with Eichmann and other architects of the Holocaust. Reliable evidence for the visit is missing, though.[33] There is evidence, instead, that a number of representatives of al-Husseini and al-Kailani went on a guided tour of the Sachsenhausen concentration camp near Oranienburg north of Berlin in the summer of 1942, but without their bosses. The Arab visitors spent two hours in the camp. The camp commander lectured to the visitors about the "educational value" of internment. They inspected inmates, among them Jews, who apparently aroused special interest among the Arab visitors. The living quarters, the sick bay and the furniture workshop left a positive impression.[34] This visit was nothing unusual, though. Sachsenhausen was established in 1936 as the successor of the Oranienburg camp. As a "model camp," the Nazis presented parts of it to domestic visitors and to the international press, as well as to representatives of allied countries. Terror, oppression, and annihilation raged in the other, less 'presentable' parts of the camp.[35] The Arabs' endorsement of the camp as they had seen it had therefore little to do with the realities of oppression and violence in Nazi concentration camps.

In his memoirs, the Mufti did in fact confirm that he had knowledge of the Final Solution, which makes his actions on behalf of the Nazi regime and against the ransoming of Jewish children even more deplorable.[36] It is, however, inappropriate to assume that the Mufti's stance was representative for all of Arab nationalism. A majority of Arabs in the Middle East supported the Allies during the war – for reasons that went beyond political exigencies and the pressures of press censorship. The war economy presented a business opportunity; moreover, intellectuals and publicists realized that Germany's expansionism represented yet another form of imperialism.[37]

Arabs in Nazi-Germany

When looking at the interaction between Arab exiles and the Nazi authorities, it should be taken into account that Germany's Arab politics were a side theater even during Rommel's North African campaign, when Hitler's expansionist goals were entirely focused on the Soviet Union. Consequently, he had little actual interest in the Middle East, which made the region a terrain that ambitious second row German diplomats and Nazi officials could use to cut out a sphere of influence for themselves without having to fear much interference from above. The interaction between Arab exiles in Berlin and the Nazi authorities should be seen in this context.[38]

The politically most visible group of Arab residents of Nazi Germany were students. Their associations were important hubs for nationalist activities in the 1930s. Egyptians, especially, belonged to the largest and most politicized groups of foreign students in Germany after World War I, but their numbers dwindled after the Nazi takeover, not least because of xenophobic assaults. Only around

170 remained in Germany.[39] Still, Egyptians and other students from Arab lands appeared on the payroll of the German propaganda apparatus, or in the entourage of Amin al-Husayni and Rashid 'Ali al-Kailani during the war. For some, this was a way to keep their student status while others were interned and pressed to leave, as happened to Egyptian citizens at the beginning of the war. German propaganda offered employment to Arab students, who became involved in editing newspapers such as *Barid al-Sharq*, which appeared in Berlin from October 1939 to 1944, at first out of the *Reichs-Rundfunk-Gesellschaft* as part of its foreign language service, and from 1941 under the immediate control of the Propaganda Ministry with a strong propagandistic, anti-British and anti-Semitic inclination. Many of Amin al-Husayni's speeches were printed there. It was widely available in the Arab world; in addition, it was distributed to exiles in European countries and, in very limited numbers, among Arab POWs, with a peak circulation of 5000 copies in March 1943.[40]

Arab employees of the German propaganda apparatus also populated the board of the *Islamisches Zentral-Institut* (*al-Ma'had al-Islami al-'Amm*, Central Islamic Institute) in Berlin. The origins of the institute went back to 1927, when it was called *Islam Institut* (*Ma'had al-Islam*) and functioned as an association for exchange between Muslims and non-Muslims, and as a center catering for the spiritual and personal needs of Muslims in Berlin and Germany. By the late 1930s, members of the Arab community in Berlin discovered it as a vehicle to further their ambitions and move closer to the regime. A new statute in 1939 excluded Jews from membership in the institute. When German authorities in Berlin developed a clear-cut interest in the Middle East in 1941, they discovered the institute as a propaganda instrument and a means to control the Muslim community in Berlin. The Institute was re-established in September 1941 as *Islamisches Zentral-Institut zu Berlin*, and Amin al-Husayni gave a speech at the official opening ceremony on December 18, 1942, which was broadcast to the Arab world and is one of his more infamous anti-Semitic diatribes.[41]

Most Arabs in Germany merely had the desire to explain themselves and their political cause to the German public, though. They sought support for Arab nationalism and the anti-colonial struggle in articles published in German language publications. The authors made strong efforts to adapt their speech to the language that was expected by the editors of the media they used, including anti-Semitic topoi, but it was the Arabs' own proper nationalist interests that played the central role in their texts.

One such author was Jabir 'Umar, born 1909 in 'Ana, Iraq. His case represents a comparatively well-documented Arab encounter with National Socialism. He attended the Teachers' Training College in Baghdad and worked as a teacher in Iraq when the Iraqi government sent him on a stipend to Germany in 1935 to study pedagogy at the University of Berlin.[42] In 1938, he transferred to the University of Jena, before his government made him move to Zurich after the outbreak of war in 1939, where he submitted his doctoral dissertation to the Philosophical Faculty of Zurich University in 1940.[43] In 1941, he can be found in Iraq and Syria as an officer in Fawzi al-Qawuqji's guerilla troop fighting the British. He returned to Germany together with his commander after the latter was wounded in Syria, and enrolled again at Berlin University for the 1941/42 winter semester for what was now indeed a political exile. In the summer semester of 1944 he moved once more to Jena, probably to escape the relentless bombing of the capital. In 1946 he did not report back for the winter semester and was therefore exmatriculated.[44] By this time he was already on his way back to the Middle East.

In July 1939, Jabir 'Umar published an article on British imperialism in the Arab world with clear cut anti-Semitic references in the Nazi organ *Völkischer Beobachter*.[45] The article was about the Palestine conflict, the main target being Britain and its policy, but with a strong link between Britain and its supposed Jewish allies, with racist undertones. According to 'Umar, the conflict in Palestine was a "struggle against the English, who took away our freedom, and a defense against the Jews, who were racially alien intruders with no right to claim Palestine as a home."[46] The article was full of Nazi jargon. 'Umar described Palestine as part of an Arab "Lebensraum," as a land bridge between different parts of the Arab world which was important for their economic "ability to live" ("Lebensfähigkeit"), and as a wedge between different Arab lands, cutting off centers of Arab culture from the desert areas, which were so important to rejuvenate the Arab population in the cities, an argument that combined Ibn Khaldun's fourteenth-century vision of the cyclical development of Arab civilizations with seemingly *völkisch* ideas about the constant need for refreshment of the areas of culture ("Kulturgebiete"), which was an issue of Arab survival ("Lebensfrage").

The identification of the Palestine conflict with racial issues also appeared in the introduction to 'Umar's doctoral dissertation in Zurich, where he compared the educational systems of England, France, Germany, Italy, and Switzerland in order to develop a future civics education for the Arab lands.[47] 'Umar's evaluation of the British and French systems was quite positive, but that of the German system was full of admiration. He referenced some stereotypes, such as the appreciation for German nationalism and militarism that had set in during the Ottoman German military partnership before and during World War I, and the model character that Germany's national unification had for the Arabs.[48] He wrote that German education was so attractive to Arabs because it combined militarism with humanism, and – since the Nazi takeover – had emphasized vocational education, too. Arabs and Germans not only shared the will to unite their peoples, but also, notably, shared a "Jewish problem" ("Deutschland steht vor einem Judenproblem, und die Araber kämpfen ebenfalls gegen die Juden.") According to 'Umar, the Arab youth was impressed with the German youth movement and tried to copy it, but he also criticized the developments in Germany as confusing and still incomplete.

Confusion about the cultural framework of the host country also shaped the contributions of Arab participants in a lecture series that took place at the University of Jena in the summer of 1939. Jabir 'Umar was among them. The *Workgroup on Questions of Arab Life* ("Arbeitsgemeinschaft über arabische Lebensfragen") brought together Arab students and professors with Nazi functionaries and members of the *Wehrmacht* and police to discuss Arab politics and society, past and present. This kind of collaboration between leading German Orientalists and Nazi authorities was nothing unusual. Just as many other German academics, they were as prone as the diplomats of the Foreign Office to use their connections in the Arab world to further personal interests.[49] The work group offered a series of widely advertised lectures by German and Arab members of Jena University between May and July.[50] In the first half, German professors presented papers about contemporary and historical topics. Oluf Krückmann, a professor of Oriental languages at Jena, who had co-organized the lecture series together with a functionary of the *NSD-Dozentenbund* (Association of National Socialist German University Lecturers), gave the opening talk about the historical evolution of the Arab "Lebensraum."[51] Interspersing racial and xenophobic jargon, he spoke about the growing influence of Arabophonic Persians in early Islam who "infiltrated the Arab spirit with so many alien elements, that this world empire was bound to lose its Arab character." Krückmann, who had spent the better part of the 1930s in Iraq, was familiar with this topic from a classic Iraqi–Arab nationalist narrative that blamed the decline of Arab power in the Middle Ages after the heyday of the Abbasid dynasty on the growing political influence of perceived "foreigners" like Persians and Turks. Applying this argument to modern Iraq, Arab nationalists in Iraq accused left leaning opponents of being partisans of foreign elements.[52] Coming from a German professor in Jena, and in the context of völkisch Nazi ideology, this argument suggested very different, in fact racial connotations, however. Krückmann gave assurance that the Arabs were in an all out struggle for existence. Like the Greater German Empire, they perceived themselves as a "community of fate" ("Schicksalsgemeinschaft"), based on racial, rather than religious bonds. It is worth noting, though, that there is no mention of Jews in Krückmann's talk, in stark contrast to that of Johann von Leers, who left a deep imprint on the *Arbeitsgemeinschaft* in two presentations with a strong anti-Semitic content. Von Leers, one of the leading anti-Semitic ideologues of Nazi Germany, held a professorship for the History of Law and Economic Policy at Jena University.[53] In an analysis of "Trajectories of Political Force in the Near East" von Leers gave a new meaning to the topos of Arab alienation, based on anti-Semitism. The Palestine conflict was for him an extension of the epic struggle of the Arabs against Jewish power, in which the Prophet Muhammad "had initiated the entry of Arabdom into world history." Von Leers was confident that the Arabs would prevail because of their solid racial foundations and the Islamic religion, which he believed was in accordance with Arab nature.[54] The Nazi demagogue's second lecture on "Islam and Judaism" was even more explicit. It was a diatribe that traced the evolution of the Jewish people in an anti-Semitic re-interpretation of early and medieval Islamic history. Von Leers stated that hardly anywhere was there more understanding of the "Führer's solution of the Jewish question" than in the Arab world. The Arabs were fighting the Jews to preserve "their own racial purity." He added, however, that "[w]e are opponents of the Jews by conviction, but we are no 'anti-Semites.'" The term was wrong, he said, because it referred to linguistics and the tongues of many "peoples of culture" ("Kulturvölker"). It therefore contradicted the Nazi's true conviction, "which does not deny recognition and respect to people of culture, but which rejects the Jews." Thus, von Leers forestalled a concern among Arabs that the concept of *anti-Semitism* might discriminate against them, too.[55]

Did Arab participants actually reflect the racial, anti-Semitic and ethnic-biologistic pathos of the German speakers in their presentations? There are hints that they felt uneasy about this appropriation of the Arab nationalist cause, which they did not see so much as a racial struggle, but rather as anti-imperialist, where the Jews took sides with the foreign intruder. 'Abd al-Karim Kannuna from Ba'quba in Iraq presented the Arabs in an almost romantic fashion as "lovers of freedom."[56] He, too, said that despotic and absolute rule had derived from the entry of foreign elements into Arab life in the cities, such as the Persians, but he did not mention the Jews. Kannuna emphasized that Arab life was so peculiar in its foundations, based on customary law and a desire for honor, that European terms were insufficient to grasp it – a remark that one could read as a reply to the *völkisch* rhetoric of the Germans' presentations. Arabs were proud, self-aware, and tolerant, but this neither led to "denigrating judgments over other peoples and cultures, nor to shallow liberalism." A cautious desire for equidistance from diverse European ideologies speaks out of this statement, as it was quite common in the Middle East of the time, but it is also a rejection of racism. Jabir 'Umar's presentation on the Arab Youth movement, flew – either consciously or not – in the face of attempts by the German speakers to draw parallels between the desires of Arab and German youth: "The youth movement in Europe is principally different in its kind and its emergence from the Arab one." European youth, he said in a rather obscure statement, desired order and distance from conventions of old life, but the Arab youth lived in accordance with nature and had no need for renewal. He certainly found the state of youth in Germany as confusing as he expressed it in his dissertation. Apparently, 'Umar was equally unsure how to handle Nazi racist ideology. Racism, after all, had a bad name in the history of Arab nationalism. He said that the Young Turks had made a grave mistake before World War I: They adopted racial thinking (which he knew was a positive thing in the eyes of his hosts) but they applied it to the Arabs in their Turkification policy. 'Umar found racism at odds with a major topos of his own nationalist tradition. Yet 'Umar also decided – as in his other articles – to adopt some Nazi jargon when he propagated that the Arab character should be reshaped according to "völkisch" principles.[57]

There is no doubt that the Arab students felt honored that Jena University allowed them to present their nationalist cause to the academic and political public of the city. The German professors used the opportunity to show off their Oriental expertise to party functionaries and peppered their own speeches with references to Nazi ideology. In hindsight, the association between the renowned Orientalist Krückmann and the Nazi demagogue and anti-Semite von Leers is particularly defeating. It is therefore all the more heartening to notice the cautious skepticism that speaks out of the presentations by the Arab guests.

It is hard to discern what kind of impact long student years and exile in Germany had on young Arab nationalists. The case of Jabir 'Umar is a useful point of orientation because he had a traceable postwar career in Iraq. After returning to his home country, he became a functionary in the education sector and a well-known nationalist figure, who even entered the first short-lived governing council under 'Abd al-Karim Qasim after the Iraqi Revolution of 1958.[58] In 1948, he published a book on Arab nationalism containing a collection of talks he had given in clubs and a radio station in Damascus.[59] His German past and the involvement in the 1941 war probably prevented his return to a British-controlled Iraq immediately after the war, but it must have worked in his favor when 'Umar was appointed Iraqi Ambassador to the Federal Republic of Germany in 1963, after 'Abd al-Salam 'Arif came to power in Baghdad. He stayed in Bonn until Germany severed relations with Iraq in mid-1965.[60]

'Umar gave his first talk in Damascus in late January 1947 under the title "Reflections on Arab Nationalism."[61] 'Umar argued for a strong philosophical and scholarly grounding of Arab nationalism: To weather the current storm in the world, Arabs would have to follow the path of European nationalism. 'Umar's choice of examples was remarkable, though, because it ignored that German nationalism had just received a deadly blow; he promoted a German model of national awakening that reflected a prewar mindset featuring the rise of the German nation, and this was how not only German, but also Iraqi high school students would have heard about it in history classes.[62] From Fichte's *Addresses to the German Nation*, 'Umar moved to Prussian military reform by Scharnhorst, Blücher, and Clausewitz, and to Jahn's *Turner* movement, with only a nod to the French Revolution as a catalyst of nationalist thought.[63] 'Umar's lecture reflected an optimism about the Arabs' ability to take their fate into their own hands as it was still possible before the disaster of the 1948 Arab–Israeli war. Nevertheless, references to European nationalism may not have resonated so well with a Damascus audience of bourgeois politicians and radical Arab nationalist students, who were heading towards a power struggle. They had observed the downfall of Germany in 1945, as well as the weakness of the Great Powers that were deeply submerged in painful decolonization politics. None of this made them great models of nationalism.[64]

'Umar's speech was, however, not exclusively about German nationalism. He also admired the patriotism of the Swiss and the love of the English and French for their intellectual heritage. In addition, he had quite a sophisticated theoretical understanding of nationalism. He stated that pride in the Great Men of a nation

> is only pride in one's bygone forefathers, and pride that one belongs to the same race as these great men. What is most important about race is not the proof of origin, or the absence of a doubt that a person belongs to it. Belief in one's descent from a race, and the pride in the qualities of a race and its peculiarities are more important than actual descent itself.[65]

This sociological reasoning about the discursive nature of nationalism may have been based on academic reading of Renan and Weber, but it is all the more remarkable that it did not raise more skepticism in 'Umar about German nationalism and, by extension, Nazi racism.

'Umar appeared out of touch both ways. Exile made him ignore the postwar realities in both Europe and the Middle East. There are, however, also traces of an anti-Semitic ideological conditioning that 'Umar took along when he left Germany. 'Umar presented anti-Semitic topoi in a radio speech in 1947 that were almost a one-to-one transfer of Johann von Leer's theses of 1939. Though anti-Semitism was not the central theme of 'Umar's talk on "The Arab Cause in Recent History" there was a strong parallel to von Leers' ideas in al-'Umar's statement that the Arabs in Islamic times did not fight any race or religion but the Jews.[66] Religious division had entered Arab society only under the Ottomans, 'Umar argued, alluding to the millet system of separate administration for the religious communities, and the protection European consuls granted to minorities under the provisions of the Capitulation treaties. 'Umar Ibn al-Khattab, the second Caliph of Islam, however, had banned Jews from the "cradle of Arabism" (a reference to the Arabian Peninsula) so that it would not get "soiled" by their wickedness. In this, 'Umar referred to the expulsion of the Jews from the Oasis of Khaybar in the year 642.[67]

A language that joined references to Islamic tradition with modern anti-Semitic topoi was familiar to Arab audiences from German radio broadcasts, such as those of Amin al-Husayni between 1942 and the end of the war.[68] As seen above, there is no substantial evidence that this discourse had a strong effect during the war when loyalty to the imperialist power of Britain and France trumped experiments based on the vague promises of German propaganda. After the war, however, the ground was fertile for an entirely different reception of anti-Semitic ideas, and the general political instability in the Arab lands made young activists in particular more receptive to conspiracy theories. The young nationalists that listened to 'Umar's speeches in 1947 imbibed anything that sounded radical and at odds with the politics of honorable cooperation with the imperialist powers that had dominated the interwar period. The fact that 'Umar had an audience for seven consecutive speeches points out that people found his ideas at least worthy of consideration. It would take decades, however, until the religiously embellished anti-Semitism as people like von Leers cooked it up, and as the Mufti promoted it, would become commonplace in the Arab anti-Israeli discourse.

Fascism in the Arab lands

Biographical studies, such as that of Jabir 'Umar, help to complicate an image of Arab involvement in Nazi affairs that is based on generalizations grounded on the actions of towering figures such as Amin al-Husayni. It is necessary, however, to return to a general perspective in order to entertain the question of how deep Arab sympathy for Nazism and fascism as ideologies actually went. How valid are arguments, raised by proponents of the Islamofascism paradigm, that Islam and fascism are not only compatible, but in principle complementary? So far, existing research only allows for substantial remarks about fascist affinities in the Arab world during the period when fascism was at its height in its worldwide appeal, which was during the period between the two world wars and the first few years of World War II.[69] It would be inappropriate to label such affinities as outright fascism. Rather, they should be categorized as part of a *phenomenology* of pro-totalitarian and pro-fascist inclinations, in reference to a historiographical debate about the existence of a fascist *typology* that transcended the boundaries of Europe at the time. According to a phenomenological reading, the respective phenomena in the Arab world were indeed manifestations of broader trends, but have to be seen in light of the immediate contexts of their occurrences. It is important to note, though, that the usage of the term *phenomenology* that is applied here is not an endorsement of the positions of the German historian Ernst Nolte in the so-called German *Historikerstreit* of the mid-1980s. Nolte's thesis that German Nazism and Soviet Stalinism were only two phenomenologically different manifestations of the same fascist type was fiercely rejected by many of his colleagues as apologetic of Nazi crimes, especially his assertion that the Holocaust was a mere reaction to chronologically earlier Stalinist crimes.[70]

Nolte's alignment of Nazism with Stalinism rests on the premise that any comparison of communist and fascist regimes has to contrast them in terms of their actions because of the lack of ideological rigidity in fascism. Nolte's critics argue, however, that fascism should certainly be taken seriously as an ideology, not least because of the massive output of – in a broad sense – proto- or pro-fascist literature that occurred in Europe since the late nineteenth century. Nazism and Stalinism were not as weakly developed ideologically (in contrast to Marxism and Leninism per se) as proponents of the phenomenological argument like Nolte suggest.[71] It is arguable, though, that a modified phenomenological approach has to offer a great deal in a debate about fascism in the Arab world. While terminology as Nolte used it has been described as vague or even ill-defined,[72] it offers a greater analytical flexibility than a rigid typology that establishes a set of broadly shared characteristics of non-European authoritarian regimes that would justify putting them into the fold of transnational or international fascism. Rather than that, a phenomenology analyzes local peculiarities of individual cases of seemingly fascist movements in the Arab world, thus avoiding the broad brush.

Within the context of the massive paradigmatic change that accompanied the dissolution of the Ottoman Empire and the ensuing integration of most of its successor states into an imperialist world system, interwar pro-fascist trends, and in particular those of the 1930s, were just one variety of a theme of political radicalism in the Arab world and the fascination it exerted on those who were in their late teens and twenties. The phenomenon was not even entirely new, but built on a pre-World War I culture of radicalism – mostly on the left, predating the emergence of nationalism as a viable ideological option – in the Mediterranean, with a free flow of ideas and political practices that traveled with the streams of Mediterranean migrants.[73] Anarchism, futurism, and left- as well as right-wing radicalism were not clearly discernible ideas at the time and especially not in the chaotic first years after 1918. Even later, during the interwar period, radicalism held a lot of temptations as a trait of the global market of ideas, especially in the colonial world where young educated men became increasingly politicized, but were most of the time barred from effecting their convictions in political functions.

As members of the Young Effendiyya – intellectuals, writers, and publicists – some of these men developed pro-totalitarian and pro-fascist ideas within a discursive field that moved rather freely between pro-totalitarian, pro-fascist, and pro-Nazi references without a clear commitment to any of these positions. They borrowed in a highly eclectic manner, and did not worry too much about consistency. They re-worked what they adopted and adapted it to local debates in their nation states, or a broader Arab regional context, overshadowed by the demands of decolonization.[74]

The use of fascist symbols was widespread in the political public, such as the fascist salute and the omnipresence of uniforms, and all political parties established youth organizations that resembled the European fascist youth. Rather than being *fascist*, these signs and organizations belong to a form of public representation through *fascist imagery*, because there are many characteristics that they do not share with either their Italian or German counterparts. A major example of such a youth organization, Iraq's Futuwwa movement, was not attached to a party, but was established as a state organization during Yasin al-Hashimi's term as Prime Minister from 1935 to 1936. It was endorsed by a broad coalition of the political establishment, including British diplomats who regarded it as an offshoot of the Boy Scout movement rather than a fascist organization that could threaten the hegemony of a pro-monarchical elite over the state. Originally, Futuwwa was ethnically and religiously inclusive; even Iraqi Jews participated in its activities, which formed part of school curricula.[75]

In other Arab countries, youth organizations were strike forces of political parties, and not an unambiguous representation of a fascist trend. In some cases, they represented partisan interest (such as the Christian *White Badges* in Aleppo) instead of a nationalist agenda. The uniforms of the Damascene (and Aleppine) *Iron Shirts* concealed that these were groups of urban rough that represented the clientele politics of the bourgeois National Bloc party and its control over traditional networks in the city, rather than the spirit and desires of young nationalist extremists.[76] Some examples stand out, however, such as the SSNP that Antun Sa'ada founded in the 1930s. The mere adoption of the name and the party symbol *al-zawba'a*, which is reminiscent of a swastika, are probably the closest mimicry of Nazi symbols of all Middle Eastern parties we know, but Sa'ada's explicit rejection of ethnic racism, though not of racial thinking, in his vision of the ethnic mix of the Syrian nation is a crucial example for the adaptation of European ideology to a specific local context.[77] But even then, ideology only played a minor role in many of the young followers' allegiance to their leader: They cared less about contents of books and treatises, but enjoyed the feeling of communal activism and the display of strength.[78] This was more "showing off" than pressing a point. Differentiation and contextualization are therefore, once more, of paramount importance.

Placing individual youth movements in the context they emerged from, and evaluating the usage of fascist imagery, and the manifestations of a pro-totalitarian discourse in the media of the time, highlights them as distinctive, singular phenomena that have to be understood within the more or less narrow contexts of local grievances and various political or social agendas. In the case of Middle Eastern countries of the interwar period, not only did the demands of decolonization loom large, but also the necessity for elite politicians to adopt what they perceived as a modern outlook that concealed their paternalistic vision of a disciplined society. A fascist self-fashioning of parties or their leaders thus provided a bridge between different generations of political activists in order to prevent the upheaval of a younger generation against the bourgeois nationalists of Syria and Iraq. This older generation had grown into an elite, unwilling to let go of power and privilege, but at the same time tainted by cooperation with the colonial power, such as, for instance, in the case of the Syrian National Bloc.[79] The bridging of the generations happened at the expense of the youth and no doubt contributed to its radicalization and openness for totalitarian ideas. According to a phenomenology of fascism in the Middle East, the adoption of fascist principles was very superficial, however, because it happened out of a defensive position, and out of a concern for "Being Modern"[80] in a way that would not challenge the comparatively liberal nationalist leanings of an older generation – until the post-World War II period.

These trends in the Arab world were reflections of a global phenomenon where nationalist movements used fascist imagery to highlight topics of national strength and renewal in light of a chauvinistic exaggeration of the masculine qualities necessary to get rid of foreign domination. Nevertheless, the term *global fascism* is, strictly speaking, an aporia. Fascism, like all nationalisms, is exclusivist in its nationalism and rests on an ever clearer, if not radical or even brutally violent definition of the *other*. Fascism is therefore necessarily compartmentalized. At most, it exists as various "fascisms." What we can speak of, though, is fascism as a global phenomenon, and we can look for a comparative *taxonomy*, or *typology* of fascism, and for international contacts and transnational channels of ideological exchange, as has already happened in this chapter. It is, however, difficult to establish such a taxonomy in the presence of the dominant, clearly shaped and colorful imagery of Italian fascism and German Nazism – the often referred to aesthetics of fascism that overshadow local peculiarities. Italy and Germany set the parameters of the fascist imaginary for an early version of a global media culture; they defined the fascist brand in popular culture as an effective vehicle for spreading the message. In advertising, however, the brand says little about the content.[81]

With regard to ideological content, there is no shortage of theories of fascism that are often ambiguous and hardly withstand critical case-by-case testing. They extend from a Marxist critique of fascism as *capitalism in crisis*, to theories that are so vaguely formulated that every occurrence requires the opening of a new category.[82] Many theories point to anti-communism and anti-liberalism, mass following and mass party organization, the cult of violence and the Führer-principle, as well as radical nationalism as common traits of fascism, often combined with racism and a specific fascist style of politics. For some, the problem in pinpointing fascism is that there is no single foundational text for all its colors: There is no Fascist Manifesto. (It would be remiss, though, to draw the conclusion that fascism as a phenomenon was void of ideology.)

One theory presents fascism as a product of late-nineteenth-century anti-Enlightenment trends, evolving out of a mythical understanding of the world at a breaking point offering "palingenesis," or a re-birth of the individual into a meaningful national community, to leave behind the fragmented and allegedly overly scientistic world of the early twentieth century that imploded during World War I.[83] Many theorists of fascism consider the World War I frontline experience as instrumental in bringing about fascist movements of like-minded seekers of new meaning that were channeled by the communitarianism and "festival culture" of the fascist movements. But fascist ideology went beyond mere representation in that it claimed to offer a "radical third way" based on the creation of an integrative (and exclusive as well as totalitarian) national community. In this view, the fascist style (of the shirt movements), the obsession with action over theory, the cult of violence, and the demonization of the *other* were only accidental matters of appearance. So were the *negatives* of other definitions of fascism (anti-communism, anti-liberalism). They were part of fascism's propaganda but not its substance.[84] Such an approach to define fascism might prove more useful when assessing in future research post-1945 movements in the Arab world, such as Ba'thism and Nasserism and the regimes that drew on them, because it avoids the rather simplistic focus on the slogans and uniforms of fascist self-fashioning. Aside from its appearance, and the shared war experience of those who submitted to it, fascism had a core of ideas, and cannot be reduced to a reaction to the destruction of nineteenth-century society, and to the emergence of Leninist and Stalinist systems – as Nolte's phenomenology would suggest. Instead, the revolutionary roots of fascist thought are in its hatred of the Enlightenment and the modernity it shaped.[85]

The same anti-Enlightenment reasoning did, however, not exist in the Middle East. During the interwar period, admirers of fascism such as Salama Musa (only in the early 1930s) or the young enthusiasts of Iraq and Syria saw themselves in the tradition of the modernizing forces of the Enlightenment, to free up, or make better use of, the potentials of the individual.[86] The authoritarianism of the interwar and immediate post-World War II Arab states was based on paternalistic authoritarian traditions of the late Ottoman polity rather than on the adoption of totalitarian ideas.[87] It has, nevertheless, been argued that the second half of the 1930s in Egypt in particular, but also in the Middle East in general, represents a period of a "crisis of orientation" among intellectuals and a frustration with the perceived failure of the so-called "liberal experiment."[88] Once more, this argument evokes Ernst Nolte's reasoning about the foundations of radical political movements in the interwar period. Nolte suggested that the liberal system – not as a political actuality, but as the dominant worldview of the bourgeoisie – offered the "radical freedom to realize its opposite," and to give in to a "totalitarian temptation."[89] In the Middle East before World War II, generational conflict created a socio-political situation that incited young intellectuals to play with all sorts of radical temptations, but it is almost banal to argue that colonial dependence did not offer Arab politicians and intellectuals enough opportunity to actually "give in" to these temptations in any significant way. The only example of a totalitarian experiment in the Arab Middle East during the first half of the twentieth century was arguably the so-called Rashid 'Ali Movement in Iraq of 1941, which was, however, ambiguous in its orientation, geographically limited and did not last long enough to allow for broad conclusions about the feasibility of totalitarian radicalism in an Arab state.[90] The multipolar relationship between local elites in the Arab lands and their contenders of a younger generation on the one hand, and the British and French imperialist hegemons, as well as the Nazi and fascist challengers of the post-World War I world order (as many Arabs perceived them) on the other created a highly complex cocktail of political opinions and opportunities that is unlike the socio-political situation of sovereign states that paved the way for the ascendance of fascist movements in Europe after 1918. Authoritarian and pro-fascist voices were just a few in a plurality of opinions in the Arab intellectual field, and no one argued for a radical rejection of humanism and reason at the time. In a similar way, the deliberations of Arab politicians in favor of Nazi Germany, and, in a few cases, their decisions about alliances, were conditioned by the peculiar geostrategic contingencies of World War II and should not be interpreted as an ideological endorsement of Nazi worldview, as in Iraq in 1941, or in Tunisia during the German occupation between 1942 and 1943 when monarch Moncef Bey tried to remain equidistant from both the Allies and the Axis powers, or in Egypt during the February Fourth Incident of 1942 when the British, with Rommel advancing, forced King Faruq at gunpoint to give up his idea of appointing his pro-Axis confidant Ali Mahir as Prime Minister.

There is no doubt that right-wing political radicalism did exist in the Arab lands, and it bore resemblances to fascist movements in Europe and worldwide during the interwar period. In other places, like for example Argentina, fascism was received and adopted in a chaotic and unsystematic process, yet one that was pursued by its actors in a very self-conscious manner, in a process of making sense of models perceived from a distance, but in a local context. In a similar way, historians of South Asia are grappling with the question of how to contextualize the manifestations of fascist-inspired thinking among intellectuals like Inayatullah Khan al-Mashriqi and the fascist aesthetics of his *Khaksar* youth movement in the 1930s. In this regard, while there was no such thing as global fascism, it nevertheless became a traveling transnational ideology and a reference point.[91] An open, flexible taxonomy constituting a field of possible manifestations of fascist or fascistic trends is therefore quite useful for a researcher of comparative, global political and ideological movements and their transnational dispersion. This approach is the opposite of what proponents of the Islamofascism paradigm are seeking. They differ, in turn, from researchers who accept only European manifestations of fascism as truly fascist and consider equivalent non-European groups and parties as performing mere mimicry. The proponents of the Islamofascism-thesis use insufficient evidence of individual personal contacts, such as those between the Mufti and Himmler, and a superficial assessment of representations such as those of the nationalist youth movements of the 1930s, to extend the fascist epithet to Arab nationalists and politicized Muslims in their entirety, with the intention to present them as indistinct from fascism's or Nazism's rigorous ideological systems and forms of political practice and extreme violence. The phenomenological approach presented above counters the equation between fascism and Arab nationalism; but even Eurocentric fascism theory itself, if rigidly applied, offers arguments against the conflation of modern Islamism and fascism. On the level of abstraction that recent theorists apply, the essential core of fascism is in the negation of humanist reasoning[92] and the rejection of the Enlightenment. It is arguable, though, that the origins of modern Islamism are precisely on the opposite side. They do not lie in the rejection of reason and science, but in debates about Islamic reform of the nineteenth century and their engagement with reason and science. It would be a matter of debate whether the militant, radical and murderous manifestations of Islamism today are simply aberrations and hence accidental and not essential characteristics of modern Islamism – or whether they are symptomatic of a digression into a "darker" terrain that Islamism entered in the 1960s or so.[93] Nineteenth-century Reformers such as Rifa'a al-Tahtawi, Khayr al-Din al-Tunisi, the Amir 'Abd al-Qadir, Muhammad 'Abduh, and twentieth-century figures like Rashid Rida and 'Abd al-Hamid Ben Badis tried to reconcile the achievements of the European age of reason with the Islamic heritage. Their agenda was to protect the Islamic community against superstition and to claim science and reason for an alternative, Islamic modernity.[94] In the late 1930s, Hassan al-Banna, the Muslim Brotherhood's founder, rejected fascism explicitly, as well as the nationalism and racism raging in Europe, including the persecution of the Jews by the Nazis. Thus he wanted to present the Muslims of his organization not only on a par with Europeans, but even morally superior.[95] If mass organization, fascist-style, and the cult of violence are accidental to fascism, as has been argued, then the same would apply to the extreme manifestations of political Islam – in violence and rhetoric. Consequently, fascism and Islamism would be essentially different in their core: the former rejects, and the latter endorses reason. On a different note, there is also no similarity between Islamism and the *clericofascism* of the extreme right in catholic countries, as the shared religious reference might suggest. Clericofascism represented an alignment between fascist movements and the institutional church.[96] The origins of modern Islamism are, however, in a movement that opposed the religious establishment of Muslim countries, which was perceived as inflexible and hostile to rationality.

In sum, there were movements in the Middle East during the 1930s that consciously chose a discernible fascist outlook, but no groups or parties existed at the time, if ever, that were explicitly fascist by name – unlike Argentina, for example.[97] In contrast, there was a desire among radicals to dissociate themselves from European right-wing ideology, because, among other reasons, they perceived it in the context of a colonial power relationship.

Overall, Middle Eastern movements were *fascistic*,[98] hence merely mimicking fascist style (discipline, uniforms, a discourse of violence) but did not meet the core criterion of fascism to be based on revolutionary expectations and a radical rejection of the Enlightenment – at least during the interwar period, if not beyond. The state-run Futuwwa movement of Iraq, or the militias of the

bourgeois Wafd party in Egypt or the Syrian National Bloc, while at times violent, did not represent a radical agenda. There was no clear-cut anti-communism
or emphasis on racial distinctiveness in these movements. The SSNP in Lebanon
and Syria and Young Egypt are arguably the most explicit manifestations of the
fascistic trend, but obviously they did not build on a World War I trench experience and the ensuing mindset. Their membership was relatively small and
socially, their members were too close to the elites.[99] They did not demand revolutionary change and rebirth, but vied for recognition and generational change.
The name of the nascent Ba'th (Re-birth or Renaissance) party of the 1940s suggests a palingenetic worldview, but it built a substantial social base only when
fusing in Syria with Akram al-Hourani's rurally oriented Arab Socialist Party in
1953, or in Iraq only once permanently in government after 1968. In comparison,
far right nationalism was already a mass movement in the 1930s and 1940s in
Argentina.[100] Both the SSNP's Sa'ada and the founders of the Ba'th party put
"feeling" over "thoughts" in the propagation of political will, which is an element
of fascism theory. But how do we deal with an ideologue like Antun Sa'ada, who
did adopt elements that some consider part of generic fascism, most prominently
the leadership principle and the communitarian vision of society, but who at the
same time explicitly denounced that his party was in any way fascist or pro-Nazi
and even warned his followers not to believe Italian and German propaganda?[101]
This statement is similar to Hassan al-Banna's anti-fascist stance, in that it represents a genuine desire to differ from European models.

A phenomenological approach to Middle Eastern fascist style movements offers the possibility to locate them on a map of social conflicts specific to their
environment rather than giving them too much ideological weight. Some scholars use governmental action as a criterion to distinguish between authoritarian
movements and truly fascist ones once they are in power. The former use propaganda and stylistic motifs that remind of fascism, but accept economic prerog-
atives that contradict their revolutionary agenda; in contrast, true fascists deal
uncompromisingly with existing elite structures.[102] None of the movements we
are looking at in the Arab world ever achieved meaningful political influence
during the 1930s, but even when extreme nationalists took over government in
the second half of the twentieth century, the disconnect between their rhetoric on
the one hand and the actual elite and leadership structures of regimes such as in
Ba'thist Iraq or Syria on the other, shows that official ideology was only a means
to an end where cliques used parties to usurp power, adjusting ideology to their
own immediate needs in the most arbitrary manner.[103]

* * *

To sum up, conventional research about Arab nationalism put a great deal of
emphasis on the nexus between ideology and politics in explaining the confrontational nature and erratic acts of national leaders in the Arab–Israeli conflict,
as well as the nature of dictatorial regimes such as those in Syria and Iraq. More
recently, some publicists have added essentialist visions of Islam as an irrational,

oppressive and xenophobic religion to this brew in order to make sense of a perceived *Clash of Civilizations*, comfortably assigning the roles of friend and foe. This chapter has turned around the vantage point in order to present the usage of ideology and its language as driven by domestic factors and situational as well as personal contingencies. According to this point of view, ideology is a form of representation among others in an endeavor to position Arab states and societies vis-à-vis dominant European paradigms of social organization. In this context, the borrowing and copying of fascistic imagery has been a provocative stance, and language and symbols of totalitarian state organizations have worked as a veneer to conceal the cracks and fissures inside the societies of Arab states, along the lines of class, ethnicity, or sect. In this process, the Jews of Arab lands became a token for the humiliation of Arab societies at the hands of the colonial powers, and therefore served as classic scapegoats. It has been argued that the use of anti-Semitism for scapegoating has been accidental and not an essential element of Arab perceptions of minorities, but it had drastic consequences as the result was the mass exodus of Jews from Arab lands, and the incorporation of anti-Semitic stereotypes into Arab popular culture today.

World War II and the different levels of exposure of Arabs to its implications of violence and worldview have been a crucial trigger in the creation of a myth related to Arab political culture as being prone to fascist style totalitarianism and the rejection of Jews. In a reversal of cause and consequences, proponents of the Islamofascism paradigm argue that Arab inclinations towards fascist symbolism, the (rare) cases of collaboration between Arab nationalist grandees and Nazi politicians, and the deep hostility towards the State of Israel are based on a cultural conditioning in favor of blind obedience and erratic tyranny, as well as deeply rooted anti-Semitism. On the contrary, this chapter argues in concert with other findings of this book that the colonial situation, the late Ottoman heritage of militarism, and the paternalistic tradition of rule combined with the violent potentials of conflicts of class and generational order produced a situation in which Middle Eastern political and social leaders indulged in the mimicry of chauvinistic images of strength and prowess. At times of relative liberal freedom in public opinion, such as the 1930s, there was no shortage of criticism of these approaches, but there was less criticism when dictatorial regimes increasingly curbed these freedoms from the 1950s onwards with sometimes drastically violent consequences.

8 Epilogue and conclusion

Broken narratives

Baikonur, Soviet Kazakhstan, 1987

On July 22, 1987, a Soviet Soyuz spacecraft took off towards the Mir space station carrying Syrian military pilot Lt. Col. Muhammad Faris as one of three crewmembers. The 36-year-old Aleppo resident was supposed to conduct several experiments and to take a number of photographs surveying Syrian land. As more than an added benefit, Syria's dictator Hafiz al-Assad certainly expected significant propagandistic gain from a widely televised video conference with the cosmonauts. The iconic images from Syrian TV, remembered by Syrians to this day, start with a close-up of a small screen on a monitor showing Faris on the left and his four cosmonaut comrades in the background. Faris greeted viewers from "above the skies" and welcomed the opportunity to send his warm regards to President al-Assad and the Arab masses while the camera was zooming out to reveal a frail looking Hafiz al-Assad crouched behind his desk, looking at three tv screens mimicking a control room. room. Assad asked Faris to pass on his greetings to his comrades and inquired about his well-being. "But now, what do you see from so high above the earth?" he asked.

> Mister President, I am very happy because I see my beloved country, protecting and beautiful as it truly is. ... I see majestic Jabal al-Shaykh and the beloved Golan ... I am very happy about this sight.[1]

What stood out for Faris was therefore not Damascus or his home town Aleppo, or the Euphrates, but the two sites that represented in their essence Syria's modern struggle, on behalf of the Arab nation, against the Zionist enemy: Jabal al-Shaykh or Mount Hermon, as well as the Golan. Both places had witnessed short-lived Syrian victories in the 1973 war. They stood for Syria's mission to make good on Israel's incursions into Arab territory. It is more than likely that Faris' remarks were not spontaneous, but had been rehearsed to convey a well-known propagandistic message, even from space.

A quarter century later, Muhammad Faris was on television again, being interviewed on Arabic news stations as the Syrian hero who had defected from Assad's military to join the opposition of the Free Syrian Army in 2012. He was in the spotlight as a hero-celebrity, but interviewers also questioned him about his past as a symbol of loyalty to the regime's controlled narrative, which had now become a broken narrative.[2]

Baghdad, June 1989

Michel 'Aflaq, the founder of the Ba'th party, who had left Syria in the wake of the 1966 military coup to take up exile in Baghdad, had died in a Paris hospital on June 23. Iraq's President, Saddam Hussein, did not miss the opportunity to use the funeral and burial of the grand old man to legitimize his rule less than a year after the end of the Iran–Iraq war. In the reports and the coverage of the funerary festivities that followed 'Aflaq's death, Saddam Hussein featured as prominently as 'Aflaq himself: 'Aflaq was depicted as the "Founding Leader," Hussein as the "Leader President." It was Hussein, not 'Aflaq's family, who at first accepted condolences from heads of states and associations and individuals that came in via national and international telegraph. There are countless pictures in the press of these days showing 'Aflaq sitting with Hussein. In a contextual reading of the texts and images, the relationship of 'Aflaq and Hussein appeared as one of true father and son, where Hussein, who marched at the front of 'Aflaq's funerary cortège, accepted the legacy of the founder of the Ba'th, rather as a legitimate inheritance from father to son, than merely as a bequest from one generation to the next.[3]

The vulgarity of this approach and its brazenness became manifest in a bombshell that is hidden as a quasi-casual comment between the lines of a front-page article of the June 25 issue of *al-Jumhuriyya*. In the middle of the announcement of 'Aflaq's death and his praise as a nationalist leader, in no particular context, the article mentioned:

> The national and regional leaderships would like to announce on the occasion of the death of the grand deceased that he – God have mercy on him – had just embraced Islam as his religion. He and his comrades in leadership did not want to make this public in order to avoid that any political meaning would be given to this choice.[4]

This is as far as references to religious orientations in the countless articles and references to 'Aflaq go in the newspapers of the day. It is tempting to interpret the Islamization of 'Aflaq as a way for Saddam Hussein to avoid having to attend a Christian funerary ceremony at a time when he was trying to bolster his credentials as a Muslim.

On June 26, 'Aflaq was buried in the garden of the headquarters of the Ba'th party, near the Tigris river. According to the newspaper, there were no public speeches, eulogies or any other attempts to give the event an immediate meaning in a public space. No onlookers were mentioned, and none appear on the photos printed in the newspapers. It is unlikely that the "sons of the people" that allegedly took part were spontaneous participants in this highly controlled and restricted location. Obviously, 'Aflaq's funeral was staged in its entirety for television cameras as a festival of vulgar nationalism with no room for public contestation.[5]

Since the US-led conquest of Baghdad in April 2003, 'Aflaq's mausoleum has been in the center of the Green Zone, across from a former presidential palace, and a stone's throw from the new American embassy. For a while in 2006, US soldiers used the mausoleum as a recreation room, including weights and a foosball table, completing the degradation of the man.[6]

Cairo, April 2012

In the spring of 2012, steadfast protesters still occupied the central traffic circle of Tahrir Square a year after the revolution. A liberal atmosphere prevailed during the days before Muhammad Mursi's temporary takeover in presidential elections, and a year before a new round of violent confrontations would lead to the downfall of Mursi's Muslim Brotherhood and the return of the military to rule with an even tighter fist than before.

On the Gezira Island, across the Nile from Tahrir Square and to the right, near the Cairo Opera complex, massive boxwood hedges concealed a wrought iron gate that once opened to the Al-Andalus Garden. A commemorative plaque marked the 1985 renovation of *Hadiqat al-Andalus* having taken place in the "era of Mister President Husni Mubarak" ("fi 'ahd al-sayyid al-ra'is …"). Mubarak's name has been inscribed on monuments all over the city, in a way reminiscent of the markings that ancient pharaohs left on the country's heritage. In the spring of 2012, graffiti had been sprayed over the name of this most hated president to counteract the hegemonic definition of space – a futile effort because the incised letters remained visible underneath. There were probably too many of these plaques in Cairo, from Mamluk mosques to early twentieth century residences, for Mubarak's name to be easily erased within a short period of time – a fact that spoke to the inertia of inscribed memory. An additional plaque next to the entrance gate reminded visitors that the name *al-Andalus* is not only a direct reference to the gardens of Muslim Spain but contains an entire Arab dream space: the park is "Hadiqat al-Firdaus al-'Arabiyya" – "The Garden of the Arab Paradise." Founded in the 1930s, the park occupies a space in Cairene urban life today as an oasis amidst the buzz of the city and is a popular meeting place for amorous couples. The entrance has been moved around the corner onto Al-Gesira Street; originally, visitors coming from the iron gate would have passed a marble structure that mimics the lion fountain in the Alhambra of Granada, with a massive column in the center. The bark of the palm trees surrounding the fountain is covered with carved romantic messages. Behind it, a water basin stretches out, with stairs at its far end leading up to a terraced rectangular structure with bronze lions as water spouts. A pavilion on top of the terrace completes an ensemble that is reminiscent of the Generalife gardens in Granada. In the center of the pavilion thrones an effigy of Ahmad Shawqi, the Prince of Poets and father of the *al-Andalus* revival in the modern Arab world. Many streets, squares and public spaces bear the *al-Andalus* name in the Arab world. Like in Cairo, such places inscribe the interplay of nostalgia, concrete architectural references, and official public commemoration onto the topography of the city.[7]

The capital on top of the column at the old entrance bears as an inscription a verse from the *al-Kahf* Sura of the Qur'an describing Paradise as a place "[w]herein they will abide, with no desire to be removed from thence" (18:108, The Cave, trsl. M.M. Pickthall). The future tense of the verse turns nostalgia for a Golden Age of civilizational splendor into longing for deliverance and a return to the lost paradise – a timeless paradise that seems out of reach even further since the descent into chaos and violence cast a deep shadow over enthusiasm and hope that seemed to unite the Arab lands in the wake of the revolutions of 2011.

Damascus, March 2013

On the twenty-first of the month, a bomb exploded in the Al-Iman Mosque, killing the Syrian State Mufti Salah al-Din al-Buti, who had just set out to deliver a sermon. Born in 1929, al-Buti had a significant career as one of the most favored Sunni scholars of the regime, which made him head preacher of the Umayyad Mosque in 2008, and as a steadfast proponent of a moderate Sunni orthodoxy. The bombing allegedly killed dozens of people in the audience, but there is disagreement in the media whether the assassination was the work of the Syrian opposition or had been instigated by the regime itself. Two days after the crime, crowds streamed into the Umayyad Mosque to attend al-Buti's funeral and to listen to the sheikh's son thanking Bashar al-Assad for the personal condolences that he had delivered over the phone, and to watch how after prayers, al-Buti's body was carried out of the courtyard, in a quasi-replay of 1937, towards Salah al-Din's mausoleum, where he was lowered into a grave that had been dug inside the tomb, next to the two sarcophagi of the medieval Sultan. Opposition members condemned the appropriation of the site as a travesty. Like Salah al-Din, al-Buti was of Kurdish origin, but that aside, what other connection did the regime see between the two men? If nothing else, the mausoleum retained its function as a Panthéon in 2013, though in the familiar vulgarized style of late Ba'thist nationalism.[8]

* * *

The chapters of this book have presented many broken narratives like the ones that appear in these four more or less contemporary vignettes – between the rather lofty goal of an Arab conquest of Space, the desperate attempts to claim the legacy of legendary forbears ('Aflaq, Salah al-Din), and the longing for a realm of love rooted in the past of an Andalusian Arab Elysium in the midst of rupture and unrest. The narratives of this book consist of sub- and supra-texts clashing with each other, they reveal frictions between hegemonic aspirations and unwieldy populism, or between intended meanings projected onto space and its usage in people's daily routines. The events that have been unfolding in the Arab world since the turn of the year 2011 are just one such breaking point after a century of revolutions, coups, or world and regional wars, on top of the *longue-durée* transformations that resulted from imperialist entanglement. But even though the world of Fu'ad al-Khatib is no more, and even if the grand expectations of his youth may have been betrayed by the vicissitudes of twentieth-century politics and social disruptions, his voice of nostalgia, speaking out of his poetry, still rings with Arabs of today as a form of cultural self-assertion against the odds of historical dynamics beyond the control of individuals. Shared myths constitute a vehicle to define the place of Arabs, across a vast geographical space stretching over several continents. Next to benign references to a shared heritage, there is belligerent imagery such as that of Tariq Ibn Ziyad's conquest of al-Andalus or the warrior leadership of Salah al-Din, which are common identifiers for Arabs, too. They are malleable enough to function as unifying braces for Muslims and Christians, the secular and the religiously conservative alike, though admittedly to different degrees at different times. Still, the narrative remains intact.

Arab cultural identity has been and continues to be contested, though. Areas of contestation exist within nation states, as the chapter about museology in Egypt and the debates about a defining narrative in the context of Cairo's Civilization Museum has indicated, but they also exist between nation states and their specific ideological pre-dispositions that are represented in ideological movements. The various efforts of Syrian parties and Iraqi or Algerian rulers at different times highlight these tensions, as the chapter on nationalist funerary practices and con-testations has shown. Belligerence, rejection, and a cult of military prowess have become an essential part of the symbolism, imagery, and performative practice of Arab nationalism – a trend that goes back to the central role that military prowess took on during the period of the formation of nationalist discourse in the Arab lands in the interwar period – but even this discourse has its roots in the militari-zation of Ottoman patriotism before World War I. The chapter on the esthetics of militarism in Egypt and Syria described the increasing vulgarity of this military symbolism, and how it coincided with an increase in the monumentality of pic-torial and architectural representations of Arab military authoritarianism, taking its purest form as a vehicle for clique and family interest in regimes such as those of Assad, Mubarak, and Saddam Hussein. Not only the defeats of Arab armies in consecutive wars (1948, 1956, 1967, 1973, 1991, 2003, to name only the most prominent ones) point to the hollowness of militarist representation. The descent of Arab armies into willing tools of mere regime protection has discredited mili-tarist imagery for good: in Iraq during and after Saddam Hussein's rule, in Egypt during the re-emergence of military rule since 2013 – even if many Egyptians still seem to cling to a picture of the army as the protector of national integrity, in the apparent absence of a viable alternative – and most clearly in the Syrian civil war since 2011. The decreasing ambivalence in the relationship and references by Arab nationalists to fascist ideology and its anti-Semitic content attest to a similar trend in the ideological positioning among Arab regimes and a signifi-cant number of intellectuals towards vulgarity and simplicity. It remains to be seen if this vulgarity can prevail. Migrations, exposure to modern media, and the disillusionment with demagogues, military technocrats and dictators motivated people to challenge the status quo in 2011, and some of the corrupt proponents of clientelism and clique-rule disguised as sectarianism have fallen. In spite of the recent backlash of authoritarianism, the pluralism of the modern world, and the movement of people between societies might ultimately promote positive identification and interactions based on mutual respect, even if many Arabs today still express their frustration about hierarchies of power rooted in a colonial past in terms of a culture war. Middle Eastern and Western, Arab and European, Muslim and Christian identities are as entangled today as they always have been – in a process of constant mirroring and positive as well as negative identification. This entanglement has been a sub-topic that runs through all the chapters of this study.

Another primary argument of this book has been about the adoption and adaptation of Western means of expression and media in Arab nationalism. While an assessment would fall short that Arab nationalism is a mere copycat of European ideology, it is nonetheless clear that the culture of Arab nationalism as presented here built on the hegemonic incursion of Western media (novel, theater, film, pamphlet, newspaper, monumental art) into the Middle Eastern realm. In fact, the culture of Arab nationalism is in the creative appropriation of these media, at times in subtle, at other times in vulgar ways. The goal of this book has been therefore to identify, or at least inquire about agency in this appropriation process. Actors drew from a wide variety of sources in the different eclectic pursuits that have been showcased here. It remains a challenge for the historian to identify grass-roots responses and dissidence to the appropriations that were dominated by the elites most of the time. Only echoes of these responses tend to appear in the sources. Hence, this book constitutes only one step in a critical re-assessment of the twentieth-century roots of Arab nationalist cultural identities in the twenty-first century.

Notes

Avant-Propos

1 Peter Wien, "The Long and Intricate Funeral of Yasin Al-Hashimi: Pan-Arabism, Civil Religion, and Popular Nationalism in Damascus, 1937," *International Journal of Middle East Studies* 43 (2011): 271–92; "Arabs and Fascism: Empirical and Theoretical Perspectives," *Die Welt des Islams* 52 (2012): 331–50; "The Culpability of Exile. Arabs in Nazi Germany," *Geschichte und Gesellschaft* 37 (2011): 332–58.

1 Introduction

1 There is a modern school of theoretical literature on nationalism by authors such as Benedict Anderson, Dipesh Chakrabarty, Partha Chatterjee, Ernest Gellner, Miroslav Hroch, and Anthony D. Smith, to name only the most outstanding representatives, who have set the parameters for all modern scholarly debates about nationalism. Their terminology is common enough that it does not require detailed elaboration or referencing in this context. Particular aspects of works will be quoted where needed in subsequent chapters.

2 On modernization theory see Nils Gilman, *Mandarins of the Future: Modernization Theory in Cold War America* (Baltimore: Johns Hopkins University Press, 2003), 1–12 and passim. A classic work based on the "rise and decline" narrative of Arab nationalism as a political ideology, based on a dichotomy between secularism and religiosity, is Bassam Tibi, *Arab Nationalism: A Critical Enquiry*, eds. Marion Farouk-Sluglett and Peter Sluglett (New York: St. Martin's Press, 1981); first published as Bassam Tibi, *Nationalismus in der Dritten Welt am arabischen Beispiel* (Frankfurt am Main, 1971); and now in its third, updated revision as Bassam Tibi, *Arab Nationalism: Between Islam and the Nation-State* (New York: St. Martin's Press, 1997). Most recently, the story of "rise and decline" has been pronounced in a pointed way in Adeed Dawisha, *Arab Nationalism in the Twentieth Century: From Triumph to Despair* (Princeton, NJ: Princeton University Press, 2003). A broad historiographical approach is in Youssef M. Choueiri, *Arab Nationalism: A History. Nation and State in the Arab World* (Oxford, Malden: Blackwell, 2000).

3 Israel Gershoni, "Rethinking the Formation of Arab Nationalism in the Middle East, 1920–1945. Old and New Narratives," in *Rethinking Nationalism in the Arab Middle East*, eds. James P. Jankowski and Israel Gershoni (New York: Columbia University Press, 1997), 3–25. More recently, Stephen Sheehi re-examined works of eminent writers of the *nahda* period, or the Arab cultural renaissance, in the nineteenth and early twentieth centuries to identify notions of an Arab subjectivity that emerged in the literary field, in *Foundations of Modern Arab Identity* (Gainesville: University Press of Florida, 2004), 12–14, passim.

4 Whether these people focused their desires on the creation of a unified state with defined borders is of lesser concern to this study. Compare the controversy between Israel Gershoni and James Jankoski on the one hand and Charles D. Smith on the other in *IJMES*: Charles D. Smith, "'Imagined Identities, Imagined Nationalisms: Print Culture and Egyptian Nationalism in Light of Recent Scholarship.' A Review Essay of Israel Gershoni and James P. Jankowski, Redefining the Egyptian Nation, 1930–1945, Cambridge Middle East Studies (New York: Cambridge University Press, 1995), p297," *International Journal of Middle East Studies* 29 (1997): 607–22; Israel Gershoni and James Jankowski, "Print Culture, Social Change, and the Process of Redefining Imagined Communities in Egypt; Response to the Review by Charles D. Smith of Redefining the Egyptian Nation," *International Journal of Middle East Studies* 31 (1999): 81–94; Charles D. Smith, "'Cultural Constructs' and Other Fantasies: Imagined Narratives in Imagined Communities; Surrejoinder to Gershoni and Jankowski's 'Print Culture, Social Change, and the Process of Redefining Imagined Communities in Egypt,'" *International Journal of Middle East Studies* 31 (1999): 95–102. Compare also Dawisha, *Arab Nationalism*, 1–13.

5 A recent example for a monograph that transcends the usual geographical boundaries of Arab nationalism research is Amal N. Ghazal, *Islamic Reform and Arab Nationalism: Expanding the Crescent from the Mediterranean to the Indian Ocean (1880s–1930s)* (London: Routledge, 2010), passim.

6 Peter Gran, *Islamic Roots of Capitalism: Egypt, 1760–1840*, 2nd edn. (Syracuse, NY: Syracuse University Press, 1998), 56–75; Nelly Hanna, *In Praise of Books: A Cultural History of Cairo's Middle Class, Sixteenth to the Eighteenth Century* (Syracuse, NY: Syracuse University Press, 2003), passim. Detailed references for the "Enlightenment" debate are below.

7 For a balanced discussion of these arguments see the introduction to Nehemia Levtzion and John Obert Voll eds. *Eighteenth-Century Renewal and Reform in Islam* (Syracuse, NY: Syracuse University Press, 1987), 3–20; and John O. Voll, "Linking Groups in the Networks of Eighteenth-Century Revivalist Scholars: The Mizjaji Family in Yemen," in *Eighteenth-Century Renewal and Reform in Islam*, ed. Nehemia Levtzion and John Obert Voll (Syracuse, NY: Syracuse University Press, 1987), 81–90. Dale F. Eickelman and Armando Salvatore, "Muslim Publics," in *Public Islam and the Common Good*, eds. Armando Salvatore and Dale F. Eickelman, Social, Economic, and Political Studies of the Middle East and Asia, 95 (Leiden, Boston: Brill, 2004), 12, endorses the argument that Neo-Sufism played a distinctive role in creating a public sphere in Muslim societies.

8 See the example in Bernd Radtke, "Erleuchtung und Aufklärung: Islamische Mystik und europäischer Rationalismus," *Die Welt des Islams* 34 (1994): 57–60.

9 The most important critical engagement with the Neo-Sufism paradigm is R.S. O'Fahey and Bernd Radtke, "Neo-Sufism Reconsidered," *Der Islam* 70 (1993): 52–87. A more up-to-date summary and reply is in John O. Voll, "Neo-Sufism: Reconsidered Again," *Canadian Journal of African Studies* 42 (2008): 314–30. See also the nuanced critique in Khaled El-Rouayheb, "Was There a Revival of Logical Studies in Eighteenth-Century Egypt?" *Die Welt des Islams* 45 (2005): 1–19. He develops a much broader argument in Khaled El-Rouayheb, *Islamic Intellectual History in the Seventeenth Century: Scholarly Currents in the Ottoman Empire and the Maghreb* (Cambridge: Cambridge University Press, 2015), passim.

10 R.S. O'Fahey, *Enigmatic Saint: Ahmad Ibn Idris and the Idrisi Tradition* (Evanston: Northwestern University Press, 1990), 2–9.

11 The controversy took place primarily in German academic circles. See, in chronological order, Reinhard Schulze, "Das islamische achtzehnte Jahrhundert: Versuch einer historiographischen Kritik," *Die Welt des Islams* 30 (1990): 140–59; Rudolph Peters, "Reinhard Schulze's Quest for an Islamic Enlightenment," *Die Welt des*

Islams 30 (1990): 160–2; Radtke, "Erleuchtung und Aufklärung," 48–66; Reinhard Schulze, "Was ist die islamische Aufklärung?," *Die Welt des Islams* 36 (1996): 276–325; Gottfried Hagen and Tilman Seidensticker, "Reinhard Schulzes Hypothese einer islamischen Aufklärung. Kritik einer historiographischen Kritik," *Zeitschrift der Deutschen Morgenländischen Gesellschaft* 148 (1998): 83–110. Much criticism was leveled against the inaccuracies of Schulze's philological record. See also, most recently, El-Rouayheb, *Islamic Intellectual History*, 8–10.

12 In a 1996 article, Radtke conceded on the basis of close readings of eighteenth-century Sufi literature that there was a striking focus on Muhammad among many Sufi authorities of the time, including a certain humanization of God ("God does draw closer") and a tendency towards "anthropocentrism" and "a rejection of 'supra-personal' authority." Nevertheless, Radtke did not accept the notion of an Enlightenment tendency in Islam at the time, as he could not identify rationalist approaches to law and jurisprudence in the texts he read. See Bernd Radtke, "Sufism in the 18th Century: An Attempt at a Provisional Appraisal," *Die Welt des Islams* 36 (1996): 360–61 and passim; quotes on p361. Arguably, rationalism had not played a central role as an Enlightenment characteristic in Schulze's argumentation in the first place.

13 See the discussion of *class* as a historical category in Sami Zubaida, *Islam, the People and the State: Essays on Political Ideas and Movements in the Middle East*, 2nd edn. (London; New York: I.B. Tauris, 1993), 83–98. For a summary of economic transformations see Roger Owen, *The Middle East in the World Economy, 1800–1914* (London; New York: Methuen, 1981), 287–93. For the emergence of a working class see Joel Beinin and Zachary Lockman, *Workers on the Nile: Nationalism, Communism, Islam, and the Egyptian Working Class, 1882–1954* (Cairo: The American University in Cairo Press, 1998), 23–47 and passim.

14 As described in Peter Wien, *Iraqi Arab Nationalism: Authoritarian, Totalitarian and Pro-Fascist Inclinations, 1932–1941* (London; New York: Routledge, 2006), passim.

15 The effects of the imperialist encounter are summarized in Julia A. Clancy-Smith, *Rebel and Saint: Muslim Notables, Populist Protest, Colonial Encounters (Algeria and Tunisia, 1800–1904)* (Berkeley, CA: University of California Press, 1994), 254–65. On press and propaganda see Kemal H Karpat, *The Politicization of Islam: Reconstructing Identity, State, Faith, and Community in the Late Ottoman State* (Oxford: Oxford University Press, 2001), 117–35. On World War I in the Arab East see Hasan Kayali, *Arabs and Young Turks: Ottomanism, Arabism, and Islamism in the Ottoman Empire, 1908–1918* (Berkeley; Los Angeles; London: University of California Press, 1997), 174–205.

16 Stefan Wild, "Islamic Enlightenment and the Paradox of Averroes," *Die Welt des Islams* 36 (1996): 379–90. For the continuing heritage ("turath") and authenticity debate in the Arab world see: Sabine Damir-Geilsdorf, "Politische Utopie und Erinnerung: Das 'Goldene Zeitalter' in islamischen Diskursen heute," in Angelika Hartmann (ed.) *Geschichte und Erinnerung im Islam*, Formen der Erinnerung 15 (Göttingen: Vandenhoeck & Ruprecht, 2004), 77; Joseph Massad, *Desiring Arabs* (Chicago: University of Chicago Press, 2007), 16–29; Geert Hendrich, *Islam und Aufklärung: Der Modernediskurs in der arabischen Philosophie* (Darmstadt: Wissenschaftliche Buchgesellschaft, 2004), 153–63. (The author would like to thank Niels Riecken for pointing out some of these references.) Recently, Thomas Bauer has added another dimension to this debate, identifying a general move away from ambiguity to strict Cartesian logic among modern Muslim thinkers. Bauer, however, does not comment on the Islamic Enlightenment debate. See Thomas Bauer, *Die Kultur der Ambiguität: Eine andere Geschichte des Islams* (Berlin: Verlag der Weltreligionen, 2011), passim.

17 Compare El-Rouayheb, *Islamic Intellectual History*, part iii.

18 The arguments are laid out in Itzchak Weismann, *Taste of Modernity: Sufism, Salafi-yya, and Arabism in Late Ottoman Damascus*, Islamic History and Civilization 34 (Leiden; Boston: Brill, 2001), 5, 16–19, 105–9, 127–33, 147–303. See also the contro-versy over the Rifaʻi sheikh and Sultan's favorite Abu'l-Huda al-Sayyadi in Thomas Eich, "The Forgotten salafi – Abul-Huda as-Sayyadi," *Die Welt des Islams* 43 (2003): 61–87; the response in Itzchak Weismann, "Abu L-Huda L-Sayyadi and the Rise of Islamic Fundamentalism," *Arabica* 54 (2007): 586–92; and again Thomas Eich, "Abu L-Huda L-Sayyadi: Still Such a Polarizing Figure (Response to Itzchak Weismann)," *Arabica* 55 (2008): 433–44. See also David Dean Commins, *Islamic Reform: Poli-tics and Social Change in Late Ottoman Syria* (New York: Oxford University Press, 1990), passim. Consider the criticism of terminology in Henri Lauzière, "The Con-struction of Salafiyya: Reconsidering Salafism From the Perspective of Conceptual History," *International Journal of Middle East Studies* 42 (2010): 369–89.

19 Compare Sheehi, *Foundations of Modern Arab Identity*, 71–5.

20 Arab nationalist thought and ideology are embedded in discourses of the majority religion in a deeper sense than a mere integration into an "Islamicate" realm – the Islamicness of this realm is essential, and not merely accidental. Compare and con-trast Marshall G.S. Hodgson, *The Venture of Islam: Conscience and History in a World Civilization*, vol. 1 (Chicago: University of Chicago Press, 1974), 57–60.

21 Angelika Hartmann, "Einleitung," in Angelika Hartmann (ed.) *Geschichte und Erin-nerung im Islam*, Formen der Erinnerung 15 (Göttingen: Vandenhoeck & Ruprecht, 2004), 13.

22 I. Gershoni and James P. Jankowski, *Redefining the Egyptian Nation, 1930–1945* (Cambridge; New York: Cambridge University Press, 1995), 55–61, esp. 57; Charles D. Smith, *Islam and the Search for Social Order in Modern Egypt: A Biography of Muhammad Husayn Haykal* (Albany: State University of New York Press, 1983), 109–30. Haykal's book has been published in numerous editions, an early one be-ing Muhammad Husayn Haykal, *Hayat Muhammad* (Cairo: Matbaʻat Dar al-Kutub al-Misriyya, 1936).

23 Rashid Khalidi, "Arab Nationalism: Historical Problems in the Literature," *American Historical Review* 96.5 (1991): 1369–71. He refers to Sylvia Haim and Elie Kedourie in this context, and introduces Albert Hourani's and C. Ernest Dawn's writings as more nuanced.

24 Sami Zubaida, "Islam and Nationalism: Continuities and Contradictions," *Nations and Nationalism* 10 (2004): 407f. The article puts into print Zubaida's 2003 Ernest Gellner Nationalism Lecture.

25 See the portrayals of the era and the place in Stefan Wild, "Gott und Mensch im Libanon: Die Affäre Sadiq al-ʻAzm," *Der Islam* 48 (1972): 206–53; Omar Kamil, *Der Holocaust im arabischen Gedächtnis: Eine Diskursgeschichte 1945–1967*, Schriften des Simon-Dubnow-Instituts 15 (Göttingen: Vandenhoeck & Ruprecht, 2012), 127–66. For a taste of al-ʻAzm's criticism of the political usage of religion see Akram Fouad Khater (ed.) "Sadiq Al-ʻAzm, an Arab Intellectual, Critiques the Arab State and Clergy for Their Use of Religion, 1968," in *Sources in the History of the Modern Middle East*, 2nd edn. (Boston: Houghton Mifflin, 2011), 225–8. The chapter translates an excerpt from Sadiq Jalal ʻAzm, *Naqd al-fikr al-dini* (Beirut: Dar al-Taliʻa, 1969), the author's key work. See also Wild, "Gott und Mensch," 224–6.

26 On the term *hybridity* in the context of education see Benjamin C. Fortna, "Islamic Morality in Late Ottoman 'Secular' Schools," *International Journal of Middle East Studies* 32 (2000): 390 n15.

27 Ibid., 370–3, quotes on 370, 371, 373. The last quote refers to comments that Şerif Mardin delivered at a conference in 1997.

28 Published as Michel ʻAflaq, *Dhikra al-Rasul al-ʻArabi* (Beirut: Al-Muʼassasa al-ʻArabiyya li'l-Dirasat wa'l-Nashr, 1972).

29 On the master and disciple relationship and the secrecy see Christoph Schu-mann, *Radikalnationalismus in Syrien und Libanon: Politische Sozialisation und*

Elitenbildung 1930–1958 (Hamburg: Deutsches Orient-Institut, 2001), 280f, 292–5, 300f; Keith D. Watenpaugh, "'Creating Phantoms': Zaki Al-Arsuzi, the Alexandretta Crisis, and the Formation of Modern Arab Nationalism in Syria," *International Journal of Middle East Studies* 28 (1996): 381f. According to Batatu, Arsuzi "remained much of a 'Alawi" in the spirituality of his thought. Both 'Aflaq and Bitar grew up in Damascus' Midan quarter when it was a center of religious agitation. See Hanna Batatu, *The Old Social Classes and the Revolutionary Movements of Iraq: A Study of Iraq's Old Landed and Commercial Classes and of Its Communists, Ba'thists, and Free Officers* (Princeton, NJ: Princeton University Press, 1978), 723–5, quote on 723.

30 'Aflaq, *Dhikra al-Rasul al-'Arabi*, 9, 11f.

31 Samir al-Khalil, *Republic of Fear: The Politics of Modern Iraq* (Berkeley; Los Angeles: University of California Press, 1989), 129–31 (the historical parallel), 197–201 ('Aflaq's speech); for a critique see Dina Rizk Khoury, "History and Historiography of Modern Iraq," *Middle East Studies Association Bulletin* 39, no. 1 (June 1, 2005): 70–2. In the run-up to the 2003 US-led invasion of Iraq, many supporters of the American intervention used Makiya's historical parallels as legitimating evidence.

32 Khalil, *Republic of Fear: The Politics of Modern Iraq*, 199–201, quote on 200; Batatu, *The Old Social Classes*, 733.

33 'Aflaq, *Dhikra al-Rasul al-'Arabi*; an English translation of the speech is in Akram Fouad Khater, *Sources in the History of the Modern Middle East*, 2nd edn. (Boston: Houghton Mifflin, 2011), 130–5.

34 Schumann, *Radikalnationalismus in Syrien und Libanon*, 282–5.

35 *Al-Istiqlal*, August 8, 1940, pp1,4.

36 Compare Wien, *Iraqi Arab Nationalism*, 52–112.

37 On the heroism of early Muslim warriors see ibid., 100. On the "salafiyya," see Lauzière, "The Construction of Salafiyya," passim.

38 On the respective *shu'ubiyya* debate see Orit Bashkin, *The Other Iraq: Pluralism and Culture in Hashemite Iraq* (Stanford: Stanford University Press, 2008), 170–1; Eric Davis, *Memories of State: Politics, History, and Collective Identity in Modern Iraq* (Berkeley: University of California Press, 2005), 184–8. On the socio-linguistic dimension of the terms *'ajam/a'ajim* and *shu'ubiyya* see also Yasir Suleiman, *The Arabic Language and National Identity: A Study in Ideology* (Edinburgh: Edinburgh University Press, 2003), 55–63.

39 Quotes in *al-Istiqlal*, August 8, 1940, pp1,4: "Dustur Muhammad wa'l-quwa al-manshuda."

40 *Al-Ahram*, July 29, 1908, p1: "'Id al-Dustur." On the 1861 constitution in Tunisia see Nathan J. Brown, *Constitutions in a Nonconstitutional World: Arab Basic Laws and the Prospects for Accountable Government* (Albany: State University of New York Press, 2002), 16. See also: ed.; B. Lewis, M. Khadduri, A.K.S. Lambton, J.A.M. Caldwell, A. Gledhill, Ch. Pellat, "Dustur." *Encyclopaedia of Islam, Second Edition*, eds. P. Bearman, Th. Bianquis, C.E. Bosworth, E. van Donzel, W.P. Heinrichs Brill Online, 2015. Reference. University of Maryland – College Park, http://referenceworks.brillonline.com/entries/encyclopaedia-of-islam-2/dustur-COM_0199, date of access: May 21, 2015. In Ottoman Turkish, "düstur" denoted a published government register of new laws, but not a constitution.

41 On the nineteenth and early twentieth-century tradition of Islamic reform in Baghdad see Itzchak Weismann, "Genealogies of Fundamentalism: Salafi Discourse in Nineteenth-Century Baghdad," *British Journal of Middle Eastern Studies* 36 (2009): 267–80.

42 Similar thoughts are outlined in James L. Gelvin, "Pensée 1: 'Arab Nationalism' Meets Social Theory," *International Journal of Middle East Studies* 41 (2009): 11–12. See also Albert Hourani's quote: "… how was complete secularism compatible with the existence of an Arab sentiment? In real life dilemmas need not be resolved, they can be lived, and most Arabs who thought about the subject were

content to affirm both terms of it; non-Muslim Arabs are fully a part of the Arab nation, but Islam is the basis of the corporate sense of the Arabs." Albert Habib Hourani, *Arabic Thought in the Liberal Age, 1798–1939* (Cambridge: Cambridge University Press, 1983), 297, see also 296–307.

43 Talal Asad, *Formations of the Secular: Christianity, Islam, Modernity* (Stanford, CA: Stanford University Press, 2003), 190–4; Charles Taylor, *A Secular Age* (Cambridge, MA: Belknap Press of Harvard University Press, 2007), 19–21, passim.

44 Asad, *Formations of the Secular*, 196–201, quotes on 197.

45 Ibid., 181–7, "deprivatized" quote on 186; see also Armando Salvatore and Dale F. Eickelman, "Preface," in *Public Islam and the Common Good*, eds. Armando Salvatore and Dale F. Eickelman, Social, Economic, and Political Studies of the Middle East and Asia, 95 (Leiden, Boston: Brill, 2004), xv–xvii, "social imaginary" quote on xvii, quoting Charles Taylor; compare Eickelman and Salvatore, "Muslim Publics," 13–24. The present and other theses about "secularity" and socio-cultural transformation that are made in the present book should be weighed against the chapter "The Age of Mobilization" in Taylor, *A Secular Age*, 423–72.

46 Hartmann, "Einleitung," 14.

47 Quote in Gelvin, "Pensée 1," 10. The classic work of this intellectual history approach is still Hourani, *Arabic Thought in the Liberal Age, 1798–1939*, for example 307–23. A close reading of Hourani's book reveals, however, many more subtleties than works such as the various editions of Tibi, *Arab Nationalism*; or Choueiri, *Arab Nationalism*; and Dawisha, *Arab Nationalism*. See the critique in Fred Halliday, "Pensée 3: The Modernity of the Arabs," *International Journal of Middle East Studies* 41 (2009): 16–18; Fred H. Lawson, "Pensée 4: Out With the Old, in With the New," *International Journal of Middle East Studies* 41 (2009): 19–21.

48 See the persistence of hegemonic nationalist narratives in the interviews in Ted Swedenburg, *Memories of Revolt: The 1936–1939 Rebellion and the Palestinian National Past* (Minneapolis: University of Minnesota Press, 1995), 19–26, 78–106. See also Emmanuel Sivan, "Arab Nationalism in the Age of the Islamic Resurgence," in *Rethinking Nationalism in the Arab Middle East*, eds. Israel Gershoni and James P. Jankowski (New York: Columbia University Press, 1997), 211–18. Note that Sivan's observations predate the era of the internet and its social media.

49 Timothy Mitchell, *Colonising Egypt* (Berkeley, CA; Los Angeles; London: Cambridge University Press, 1991), 131–54; Hanna, *In Praise of Books: A Cultural History of Cairo's Middle Class, Sixteenth to the Eighteenth Century*, 2–5, 79–103, 139–70. See also El-Rouayheb, *Islamic Intellectual History*, 97–128. He argues that the individual practice of a "deep reading" of books and a loosening of the scholar–disciple relationship, too, started in the seventeenth and eighteenth century already.

50 Juan Ricardo Cole, *Colonialism and Revolution in the Middle East: Social and Cultural Origins of Egypt's 'Urabi Movement*, Princeton Studies on the Near East (Princeton, NJ: Princeton University Press, 1993), 110–31; Mitchell, *Colonising Egypt*, 114–27. On the "open" and discursive nature of authoritative text in Islamic society and the impact of print see Brinkley Morris Messick, *The Calligraphic State: Textual Domination and History in a Muslim Society*, Comparative Studies on Muslim Societies 16 (Berkeley, CA: University of California Press, 1993), 21–36, 115–31.

51 Ziad Fahmy, *Ordinary Egyptians: Creating the Modern Nation Through Popular Culture* (Stanford, CA: Stanford University Press, 2011), 3–95, 156–63. Suleiman, *The Arabic Language*, 9–10, argues in a history-of-ideas approach for the prominence of the high language in Arab nationalism.

52 James L. Gelvin, *Divided Loyalties: Nationalism and Mass Politics in Syria at the Close of Empire* (Berkeley, CA: University of California Press, 1998), 1–22 and passim; Fahmy, *Ordinary Egyptians*, 134–66; Abbas K. Kadhim, *Reclaiming Iraq: The 1920 Revolution and the Founding of the Modern State* (Austin: University of Texas Press,

2012), passim. See especially the analysis of the intersection between urban protest, consumer culture, world market entanglement, and a nationalist public sphere in Nancy Y. Reynolds, *A City Consumed: Urban Commerce, the Cairo Fire, and the Politics of Decolonization in Egypt* (Stanford, CA: Stanford University Press, 2012), passim.

53 A recent study that shares some of the conceptual points of departure of this book, and that approaches them from a grass-roots perspective is Mériam N. Belli, *An Incurable Past: Nasser's Egypt Then and Now* (Gainesville: University Press of Florida, 2013), passim.

2 The trials and tribulations of the poet Fu'ad al-Khatib

1 Edmund Burke, "Middle Eastern Societies and Ordinary People's Lives," in *Struggle and Survival in the Modern Middle East*, ed. Edmund Burke (Berkeley: University of California Press, 1993), 1–27; Gershon Shafir and Mark LeVine, "Introduction: Social Biographies in Making Sense of History," in *Struggle and Survival in Palestine/Israel*, eds. Mark LeVine and Gershon Shafir (Berkeley, CA: University of California Press, 2012), 1–20; For the usage of biography to trace historical experience see Christoph Schumann, "The Generation of Broad Expectations: Nationalism, Education and Autobiography in Syria and Lebanon, 1930–1958," *Die Welt Des Islams* 41 (2001): 174–205; and more broadly Christoph Schumann, *Radikalnationalismus in Syrien und Libanon: Politische Sozialisation und Elitenbildung 1930–1958* (Hamburg: Deutsches Orient-Institut, 2001), passim. For examples of the benefits of using biography to illustrate broader lines in the history of the Arab lands see Eugene Rogan, *The Arabs: A History* (New York: Basic Books, 2009). An especially rich collection of scholarship on biographical and autobiographical writing in the Middle East, including articles on early modern subjects, is in Mary Ann Fay (ed.) *Auto/biography and the Construction of Identity and Community in the Middle East* (New York: Palgrave, 2001), passim.

2 Compare Dina Rizk Khoury, "Ambiguities of the Modern: The Great War in the Memoirs and Poetry of the Iraqis," in *The World in World Wars: Experiences, Perceptions and Perspectives from Africa and Asia*, eds. Heike Liebau et al., *Studies in Global Social History* 5 (Leiden, Boston: Brill, n.d.), 313–40.

3 Searches in a wide array of newspapers in the Reading Room of the Africa and Middle East Division of the Library of Congress did not yield any results.

4 Ihsan Fu'ad Khatib, *Wamadat min 'umr al-zaman: Qabasat min hayat al-Shaykh Fu'ad al-Khatib, sha'ir al-thawra al-'Arabiyya al-kubra* (Beirut: Dar al-'Ilm li'l-Malayin, 1994).

5 Fu 'ad al-Khatib, *Diwan al-Khatib*, ed. Riyad al-Khatib (Cairo: Dar al-Ma'arif, 1959); Imtinan al-Samadi, *Shi'r Fu'ad al-Khatib fi'l-thawra al-'Arabiyya al-kubra wa'l-Hashimiyya* (Amman: Wizarat al-Thaqafa, 2010). There are a few references to his political role in Joshua Teitelbaum, *The Rise and Fall of the Hashemite Kingdom of Arabia* (New York: New York University Press, 2001), passim.

6 Khatib, *Wamadat min 'umr al-zaman*, 16f, 35; Khatib, *Diwan al-Khatib*, 8f (introduction by the editor).

7 Khatib, *Wamadat min 'umr al-zaman*, 31–3. On photography and modernity in the Ottoman Empire see Nancy Micklewright, "An Ottoman Portrait," *International Journal of Middle East Studies* 40.3 (2008): 372–3. On family politics see Lisa Pollard, *Nurturing the Nation: The Family Politics of Modernizing, Colonizing and Liberating Egypt, 1805–1923* (Berkeley, CA: University of California Press, 2005), 132–49. On family photography in Khedive Isma'il's household see Mona L. Russell, *Creating the New Egyptian Woman: Consumerism, Education, and National Identity, 1863–1922* (New York: Palgrave Macmillan, 2004), 15f. On the paternalistic caliphate see Kemal H. Karpat, *The Politicization of Islam: Reconstructing Identity, State,*

Faith, and Community in the Late Ottoman State (Oxford: Oxford University Press, 2001), 188.

8 Khatib, *Wamadat min 'umr al-zaman*, 15f.

9 Originally published in 1938 in London by Hamish Hamilton. The reference here is in George Antonius, *The Arab Awakening: The Story of the Arab National Movement* (New York: Capricorn Books, 1965), 35–60. See William L. Cleveland, "The Arab Nationalism of George Antonius Reconsidered," in *Rethinking Nationalism in the Arab Middle East* James P. Jankowski and Israel Gershoni (New York: Columbia University Press, 1997), 65–86 and 302, n1.

10 For a summary of the arguments see Rashid Khalidi, "Arab Nationalism: Historical Problems in the Literature," *American Historical Review* 96.5 (1991): 1363–73. See also the path breaking C. Ernest Dawn, *From Ottomanism to Arabism: Essays on the Origins of Arab Nationalism* (Urbana: University of Illinois Press, 1973), esp. 122–47; Karpat, *The Politicization of Islam*, 241–57; Hasan Kayali, *Arabs and Young Turks: Ottomanism, Arabism, and Islamism in the Ottoman Empire, 1908–1918* (Berkeley; Los Angeles; London: University of California Press, 1997), 81–143; Albert Habib Hourani, *Arabic Thought in the Liberal Age, 1798–1939* (Cambridge: Cambridge University Press, 1983), 268–73; Samir Seikaly, "Shukri Al-'Asali: A Case Study of a Political Activist," in *The Origins of Arab Nationalism*, eds. Rashid Khalidi et al. (New York: Columbia University Press, 1991), 83–91. On educational reform see Benjamin C. Fortna, *Imperial Classroom: Islam, the State, and Education in the Late Ottoman Empire* (Oxford; New York: Oxford University Press, 2002), passim.

11 Khatib, *Wamadat min 'umr al-zaman*, 16; Khatib, *Diwan al-Khatib*, 12. See also James L. Gelvin, *Divided Loyalties: Nationalism and Mass Politics in Syria at the Close of Empire* (Berkeley: University of California Press, 1998), 65–86; Rashid Khalidi, "Ottomanism and Arabism in Syria Before 1914: A Reassessment," in *The Origins of Arab Nationalism* eds. Rashid Khalidi et al. (New York: Columbia University Press, 1991), 55–65.

12 Michael Provence, "Ottoman Modernity, Colonialism, and Insurgency in the Interwar Arab East," *International Journal of Middle East Studies* 43.2 (May 1, 2011): 207–15; See for example Yücel Güçlü, "The Role of the Ottoman-Trained Officers in Independent Iraq," *Oriente Moderno* 21.2 n.s. (2002): 441–58.

13 Khatib, *Diwan al-Khatib*, 9. On the Syrian Protestant College/AUB see Betty S. Anderson, *The American University of Beirut: Arab Nationalism and Liberal Education* (Austin: University of Texas Press, 2011), 17–20 and passim. For an urban history of Beirut at the time see Jens Hanssen, *Fin de Siècle Beirut: The Making of an Ottoman Provincial Capital* (Oxford, New York: Oxford University Press, 2005), passim; on institutions of learning: 163–89.

14 Khatib, *Wamadat min 'umr al-zaman*, 10–12. On the press see Ami Ayalon, *The Press in the Arab Middle East: A History* (New York, Oxford: Oxford University Press, 1995), 147–63.

15 Khatib, *Diwan al-Khatib*, 25; Samadi, *Shi'r Fu'ad al-Khatib*, 27. The title used in the *Diwan* is "Amal wa-Alam."

16 Compare and contrast the modernism in the life and work of Jamil Sidqi al-Zahawi (1863–1936), who belonged to an earlier generation of poet-intellectuals, in Dina Rizk Khoury, "Looking for the Modern: A Biography of an Iraqi Modernist," in Mary Ann Fay (ed.) *Auto/biography and the Construction of Identity and Community in the Middle East* (New York: Palgrave, 2001), 109–24.

17 Khatib, *Diwan al-Khatib*, 5–6 (new pagination after editor's intro); on "those who pronounce the dad" see Yasir Suleiman, *The Arabic Language and National Identity: A Study in Ideology* (Edinburgh: Edinburgh University Press, 2003), 59f.

18 Khatib, *Diwan al-Khatib*, 25 (quote), 28.

19 See his poem "Ayyuha al-Turk wa'l-'Arab" in ibid., 31–5; Samadi, *Shi'r Fu'ad al-Khatib*, 78–82.

20 He wrote "What are the Arabs if not Turks in their honor and vigor – what are the Turks if not Arabs in their [religious] ways" in "Ila'l-'Arab wa-Shawkat Basha," *al-Ahram*, July 1, 1909, p1. The poem praised Mahmud Shawkat Pasha's leadership, but expressed that Arabs had doubts about his affiliation. Shawkat Pasha, who played a decisive role in the second constitutional period and the suppression of the counter-revolution in April 1909, stemmed from an Arabized Georgian family in Baghdad. Kayali, *Arabs and Young Turks*, 20.
21 Khatib, *Wamadat min 'umr al-zaman*, 12.
22 Hans Wehr and J. Milton Cowan, *A Dictionary of Modern Written Arabic (Arabic–English)*, 4th edn. (Wiesbaden: Harrassowitz, 1979), 593, 1151f.
23 Khatib, *Wamadat min 'umr al-zaman*, 13f. Only the original print version of the poem gives the derogatory title: *Al-Ahram*, October 19, 1909, p1: "Nafthat masdur."
24 Heather J. Sharkey, *Living with Colonialism: Nationalism and Culture in the Anglo-Egyptian Sudan*, Colonialisms 3 (Berkeley: University of California Press, 2003), 3–4, 7–11, 21, 51–5, 60–63, 104–7. Apparently, Isma'il al-Azhari was among al-Khatib's students. He later became Sudanese prime minister and president. Khatib, *Diwan al-Khatib*, 4f, 9; Khatib, *Wamadat min 'umr al-zaman*, 14.
25 Khatib, *Wamadat min 'umr al-zaman*, 14–20.
26 Ibid., 24–6.
27 Ibid., 22f; Khatib, *Diwan al-Khatib*, 10. On officers joining Faysal see Güçlü, "The Role of the Ottoman-Trained Officers in Independent Iraq," 125–7. On continuing Ottoman loyalty see Provence, "Ottoman Modernity," 215–20. On Khatib's role in the Arab revolt see Teitelbaum, *Hashemite Kingdom*, 83 etc.
28 See an opening article of *al-Qibla* of August 28, 1916, and the poem "Tahya al-nahda," first recited after the proclamation of the Arab Revolt on June 10, 1916. Samadi, *Shi'r Fu'ad al-Khatib*, 7–9, 121–8, quotes on 122, 125.
29 For the preceding paragraphs see Kayali, *Arabs and Young Turks*, 116–205.
30 Khatib, *Wamadat min 'umr al-zaman*, 23f; other versions of the origin story and information about the Literary Society in Gelvin, *Divided Loyalties*, 66–9, 244–5n; Elie Podeh, "The Symbolism of the Arab Flag in Modern Arab States: Between Commonality and Uniqueness," *Nations and Nationalism* 17 (2011): 423–5, and passim. Al-Khatib's explanation of the colors is partly confirmed by "The New Flag of the Kingdom of the Hedjaz," *The Muslim World* 8.1 (January 1918): 190; Whitney Jr. Smith, "Arab National Flags," *Middle East Forum* 36.8 (1960): 22.
31 Khatib, *Wamadat min 'umr al-zaman*, 36–47 (period of Faysal's rule in Damascus), 51–69 (in the Hijaz with Husayn), 75–9 (Foreign Minister under 'Ali in the Hejaz); 82–133 (with 'Abdallah in Jordan), 151–78 (in Saudi service and in Afghanistan).

3 Holding up the mirror

3.1 Saladin the Victor

1 Compare similar arguments in Stefan Heidemann, "Memory and Ideology: Images of Saladin in Syria and Iraq," in *Visual Culture in the Modern Middle East: Rhetoric of the Image*, eds. Christiane Gruber and Sune Haugbolle (Bloomington, Indianapolis: Indiana University Press, 2013), 57–81.
2 Anne-Laure Dupont, "Le grand homme, figure de la 'Renaissance' arabe," in Catherine Mayeur-Jaouen (Ed.) *Saints et héros du moyen-orient contemporain: actes du colloque des 11 et 12 décembre 2000, à l'institut universitaire de France* (Paris: Maisonneuve et Larose, 2002), 47–73; Werner Ende, "Wer ist ein Glaubensheld, wer ist ein Ketzer? Konkurrierende Geschichtsbilder in der modernen Literatur islamischer Länder," *Die Welt des Islams* 23/24 (1984): 70–9.

3 Thomas Carlyle, *On Heroes, Hero-Worship, and the Heroic in History* (New York: Wiley and Putnam, 1846). See Ende, "Wer ist ein Glaubensheld," 71.
4 Dupont, "Le grand homme," 62.
5 Emile Durkheim, *The Elementary Forms of the Religious Life* (London: George Allen & Unwin Ltd., 1968), 415ff.
6 Reinhart Koselleck, *Vergangene Zukunft: Zur Semantik geschichtlicher Zeiten* (Frankfurt am Main: Suhrkamp, 1979), 61.
7 Salah al-Din's name ranks among the highest in numbers of internet searches for historical figures in the Arab world. Mark Sedgwick, "Modern and Islamic Icons in Arab-Islamic Popular Historical Memory," in *Islamic Myths and Memories: Mediators of Globalization*, eds. Itzchak Weismann, Mark Sedgwick, and Ulrika Mårtensson (Surrey, Burlington: Ashgate, 2014), 25f.
8 Lisa Wedeen, *Ambiguities of Domination: Politics, Rhetoric, and Symbols in Contemporary Syria* (Chicago: University of Chicago Press, 1999), 3. On Saladin in Iraqi propaganda see Ofra Bengio, *Saddam's Word: Political Discourse in Iraq* (New York: Oxford University Press, 1998), 82–4.
9 Ende, "Wer ist ein Glaubensheld," 83–7; Elizabeth Thompson, *Colonial Citizens: Republican Rights, Paternal Privilege, and Gender in French Syria and Lebanon* (New York: Columbia University Press, 2000), 69; on the mausoleum see Stefan Weber, *Damascus: Ottoman Modernity and Urban Transformation (1808–1918)*, vol. 2, Proceedings of the Danish Institute in Damascus 5 (Aarhus: Aarhus Universitetsforlag, 2009), 241f.
10 See Ende, "Wer ist ein Glaubensheld," 79–86; Carole Hillenbrand, *The Crusades: Islamic Perspectives* (Chicago: Fitzroy Dearborn Publishers, 1999), 593–600; Abdel-Raouf Sinno, "The Emperor's Visit to the East as Reflected in Contemporary Arabic Journalism," in *Baalbek: Image and Monument 1898–1998*, ed. Helene Sader, Thomas Scheffler, and Angelika Neuwirth, Beiruter Texte und Studien, Bd. 69 (Stuttgart: Steiner, 1998), 129–33; Emmanuel Sivan, "Modern Arab Historiography of the Crusades," *Asian & African Studies* 8.2 (1972): 109–17; Weber, *Damascus*, 2: 241f; Emma Aubin-Boltanski, "Salah al-Din, un héros à l'épreuve: Mythe et pèlerinage en Palestine," *Annales* 60 (2005): 95–99.
11 On the Paris Panthéon: Avner Ben-Amos, *Funerals, Politics, and Memory in Modern France, 1789–1996* (Oxford; New York: Oxford University Press, 2000), 20ff. The Panthéon is a monumental building in the Quartier Latin, initially erected as a church in the eighteenth century. The French nation has been burying and venerating its Great Men and secular saints there since the French Revolution.
12 'Abdallah Hanna, *'Abd al-Rahman al-Shahbandar, 1879–1940: 'Alam nahdawi wa-rajul al-wataniyyah wa'l-taharrur al-fikri* (Damascus: Al-Ahali li'l-Tiba'a wa'l-Nashr wa'l-Tauzi', 1989), 171–215; Philip S. Khoury, *Syria and the French Mandate: The Politics of Arab Nationalism, 1920–1945* (Princeton: Princeton University Press, 1987), 587–9.
13 Stefan Weber, *Damascus: Ottoman Modernity and Urban Transformation (1808–1918)*, vol. 1, Proceedings of the Danish Institute in Damascus 5 (Aarhus: Aarhus Universitetsforlag, 2009), 451, 453. Weber dates the accident to 1912, which is the year when, according to his account, the first airplane landed in Damascus. It is possible that these were in fact two separate incidents. See also the commemoration of the fliers at Istanbul's "Monument for the Victims of Aviation" ("Tayyare Şehitleri Abidesi"), Klaus Kreiser, "Public Monuments in Turkey and Egypt, 1840–1916," *Muqarnas* 14 (January 1, 1997): 112f. See also numerous reports in the Cairene *al-Ahram* between February and March 1914.
14 As an appendix to his historical novel *Riwayat waraqat al-As.* Carl Brockelmann, "A. Shauqi," in *Geschichte der arabischen Literatur, Suppl. 3* (Leiden: E.J. Brill, 1942), 21–3, 27. The poem is printed in Ahmad Shawqi, *Al-Shawqiyyat*, vol. 3 (Cairo:

Matba'at al-Istiqama, 1964), 116–20. It was apparently necessary to explain in this reprint that Egyptians grieved over the Ottoman pilots because "the Islamic caliphate still created a bond between Egyptians and Ottomans" at the time, which had since been forgotten and replaced by a negative Arab nationalist perception of the Arab-Ottoman past.

15 Ludvík Mucha, *Webster's Concise Encyclopedia of Flags & Coats of Arms*, W.G. Crampton (Ed.), trans. Jiří Louda (New York: Crescent Books, Distributed by Crown Publishers, 1985), 123. The eagle was replaced with the "Hawk of the Quraysh" as the national emblem between 1972 and 1984. See also Doris Behrens-Abouseif, *Islamic Architecture in Cairo: An Introduction*, Studies in Islamic Art and Architecture, v3 (Leiden; New York: E.J. Brill, 1989), 80; Nasser O. Rabbat, *The Citadel of Cairo: A New Interpretation of Royal Mamluk Architecture*, Islamic History and Civilization, v14 (Leiden; New York: E.J. Brill, 1995), 24.

16 Youssef Chahine used the eagle as Saladin's symbol in his film *al-Nasir Salah al-Din*, too. Hala Halim, "The Signs of Saladin: A Modern Cinematic Rendition of Medieval Heroism," *Alif: Journal of Comparative Poetics*, 12 (1992): 79–80. Halim does not refer to the eagle as a popular symbol for the Sultan, however. See more on the film below.

17 Salih Jawad al-Tu'ma, *Salah al-Din fi'l-shi'r al-'arabi al-hadith: dirasa wa-nusus*, 2nd edn. (Damascus: Dar Kutha, 1997), 16–21 (on Shawqi), passim. Shawqi also wrote a poem on the occasion of Wilhelm II's visit to the Damascus tomb in 1898: "Tahiyya Ghalyum al-Thani li-Salah al-Din fi'l-qabr" ("Greetings of Wilhelm II to Saladin in the Grave"), see ibid., 105f.

18 J. Pedersen, "Djabra'il." *Encyclopaedia of Islam, Second Edition*, eds. P. Bearman, Th. Bianquis, C.E. Bosworth, E. van Donzel, W.P. Heinrichs. Brill Online, 2015. Reference. University of Maryland – College Park, http://referenceworks.brillonline.com/entries/encyclopaedia-of-islam-2/djabrail-SIM_1903, date of access: May 19, 2015; B. Schrieke; J.E. Bencheikh; J. Knappert; and B.W. Robinson, "Mi'radj." *Encyclopaedia of Islam, Second Edition*, eds. P. Bearman, Th. Bianquis, C.E. Bosworth, E. van Donzel, W.P. Heinrichs. Brill Online, 2015. Reference. University of Maryland – College Park, http://referenceworks.brillonline.com/entries/encyclopaedia-of-islam-2/miradj-COM_0746, date of access: May 19, 2015.

19 *Al-Istiqlal*, January 21, 1938, 3: "Tafat zahar 'ala qabar Yasin al-Hashimi." Translation in Peter Wien, "The Long and Intricate Funeral of Yasin Al-Hashimi: Pan-Arabism, Civil Religion, and Popular Nationalism in Damascus, 1937," *International Journal of Middle East Studies* 43 (2011): 287.

20 See the images of the festival between 1898 and 1917 in the Matson Photograph Collection, Library of Congress, http://loc.gov/pictures/resource/matpc/, date of access: January 31, 2015.

21 See Ende, "Wer ist ein Glaubensheld," 86. On the Arabization of Saladin, Sivan, "Modern Arab Historiography," 127–34.

22 Sivan, "Modern Arab Historiography," 115.

23 Aubin-Boltanski, "Salah al-Din," 99–107.

24 For this and the following see Ende, "Wer ist ein Glaubensheld," 83–92.

25 See Edward W. Said, *Orientalism* (New York: Pantheon Books, 1978), 31–73 etc., 101, 192. *Talisman* was originally published as part of a trilogy in Walter Scott, *Tales of the Crusaders*. (Philadelphia: James Crissy, 1825). See also Paul Pelckmans, "Walter Scott's Orient: The Talisman," in *Oriental Prospects: Western Literature and the Lure of the East*, eds. C.C. Barfoot and Theo d'Haen (Amsterdam, Atlanta: Editions Rodopi, 1998), 97–109.

26 Ende, "Wer ist ein Glaubensheld," 84; Anis al-Nusuli, *Asbab al-nahda al-'Arabiyya fi'l-qarn al-tasi' 'ashar*, ed. 'Abd Allah Anis Tabba' (Beirut: Dar Ibn Zaydun, 1985), 199. Ben Halima presents the play as "inspirée" by Scott: Hamadi Ben Halima, *Un*

demi siècle de théâtre arabe en tunisie, 1907–1957, Publications de l'Université de Tunis, Faculté des lettres et sciences humaines de Tunis : 6. sér., Philosophie-littérature; v. 6 (Tunis: Université de Tunis, 1974), 40. Brockelmann emphasizes that Salah al-Din was Haddad's own work. Carl Brockelmann, "Najib al-Haddad," in *Geschichte der arabischen Literatur, Suppl. 3* (Leiden: E.J. Brill, 1942), 268.

27 Najib al-Haddad, *Riwayat Salah al-Din al-Ayyubi* (Alexandria, 1893), passim.

28 See Rudi Paret, "Sirat Baybars." *Encyclopaedia of Islam, Second Edition,* eds. P. Bearman, Th. Bianquis, C.E. Bosworth, E. van Donzel, W.P. Heinrichs. Brill Online, 2015. Reference. University of Maryland – College Park, http://referenceworks.brillonline.com/entries/encyclopaedia-of-islam-2/sirat-baybars-SIM_1306, date of access: May 19, 2015. Paret writes: "... it represents the type of intellectual nourishment accepted by large parts of the Muslim population in Cairo in the late Middle Ages and in the following centuries." See also Ende, "Wer ist ein Glaubensheld," 82.

29 Jurji Zaydan, *Salah al-Din al-Ayyubi* (Cairo: Dar al-Hilal, 1965), passim; Ende, "Wer ist ein Glaubensheld," 85. Like many of Zaydan's books, *Salah al-Din* was translated into other Middle Eastern and Asian languages, such as Turkish and Kurdish.

30 Luc-Willy Deheuvels, "Le Saladin de Farah Antun du mythe littéraire arabe au mythe politique," *Revue des mondes musulmans et de la Méditerranée,* 89–90 (2000): 191.

31 M. Perlmann, "Farah Antun." *Encyclopaedia of Islam, Second Edition,* eds. P. Bearman, Th. Bianquis, C.E. Bosworth, E. van Donzel, W.P. Heinrichs. Brill Online, 2015. Reference. University of Maryland – College Park, http://referenceworks.brillonline.com/entries/encyclopaedia-of-islam-2/farah-antun-SIM_2269, date of access: May 19, 2015.

32 New editions have confirmed the play's legacy, such as: Farah Antun, *Al-Sultan Salah al-Din wa-mamlakat Urshalim: Riwaya tamthiliyya dhat arba'at fusul* (Misr: [s.n.], 1923); Farah Antun, *Al-Sultan Salah al-Din wa-mamlakat Urshalim* (Beirut: Dar Marun 'Abbud, 1981). There may have been more. A reference to a performance of the play is in James L. Gelvin, *Divided Loyalties: Nationalism and Mass Politics in Syria at the Close of Empire* (Berkeley: University of California Press, 1998), 254.

33 Still, Christian characters play a central role in the plot, even as carriers of tragic sympathy. The anti-crusader message is interspersed with elements of love and jealousy, and the topos of a Christian princess in disguise as a male servant at Saladin's court. It even carries traces of feminist debates of the time. Antun, *Al-Sultan Salah al-Din,* 173 (quote), and passim. See also Muhammad Mustafa Badawi, *Early Arabic Drama* (Cambridge; New York: Cambridge University Press, 1988), 72. It is a sign for the fluidity of nationalist identities at Antun's time that Donald M. Reid, *The Odyssey of Farah Antun: A Syrian Christian's Quest for Secularism,* Studies in Middle Eastern History, no. 2 (Minneapolis: Bibliotheca Islamica, 1975), 128, identifies undertones of Egyptian nationalism in the work; Ilham Khuri-Makdisi, *The Eastern Mediterranean and the Making of Global Radicalism, 1860–1914* (Berkeley: University of California Press, 2010), 80, in turn, considers Antun a proto-Arab nationalist.

34 Compare Michelle U. Campos, *Ottoman Brothers: Muslims, Christians, and Jews in Early Twentieth-Century Palestine* (Stanford: Stanford University Press, 2011), passim.

35 Reid, *The Odyssey of Farah Antun,* 63–70, 99–108.

36 Khuri-Makdisi, *The Eastern Mediterranean,* 62.

37 Ibid., 7, 60–71.

38 al-Tu'ma, *Salah al-Din fi'l-shi'r al-'Arabi,* 117. The information about the play is in Arslan's introduction to his poem "Salah al-Din al-Ayyubi." Arslan wrote that the events took place a year before the war. However, the Ottoman Parliament convened in May 1914 only. See Hasan Kayali, "Elections and the Electoral Process in

the Ottoman Empire, 1876–1919," *International Journal of Middle East Studies* 27 (1995): 278–80. On Arslan's convictions see William L. Cleveland, *Islam Against the West: Shakib Arslan and the Campaign for Islamic Nationalism* (Austin: University of Texas Press, 1985), 12–27. See also Philip S. Khoury, *Urban Notables and Arab Nationalism: The Politics of Damascus, 1860–1920* (Cambridge; New York: Cambridge University Press, 1983), 67; Khoury, *Syria and the French Mandate*, 265, 268–9.

39 Ben Halima, *Un demi siècle de théâtre arabe en tunisie, 1907–1957*, 39–44, 55, 58, 88, 91, 137f, 171f.

40 al-Nusuli, *Asbab al-nahda*, 23–33 (the editor's introduction does not mention the affair); Werner Ende, *Arabische Nation und islamische Geschichte: Die Umayyaden im Urteil arabischer Autoren des 20. Jahrhunderts* (Beirut, 1977), 132–45; Jennifer Marie Dueck, *The Claims of Culture at Empire's End: Syria and Lebanon under French Rule* (Oxford; New York: Oxford University Press, 2010), 187f.

41 Anis al-Nusuli, "Al-Tamthil," in *Asbab al-nahda al-'Arabiyya fi'l-qarn al-tasi' 'ashar* (Beirut: Dar Ibn Zaydun, 1985), 196, 199–200.

42 Khuri-Makdisi, *The Eastern Mediterranean*, 71–8; Gelvin, *Divided Loyalties*, 252–9.

43 Youssef Chahine and Joseph Massad, "Art and Politics in the Cinema of Youssef Chahine," *Journal of Palestine Studies* 28 (1999): 77–80. Cinema started out in the Middle East as part of the same traveling popular entertainment and education business as theater, with deep political implications. See Thompson, *Colonial Citizens*, 197–210.

44 Maureen Kiernan, "Cultural Hegemony and National Film Language: Youssef Chahine," *Alif: Journal of Comparative Poetics*, 15 (1995): 139–40.

45 Ibid., 130–52.

46 Malek Khouri, *The Arab National Project in Youssef Chahine's Cinema* (Cairo; New York: The American University in Cairo Press, 2010), 49; Joel Gordon, *Revolutionary Melodrama: Popular Film and Civic Identity in Nasser's Egypt*, Chicago Studies on the Middle East (Chicago: Middle East Documentation Center, 2002), 79–80. Critics are divided, either praising its cinematic quality, or considering it, due to a lack of mastery of the cinemascope technology, as "an occasionally brilliant failure." Kiernan, "Cultural Hegemony and National Film Language," 138.

47 Chahine and Massad, "Art and Politics in the Cinema of Youssef Chahine," 81.

48 Youssef Chahine, *Al-Nasir Salah al-Din*, 1963; Khouri, *The Arab National Project in Youssef Chahine's Cinema*, 48.

49 Halim, "The Signs of Saladin," 79.

50 Khouri, *The Arab National Project in Youssef Chahine's Cinema*, 44–52; Kiernan, "Cultural Hegemony and National Film Language," 135–8; Halim, "The Signs of Saladin," 78–80.

51 Ende, "Wer ist ein Glaubensheld," 86–92.

52 Bengio, *Saddam's Word*, 82–4.

3.2 *From the glory of conquest to paradise lost*

1 Compare Bernard Lewis, *History – Remembered, Recovered, Invented* (Princeton, NJ: Princeton University Press, 1975), 71–87. Lewis' observations in this essay are accurate, the author's propensity to Orientalist stereotypes notwithstanding.

2 Salih Jawad al-Tu'ma, *Salah al-Din fi'l-shi'r al-'arabi al-hadith: dirasa wa-nusus*, 2nd edn. (Damascus: Dar Kutha, 1997), 20. There is a reference to the performance of a play about the fall of Edirne in late Ottoman Damascus in James L. Gelvin,

Divided Loyalties: Nationalism and Mass Politics in Syria at the Close of Empire (Berkeley: University of California Press, 1998), 255.

3   Ahmad Shawqi, *Al-Shawqiyyat*, vol. 1 (Cairo: Matba'at al-Istiqama, 1964), 230, 231. A French translation of these parts of the poem (but not the following) is also in Henri Pérès, *L'Espagne vue par les voyageurs musulmans de 1610 à 1930*, Publications de l'Institut d'études orientales, Faculté des lettres d'Alger 6 (Paris: Librairie d'Amerique et d'Orient, A. Maisonneuve, 1937), 102–103.

4   Shawqi, *Al-Shawqiyyat*, 1964, 1: 234.

5   For a critical engagement see Nouri Gana, "In Search of Andalusia: Reconfiguring Arabness in Diana Abu-Jaber's Crescent," *Comparative Literature Studies* 45 (2008): 228–46. *Al-Andalus* appears as an "interfaith utopia" in William Granara, "Nostalgia, Arab Nationalism, and the Andalusian Chronotope in the Evolution of the Modern Arabic Novel," *Journal of Arabic Literature* 36 (2005): 58. About *al-Andalus* as a literary topos see also Reuven Snir, "'Al-Andalus Arising from Damascus': Al-Andalus in Modern Arabic Poetry," in *Charting Memory: Recalling Medieval Spain*, ed. Stacy N. Beckwith (New York: Garland, 2000), 263–93. A recent article combining many of these aspects is Nizar F. Hermes, "Nostalgia for al-Andalus in Early Modern Moroccan *Voyages en Espagne*: al-Ghassani's *Rihlat al-wazir fi iftikak al-asir* (1690–91) as a Case Study," *The Journal of North African Studies* 21 (2016): 433–52.

6   Taieb Belghazi, "Festivalization of Urban Space in Morocco," *Critique: Critical Middle Eastern Studies* 15 (2006): 97–107.

7   L. Rouhi, "Miguel de Cervantes, Early Modern Spain, and the Challenges to the Meaning of Islam," *Middle East Journal of Culture and Communication* 4 (2011): 7–10.

8   Compare similar notions in literary studies in Granara, "Nostalgia, Arab Nationalism, and the Andalusian Chronotope," 60; Jonathan H. Shannon, "There and Back Again: Rhetorics of Al-Andalus in Modern Syrian Popular Culture," *International Journal of Middle East Studies* 48 (2016): 5–24.

9   Anthony D. Smith, *The Ethnic Origins of Nations* (Oxford, Malden: Blackwell, 1986), 191.

10 Sabine Damir-Geilsdorf, "Politische Utopie und Erinnerung: Das 'Goldene Zeitalter' in islamischen Diskursen heute," in *Geschichte und Erinnerung im Islam*, ed. Angelika Hartmann, Formen der Erinnerung 15 (Göttingen: Vandenhoeck & Ruprecht, 2004), 77f; Dennis Walker, "Egypt's Arabism: Mustafa Kamil's 1893 Play (Fath Al-Andalus) on the Muslim Conquest of Spain," *Islamic Studies* 33.1 (1994): 71. See the references to the "authenticity debate" in the first chapter of this book.

11 Ahmad Hasan al-Zayyat, "Athr al-thaqafa al-'Arabiyya fi'l-'ilm wa'l-'alam, part 3," *al-Risala* 4 (1933), 10.

12 Israel Gershoni, "Eine Stimme der Vernunft: Muhammad Abdallah Inan und die Zeitschrift Al-Risala," in *Konstellationen: Über Geschichte, Erfahrung und Erkenntnis. Festschrift für Dan Diner zum 65. Geburtstag*, eds. Nicolas Berg et al. (Göttingen: Vandenhoeck & Ruprecht, 2011), 107–10.

13 Muhammad 'Abdallah 'Inan, "Tarikh al-'Arab wa'l-Islam fi Urubba bayna tahamul al-gharb wa-nisyan al-sharq," *al-Hilal* 42 (1934): 665, 668; see also Muhammad 'Abdallah 'Inan, "Watha'iq majhula 'an: Ma'sat al-Muriskiyyin aw al-'Arab al-muntasarin," *al-Hilal* 42 (1934): 565–9.

14 Muhammad 'Abdallah 'Inan, *Dawlat al-Islam fi'l-Andalus min al-fath ila nihayat mamlakat Gharnata* (Cairo: Matba'at Lajnat al-Ta'lif wa'l-Tarjama wa'l-Nashr, 1943), 4–5; see also: Joseph Aschbach, *Tarikh al-Andalus*, trans. Muhammad 'Abd Allah 'Inan (Cairo: Matba'at Lajnat al-Ta'lif wa'l-Tarjama wa'l-Nashr, 1940); the original: Joseph Aschbach, *Geschichte der Ommaijaden in Spanien, nebst einer Darstellung des Entstehens der spanischen christlichen Reiche* (Frankfurt/Main: Franz Barrentrapp, 1829).

15 Muhammad 'Abdallah 'Inan, "Al-Andalus fi jamal al-fann al-Islami," *al-Hilal* 44 (1935): 109.

16 Muhammad 'Abdallah 'Inan, "Qisas wa-asatir: Hamra' Gharnata: Hal banathu al-sahra wa'l-shayatin," *al-Hilal* 44 (1936): 425.

17 To access the topic see Dwight F. Reynolds, "Musical 'Membrances of Medieval Muslim Spain," in *Charting Memory: Recalling Medieval Spain*, ed. Stacy N. Beckwith (New York: Garland, 2000), 229–62; Jonathan Holt Shannon, "Performing Al-Andalus, Remembering Al-Andalus: Mediterranean Soundings from Mashriq to Maghrib," *Journal of American Folklore* 120 (2007): 308–34; and Jonathan Holt Shannon, *Among the Jasmine Trees: Music and Modernity in Contemporary Syria* (Middletown: Wesleyan University Press, 2006), passim. They share many of the arguments of the preceding paragraphs.

18 Hasan Kamil al-Sairafi, "Wada' al-Hamra' (min Diwan 'Raj' al-Sada')," *al-Risala* 317 (1939): 1508.

19 Shakib Arslan, *Al-Hulal al-sundusiyya fi'l-akhbar wa'l-athar al-Andalusiyya*, vol. 1 (Cairo: al-Matba'a al-Rahmaniyya, 1936), (title page); about the journey see Umar Ryad, "New Episodes in Moroccan Nationalism Under Colonial Role: Reconsideration of Shakib Arslan's Centrality in Light of Unpublished Materials," *The Journal of North African Studies* 16 (2011): 120; about the title: Mikel de Epalza, "Dos literatos arabes viajan por sharq al-Andalus: Shakib Arslan (1939) y Husain Mones (1963)," *Sharq Al-Andalus: Estudios Árabes* 1 (1984): 175. Further examples for "silk clothes" are in Carl Brockelmann, "Siragaddin Abu'l-'Abbas Ahmad Ibn 'Abdalhaiy al-Halabi (d. 1708)," in *Geschichte der arabischen Literatur, Suppl. 2* (Leiden: E.J. Brill, 1938), 683f; Carl Brockelmann, "Muhammad Abu Ra's Ibn Ahmad Ibn 'Aqqad an-Nasiri (1751–1823)," in *Geschichte der arabischen Literatur, Vol. 2* (Leiden: E.J. Brill, 1949), 654f.

20 Ryad, "New Episodes in Moroccan Nationalism Under Colonial Role," 117–42.

21 Shakib Arslan, *Al-Hulal al-sundusiyya*, 3:5–6.

22 Arslan, *Al-Hulal al-sundusiyya*, 1936, 1:1.

23 Compare Manuel Nieto Cumplido and Carlos Luca de Tena y Alvear, *La Mezquita de Córdoba: planos y dibujos* (Córdoba: Colegio Oficial de Arquitectos de Andalucía Occidental, 1992), 26–32, 69, 82, 133, 164.

24 Images in William L. Cleveland, *Islam Against the West: Shakib Arslan and the Campaign for Islamic Nationalism* (Austin: University of Texas Press, 1985), 15, 22, 51, 153.

25 First edition of the Arabic text in Bulaq, 1862/3. First English translation: Ahmad ibn Muhammad Maqqari, *The History of the Mohammedan Dynasties in Spain; Extracted from the Nafhu-T-Tib Min Ghosni-L-Andalusi-R-Rattib Wa Tárikh Lisánu-D-Dín Ibni-L-Khattíb* (London: Printed for the Oriental translation fund of Great Britain and Ireland, 1840).

26 E. Lévi-Provençal, E. and Ch. Pellat, "al-Makkari." *Encyclopaedia of Islam, Second Edition*, eds. P. Bearman, Th. Bianquis, C.E. Bosworth, E. van Donzel, W.P. Heinrichs. Brill Online, 2015. Reference. University of Maryland – College Park, http://referenceworks.brillonline.com/entries/encyclopaedia-of-islam-2/al-makkari-SIM_4832, date of access: May 19, 2015.

27 On North African migrants in Cairo see André Raymond, *Artisans et commerçants au Caire au XVIIIe siècle*, vol. 2 (Damas: *Institut français de Damas*, 1974), 470–6. On al-Maqqari's journeys to the East see Khaled El-Rouayheb, *Islamic Intellectual History in the Seventeenth Century: Scholarly Currents in the Ottoman Empire and the Maghreb* (Cambridge: Cambridge University Press, 2015), 154f. Suraiya Faroqhi's study of the *hajj* in early modern times does not cover North African itineraries in detail, but includes a synopsis of the pre-modern account of the pilgrimage by the Andalusian courtier, scholar and travel writer Ibn Jubayr (1145–1217),

in: *Pilgrims and Sultans: The Hajj under the Ottomans, 1517–1683* (London: Tauris, 1994), 15–26, 142f.

28 This and much of the following section is based on the invaluable monograph by Pérès, *L'Espagne vue par les voyageurs musulmans*. Pérès only covers travelogues and reports in Arabic, therefore he does not include, for instance, the delegation led by Ottoman Ambassador Ahmed Vasif Effendi that visited Spain in 1787. Ahmed Vasif did apparently not make any references to Muslim Spain at all, except for a mentioning of the Arabic manuscripts that he was allowed to see in the library of the Escorial. See Markus Köhbach, "Die osmanische Gesandtschaft nach Spanien in den Jahren 1787/88: Begegnung zweier Kulturen im Spiegel eines Gesandtschaftsberichts," *Wiener Beiträge zur Geschichte der Neuzeit* 10 (1983): 143–52, esp. 150.

29 Pérès, *L'Espagne vue par les voyageurs musulmans*, 41–51. Recently, Nizar F. Hermes has argued that the late seventeenth-century Moroccan travelogue by Muhammad Ibn 'Abd al-Wahhab al-Ghassani already displayed a kind of nostalgia akin to that of modern travelers. In contrast to writers of the twentieth century, al-Ghassani's vision still foregrounds his disdain over the difference between a golden past and a corrupt present, however, instead of the immersion into a very present, idealized realm of imagination as authors like Ahmad Shawqi displayed it. See Hermes, "Nostalgia for al-Andalus," 434, 444–46, and passim.

30 Ibid., 53. A.G. Karam, "Faris al-Shidyak." *Encyclopaedia of Islam, Second Edition*, eds. P. Bearman; Th. Bianquis; C.E. Bosworth; E. van Donzel; and W.P. Heinrichs. Brill, 2012. Brill Online. Library of Congress, http://www.brillonline.nl/subscriber/entry?entry=islam_SIM-2289, date of access: March 28, 2012; Albert Habib Hourani, *Arabic Thought in the Liberal Age, 1798–1939* (Cambridge: Cambridge University Press, 1983), 97–9.

31 Muhammad Mahmud Shinqiti, *Al-Hamasa al-saniyya al-kamila al-maziyya fi'l-rihla al-'ilmiyya al-Shinqitiyya al-Turkuziyya*, ed. Muhammad Wuld Khabbaz (Mauritania: s.n., 2000), ba, jim, 1–2.

32 'Ali Ibn Salim al-Wardani, *Al-Rihla al-Andalusiyya*, ed. al-Habib 'Awwadi (Tunis: Matba'at Fann al-Tiba'a, 2008), 24–6.

33 See the poems in Shinqiti, *Al-Hamasa al-saniyya*, 13ff.

34 Pérès, *L'Espagne vue par les voyageurs musulmans*, 55–61.

35 Ibid., 62–72.

36 al-Wardani, *Al-Rihla al-Andalusiyya*, 63–145, esp. 126–7.

37 Ahmad Zaki, *Al-Safar ila'l-mu'tamar* (Cairo: Al-Dar al-Misriyya al-Lubnaniyya, 2000), 21–2; see also Carl Brockelmann, "A. Zaki Bek," in *Geschichte der arabischen Literatur, Suppl. 3* (Leiden: E.J. Brill, 1942), 281–3.

38 Zaki, *Al-Safar ila'l-mu'tamar*, 339–40.

39 Pérès, *L'Espagne vue par les voyageurs musulmans*, 47f. He quotes Ahmad Zaki, "Sur les relations entre l'Egypte et l'Espagne pendent l'occupation musulmane," in *Homenaje á D. Francisco Codera en su jubilación del profesorado: Estudios de erudición oriental con una introducción de D. Eduardo Saavedra*, ed. Eduardo Saavedra (Zaragoza: M. Escar, tipógrafo, 1904), 457–8.

40 Pérès, *L'Espagne vue par les voyageurs musulmans*, 75n2. He quotes from Zaki's *Rapport sur les manuscrits arabes conservés à l'Escurial en Espagne* (Cairo, 1894), 14.

41 Zaki, *Al-Safar ila'l-mu'tamar*, 289.

42 Pérès, *L'Espagne vue par les voyageurs musulmans*, 83–85 quotes Zaki in French translation.

43 Zaki, *Al-Safar ila'l-mu'tamar*, 335.

44 Ibid., 289–90. For this section altogether Pérès, *L'Espagne vue par les voyageurs musulmans*, 72–87.

45 Next to the edition used above see, for instance, the reprint of the *al-Andalus* part in Ahmad Zaki, *Rihla ila'l-Andalus, 1893*, ed. Muhammad Kamil al-Khatib

(Damascus: Wizarat al-Thaqafa fi'l-Jumhuriyya al-'Arabiyya al-Suriyya, 1990). See also the letters and responses in Zaki, *Al-Safar ila'l-mu'tamar*, 366–84.

46 Carl Brockelmann, "A. Shauqi," in *Geschichte der arabischen Literatur, Suppl. 3* (Leiden: E.J. Brill, 1942), 21–32; J. Brugman, *An Introduction to the History of Modern Arabic Literature in Egypt*, Studies in Arabic Literature 10 (Leiden: E.J. Brill, 1984), 35–45. Shawqi was called "Prince of Poets" before World War I already.

47 See the verse: "Khosroe's palace was an exhortation for al-Buhturi, but I was healed by the palaces of the 'Abd Shams," referring to the ruins of *Madinat al-Zahra*, the residence of the Umayyad Caliphs of Spain, who were descendants of the clan of 'Abd Shams. In Ahmad Shawqi, *Al-Shawqiyyat*, vol. 2 (Cairo: Matba'at al-Istiqama, 1964), 47; French trsl. in Pérès, *L'Espagne vue par les voyageurs musulmans*, 107. The verse is also quoted in Yaseen Noorani, "The Lost Garden of Al-Andalus: Islamic Spain and the Poetic Inversion of Colonialism," *International Journal of Middle East Studies* 31.2 (May 1, 1999): 238. On questions of style and technique, and a detailed analysis of the juxtaposition of Egypt and *al-Andalus*, see ibid., 238–47, 251. See also Ch. Pellat "al-Buhturi, Abu 'Ubada al-walid b. 'Ubayd (Allah)." *Encyclopaedia of Islam, Second Edition*, eds. P. Bearman, Th. Bianquis, C.E. Bosworth, E. van Donzel and W.P. Heinrichs. Brill, 2012. Brill Online. Library of Congress, http://www.brillonline.nl/subscriber/entry?entry=islam_SIM-1500, date of access: April 6, 2012.

48 Shawqi, *Al-Shawqiyyat*, 1964, 2:48–50, verse on 49; Pérès, *L'Espagne vue par les voyageurs musulmans*, 111–14, French trsl. of verse (quite free) on 112.

49 Literally: "The face of consolation is concealed from you." Shawqi, *Al-Shawqiyyat*, 1964, 2:51; French trans., slightly different, in Pérès, *L'Espagne vue par les voyageurs musulmans*, 115. Another translation of the verses is in Noorani, "The Lost Garden of Al-Andalus," 238. He interprets the lines as a statement that the past offers consolation to the poet. In fact, it is a bitter indictment of Egypt's youth and its disregard for the past.

50 Pérès, *L'Espagne vue par les voyageurs musulmans*, 101–120. See Zaki Mubarak's evaluation of Shawqi's poetry as quoted in Noorani, "The Lost Garden of Al-Andalus," 245.

51 Both in Shawqi, *Al-Shawqiyyat*, 1964, 2: 170–6 and 103–107, respectively. "Saqr Quraysh" was posthumously reprinted in Ahmad Shawqi, *Duwal al-'Arab wa-'uzama' al-Islam* (Beirut: Dar al-Kitab al-'Arabi, 1970), 78–86. (First published in 1933.) The Syrian poet Adunis (b. 1930) picked up the topic of exile in his early 1960s poem of the same name. Salma Khadra Jayyusi (ed.), *Modern Arabic Poetry: An Anthology* (New York: Columbia University Press, 1987), 23–4.

52 Noorani, "The Lost Garden of Al-Andalus," 239 (quote), 245–6.

53 Mustafa Farrukh, *Rihla ila bilad al-majd al-mafqud*, 1933, 101, and again 110.

54 Ibid., 123.

55 Ibid., 5; See also Pérès, *L'Espagne vue par les voyageurs musulmans*, 163, 168, the entire section on Farrukh on 159–71.

56 Arslan, *Al-Hulal al-sundusiyya*, 1936, 1:(title page). Pérès mentions the book, but writes that it appeared too late to consider it. Pérès, *L'Espagne vue par les voyageurs musulmans*, 171, n1.

57 Ryad, "New Episodes in Moroccan Nationalism Under Colonial Role," 127f; Haggai Erlich, "The Tiger and the Lion: Fascism and Ethiopia in Arab Eyes," in *Arab Responses to Fascism and Nazism: Attraction and Repulsion*, ed. I. Gershoni (Austin, TX: University of Texas Press, 2014), 281–6; Cleveland, *Islam against the West*, 135–59.

58 Muhammad Musa, "Salat 'asr fi masjid Qurtuba 'am 1368h," *al-Risala* 797 (1948): 1145. The Indian Muslim poet Muhammad Iqbal (1873–1938) prayed in the Mezquita in 1933. The experience inspired him to write the Urdu poem "Masjid-i Qurtubah."

Noorani, "The Lost Garden of Al-Andalus," 237; Werner Ende, "Der Mihrab in der Kathedrale: Die Mezquita in Cordoba und der muslimisch-christliche Dialog," in *Zwischen Orient und Okzident: Studien zu Mobilität von Wissen, Konzepten und Praktiken*, eds. Anke Bentzin et al. (Freiburg im Breisgau: Herder, 2010), 113–14.

59 Ryad, "New Episodes in Moroccan Nationalism Under Colonial Role," 128 (letter to Arslan).

60 Mikaela Rogozen-Soltar, "Al-Andalus in Andalusia: Negotiating Moorish History and Regional Identity in Southern Spain," *Anthropological Quarterly* 80.3 (2007): 863–9, 874–80; Ende, "Der Mihrab in der Kathedrale." See also *The Guardian*, April 19, 2004: "Cathedral May See Return of Muslims," http://www.theguardian.com/world/2004/apr/19/spain, date of access: August 19, 2013; The Guardian, December 28, 2006: "Pope Asked to let Muslims Pray in Cathedral." http://www.theguardian.com/world/2006/dec/28/spain.catholicism?INTCMP=ILCNETTXT3487, date of access: August 19, 2013.

61 *The Guardian*, April 1, 2010: "Two Arrested After Fight in Cordoba's Former Mosque," http://www.theguardian.com/world/2010/apr/01/muslim-catholic-mosque-fight?INTCMP=ILCNETTXT3487, date of access: August 19, 2013; *Der Standard*, April 2, 2010: "Muslimisches Gebet in Kathedrale: Jugendliche 'wollten nicht provozieren,'" http://derstandard.at/1269448780775/CordobaWien-Muslimisches-Gebet-in-Kathedrale-Jugendliche-wollten-nicht-provozieren, date of access: August 19, 2013; *The New York Times*, November 4, 2010: "Name Debate Echoes and Old Clash of Faiths," http://www.nytimes.com/2010/11/05/world/europe/05cordoba.html?pagewanted=all&_r=0, date of access: August 19, 2013. The conservative commentary is by Soeren Kern: "Ban Remains on Muslim Prayer in Spanish Cathedral," The Gatestone Institute, February 14, 2013, http://www.gatestoneinstitute.org/3589/cordoba-cathedral-muslim-prayer, date of access: August 19, 2013.

62 Shawqi, *Al-Shawqiyyat*, 1964, 1:237. Pérès' French translation only contains the first verse, and he changes the personal pronoun: "Le Temps nous imposa la même attitude qu'a Târiq: le désespoir était derrière [vous] et l'espérance, devant." Pérès, *L'Espagne vue par les voyageurs musulmans*, 103.

63 Ahmad Ibn Muhammad al-Maqqari, *Nafh al-tib*, ed. Muhammad Muhyi al-Din 'Abd al-Hamid, vol. 1, 1967, 225. Arabic: "Ayyuha al-nas, ayna al-mafarr? Al-bahr min wara'ikum, wa'l-'udw amamakum, wa laysa lakum wa'llah illa al-sidq wa'l-sabr…"

64 See the relevant sections in "Medieval Sourcebook: Ibn Abd-El-Hakem: The Islamic Conquest of Spain," accessed July 11, 2012, http://www.fordham.edu/halsall/source/conqspain.asp. Arabic text in Ibn 'Abd al-Hakam, *The History of the Conquest of Egypt, North Africa and Spain, Known as the Futuh Misr of Ibn 'Abd Al-Hakam*, ed. Charles Cutler Torrey, Yale Oriental Series. Researches 3 (New Haven: Yale University Press, 1922), 204–206. For Christian chronicles see Elizabeth Drayson, *The King and the Whore: King Roderick and La Cava* (New York: Palgrave Macmillan, 2007), 15, 17–19.

65 "Tarik b. Ziyad," Encyclopaedia of Islam, Second Edition. Brill Online, 2012. Reference. University of Maryland, http://referenceworks.brillonline.com.proxy-um.researchport.umd.edu/entries/, encyclopaedia-of-islam-2/tarik-b-ziyad-COM_1182, date of access: July 11, 2012.

66 In July 2012, an internet search of "al-bahr min wara'ikum" yielded more than 100,000 hits. See also 'Abd al-Halim 'Uways, *Qadiyat ihraq Tariq Ibn Ziyad li'l-sufun: Bayna al-ustura wa'l-tarikh* (Cairo: Dar al-Sahwa, 1987). The book is dedicated in its entirety to the question whether the burning of the ships actually took place or not.

67 Ahmad Mukhtar 'Abd al-Fattah 'Abbadi, *Fi Tarikh al-Maghrib wa'l-Andalus* (Alexandria: Mu'assasat al-Thaqafa al-Jami'iyya, 1975), 63–5; 'Uways, *Qadiyat ihraq Tariq Ibn Ziyad li'l-sufun*, 6–17. See also Bosch-Vilá, J. "Ibn al-Kutiyya," Encyclopaedia of Islam, Second Edition. Brill Online, 2012. Reference. University of Maryland,

http://referenceworks.brillonline.com.proxy-um.researchport.umd.edu/entries/ency-clopaedia-of-islam-2/ibn-al-kutiyya-SIM_3265, date of access: July 11, 2012; Oman, G., "al-Idrisi," Encyclopaedia of Islam, Second Edition. Brill Online, 2012. Reference. University of Maryland, http://referenceworks.brillonline.com.proxy-um.researchport. umd.edu/entries/encyclopaedia-of-islam-2/al-idrisi-SIM_3494, date of access: July 11, 2012; Lewicki, T., "Ibn 'Abd al-Mun'im al-Himyari," Encyclopaedia of Islam, Second Edition. Brill Online, 2012. Reference. University of Maryland, http://referenceworks. brillonline.com.proxy-um.researchport.umd.edu/entries/encyclopaedia-of-islam-2/ ibn-abd-al-munim-al-himyari-SIM_3030, date of access: July 12, 2012.

68 'Abd al-Malik Ibn Habib, *Kitab Al-Ta'rij: (La Historia)*, ed. Jorge Aguadé, Fuentes Arábico-Hispanas 1 (Madrid: Consejo Superior de Investigaciones Científicas, Instituto de Cooperación con el Mundo Arabe, 1991), 136–8.

69 Very brief sketch in Carl Brockelmann, "Abu Marwan 'Abdalmalik b. al-Kardabus at-Tauzari," in *Geschichte der arabischen Literatur, Vol. 1* (Leiden: E.J. Brill, 1943), 345.

70 al-Tabari, *The Sasanids, the Byzantines, the Lakhmids, and Yemen*, trans. Clifford Edmund Bosworth, The History of Al-Tabari 5 (Albany: State University of New York Press, 1999), 247; 'Abbadi, *Fi Tarikh al-Maghrib wa'l-Andalus*, 66–8; 'Uways, *Qadiyat ihraq Tariq Ibn Ziyad li'l-sufun*, 19–23, 30–36. Lévi-Provençal, E., Ch. Pellat, "al-Makkari," Encyclopaedia of Islam, Second Edition. Brill Online, 2012. Reference. University of Maryland, http://referenceworks.brillonline.com.proxy-um. researchport.umd.edu/entries/encyclopaedia-of-islam-2/al-makkari-SIM_4832, date of access: July 12, 2012; Huici Miranda, A., "Ibn Habib," Encyclopaedia of Islam, Second Edition. Brill Online, 2012. Reference. University of Maryland, http://referenceworks.brillonline.com.proxy-um.researchport.umd.edu/entries/ encyclopaedia-of-islam-2/ibn-habib-SIM_3175, date of access: July 16, 2012.

71 Fu'ad al-Khatib, *Fath al-Andalus* (Amman, 1931).

72 Ibid., 48.

73 Ibid., 49. "Labbaika nahnu al-'Arab / nahnu al-suyuf al-qadab…" On Arabic nation-alist terminology see William L. Cleveland, *The Making of an Arab Nationalist: Ottomanism and Arabism in the Life and Thought of Sati' Al-Husri* (Princeton, NJ: Princeton University Press, 1971), 92–6.

74 Fu 'ad al-Khatib, *Diwan al-Khatib*, ed. Riyad al-Khatib (Cairo: Dar al-Ma'arif, 1959), 3.

75 Ibn Habib, *Kitab Al-Ta'rij*, 136.

76 Ibn 'Abd al-Hakam, *Futuh Misr*, 205. There is a tradition that Yulyan's descendants eventually converted to Islam, and that one even became a revered scholar in Iraq. See Ibn Khaldun, *Histoire des Berbères et des dynasties musulmanes de l'Afrique septentrionale*, ed. Paul Casanova, trans. William MacGuckin Slane, vol. 1 (Paris: P. Geuthner, 1968), 346n3.

77 Ibn Khaldun, *Histoire des Berbères et des dynasties musulmanes de l'Afrique septentrionale*, 1:345f (appendix, "Conquête de l'Afrique septentrionale par les musulmans et histoire de ce pays sous les émirs arabes," taken from En-Noweiri's work, published in Paris, 1841, by M. Noël as Histoire de l'Afrique sous la dynastie des Aghlabites etc.).

78 al-Maqqari, *Nafh al-tib*, 1: 235–6. E. Lévi-Provençal, Ch. Pellat, "al-Makkari," Encyclopaedia of Islam. On Cairo's book culture see Nelly Hanna, *In Praise of Books: A Cultural History of Cairo's Middle Class, Sixteenth to the Eighteenth Century* (Syracuse, NY: Syracuse University Press, 2003), 79–103.

79 Mughith was a historical figure, a lieutenant of Tariq and freedman, as his byname "al-Rumi" indicates. Hitoriography does not associate him with Yulyan, though. C.F. Seybold, M. Ocaña Jiménez, "Kurtuba," Encyclopaedia of Islam, Second Edi-tion. Brill Online, 2012. Reference. University of Maryland, http://referenceworks. brillonline.com.proxy-um.researchport.umd.edu/entries/encyclopaedia-of-islam-2/ kurtuba-SIM_4552, date of access: July 19, 2012.

80 Khatib, *Fath al-Andalus*, 1–4.
81 ʿAli Mubarak, *Khulasat Tarikh Al-ʿArab* (Cairo: Matbaʿat Muhammad Afandi Mustafa, 1309), 95–6; L.-A. Sédillot, *Histoire des Arabes* (Paris: L. Hachette et Cie, 1854), 147–50.
82 Mustafa Kamil, *Fath al-Andalus: al-nass al-kamil lil-masrahiyya al-wahida allati katabaha al-zaʿim al-khalid Mustafa Kamil*, eds. Rishad Rushdi, Masrahiyyat Mukhtara 19 (Cairo: Matabiʿ al-Haiʾa al-Misriyya al-ʿAmma liʾl-Kitab, 1973), 33–4. Kamil may have been familiar with Mubarak's translation. See Walker, "Egypt's Arabism," 51.
83 Kamil, *Fath al-Andalus*, 35; Walker, "Egypt's Arabism," 51–66; compare Israel Gershoni and James P. Jankowski, *Egypt, Islam, and the Arabs: The Search for Egyptian Nationhood, 1900–1930* (Oxford, New York: Oxford University Press, 1987), 3–20.
84 A superficial worldwide online library search through *WorldCat* alone yielded nearly twenty different Arabic editions between 1903 and 2007 in Cairo and Beirut, the Arab world's publishing capitals (as of July 26, 2012).
85 A list of novels in Thomas Philipp, *Gurgi Zaidan, His Life and Thought*, Beiruter Texte und Studien 3 (Beirut, Wiesbaden: Orient-Institut der Dt. Morgenländischen Gesellschaft; Steiner, 1979), 235–39. Some of the information is based on anecdotal accounts by the late Thomas Philipp, and on Yoav Di-Capua, *Gatekeepers of the Arab Past: Historians and History Writing in Twentieth-Century Egypt* (Berkeley, CA: University of California Press, 2009), 53–9. See also the chapter on Zaydan in Stephen Sheehi, *Foundations of Modern Arab Identity* (Gainesville: University Press of Florida, 2004), 159–88. See Indonesian translations such as Jirji Zaydan, *Rahasia Tjintjin Nukman. Roman Sedjarah Karya Djirdji Zaidan, Alih Bahasa A. Fuad Said*, trans. A. Fuad Said (Medan: Firma Harris, 1965) (trans. of Fatat Ghassan); Jirji Zaydan, *Penaklukan Andalus*, trans. A. Fuad Said (Medan: Pustaka "Budaja," 1964) (trans. of *Fath al-Andalus*); Jirji Zaydan, *Dibawah Rajuan Setan*, trans. A. Fuad Said (Medan: Dian, 1964); Jirji Zaydan, *Pengantin Fergana*, trans. A. Fuad Said (Medan: Dian, 1965) (both trans. of *ʿArus Ferghana*).
86 Jirji Zaydan, *Fath al-Andalus* (Cairo: Dar al-Hilal, 1965), 4. A brief analysis of another one of Zaydan's *al-Andalus* novels, *Sharl wa-ʿAbd al-Rahman* (1904), is in Granara, "Nostalgia, Arab Nationalism, and the Andalusian Chronotope," 63–5.
87 See motifs in Zaydan, *Fath al-Andalus*, 28–9, 70–74, 148–84.
88 Al-Maqqari conveys this tradition, too, and introduces the ensuing disunity as one of the reasons for the weakness of the Visigoths. Maqqari, *The History of the Mohammedan Dynasties in Spain*, 254, 269–70.
89 Reinhart Pieter Anne Dozy, *Spanish Islam: A History of the Moslems in Spain* (London: Chatto & Windus, 1913), 215–32. Zaydan had great esteem for al-Maqqari: Khaled El-Rouayheb, *Islamic Intellectual History in the Seventeenth Century: Scholarly Currents in the Ottoman Empire and the Maghreb* (Cambridge: Cambridge University Press, 2015), 155.
90 Di-Capua, *Gatekeepers of the Arab Past*, 53; Philipp, *Gurgi Zaydan*, 26. Zaydan received an important induction to Orientalist literature in the British Library during a short stay in London in 1886. On Rida's criticism see Sheehi, *Foundations of Modern Arab Identity*, 160.
91 Drayson, *The King and the Whore*, 1, 4–6.
92 An early print is in the Library of Congress, Washington DC: Miguel de Luna, *La verdadera historia del rey Don Rodrigo* (Valencia: En casa de P.P. Mey, a costa de B. Simon, 1606).
93 Drayson, *The King and the Whore*, 22–47, 53–6.
94 Ibid., 58–127.
95 Ibid., 129–56; Robert Southey, *Roderick: The Last of the Goths*, vol. 1 (London: Longman, Hurst, Rees, Orme, and Brown, 1816).

96 Sade, "Rodrigue ou la tour enchantée: Conte allégorique," in *Les crimes de l'amour: nouvelles héroïques et tragiques ; précédées d'une Idée sur les romans* (Cadeilhan: Zulma, 1995), 257–71; Washington Irving, *Legends of the Conquest of Spain* (London: John Murray, 1836), 27–157; T.H. Chivers, "Count Julian, or the Virgin of the First Fond Love. A Tragedy, in Five Acts," in *The Unpublished Plays of Thomas Holley Chivers* (Delmar, NY: Scholars' Facsimiles & Reprints, 1980), 1–112.

97 Drayson, *The King and the Whore*, 156–210; Felix Dahn, *König Roderich: Ein Trauerspiel in fünf Aufzügen*, 2nd edn. (Leipzig: Breitkopf und Härtel, 1876). The evaluation of the musical is based on the CD recording *La Cava the Musical*. (London: Dress Circle, 2000).

98 Dozy, *Spanish Islam*, 230n1, 231–2; Zaydan, *Fath al-Andalus*, 302–48.

99 Ibn Habib, *Kitab Al-Ta'rij*, 137 (Ludhriq); Ibn 'Abd al-Hakam, *Futuh Misr*, 205, see also n6&8 (Ludhriq, Yulyan); al-Maqqari, *Nafh al-tib*, 1:214; Maqqari, *The History of the Mohammedan Dynasties in Spain*, 1: 509–510n4–5.

100 Zaydan, *Fath al-Andalus*, 4; Mubarak, *Khulasat Tarikh Al-'Arab*, 95.

101 Hamadi Ben Halima, *Un demi siècle de théâtre arabe en tunisie, 1907–1957*, Publications de l'Université de Tunis, Faculté des lettres et sciences humaines de Tunis: 6. sér., Philosophie-littérature; v. 6 (Tunis: Université de Tunis, 1974), 40, 66, 83, 91, 114, 137.

102 *Tariq Ibn Ziyad: Fatih al-Andalus* (Beirut: Dar al-'Ilm li'l-Malayin, 2000), (quote on back cover). [no author, 1st edn, 1994.] The book contains reading questions with an instructive purpose.

103 Mahmud Shalabi, *Hayat Tariq Ibn Ziyad, Fatih al-Andalus* (Beirut: Dar al-Jil, 1992), 77f; *Tariq Ibn Ziyad, Fatih al-Andalus*, Abtal al-'Arab 10 (Beirut: Dar al-'Awda, 1975), 19, 30f.

104 Refers to Mahmud Salim, *Qisas tarikh al-Islam li'l-fityan wa'l-fatayat* (Beirut: al-Mu'assasa al-'Arabiyya li'l-Dirasat wa'l-Nashr, 1977).

105 Muhammad Bassam Mals, *Fath al-Andalus fi adab al-atfal: dirasa naqdiya*, Buhuth fi thaqafat al-tifl al-Muslim 8 (Riyadh: al-Mamlaka al-'Arabiyya al-Sa'udiyya, Wizarat al-Ta'lim al-'Ali, Jami'at al-Imam Muhammad ibn Sa'ud al-Islamiyya, Idarat al-Thaqafa wa'l-Nashr, 1994), 3–12, 16, 19–23, 36–38.

106 'Uways, *Qadiyat ihraq Tariq Ibn Ziyad li'l-sufun*, 41–58.

107 Muhammad 'Abd al-Raziq Manna', *Batal al-Andalus Tariq Ibn Ziyad*, Abtal al-Islam (Benghazi: Mu'assasat Nasir li'l-Thaqafa, 1978), first quote 86, second quote 5–6, see also 24–31.

108 Sawadi 'Abd Muhammad, *Tariq Ibn Ziyad: Hayatuhu, zuhuruhu, nasabuhu, khitatuhu al-'askariyya wa-waqa'i'uhu fi'l-Andalus wa'l-Maghrib* (Baghdad: Dar al-Shu'un al-Thaqafiyya al-'Amma "Afaq 'Arabiyya," 1988), 4, 34–5; the burning of the ships is on 92–4. On regime historians see Eric Davis, *Memories of State: Politics, History, and Collective Identity in Modern Iraq* (Berkeley: University of California Press, 2005), 148–75, 185–9; Stefan Wild, "Der Generalsekretär und die Geschichtsschreibung: Saddam Husayn und die irakische Geschichtswissenschaft," in *The Challenge of the Middle East. Middle Eastern Studies at the University of Amsterdam*, eds. Ibrahim A. El-Sheikh et al. (Amsterdam, 1982), 161–72.

109 In addition to being widely distributed as a download on the internet, the film is available on *YouTube*: http://www.youtube.com/watch?v=TWNGn4okAYs&feature= related; date of access: July 27, 2012.

110 Since 2000, several TV series, Syrian productions or co-productions involving Syria, Morocco and other Arab countries, have covered Andalusian topics, including a 2004 production entitled *Tariq*. The elaborately staged series were first broadcast during Ramadan to wide audiences throughout the Arab world, but have become a mainstay of Arab television programs since. The not so subtle message of these

productions is one of unity and civilizational splendor under threat by foreign powers, but more importantly by internal rifts, in a reflection of contemporary Arab politics. Interestingly, the series gives a lot of room to Berbers as faithful to the cause of Islam, and to Arab induced rifts among the Muslims as a reason for weakness. Aside from these novelties, the series takes over many of Zaydan's characters, including Count Julian, Florinda and Alfons. See John Shoup, "As It Was, and As It Should Be Now: Al Andalus in Contemporary Arab Television Dramas," *Transnational Broadcasting Studies*, no. 15 (Fall 2005), http://www.tbsjournal.com/Archives/Fall05/Shoup.html. The series is available on *You Tube*, for example on: http://www.youtube.com/playlist?list=PLD9D03445EE04F314, date of access: February 6, 2015.

111 Zaydan, *Fath al-Andalus*, 27–9, 63–6, 148–84, 188–92, 360.
112 Granara, "Nostalgia, Arab Nationalism, and the Andalusian Chronotope," 58–9, 62–3.
113 "Al-Andalus al-Jadida [Letter to the Editor]," *al-Risala* 292 (1939): 282–3. On similar notions see Amal N. Ghazal, *Islamic Reform and Arab Nationalism: Expanding the Crescent from the Mediterranean to the Indian Ocean (1880s–1930s)* (London: Routledge, 2010), 1, 125.
114 James Jankowski, "Egyptian Responses to the Palestine Problem in the Interwar Period," *International Journal of Middle East Studies* 12 (1980): 21, 23.
115 Muhammad 'Abdallah 'Inan, "Khatimat al-Ma'sat al-Andalusiyya: Al-Sira' al-akhir bayna'l-Muriskiyyin wa-Isbaniya, 1," *al-Risala* 203 (1937): 853. The text of the convention is available on http://www.worldlii.org/int/other/LNTSer/1937/174.html, date of access: August 22, 2013. See Article 3, paragraph 4 on p45 (p5 of the online document).
116 Isabelle Rohr, *The Spanish Right and the Jews, 1898–1945: Antisemitism and Opportunism* (Brighton; Portland: Sussex Academic Press, 2007), 15–16, 20, 40–48. The restrictive immigration policy towards German Jews at the time contradicted this pro-Jewish image, though.
117 'Inan, "Khatimat al-Ma'sat al-Andalusiyya…," *al-Risala* 203 (1937): 853.
118 Granara, "Nostalgia, Arab Nationalism, and the Andalusian Chronotope," 66–71; M. Peled, "Annals of Doom: 'Palestinian Literature – 1917–1948,'" *Arabica* 29.2 (1982): 181; Snir, "'Al-Andalus Arising from Damascus': Al-Andalus in Modern Arabic Poetry," 281–3.
119 Al-Mamlaka al-Maghribiyya, Wizarat al-Tarbiyya al-Wataniyya, *Al-Qira'a: Kitab al-Talmidh. Al-Sana al-khamisa min al-ta'lim al-asasi* (Rabat: Dar Nashr al-Ma'rifa, 2001), 60. Unfortunately, the book was not available for a reproduction of the watercolor.

4 Of Kings and Cavemen

1 "Min Hadarat al-Islam: Dawr al-tuhaf al-'Arabiyya," *al-Risala* 545 (1943), p995.
2 Wizarat al-Ma'arif al-'Umumiyya, *Mathaf al-Hadara al-Misriyya 1949* (Cairo, 1949), image of the Caveman on p35, of the Pasha on p265, Khedive Isma'il p267, and Kings Fu'ad and Faruq on pp287 and 289, respectively.
3 Ibid., 24–7.
4 Ibid., 12.
5 Christel Braae, "The Early Museums and the Formation of Their Publics," in *Middle Eastern Cities, 1900–1950: Public Places and Public Spheres in Transformation*, eds. Hans Chr. Korsholm Nielsen and Jakob Skovgaard-Petersen (Aarhus: Aarhus University Press, 2001), 113–15; Carol Duncan, "Art Museums and the Ritual of Citizenship," in *Exhibiting Cultures: The Poetics and Politics of Museum Display*, eds. Ivan Karp and Steven Lavine (Washington: Smithsonian Institution Press, 1991), 96, 99. On museology in Jordan, including grass-roots activities for the assertion of community identities among the tribal population, see Irene Maffi, *Pratiques*

du patrimoine et politiques de la mémoire en Jordanie: Entre histoire dynastique et récits communautaires (Lausanne: Payot Lausanne, 2004), passim; on questions of archaeology and national heritage see Irene Maffi, "The Intricate Life of Cultural Heritage: Colonial and Postcolonial Processes of Patrimonialisation in Jordan," in *The Politics and Practices of Cultural Heritage in the Middle East: Positioning the Material Past in Contemporary Societies*, eds. Rami Daher and Irene Maffi, Library of Modern Middle East Studies 101 (London: Tauris, 2014), 66–103. Magnus Bernhardsson addresses questions of national identity, imperialism and their links to archaeology and museology in *Reclaiming a Plundered Past: Archaeology and Nation Building in Modern Iraq* (Austin, TX: University of Texas Press, 2005), passim.

6 Wizarat al-Ma'arif al-'Umumiyya, *Mathaf al-Hadara*, 35.

7 "Mathaf al-Hadara," *al-Hilal* 55 (1947), 58.

8 "Mathaf al-Hadara al-Misriyya," *al-Hilal* 53 (1945), 519.

9 Wizarat al-Ma'arif al-'Umumiyya, *Mathaf al-Hadara*, 271, 293, 299.

10 Israel Gershoni and James P. Jankowski, *Egypt, Islam, and the Arabs: The Search for Egyptian Nationhood, 1900–1930* (Oxford, New York: Oxford University Press, 1987), 35–36, 131–61.

11 Debates about Darwinism and the origins of man first flared up in the Middle East in the 1880s and continue until today. Compare Muzaffar Iqbal, *The Making of Islamic Science* (Sclangor, Malaysia: Islamic Book Trust, 2009), 181–8. On an 1882 controversy about Darwinism at the Syrian Protestant College, later American University of Beirut, see Albert Habib Hourani, *Arabic Thought in the Liberal Age, 1798–1939* (Cambridge: Cambridge University Press, 1983), 249f. On the prominence of Darwinism and its criticism among Arab intellectuals see Marwa Elshakry, *Reading Darwin in Arabic, 1860–1950* (Chicago; London: The University of Chicago Press, 2013), 287–98, 307–311, and passim. See also Omnia S. El Shakry, *The Great Social Laboratory: Subjects of Knowledge in Colonial and Postcolonial Egypt* (Stanford, CA: Stanford University Press, 2007), 10–14.

12 "Mathaf al-Hadara al-Misriyya," *al-Hilal* 53 (1945), 519.

13 "Mathaf al-Hadara," *al-Hilal* 55 (1947), 58.

14 Wizarat al-Ma'arif al-'Umumiyya, *Mathaf al-Hadara*, 189–90, 195.

15 Donald Malcolm Reid, "The Egyptian Geographical Society: From Foreign Laymen's Society to Indigenous Professional Association," *Poetics Today* 14.3 (October 1, 1993): 539–72. The history of the Agricultural Society is also in "Kanat al-Jam'iyya al-Zira'iyya wizarat al-zira'a fima mada," *al-Muqattam*, March 1, 1949, p10.

16 DWQ 0069–005661, Mathaf al-hadara al-misriyya: Mudhakkira, April 6, 1939.

17 DWQ 0069–005664, Juz' thalith awraq khassa bi-mathaf al-hadara al-misriyya al-qadima: Article "Avant son Inauguration Officielle: Visite au Musée de la Civilisation Egyptienne, par Gabriel Boctor," April 24, 1946. The author recounted the origins of the project. See also *Das Schweizerische Landesmuseum, 1898–1948: Kunst, Handwerk und Geschichte. Festbuch zum 50. Jahrestag der Eröffnung* (Zürich: Atlantis, 1948), 5,9,10,17, 28–74.

18 DWQ 0069–005661, Mathaf al-hadara al-misriyya: Mudhakkira, April 6, 1939, p1.

19 Ghurbal himself earned a Ph.D. at the University of London under the supervision of Arnold Toynbee. On the Arab reception of Toynbee as a historian and public intellectual see the chapter "Toynbee in Montreal" in Omar Kamil, *Der Holocaust im arabischen Gedächtnis: Eine Diskursgeschichte 1945–1967*, Schriften des Simon-Dubnow-Instituts 15 (Göttingen: Vandenhoeck & Ruprecht, 2012), 47–85, on Ghurbal pp67–8.

20 Yoav Di-Capua, *Gatekeepers of the Arab Past: Historians and History Writing in Twentieth-Century Egypt* (Berkeley: University of California Press, 2009), 6–10, 186–96.

21 Khaled Fahmy, *All the Pasha's Men: Mehmed Ali, His Army, and the Making of Modern Egypt*, Cambridge Middle East Studies 8 (Cambridge, New York: Cambridge

University Press, 1997), 12–26; Donald M. Reid, "Nationalizing the Pharaonic Past: Egyptology, Imperialism, and Egyptian Nationalism, 1922–1952," in *Rethinking Nationalism in the Arab Middle East*, eds. Israel Gershoni and James P. Jankowski (New York: Columbia University Press, 1997), 145. Egyptian historiography refers to Mehmet Ali as Muhammad 'Ali in an Arabized version of his name.

22 Duncan, "Art Museums," 89–93, 98.

23 Robert Musil, "Monuments," in *Selected Writings*, ed. Burton Pike, The German Library 72 (New York: Continuum, 1986), 320.

24 Eilean Hooper-Greenhill, *Museums and the Shaping of Knowledge* (London; New York: Routledge, 1992), 4–5, 23–132.

25 Ibid., 133–66.

26 Ibid., 167–90. See also Reinhart Koselleck, *Vergangene Zukunft: Zur Semantik geschichtlicher Zeiten* (Frankfurt am Main: Suhrkamp, 1979), 47–66.

27 Elliott Colla, *Conflicted Antiquities: Egyptology, Egyptomania, Egyptian Modernity* (Durham, NC: Duke University Press, 2007), 24–51, 58. The British Museum was founded in the mid-eighteenth century as an institution for highly regulated public access, but without the popular civilizing ethos of the post-revolutionary Louvre.

28 Ibid., 60.

29 Ibid., 61, 63–6.

30 Gyan Prakash, *Another Reason: Science and the Imagination of Modern India.* (Princeton, NJ; Chichester: Princeton University Press, 1999), 18–21, quote on 19; see also Donald M. Reid, *Whose Pharaohs? Archaeology, Museums, and Egyptian National Identity from Napoleon to World War I* (Berkeley, CA: University of California Press, 2002), 9–10; and compare Bernard S. Cohn, *Colonialism and Its Forms of Knowledge: The British in India* (Princeton, NJ: Princeton University Press, 1996), 95–96. Compare also Bernhardsson, *Reclaiming a Plundered Past*, 6–18, and passim.

31 See for instance Peter Gran, *Islamic Roots of Capitalism: Egypt, 1760–1840*, 2nd edn. (Syracuse, NY: Syracuse University Press, 1998); Nelly Hanna, *In Praise of Books: A Cultural History of Cairo's Middle Class, Sixteenth to the Eighteenth Century* (Syracuse, NY: Syracuse University Press, 2003).

32 Reid, *Whose Pharaohs?*, 21–36, 40–46; Colla, *Conflicted Antiquities*, 73–91.

33 Reid, *Whose Pharaohs?*, 37–9, 46–50, 120–3, 189–190.

34 Ibid., 36–37, 39–40, 50–54; Colla, *Conflicted Antiquities*, 121–6. See also D. Ayalon, "al-Djabarti." *Encyclopaedia of Islam, Second Edition*, eds. P. Bearman, Th. Bianquis, C.E. Bosworth, E. van Donzel, W.P. Heinrichs. Brill Online, 2015. Reference. University of Maryland – College Park, http://referenceworks.brillonline.com/entries/encyclopaedia-of-islam-2/al-djabarti-SIM_1894, date of access: May 19, 2015; K. Öhrnberg, "Rifa'a Bey al-Tahtawi." *Encyclopaedia of Islam, Second Edition*, eds. P. Bearman, Th. Bianquis, C.E. Bosworth, E. van Donzel, W.P. Heinrichs. Brill Online, 2015. Reference. University of Maryland – College Park, http://referenceworks.brillonline.com/entries/encyclopaedia-of-islam-2/rifaa-bey-al-tahtawi-SIM_6294, date of access: May 19, 2015.

35 Reid, *Whose Pharaohs?* 54–58.

36 Ibid., 93–106, 192–5; for Mariette's statements, see the quotations on p106.

37 Prakash, *Another Reason*, 22, 26, 30–31, 44–6, 48; Paul Sedra, "Imagining an Imperial Race: Egyptology in the Service of Empire," *Comparative Studies of South Asia, Africa and the Middle East* 24 (2004): 249–52.

38 Reid, *Whose Pharaohs?* 116–18, 173–5, 205–12.

39 C. Wendell, "Lutfi al-Sayyid," *Encyclopaedia of Islam, Second Edition*, eds. P. Bearman, Th. Bianquis, C.E. Bosworth, E. van Donzel, W.P. Heinrichs. Brill Online, 2015. Reference. University of Maryland – College Park. http://referenceworks.

brillonline.com/entries/encyclopaedia-of-islam-2/lutfi-al-sayyid-SIM_4705, date of
access: May 19, 2015.
40 "Al-Athar al-Qadima," quoted in Colla, *Conflicted Antiquities*, 149–50. See also
p151.
41 Ibid., 177, 199–210; Reid, "Nationalizing the Pharaonic Past," 133–5; Donald M.
Reid, *Contesting Antiquity in Egypt: Archaeologies, Museums & the Struggle for
Identities from World War I to Nasser* (Cairo: American University in Cairo Press,
2015), 51–79.
42 Reid, "Nationalizing the Pharaonic Past," 127–9, 131–2, 135–6, 138; Reid, *Whose
Pharaohs?*, 186–90, 201–204; Reid, *Contesting Antiquity in Egypt*, 109–133.
43 Reid, "Nationalizing the Pharaonic Past," 140–2; Reid, *Contesting Antiquity in
Egypt*, 111–114, 116–117, 120–22. See the record of Hassan's Rigorosum/Ph.D. ex-
amination in the archives of the University of Vienna on http://scopeq.cc.univie.
ac.at/Query/detail.aspx?ID=354616, date of access: January 7, 2016.
44 S.R.K. Glanville, "Reginald Engelbach," *The Journal of Egyptian Archaeology* 32
(1946): 98. On Glanville see http://www.ames.cam.ac.uk/faclib/archive/glanville.
html, date of access: June 19, 2012.
45 Reid, "Nationalizing the Pharaonic Past," 141–4; Reid, *Contesting Antiquity in
Egypt*, 278–88; Glanville, "Engelbach," 97–8. The affair is also covered in James F.
Goode, *Negotiating for the Past: Archaeology, Nationalism, and Diplomacy in the
Middle East, 1919–1941* (Austin: University of Texas Press, 2007), 118–25.
46 DWQ 0069–005624, dated Cairo, November 10, 1937: The letters (including the
interim report, dated May 16, 1937) and the memorandum contained in this file do
not have an immediate addressee, except for sporadic references to a "ministry" as a
recipient. The letters are held in French, but the memorandum was written in Arabic.
It is possible that Hassan sent a copy of his complaints to his employer, the Ministry
of Education, and another one to the Palace. At a time of growing tensions with Nazi
Germany in Europe, the affair was also shaded by British and French suspicions
because of Hassan's protégé relationship with Hermann Junker, head of the German
Archaeological Institute, Department Cairo, and Professor at Cairo University. Reid,
Contesting Antiquity in Egypt, 288.
47 In DWQ 0069–005624.
48 Ibid., Memorandum, p2.
49 Ibid., p3. Hassan himself had been attacked the previous year for not knowing Greek
or Latin in the controversy over the directorship of the Antiquities Service. Reid,
Contesting Antiquity in Egypt, 281f.
50 Reid, "Nationalizing the Pharaonic Past," 147.
51 Glanville, "Engelbach," 98; Reid, "Nationalizing the Pharaonic Past," 146–7, quote
on 144, referencing an article from Akhir Sa'a. Reid, *Contesting Antiquity in Egypt*,
273, 288–91, 365.
52 *Al-Balagh*, April 5, 1949, p4: "Al-'Arabiyya tahullu mahall al-Ingliziyya 'ala lafitat
al-Mathaf al-Misri." The reporter apparently mistook Latin for English.
53 Israel Gershoni and James P. Jankowski, *Redefining the Egyptian Nation, 1930–1945*
(Cambridge; New York: Cambridge University Press, 1995), 54–96.
54 Israel Gershoni and James P. Jankowski, *Confronting Fascism in Egypt: Dictatorship
Versus Democracy in the 1930s* (Stanford: Stanford University Press, 2010), 27–44.
55 A list of the museums that existed in 1939 is in DWQ 0069–005661, Mathaf al-hadara
al-misriyya: Mudhakkira, April 6, 1939, p1; and a list of Fu'ad's foundations is in
DWQ 0069–005664, Juz' thalith awraq khassa bi-mathaf al-hadara al-misriyya
al-qadima: 'Ahd al-maghfur lahu al-Malik Fu'ad, p2. On Fu'ad's sponsorship see
Reid, "The Egyptian Geographical Society," 555–6.
56 Colla, *Conflicted Antiquities*, 53–5.

57 Reid, *Whose Pharaohs?*, 7–9, 151–2, 161, 213–85, 294; Donald Malcolm Reid, "Cultural Imperialism and Nationalism: The Struggle to Define and Control the Heritage of Arab Art in Egypt," *International Journal of Middle East Studies* 24, no. 1 (1992): 57–76; István Ormos, *Max Herz Pasha 1856–1919: His Life and Career* (Cairo: Institut français d'archéologie orientale, 2009), passim. This section owes a great deal to Donald Reid's research about Egyptian museums. See also Reid, *Contesting Antiquity in Egypt*, 167–259.

58 DWQ 0069–026591, Musée Royal d'Agriculture d'Egypte, Le Caire, Guizeh, le 26.1.1931: "Appel à la Nation Egyptienne," pp1–3. The museum opened to the public on 17 January 1938 only. See "Al-Barid al-Adabi: Al-Mathaf al-Zira'i al-Misri," *al-Risala* 238 (1938), 156f.

59 Tony Bennett, *The Birth of the Museum: History, Theory, Politics* (London; New York: Routledge, 1995), 38–9.

60 On the role of museums in shaping historical consciousness: Gaynor Kavanagh, "Making Histories, Making Memories," in *Making Histories in Museums*, ed. Gaynor Kavanagh (London, New York: Leicester University Press, 1996), 5–7; John Reeve, "Making the History Curriculum," in *Making Histories in Museums*, ed. Gaynor Kavanagh (London, New York: Leicester University Press, 1996), 228–39.

61 DWQ 0069–005661, Mathaf al-hadara al-misriyya: Mudhakkira, 6 April 1939, pp1–2.

62 See, for example, Timothy Mitchell, *Colonising Egypt* (Berkeley, Los Angeles, London: University of California Press, 1991), 34–127.

63 Bennett, *The Birth of the Museum*, 6, 17–24, 28, 48–58. The Egyptian Museum in Cairo provides an example for this kind of architecture, even though it continued to function following the old storehouse model.

64 Ibid., 41–3.

65 Mitchell, *Colonising Egypt*, 1–33.

66 Reid, *Whose Pharaohs?* 125–30, 190–92; Zeynep Çelik, *Displaying the Orient: Architecture of Islam at Nineteenth-Century World's Fairs*, Comparative Studies on Muslim Societies 12 (Berkeley: University of California Press, 1992), 57–63, 111–119; on the opening of the Suez Canal in 1869 as an exhibition: 145–51.

67 DWQ 0069–005662, Juz' auwal auraq khassa bi-mathaf al-hadara al-misriyya al-qadima, min 4/6/1939 – 5/31/1942, Session of the Committee for Exhibitions and Conferences and the Cotton Museum, minutes, May 3, 1939.

68 Entry "Fahmi, Mustafa" in Arthur Goldschmidt, *Biographical Dictionary of Modern Egypt* (Boulder: Lynne Rienner, 2000), 52. A plaque with his name, along with the year "1936" as the date of the completion of the building, still adorns the main entrance of the Grand Pavilion.

69 Princesses participated in state functions during the rule of Khedive Isma'il (r. 1863–1879) already, but their elevation into celebrity status must have been a novelty. Mona L. Russell, *Creating the New Egyptian Woman: Consumerism, Education, and National Identity, 1863–1922* (New York: Palgrave Macmillan, 2004), 16.

70 "Jami'at sanat 1936: Al-Ma'rad al-zira'i al-sina'i al-khamis 'ashar," *al-Hilal* 44 (1936), 533–539. On Orientalism in European exhibitions see Mitchell, *Colonising Egypt*, 1–13; on the Effendiyya and "cultural consumption" see Gershoni and Jankowski, *Redefining the Egyptian Nation*, 13–14.

71 DWQ 0069–005662, Juz' auwal auraq khassa bi-mathaf al-hadara al-misriyya al-qadima, min 4/6/1939 – 5/31/1942: Session of the Committee for Exhibitions and Conferences and the Cotton Museum, Minutes, May 3, 1939.

72 Ibid.: Letter by Fu'ad 'Abd al-Malik, Owner and director of *al-Mathaf al-Misri li'l-tamathil al-sham'iyya*. Cairo, June 22, 1939, addressed to the Director General of the Royal Agricultural Society, memorandum attached. Arabic Wikipedia explains that the Museum was first located on what is today Tahrir Square, then moved to Qasr

al-'Aini Street near Garden City, and finally to its present location in the Cairo suburb Ain al-Helwan. http://ar.wikipedia.org/wiki/ معـــلشــ ا_تحف م, date of access: February 21, 2013.

73 Vanessa R. Schwartz, *Spectacular Realities: Early Mass Culture in Fin-de-Siècle Paris* (Berkeley: University of California Press, 1998), 5–6.

74 See for example Wilhelm Kretzler, "Glückauf im Bergwerk: Das Besucherbergwerk im Deutschen Museum," *Kultur & Technik – das Magazin aus dem Deutschen Museum* 12, no. 1 (1988): 2–7.

75 DWQ 0069–005662, Juz' auwal auraq khassa bi-mathaf al-hadara al-misriyya al-qadima, min 4/6/1939 – 5/31/1942: Letter by Fu'ad 'Abd al-Malik, memorandum, 1.

76 Michelle E. Bloom, *Waxworks: A Cultural Obsession* (Minneapolis: University of Minnesota Press, 2003), 3–18.

77 Schwartz, *Spectacular Realities*, 108–21, 131–2; quotes on 108, 131.

78 DWQ 0069–005662, Juz' auwal auraq khassa bi-mathaf al-hadara al-misriyya al-qadima, min 4/6/1939 – 5/31/1942: Letter and memorandum (p1) by Fu'ad 'Abd al-Malik).

79 Bloom, *Waxworks*, 21–22, 30–31.

80 DWQ 0069–005662, Juz' auwal auraq khassa bi-mathaf al-hadara al-misriyya al-qadima, min 4/6/1939 – 5/31/1942: Memorandum by Fu'ad 'Abd al-Malik, 3.

81 On the *Deutsches Museum* see Kenneth Hudson, *Museums of Influence* (Cambridge; New York: Cambridge University Press, 1987), 88–90, 96–101.

82 DWQ 0069–005662, Juz' auwal auraq khassa bi-mathaf al-hadara al-misriyya al-qadima, min 4/6/1939 – 5/31/1942: Memorandum by Fu'ad 'Abd al-Malik, 3.

83 The caveman was a work by "Professor Ahmad Uthman." Wizarat al-Ma'arif al-'Umumiyya, *Mathaf al-Hadara*, 35.

84 Reid, "Nationalizing the Pharaonic Past," 145. See also DWQ 0069–005661, Mathaf al-hadara al-misriyya: Minutes, session of the Committee of Exhibitions and Conferences and the Cotton Museum, Royal Agricultural Society, May 24, 1939, pp1, 3.

85 Ibid.: Letter by the General secretary [of the Railway Museum], dated 8 June 1939.

86 Ibid.: Letter, Egyptian Museum, to Royal Agricultural Society [?], 1939 [?]. This is probably a typed translation of a French original. The addressee and date can be derived from the context of other documents in the file.

87 DWQ 0069–005662, Juz' auwal auraq khassa bi-mathaf al-hadara al-misriyya al-qadima, min 4/6/1939 – 5/31/1942: Ministry of Defense, The War Museum, Re: the topic of the program of the representation/shaping of the military section, Cairo, June 22, 1939, addressed to the Director General of the Royal Agricultural Society (cover letter for the following); The War Museum, Concise Report about the Military Section in the Museum for Egyptian Civilization, p1.

88 Ibid.: Minutes of the session of the committee of the Museum of Civilization in the Agricultural Society, March 18, 1942, p2.

89 DWQ 0069–005661, Mathaf al-hadara al-misriyya: Al-Jam'iyya al-zira'iyya al-malikiyya, *Mathaf al-hadara al-misriyya: Majmu'at taqarir al-lijan al-far'iyya* (Collection of Memoranda of the Subcommittees), May 1942. (Matba'at 'Inani) The user of the copy of the booklet that is in the files of the Royal Diwan, probably the King's private secretary, inserted typed check lists of items and objects in the various sections that marked them as either completed or yet unfinished. The lists probably date to the second half of the 1940s.

90 Ibid., pp10–11, 18–19; DWQ 0069–005661, Mathaf al-hadara al-misriyya: Minutes, session of the Committee of Exhibitions and Conferences and the Cotton Museum, Royal Agricultural Society, May 24, 1939, p3. On Ghurbal and the French expedition see DWQ 0069–005662, Juz' auwal auraq khassa bi-mathaf al-hadara al-misriyya al-qadima, min 4/6/1939 – 5/31/1942: Letter, July 15, 1939, Royal Agricultural Society, p11. The "missing link" aspect is emphasized in the 1949 museum catalogue

as well. Compared to other sections, the actual display in the museum was relatively small. Dioramas, paintings and other exhibits represented early church life. Wizarat al-Ma'arif al-'Umumiyya, *Mathaf al-Hadara*, 121–35.

91 DWQ 0069–005661, Mathaf al-hadara al-misriyya: Al-Jam'iyya al-zira'iyya al-malikiyya, *mathaf al-hadara al-misriyya: Majmu'at taqarir al-lijan al-far'iyya*, p28; DWQ 0069–005663, Al-Juz' al-thani: Auraq khassa bi-mathaf al-hadara al-misriyya al-qadima: Royal Agricultural Society, Museum of Egyptian Civilization, Minutes of the session of the Executive and Coordination Committees, August 3, 1942, p2.

92 DWQ 0069–005662, Juz' auwal auraq khassa bi-mathaf al-hadara al-misriyya al-qadima, min 4/6/1939 – 5/31/1942: Letter, July 15, 1939, Royal Agricultural Society, p14.

93 Eve Troutt Powell, *A Different Shade of Colonialism: Egypt, Great Britain, and the Mastery of the Sudan*, Colonialisms 2 (Berkeley: University of California Press, 2003), 3–12, 26–63; see also Reid, *Whose Pharaohs?* 123–4; Reid, "The Egyptian Geographical Society," 541–5; Fahmy, *All the Pasha's Men*, 86–9; Heather J. Sharkey, *Living with Colonialism: Nationalism and Culture in the Anglo-Egyptian Sudan*, Colonialisms 3 (Berkeley: University of California Press, 2003), 4–6. The building of the Royal Geographic Society contained a small geographic and ethnographic collection, too, which opened as a museum in 1898. As an outlier in terms of timing, size and purpose, it has not been considered a part of Egypt's museum landscape for this study. El Shakry, *The Great Social Laboratory*, 27–30.

94 DWQ 0069–005662, Juz' auwal auraq khassa bi-mathaf al-hadara al-misriyya al-qadima, min 4/6/1939 – 5/31/1942: Executive Council of the Museum for Egyptian Civilization, minutes of the session on December 27, 1939, Diwan of the Ministry of Public Education, p3. When Tusun passed away on January 26, 1944, the officials involved in the Civilization Museum mourned him as a scholar who had provided guidance for the organization of the sections on the modern period and the civilization of the Sudan. DWQ 0069–005663, Al-Juz' al-thani: Auraq khassa bi-mathaf al-hadara al-misriyya al-qadima: Royal Agricultural Society, Museum of Egyptian Civilization, Minutes of the session of the Executive and Coordination Committees, February 10, 1944. In February 1923, Tusun had attended the official opening of the passageway between the antechamber and the actual tomb of Tutankhamen. King Fu'ad had declined an invitation. Colla, *Conflicted Antiquities*, 195.

95 Wizarat al-Ma'arif al-'Umumiyya, *Mathaf al-Hadara*, 217; Fahmy, *All the Pasha's Men*, 86–9; Troutt Powell, *A Different Shade of Colonialism*, 135–55; Juan Ricardo Cole, *Colonialism and Revolution in the Middle East: Social and Cultural Origins of Egypt's 'Urabi Movement*, Princeton Studies on the Near East (Princeton, NJ: Princeton University Press, 1993), 28f.

96 Wizarat al-Ma'arif al-'Umumiyya, *Mathaf al-Hadara*, 220, 223.

97 Ibid., 222: "Lawha raqm 6: Al-Khalawa." On Gordon College see Sharkey, *Living with Colonialism*, 7–9 and passim.

98 The 1942 booklet already confirmed this mindset among Egyptian nationalist intellectuals in a roadmap of goals and topics for the Sudan display, once more based on ideas of Shafiq Ghurbal. DWQ 0069–005661, Mathaf al-hadara al-misriyya: Al-Jam'iyya al-zira'iyya al-malikiyya, *mathaf al-hadara al-misriyya: Majmu'at taqarir al-lijan al-far'iyya*, p33: Assembly of the Subcommittee for the Sudan, May 9, 1942, Diwan of the Royal Agricultural Society.

99 Reid, "Nationalizing the Pharaonic Past," 145; Reid, "The Egyptian Geographical Society," 561, 563–4 (quote on 564). In 1951, the Ministry of Public Education put together a committee to create a separate "Nile Valley" section in the Civilization Museum. See the files in DWQ 0069–005667: Auraq khassa bi-mathaf al-hadara bi-qism wadi al-Nil. The folder contains no information if the project ever came to

fruition. On the "people without history" topos compare Cohn, *Colonialism and Its Forms of Knowledge*, 93.

100 Troutt Powell, *A Different Shade of Colonialism*, 7, 51–2; El Shakry, *The Great Social Laboratory*, 23–86. Maps have been interpreted as instruments of colonization. The combination of "census, map and museum" constitutes a "totalizing classificatory grid" for conquest, survey and classification. The abstract grid of longitude and latitude on a map stakes out "empty," i.e. unsurveyed territory for future power projection. In addition, maps determine shapes of borders that turn into logos for territorial nationalism. See Benedict Anderson, *Imagined Communities: Reflections on the Origin and Spread of Nationalism*, new edn. (London: Verso, 2006), 170–85, quote on 184.

101 DWQ 0069–005664, Juz' thalith awraq khassa bi-mathaf al-hadara al-misriyya al-qadima: Ministry of Public Education, Museum of Egyptian Civilization, minutes of the session of the executive subcommittee, June 22, 1947, p2. See also Mitchell, *Colonising Egypt*, 1–13.

102 Shafiq Ghurbal, *Muhammad 'Ali al-Kabir*, new edn, Kitab al-Hilal 430 (Cairo: Dar al-Hilal, 1986), 11 (original publication year unknown; Ghurbal presented it to the King on its first publication).

103 For al-Tahtawi's time in Khartoum see Troutt Powell, *A Different Shade of Colonialism*, 47–55.

104 *Al-Muqattam*, March 23, 1949, p3: "Al-Sahafiyyun al-Sudaniyyun."

105 *Al-Balagh*, March 22, 1949, pp3, 5: "Misr la turidu hukm al-Sudan – wa-la tatma'u fi istighlalihi au isti'marihi."

106 A change in the venue for committee meetings from the Society to the Ministry is an indicator for the shift in hierarchy. See, for instance, DWQ 0069–005663, Al-Juz' al-thani: Auraq khassa bi-mathaf al-hadara al-misriyya al-qadima: Ministry for Public Education, Museum of Egyptian Civilization, Program for Sudanese Civilization, January 23, 1945.

107 Reid, "The Egyptian Geographical Society," 555–6.

108 Reports and photos in *al-Balagh*, February 10, 1949, p2: "Sahib al-jalala al-malik yaftatihu al-yawm Mathaf al-Hadara;" and February 12, 1949, p1: "Sahib al-jalala al-malik wa'l-amiratan Fawziyya wa-Fa'iza fi iftitah Mathaf al-Hadara bi'l-Qahira."

109 *The New York Times*, March 6, 1949, p38: "In Israel and Egypt: New State Greets Tourists – Cairo Exposition."

110 *Al-Muqattam*, February 10, 1949, p3: "Mathaf al-Hadara: Awwal mathaf min naw'ihi, sijill al-hayat al-Misri min al-'ahd al-bida'i ila 'asr al-Faruq."

111 Ibid.

112 *Al-Muqattam*, February 25, 1949, p3: "Al-Ma'rad al-zira'i al-sina'i," same title on February 26, 1949, p3; February 28, 1949, p3; March 8, 1949, p3; April 13, 1949, p3; April 20, p4: "Intiha' ayyam al-ma'rad."

113 Sylvia G. Haim, *Arab Nationalism: An Anthology* (Berkeley, Los Angeles, London: University of California Press, 1976), 229–32.

114 Reid, "Nationalizing the Pharaonic Past," 145, 313n71.

115 Neither the 1949 museum catalogue nor the archival material cited for this study contain floor plans of the museum.

116 Marcelle Baud and Magdelaine Parisot, *Les Guides bleus: Égypte. Le Nil égyptien et soudanais du Delta à Khartoum* (Paris: Hachette, 1956), 143; Emma Brunner-Traut and Vera Hell, *Aegypten: Studienreiseführer mit Landeskunde*, 2nd edn, Führer für Studienreisen 1 (Stuttgart: Günther, 1966), 389; Dimitri Meeks and Jean Jacques Fauvel, *Les Guides bleus: Égypte. le Nil égyptien et soudanais, du delta à Khartoum* (Paris: Hachette, 1971), 328; Jean Jacques Fauvel, Dimitri Meeks, and Christine Favard-Meeks, *Les Guides bleus: Égypte. Le Nil égyptien et soudanais, du delta à Khartoum* (Paris: Hachette, 1976), 288.

117 Reid, "Nationalizing the Pharaonic Past," 145.

118 Abu Bakr 'Ali 'Abd al-'Alim, *Al-Lugha al-'Arabiyya: Iqra' wa-naqish. Al-Saff al-khamis al-ibtida'i, al-fasl al-dirasi al-awwal*, eds. Jumhuriyyat Misr al-'Arabiyya, Wizarat al-Tarbiyya wa'l-Ta'lim (Cairo: Al-Mu'assasa al-'Asriyya li'l-Nashr wa'l-Tarjama, 2001), 10–11.

119 Liqani, Ahmad Husayn al- et al., *Al-Dirasat al-Ijtima'iyya. Bi'at wa-shakhsiyyat Misriyya. Al-Saff al-khamis al-ibtida'i. Al-Fasl al-dirasi al-awwal*, eds. Jumhuriyyat Misr al-'Arabiyya, Wizarat al-Tarbiyya wa'l-Ta'lim (Cairo: Dar al-Tawfiqiyya li'l-Tiba'a, 2001), 13–18, 29–38, Liqani, Ahmad Husayn al- et al., *Al-Dirasat al-Ijtima'iyya. Bi'at wa-shakhsiyyat Misriyya. Al-Saff al-khamis al-ibtida'i. Al-Fasl al-dirasi al-thani*, eds. Jumhuriyyat Misr al-'Arabiyya, Wizarat al-Tarbiyya wa'l-Ta'lim (Cairo: Sharikat al-Islam Misr li'l-Tiba'a, 2001), 9–26, the Sudan on p12. Other textbooks consulted were: Mustafa Ahmad Sulaiman, Ahmad Ahmad Mutawalli Jad, and Nasif Mustafa 'Abd al-'Aziz, *Al-Lugha al-'Arabiyya: Iqra' wa-ta'allam. Al-Saff al-thani al-ibtida'i, al-fasl al-dirasi al-thani*, eds. Jumhuriyyat Misr al-'Arabiyya, Wizarat al-Tarbiyya wa'l-Ta'lim (Cairo: Dar Nahr al-Nil, 2001); Mustafa Ahmad Sulayman, Ahmad Ahmad Mutawalli Jad, and Nasif Mustafa 'Abd al-'Aziz, *Al-Lugha al-'Arabiyya: Iqra' wa-ta'allam. Al-Saff al-thalith al-ibtida'i, al-fasl al-dirasi al-awwal*, eds. Jumhuriyyat Misr al-'Arabiyya, Wizarat al-Tarbiyya wa'l-Ta'lim (Cairo: Sharikat al-Islam Misr li'l-Tiba'a, 2001); Mustafa Ahmad Sulayman, Ahmad Ahmad Mutawalli Jad, and Nasif Mustafa 'Abd al-'Aziz, *Al-Lugha al-'Arabiyya: Iqra' wa-ta'allam. Al-Saff al-thalith al-ibtida'i, al-fasl al-dirasi al-thani*, eds. Jumhuriyyat Misr al-'Arabiyya, Wizarat al-Tarbiyya wa'l-Ta'lim (Cairo: Sharikat al-Islam Misr li'l-Tiba'a, 2001); Liqani, Ahmad Husayn al- et al., *Al-Dirasat al-Ijtima'iyya. Al-Saff al-rabi' al-ibtida'i (muhafazati juz' min Misr). Al-Fasl al-dirasi al-awwal* (Cairo: 'Amr Ibn al-'As li'l-Tiba'a, 2001).

120 http://www.unesco.org/new/en/culture/themes/movable-heritage-and-museums/museums/museum-projects/the-national-museum-of-egyptian-civilization/, date of access: February 26, 2013. A critique of the new museum project is on http://cairobserver.com/post/29770743541/national-museum-of-egyptian-civilization, posted August 19, 2012, date of access: February 26, 2013. On a partial opening of the museum see: http://english.ahram.org.eg/NewsContent/9/44/141758/Heritage/Museums/National-Museum-of-Egyptian-Civilization-organises.aspx, date of access: March 14, 2016.

5 Damascus transfers

1 Anne-Laure Dupont, "Le grand homme, figure de la 'Renaissance' arabe," in *Saints et héros du moyen-orient contemporain: actes du colloque des 11 et 12 décembre 2000, à l'institut universitaire de France*, ed. Catherine Mayeur-Jaouen (Paris: Maisonneuve et Larose, 2002), 62.

2 Emile Durkheim, *The Elementary Forms of the Religious Life* (London: George Allen & Unwin Ltd., 1968), 415ff.

3 Avner Ben-Amos, *Funerals, Politics, and Memory in Modern France, 1789–1996* (Oxford; New York: Oxford University Press, 2000), 9f, 28f; James L. Gelvin, "The Other Arab Nationalism: Syrian/Arab Populism and Its Historical and International Contexts," in *Rethinking Nationalism in the Arab Middle East*, eds. James P. Jankowski and Israel Gershoni (New York: Columbia University Press, 1997), 231–48.

4 Catherine Mayeur-Jaouen, *Saints et héros du moyen-orient contemporain: actes du colloque des 11 et 12 décembre 2000, à l'institut universitaire de France* (Paris: Maisonneuve et Larose, 2002), 14ff, 28ff; see also Christopher S. Wilson, *Beyond Anıtkabir: The Funerary Architecture of Atatürk* (Farnham: Ashgate Publishing, 2013), 65–99, 110–16.

5 Compare James L. Gelvin, *Divided Loyalties: Nationalism and Mass Politics in Syria at the Close of Empire* (Berkeley: University of California Press, 1998), 226–7; and all of part 3.

6 Katherine Verdery, *The Political Lives of Dead Bodies: Reburial and Postsocialist Change* (New York: Columbia University Press, 1999), 47–50, 106. Quotes on 49 and 106.

7 Michael Provence, "Ottoman Modernity, Colonialism, and Insurgency in the Interwar Arab East," *International Journal of Middle East Studies* 43 (2011): 212–20; Hanna Batatu, *The Old Social Classes and the Revolutionary Movements of Iraq: A Study of Iraq's Old Landed and Commercial Classes and of Its Communists, Ba'thists, and Free Officers* (Princeton: Princeton University Press, 1978), 195ff.

8 Phebe Marr, "Yasin Al-Hashimi: The Rise and Fall of a Nationalist (A Study of the Nationalist Leadership in Iraq, 1920–1936)" (Harvard University: PhD thesis, History and Middle Eastern Studies, 1966), 302ff. Marr's unpublished thesis is the most extensive evaluation of al-Hashimi's life.

9 Michael Eppel, *The Palestine Conflict in the History of Modern Iraq: The Dynamics of Involvement 1928–1948* (London and Portland: Frank Cass, 1994), 30ff.

10 Marr, "Yasin Al-Hashimi," 351f.

11 Charles Tripp, *A History of Iraq*, 3rd edn. (Cambridge: Cambridge University Press, 2007), 86ff. On al-Ahali see Muzaffar 'Abd Allah al-Amin, *Jama'at al-Ahali: Munshi'uha, 'aqidatuha, wa-dawruha fi'l-siyasa al-'Iraqiyya, 1932–1946* (Beirut: al-Mu'assasa al-'Arabiyya li'l-Dirasat wa'l-Nashr, 2001), passim; Orit Bashkin, *The Other Iraq: Pluralism and Culture in Hashemite Iraq* (Stanford, CA: Stanford University Press, 2008), 61ff.

12 See Philip S. Khoury, *Syria and the French Mandate: The Politics of Arab Nationalism, 1920–1945* (Princeton: Princeton University Press, 1987), 402.

13 Taha al-Hashimi, born in 1887, was chief of staff in Iraq for many years in the 1930s and Iraqi prime minister from February to April 1941.

14 *Al-Ayyam*, January 24, 1937, 5: "Juthman al-Hashimi yashuqqu shawari' Dimashq bayna jamahir al-umma al-multa'a."

15 Taha al-Hashimi, *Mudhakkirat 1919–1943* (Beirut: Dar al-Tali'a, 1968), 165ff.

16 *Al-Difa'*, January 22, 1937, 1: "Ila'l-khulud ya ibn al-thawra al-'Arabiyya al-kubra,"; *Filastin*, January 22, 1937, 1: "Salat al-gha'ib fi masajid Filastin."

17 *Al-Difa'*, January 22, 1937, 1: "Mata al-Hashimi."

18 *Al-Difa'*, February 1st, 1937, 6: "Ritha' al-Hashimi."

19 *Al-Ahram*, 22 January 1937, 7: "Yas Basha al-Hashimi."

20 "Yasin al-Hashimi," *al-Fath*, 15 Dhu al-Qi'da 1355 AH (January 28, 1937 CE), 3f. On *al-Fath* and its Salafi editor Muhibb al-Din al-Khatib see Henri Lauzière, "The Construction of Salafiyya: Reconsidering Salafism from the Perspective of Conceptual History," *International Journal of Middle East Studies* 42 (2010): 376ff. On al-Khatib being close to the Muslim Brothers see Richard P. Mitchell, *The Society of the Muslim Brothers* (London: Oxford University Press, 1969), 7f, 322f.

21 'Abd al-Razzaq al-Hasani, *Tarikh Al-Wizarat Al-'Iraqiyya*, vol. 4 (Baghdad: Dar al-Shu'un al-Thaqafiyya al-'amma, 1988), 261. *Al-Qabas*, 27 January 1937, 4: "'Uquq yastankiruhu al-'Arab jami'an." Quote in: *Centre des Archives Diplomatiques de Nantes* (hereafter CADN), *Fond Beyrouth*, box 1922, "Renseignements et Presse, Revue de la presse libanaise et syrienne du 23 Janvier au 1er Février 1937," 35.

22 Batatu, *The Old Social Classes*, 319–61; Michael Eppel, "The Elite, the Effendiyya, and the Growth of Nationalism and Pan-Arabism in Hashemite Iraq, 1921–1958," *International Journal of Middle East Studies* 30 (1998): 227–50; Khoury, *Syria and the French Mandate*, passim; Elizabeth Thompson, *Colonial Citizens: Republican Rights, Paternal Privilege, and Gender in French Syria and Lebanon* (New York: Columbia University Press, 2000), passim.

23 Khoury, *Syria and the French Mandate*, 468ff.
24 A French intelligence report confirms this observation. See CADN, box 491, February 17, 1937, Capitaine Grall, French Inspector of the "Special Services" of Damascus and Hawran, "Le Délégué du Haut Commissaire auprès de la République Syrienne à Monsieur le Comte D. de Martel, Ambassadeur, Haut Commissaire de la République Française en Syrie et au Liban." On French Mandate intelligence and its quality see Martin C. Thomas, "French Intelligence-Gathering in the Syrian Mandate, 1920–40," *Middle Eastern Studies* 38 (2002): 1–32.
25 Hashimi, *Mudhakkirat 1919–1943*, 178f. *Al-Ayyam*, January 24, 1937, p5: "Juthman al-Hashimi yashuqqu shawari' Dimashq ..."; *al-Qabas*, January 24, 1937, p4: "Al-Wizara al-wataniyya wa'l-sha'b al-Suri yahtafilan bi-juthman Yasin al-Hashimi."
26 Probably the same as the *Hadiqat al-Umma*, or former *Junaynat al-Daftardariyya*, opposite the Tekkiye complex. Stefan Weber, *Damascus: Ottoman Modernity and Urban Transformation (1808–1918)*, vol. 2, Proceedings of the Danish Institute in Damascus 5 (Aarhus: Aarhus Universitetsforlag, 2009), 253.
27 Successor of the Ottoman *Maktab 'Anbar* and center of pan-Arab nationalist activities among students in the 1930s. Stefan Weber, *Damascus: Ottoman Modernity and Urban Transformation (1808–1918)*, vol. 1, 155f; Khoury, *Syria and the French Mandate*, 410ff.
28 Probably former Sa'd-Allah-Jabi Street, leading to the Hijaz Railway station. Weber, *Damascus*, 2: 281.
29 *Al-Nahar*, January 24–25, 1937, p3: "Kaifa istaqbalat Dimashq juthman al-Hashimi."
30 *Al-Ayyam*, January 24, 1937, pp1/3: "Madinat al-adahi tabki Yasin al-Hashimi."
31 *Al-Ayyam*, January 24, 1937, p3: "Al-Akalil allati sarat amama na'sh al-Hashimi," p5: "Juthman al-Hashimi yashuqqu shawari' Dimashq...;" *Al-Qabas*, January 24, 1937, p4: "Al-Wizara al-wataniyya wa'l-sha'b al-Suri ..."
32 *Al-Ayyam*, January 28, 1937, p3: "Dafn juthman al-faqid al-Hashimi fi Dimashq."
33 *Al-Ayyam*, February 3, 1937, p5: "Nahnu wa'l-'Iraq akhawan shaqiqan. Limadha lam yudfan juthman al-Hashimi fi'l-'Iraq. Al-Hukuma al-'Iraqiyya lam tamna' dafn al-juthman fi Baghdad." The article lists Fakhri al-Barudi's responses to such allegations.
34 Compare Matthew D. Esposito, "The Politics of Death: State Funerals as Rites of Reconciliation in Porfirian Mexico, 1876–1889," *The Americas* 62.1 (2005): 74f.
35 Weber, *Damascus*, 2: 244; Janine Sourdel-Thomine, "Les anciens lieux de pèlerinage damascains d'après les sources arabes," *Bulletin d'études orientales* 14 (1952–1954): 80.
36 *Al-Ayyam*, January 26, 1937, p3: "Ayna huquq Tarabulus;" *al-Qabas*, January 25, 1937, p6: "Hamah tumidu li-na'i faqid al-'Arab al-akbar."
37 *Al-Qabas*, January 24, 1937, p1: "Yawman li'l-Hashimi fi'l-Sham."
38 Khoury, *Syria and the French Mandate*, 503ff; Majid Khadduri, "The Alexandretta Dispute," *American Journal of International Law* 39 (1945): 415ff; and in most detail: Sarah D. Shields, *Fezzes in the River: Identity Politics and European Diplomacy in the Middle East on the Eve of World War II* (Oxford; New York: Oxford University Press, 2011), passim. A report on the protests is in CADN, box 1918, January 26, 1937, "Sûreté Damas."
39 Capitaine Grall, French Inspector of the "Special Services" intelligence apparatus of Damascus and Hawran, wrote that the shallow trust in France that the nationalists had developed had been shattered by the French–Turkish accord on Alexandretta just as they were trying to establish their pan-Arab credentials during Yasin's funeral. CADN, box 491, February 17, 1937, Le Délégué du Haut Commissaire auprès de la République Syrienne à Monsieur le Comte D. de Martel, Ambassadeur, Haut Commissaire de la République Française en Syrie et au Liban.
40 Khoury, *Syria and the French Mandate*, 400ff, 423, 457ff.

41 See CADN, box 1918, Beyrouth, le 4 Jan 1937, Sûreté Damas, 31.12.36, Agitation
    Sociale. Ibid., Beyrouth, le 4 Jan 1936 [should be 1937], Sûreté Damas, 29.12.36,
    Agitation sociale; and Sûreté Damas, 4.1.36 [should be 37], Grève des chauffeurs.
    (Similar reports for January 8, 9, 12 etc. and for other towns.).
42 Ibid., January 15, 1937, Sûreté Damas, 13.1, Agitation sociale, and January 19, 1937,
    Sûreté Damas, 18.1, le mécontentement general et l'opposition.
43 Khoury, *Syria and the French Mandate*, 400ff, 423.
44 See Gelvin, *Divided Loyalties*, 9; Peter Wien, *Iraqi Arab Nationalism: Authori-
    tarian, Totalitarian and Pro-Fascist Inclinations, 1932–1941* (London; New York:
    Routledge, 2006), 14ff. On popular transgression: Gelvin, "The Other Arab Nation-
    alism: Syrian/Arab Populism and Its Historical and International Contexts," 246ff;
    compare also Esposito, "The Politics of Death," 68, 93. The nationalist pomp of
    al-Hashimi's funeral did not fail to impress the League of National Action, which
    marched in the cortège. When the Alexandretta protests broke out spontaneously,
    students took the lead while the League was still lulled. It endorsed the protests only
    with a delay. See CADN, box 1918, January 30, 1937, "Sûreté Damas 29.1, agitation
    dans les milieux scolaires." Only a few days before Yasin's funeral, the League had
    opposed street protests against the government's failure to counter the economic
    crisis. CADN, box 1916, January 4, 1937, "Sûreté Damas, 29.12.36, l'opposition,";
    and box 1918, January 16, 1937, "Sûreté Damas, 15–1-37, l'opposition."
45 CADN, box 1918, January 26, 1937, Sûreté Damas; January 28, 1937, Sûreté Damas,
    27–1-37, l'attitude du gouvernement; January 30, 1937, Sûreté Damas 29–1-37,
    organisation d'une police auxiliaire par le Bloc. Al-Qabas, January 26, 1937, 4:
    "Dimashq al-jabbara tastankaru ittifaq Jinif."
46 CADN, box 1918, January 29, 1937, Sûreté Damas 28.1, funerailles de Yassine Pacha
    el Hachemi. See also *al-Nahar*, January 28, 1937, p5: "Dafn al-Hashimi fi Dimashq
    ba'da an mana'at hukumat al-'Iraq wafd al-Kutla min murafiqat juthman al-rahil
    al-'arabi al-kabir."
47 "Ibn al-'Arabi," Encyclopaedia of Islam, 2nd edn. P. Bearman, Th. Bianquis,
    C.E. Bosworth, E. van Donzel, W.P. Heinrichs, eds. Brill Online, 2013. Reference.
    University of Maryland, http://referenceworks.brillonline.com.proxy-um.researchport.
    umd.edu/entries/encyclopaedia-of-islam-2/ibn-al-arabi-COM_0316, date of access:
    August 2, 2013.
48 Nora Achrati, "Following the Leader: A History and Evolution of the Amir 'Abd
    Al-Qadir Al-Jazairi as Symbol," *The Journal of North African Studies* 12 (2007):
    140–2; Leila Tarazi Fawaz, *An Occasion for War: Civil Conflict in Lebanon and
    Damascus in 1860* (Berkeley, CA: University of California Press, 1994), 78–100.
    On 'Abd al-Qadir's role as a reformist and spiritual leader, see Itzchak Weismann,
    Taste of Modernity: Sufism, Salafiyya, and Arabism in Late Ottoman Damascus,
    Islamic History and Civilization 34 (Leiden; Boston: Brill, 2001), 148–224.
49 Achrati, "Following the Leader," 142–50. Recent historiography, however, sees 'Abd
    al-Qadir rather as a representative of a transitory model of leadership and statehood,
    comparable to that of Mehmet Ali in Egypt, than as a national leader. His authority
    was deeply rooted in the saintly lineage of his Sufi order. He rallied his supporters in
    a struggle against enemies of Islam, but he also built rational state structures through
    government offices, as well as modern forms of military organization. On the other
    hand, he compromised with the French, gaining their recognition in a treaty in 1837
    that gave the French breathing room to overcome resistance in Eastern Algeria,
    which is nothing a truly national leader would do. John Ruedy, *Modern Algeria: The
    Origins and Development of a Nation*, 2nd edn. (Bloomington: Indiana University
    Press, 2005), 62f, 66.
50 A. Le Chatelier, "Les Musulmans algériens au Maroc et en Syrie," *Revue du monde
    musulman* 2 (1907): 499–500, 508–10, 512; Mouloud Haddad, "Sur les pas d'Abd

el-Kader: la hijra des Algériens en Syrie au XIXe siècle," in *Abd el-Kader, un spirituel dans la modernité*, eds. Ahmed Bouyerdene, Éric Geoffroy, and Setty G. Simon-Khedis (Damascus: Presses de l'Ifpo, 2012), passim.

51 Gelvin, *Divided Loyalties*, 26–7; Michael Provence, *The Great Syrian Revolt and the Rise of Arab Nationalism* (Austin: University of Texas Press, 2005), 104–6.

52 *Al-Ba'th*, July 4, 1966, p7: "Thawrat al-amir 'Abd al-Qadir al-Jaza'iri satazallu ramz[an] li'l-ajyal al-sa'ida fi-mashriq al-watan al-'Arabi wa-maghribiha."

53 Itamar Rabinovich, *Syria under the Ba'th, 1963–66: The Army Party Symbiosis* (Jerusalem: Israel Universities Press, 1972), 22–3, 26–7, 36–117, 127–207. On sectarianism and power in Syria see also Nikolaos van Dam, *The Struggle for Power in Syria: Sectarianism, Regionalism, and Tribalism in Politics, 1961–1978* (New York: St. Martin's Press, 1979), passim.

54 Rabinovich, *Syria under the Ba'th*, 109–117; Hanna Batatu, *Syria's Peasantry, the Descendants of Its Lesser Rural Notables, and Their Politics* (Princeton: Princeton University Press, 1999), 133–75; Raphaël Lefèvre, *Ashes of Hama: The Muslim Brotherhood in Syria* (New York: Oxford University Press, 2013), 45–46; Thomas Pierret, *Religion and State in Syria: The Sunni Ulema under the Ba'th* (Cambridge: Cambridge University Press, 2013), 180–4. The Ottoman state made first efforts to integrate Alawites into mainstream society during the Tanzimat and late imperial periods. The creation of a separate Alawite state by the French Mandate authorities provided some political agency to members of the sect. In addition, Arab nationalism offered an opportunity to some Alawites to move closer to the middle of society such as in the case of Zaki al-Arsuzi, one of the founding fathers of Ba'thism. In addition, the French Mandate authority recruited minorities into the officer corps of the Syrian army and thus promoted the rise of Alawites in military ranks. See Mervin, Sabrina, "'Alawis, contemporary developments," Encyclopaedia of Islam, 3rd edn, eds. Gudrun Krämer, Denis Matringe, John Nawas, Everett Rowson. Brill Online, 2013. Reference. University of Maryland, http://referenceworks.brillonline. com.proxy-um.researchport.umd.edu/entries/encyclopaedia-of-islam-3/alawis-contemporary-developments-COM_22953, date of access: August 6, 2013.

55 Ruedy, *Modern Algeria*, 196–208; Rabinovich, *Syria under the Ba'th*, 206–7; Batatu, *Syria's Peasantry*, 258.

56 James McDougall, *History and the Culture of Nationalism in Algeria* (Cambridge; New York: Cambridge University Press, 2006), 97–143, quote on 181.

57 Rabinovich, *Syria under the Ba'th*, 70–2; Batatu, *Syria's Peasantry*, 145–55, 157–60.

58 On the axis of *progressive* regimes proving the *reactionaries* wrong see a commentary from the Algerian newspaper *al-Mujahid* that was reprinted in *al-Ba'th*, June 17, 1966, p3: "Baina San'a', wa'l-Jaza'ir, 'abr al-Qahira wa Dimashq." Another article confirmed that the Syrian and Algerian revolutionaries had to stand together in defense against the reactionary forces. They gathered around 'Abd al-Qadir's remains to prove to the imperialists that the Arabs still had the same resolve on the march toward the creation of a unified and socialist Arab society. "The spirit of 'Abd al-Qadir helps us grasp what this meeting grants us in terms of revolutionary and historical assurance ..." *Al-Ba'th*, June 30, 1966, p4: "Ra'y wa-khabar: Fi afaq al-liqa' al-Suri al-Jaza'iri."

59 Only *al-Ba'th* was available for this study as a newspaper that covered the events in detail.

60 The confirmation that the grave would remain appeared twice in a special issue of *al-Ba'th* on July 4, 1966 (title on p1: "'Adad khass bi-munasibat naql rufat al-batal 'Abd al-Qadir al-Jaza'iri.") first on p3: "Thawrat al-amir 'Abd al-Qadir al-Jaza'iri satazallu ramz [sic] li-l-ajyal al-sa'ida fi-mashriq al-watan al-'Arabi wa-maghribiha;" second on p6: "Hayat al-Amir 'Abd al-Qadir al-Jaza'iri: Sira hafila li-batal kabir."

61 *Al-Ba'th*, June 16, 1966, p4: "Al-Wafd al-Jaza'iri bi-ri'asat Butifliqa yasilu fi 29 Haziran;" June 20, 1966, p4: "Mawa'id wusul al-wafd al-Jaza'iri al-shaqiqa ila Dimashq. Al-Lajna al-'ulya li-tanzim al-ihtifalat wa'l-ziyarat tajtami'u al-yawm;" June 22, 1966, p5: "16 shakhsiyya 'askariyya jaza'iriyya tumaththilu al-asliha al-barriyya al-bahriyya wa'l-jawwiyya fi'l-Jaza'ir."

62 *Al-Ba'th*, June 17, 1966, p5: "Tashkil lajna 'ulya li-tanzim al-ihtifalat wa'l-ziyarat allati saturafiqu naql rufat al-batal 'Abd al-Qadir al-Jaza'iri." The book reference is probably to 'Abd al-Qadir al-Jaza'iri, *Kitab al-mawaqif fi'l-tasawwuf wa'l-wa'z wa'l-irshad* ([Damascus]: Dar al-Yaqza al-'Arabiyya li'l-Ta'lif wa'l-Tarjama wa'l-Nashr, 1966).

63 See for example *al-Ba'th*, June 26, 1966, p3: "Ara' wa-Ta'liqat: 'Abd al-Qadir al-Jaza'iri: Min awa'il ruwwad harakat al-taharrur al-watani."

64 *Al-Ba'th*, July 1, 1966, p1: "Haflat al-firaq al-fanniyya al-Jaza'iriyya."

65 *Al-Ba'th*, July 1, 1966, p7: "Muntakhaba al-jaysh wa'l-Jaza'ir yata'adilan fi liqa'ihima bi-kurrat al-qadam."

66 A military delegation arrived in the evening of June 30, whereas Bouteflika's group arrived the following day. *Al-Ba'th*, June 30, 1966, p5: "Suriyat al-thawra tastaqbilu masa' al-yawm al-wafd al-rasmi li-thawrat al-Jaza'ir wa-tu'ayyinu farhat al-liqa' al-tarikhi;" July 1, p1: "Al-Wafd al-Jaza'iri al-rasmi bi-ri'asa Butifliqa yasilu al-yawm ila Dimashq."

67 *Al-Ba'th*, July 1, 1966, p4: "Al-Jumhuriyya al-'Arabiyya al-Suriyya tukarrimu dhikra mawlid al-rasul al-'Arabi Muhammad Ibn 'Abdallah."

68 *Al-Ba'th*, July 1, 1966, pp1, 7, "Kalimat al-Ba'th: Fi milad al-rasul," here p1.

69 Ibid., here pp1, 7.

70 McDougall, *History and the Culture of Nationalism in Algeria*, 121–37.

71 Pierret, *Religion and State in Syria*, 17–63, 168–84; Joshua Teitelbaum, "The Muslim Brotherhood in Syria, 1945–1958: Founding, Social Origins, Ideology," *Middle East Journal* 65 (2011): 219–21, 230, 232; Lefèvre, *Ashes of Hama*, 43–4. Pierret argues that the Ba'thist antagonism to religious authority and the party leaders' socialist-secular vision of the state in effect protected the prominence of traditionalists among the '*ulama*' because an all out integration of their ranks into the state apparatus never took place. Teitelbaum's account highlights the variations in the ideological positioning of the Muslim Brothers in Syria, between Islamic populism and Salafism.

72 *Al-Ba'th*, July 1, p3: "Ara' wa-taftishat: Fi Dhikra milad al-tha'ir al-a'zam yaltaqi al-thuwar al-'Arab fi Dimashq."

73 *Al-Ba'th*, July 3, 1966, p5: "Mahrajan al-Futuwwa wa'l-haras al-qawmi yuwaddihu qadrat al-jaysh al-awwal li'l-difa' al-sha'bi 'ala'l-qital wa-tadmir masalih al-isti'mar," photo of the girl scouts on p8.

74 *Al-Ba'th*, July 3, 1966, pp1, 7: "Al-Wufud al-Jaza'iriyya al-shaqiqa yazuru al-khutut al-amamiyya – Butifliqa yashhadu butulat jayshina wa-tadhiyatahu," photo of the actress on p8.

75 *Al-Ba'th*, July 3, p1: "Dimashq tashhadu al-yawm al-masira al-kubra li-tawdi' rufat al-batal al-'Arabi 'Abd al-Qadir al-Jaza'iri."

76 Annette Léna, "Algérie: Le Retour d'Abdel Kader," *Jeune Afrique* 290 (July 17, 1966): 14–15, photo on 14.

77 Thomas Pierret and Ahmad Mu'adh al-Khatib helped me identify Abu'l-Faraj al-Khatib. Mu'adh is Abu'l-Faraj's son and took over the position his father had held in 1990, only to fall out with the regime soon afterwards. After 2011, he became a leading figure of the Syrian opposition to Bashar al-Assad. See Pierret, *Religion and State in Syria*, 138–41.

78 *Al-Ba'th*, July 4, 1966 ("'Adad khass …"), pp1, 7: "Dimashq tuwaddi'u al-batal 'Abd al-Qadir fi-ihtifal rasmi wa-sha'bi muhib," quote on p1.

79 Ibid., p7.

80 Ibid., p1.
81 *Al-Ba'th*, July 4, 1966, pp1, 7: "Kalimat ra'is al-dawla fi ihtifal tashyi' rufat 'Abd al-Qadir."
82 See the photo in Léna, "Algérie: Le Retour d'Abdel Kader," 15.
83 *Al-Ba'th*, July 4, 1966, pp1, 2: "Kalimat Butifliqa fi'l-ihtifal," all quotes on p2.
84 *Al-Ba'th*, June 29, 1966, p4: "Tamma ams fath qabar al-batal al-'Arabi 'Abd al-Qadir."
85 *Al-Ba'th* moved an announcement and a report about the mawlid festivities to the second page of the newspaper: June 20, 1967, p2: "Al-Bilad tahtafilu al-yawm bi-dhikra al-mawlid al-nabawi al-sharif: Ihtifal dini kabir taht ri'aya ra'is al-dawla;" June 21, p2: "Ihtifal dini kabir bi-munasabat al-mawlid al-nabawi al-sharif." The extent of the coverage is nowhere near the one of the previous year. The only further *mawlid* reference in the paper is an op-ed piece (June 20, p1: "Durus wa-'ibar fi dhikra mawlid al-nabi"), which presented the *mawlid* as an admonition to the Arabs that it had taken significant patience and sacrifices during the lifetime of the Prophet until the Arabs had vanquished their enemies, and the Jews in particular. Already in April of 1967, the confrontation between the Ba'th party and religious authorities had reached boiling point when Ibrahim Khlas, a Ba'thist officer, published an article in the army journal *Jaysh al-Sha'b* that denigrated pious men as weaklings and reactionaries. Fierce public protests followed the publication. Lefèvre, *Ashes of Hama*, 46–7.
86 On the significance of the location see Achrati, "Following the Leader," 149. He mentions that 'Abd al-Qadir's burial next to Ibn al-'Arabi had been according to his own wish. The funerary festivities in Algiers are covered in McDougall, *History and the Culture of Nationalism in Algeria*, 177–82.
87 Photos in Léna, "Algérie: Le Retour d'Abdel Kader," 15.

6 Nearly victorious

1 See for example Eliezer Be'eri, *Army Officers in Arab Politics and Society* (Jerusalem: Israel University Press, 1969), passim; P.J. Vatikiotis, *Nasser and His Generation* (New York: St. Martin's Press, 1978), 47–66; Joel Gordon, *Nasser's Blessed Movement: Egypt's Free Officers and the July Revolution* (New York: Oxford University Press, 1992), passim; Mohammad A. Tarbush, *The Role of the Military in Politics. A Case Study of Iraq to 1941* (London: Kegan Paul International, 1983), passim.
2 For this and the rest of the chapter, and a critique of the efficacy of the military message, see Mériam N. Belli, *An Incurable Past: Nasser's Egypt Then and Now* (Gainesville: University Press of Florida, 2013), 67–71.
3 "Al-Mathaf al-harbi bi'l-Qahira," *al-Hilal* 48 (1939), 105. El-Alfy, Amal M. Safwat, ed., *al-Mathaf al-Harbi al-Qawmi* (Cairo: Jumhuriyyat Misr al-'Arabiyya, Wizarat al-Difa', Hay'at al-Athar al-Misriyya, 1987), (no page numbers); *Dalil al-Mathaf al-Harbi bi'l-Qal'a wa-'Abidin* (Cairo: Matba'at al-Tahrir, 1958), 18–20.
4 *Dalil al-Mathaf al-Harbi*, 18. Only scarce biographical information on Zaki was available on http://alencyclopedia.com/8623/عبـــد_الرحمن_زكي/, date of access: May 4, 2015. According to the website, he was born in the Sudan. It lists employment as a college Professor in Baghdad and later at Cairo University. Considering that he was a man of the monarchical regime, his move to Baghdad and return to the College of Letters in Cairo may have followed the revolutions in Egypt in 1952 and in Iraq in 1958.
5 DWQ, 0069–021265, Taqrir 'an al-mathaf al-harbi wa-muqtanayatihi min al-asliha wa'l-malabis al-harbiyya wa'l-dafatir al-qadima wa'l-haditha sanat 1936m: Report [submitted to the "Cabinet de sa Majesté le Roi" (title of the dossier)], by 'Abd al-Rahman Zaki, Lieutenant at the Military Works Offices, Port Said, December 10, 1936.

6 Gaynor Kavanagh, *Museums and the First World War: A Social History* (London; New York: Leicester University Press, St. Martin's Press, 1994), 18–151; Steven Cooke and Lloyd Jenkins, "Discourses of Regeneration in Early Twentieth-Century Britain: From Bedlam to the Imperial War Museum," *Area* 33, no. 4 (December 1, 2001): 382–90; Sue Malvern, "War, Memory and Museums: Art and Artefact in the Imperial War Museum," *History Workshop Journal* 49 (2000): 177–88; Frederick P. Todd, "The Military Museum in Europe," *Military Affairs* 12 (1948): 36–45.

7 Wendy M.K. Shaw, *Possessors and Possessed: Museums, Archaeology, and the Visualization of History in the Late Ottoman Empire* (Berkeley: University of California Press, 2003), 32–5, 45–58, 185–206.

8 DWQ, 0069–021265, Taqrir 'an al-mathaf al-harbi wa-muqtanayatihi …, 3–4.

9 "Istitla' sahafi: 50 qarnan fi'l-Mathaf al-Harbi. Jaula baina athar al-madi wa'l-hadir," *al-Risala* 329 (1939), 2013.

10 *Dalil al-Mathaf al-Harbi*, (title page).

11 Ibid., 10–11, 16–18, 24–6. The renovations of the 1980s added an entire new wing that contained the Victory Hall celebrating the October War on the upper level, and a Martyrs' Hall on the ground level commemorating Egyptian fallen soldiers. See El-Alfy, Amal M. Safwat, *al-Mathaf al-Harbi al-Qawmi*, (no page numbers).

12 Mubarak used the opening ceremony to assert the prowess of the state in the face of continuing terrorist threats at the time. *Al-Ahram*, November 30, 1993, pp1,3: "Musanadat al-sha'b li'l-daula fi muqawamat al-irhab tatatallibu al-iblagh 'an al-irhabiyyin … Mubarak fi tasrihat 'aqb li'l-Mathaf al-Harbi bi'l-Qal'a: Al-Irhabiyyun ya'uduna min Afghanistan …"

13 Translation of the Arabic caption. The English caption is slightly different. "Qadesh" refers to a battle between the Egyptian and Hittite Empires in 1274 BCE in modern day Syria. "Hittin" refers to the battle between Salah al-Din's army and the Christian Crusaders at the Horns of Hittin in 1187 in modern day Israel. "October 73" stands for the Arab-Israeli war of 1973.

14 See a photograph in Eric Schewe's excellent blog post about Egyptian military museums: http://ericschewe.wordpress.com/2012/07/14/dear-leader-could-we-have-a-new-military-museum-part-ii/, date of access: April 16, 2013.

15 Obituary "Gen Mohamed Abdel Ghani al-Gamasy: Military Mastermind Behind the Yom Kippur War," in *The Guardian*, June 19, 2003. http://www.guardian.co.uk/news/2003/jun/19/guardianobituaries.israel, date of access: July 5, 2013. I am grateful to Emad Helal for his help in identifying al-Gamasy.

16 Ryom Tae Sun, "Panoramas in the Democratic People's Republic of Korea," in *Die Welt der Panoramen: Zehn Jahre Internationale Panorama Konferenzen*, eds. Gabriele Koller and Gebhard Streicher (Amberg: SPA Stiftung Panorama Altötting, 2003), 87. The Paekho Company advertised its products internationally at an exhibition at the London embassy of North Korea in the fall of 2007. See http://londonkoreanlinks.net/2007/09/24/paekhos-architectural-art/, date of access: July 10, 2013. The most recent Mansudae product has been a panorama in Angkor Wat, Cambodia, depicting the fifteenth century Cham-Vietnamese War. See http://www.theguardian.com/world/2016/feb/01/north-korea-panoramic-museum-cambodia-angkor-wat, date of access: March 30, 2016. For recent panoramas see exhibitions in Berlin, Dresden and Leipzig by the artist Yadegar Asisi. http://www.asisi.de/index.php?id=7#asisi_panoramen, date of access: July 10, 2013.

17 See the digital documents section of the North Korea International Documentation Project at the Wilson Center in Washington DC: telegram 027.498 from the Romanian Embassy in Cairo to the Romanian Ministry of Foreign Affairs, May 13, 1978. http://digitalarchive.wilsoncenter.org/document/116424, date of access: July 10, 2013. The Embassy reported that the North Korean Ambassador commented about relations with Egypt and confirmed that North Korean pilots had flown in the

October War. On economic relations in Middle Eastern arms trade see *The Christian Science Monitor*, February 7, 2011: "Why Kim Jong-il wished Egypt's Mubarak a Happy New Year," http://www.csmonitor.com/World/Asia-Pacific/2011/0207/Why-Kim-Jong-il-wished-Egypt-s-Mubarak-a-Happy-New-Year, date of access: July 10, 2013. Reference found in http://ericschewe.wordpress.com/2012/07/14/dear-leader-could-we-have-a-new-military-museum-part-ii/, date of access: July 10, 2013.

18 *Al-Akhbar*, October 6, 1989, p3: "Mubarak yaftatihu Banurama Uktubar .. Akbar banurama 'askariyya fi'l-'alam. Al-ra'is: sajjalna intisarna al-ra'i' fi-uktubar li-yushahiduhu kull muwatin." Information on the Pyongyang Panorama is on the website of the International Panorama Council, an association of art historians concerned with documentation and preservation of Panoramas worldwide: http://www.panoramapainting.com/en/what_we_do/resources/panoramas_of_the_world_database/operations_for_liberation_of_taejon/?country=north_korea, date of access: July 10, 2013.

19 Visits for documentation took place on October 3, 2010 in Damascus and April 27, 2012 in Cairo, respectively.

20 Oliver Grau, *Virtuelle Kunst in Geschichte und Gegenwart: Visuelle Strategien* (Berlin: Reimer, 2001), 25–65; See the English translation Oliver Grau, *Virtual Art: From Illusion to Immersion* (Cambridge, MA: MIT Press, 2003); Stephan Oettermann, *Das Panorama: Die Geschichte eines Massenmediums* (Frankfurt am Main: Syndikat, 1980), 7–22, 33–9, 126–7; English translation: Stephan Oettermann, *The Panorama: History of a Mass Medium* (New York: Zone Books, 1997); Ralph Hyde, *Panoramania! The Art and Entertainment of the "All-Embracing" View* (London: Trefoil, Barbican Art Gallery, 1988), 169–72.

21 Grau, *Virtuelle Kunst in Geschichte und Gegenwart*, 60–63, 66–82; Oettermann, *Das Panorama*, 60–65.

22 Svetlana Kostyuchenko, "Die Geschichte der sowjetischen Dioramenkunst," in *Panorama: Virtualität und Realitäten: 11. Internationale Panoramakonferenz in Altötting 2003*, ed. Gebhard Streicher (Amberg: SPA Stiftung Panorama Altötting, 2005), 64–6; Hyde, *Panoramania*, 199–201.

23 Grau, *Virtuelle Kunst in Geschichte und Gegenwart*, 19; term "Illusionsräume" ibid.; English trsl. in Grau, *Virtual Art*, 6.

24 Grau calls this the "entmündigende Potenz der Immersion," and its "suggestive-emotionale Wirkung." See Grau, *Virtuelle Kunst in Geschichte und Gegenwart*, 99. (English trans.: "The power of immersion to deprive the human subject of the right of decision ..." in Grau, *Virtual Art*, 110.).

25 Grau, *Virtuelle Kunst in Geschichte und Gegenwart*, 56–60, 87–100; see also Vanessa R. Schwartz, *Spectacular Realities: Early Mass Culture in Fin-de-Siècle Paris* (Berkeley, CA: University of California Press, 1998), 149–70.

26 Newspaper articles provide information about the background of Panorama visitors. For example: *'Aqidati*, January 25, 2000, p18: "Li'l-tufula kalima: Atfal janub Sina' wa-rihla ila ma'alim al-Qahira ..." reports about a week-long journey organized for children from southern Sinai to the sights of Cairo, prominently including the Panorama, next to medieval mosques etc. In *al-Ahram al-Masa'i*, October 28, 2001, p7: "Banurama Harb Uktubar," 'Abd al-Jabir Ahmad 'Ali interviewed the director about the composition of visitor groups. He replied that most traffic came from students from various universities and schools. Next were tourist groups of locals, Arabs and foreigners, followed by more and more individual Egyptian visitors. Mark Sedgwick notes, based on anecdotal evidence, that "... almost nobody in Cairo ever visits [...] the October War Panorama ..." in: "Modern and Islamic Icons in Arab-Islamic Popular Historical Memory," in *Islamic Myths and Memories: Mediators of Globalization*, eds. Itzchak Weismann, Mark Sedgwick, and Ulrika Mårtensson (Surrey, Burlington: Ashgate, 2014), 19. Arguably, it would

be a more accurate assessment that most visits are not deliberate, such as those of school children. See also Yoram Meital, "Sadat's Grave and the Commemoration of the 1973 War in Egypt," in *National Symbols, Fractured Identities: Contesting the National Narrative*, ed. Michael E. Geisler (Middlebury: Middlebury College Press, 2005), 235.

27 This is the bottom-line of the largely streamlined coverage of the panorama in the Syrian press. See, for example, *Tishrin*, August 1, 1999, p7: "Jawlat al-kamira wa'l-sura fi sarh Banurama Harb Tishrin al-Tahririyya: Li'l-watan wa'l-jaysh fi yawm 'idihi. Hadiyat al-ra'is al-qa'id;" *al-Thawra*, October 7, 2008, p13: "Nastadhkiru min khilaliha tafasil al-malhama al-tarikhiyya: Banurama Harb Tishrin al-Tahririyya, sura hayya 'an butulat jayshina wa-manara li-tarikh mushriq."

28 On public forms of commemoration of the war in Egypt see Meital, "Sadat's Grave."

29 See the description of the platform in *al-Gumhuriyya*, October 5, 1989, p4: "Banurama harb uktubir allati yushahiduha al-ra'is Mubarak al-yawm: Sura mujas-sada li-butulat al-sha'b al-Misri istaghraqa i'daduha 6 sanawat."

30 *Al-Ahali*, October 4, 1989, p10: "Fi akbar banurama 'askariyya." The "June emergency" refers to the 1967 war.

31 Ibid.

32 *Al-Gumhuriyya*, October 5, 1989, p4: "Banurama harb uktubir allati yushahiduha al-ra'is Mubarak al-yawm ..."

33 See for example: *Al-Gumhuriyya*, October 5, 1989, p4: "Akbar banurama 'alami-yya." The article contained references to the history of panorama painting, men-tioning its origins in the eighteenth century, extant European Panoramas, the Iraqi Qadisiyya Panorama, and the Korean *War of Liberation* Panorama.

34 *Al-Ahali*, October 10, 1989, p18: "Banurama 6 Uktubar: Sarh fanni 'ala mustawa al-ma'raka .. wa lakinna!"

35 *Al-Ahram*, October 6, 1989, p3: "Mubarak: Banurama Harb Uktubar 'amal majid wa-waqi'i li-taswir butulat quwwatina al-musallaha khilal al-ma'raka;" *al-Gumhuriyya*, October 6, 1989, p3: "Mubarak ma'a al-quwwat al-musallaha."

36 *Al-Thawra*, October 5, 2003, p16: "Banurama Harb Tishrin wa'l-fann."

37 Traceable recognitions of the Korean connection appeared in Syrian newspapers only years after the opening: *Tishrin*, October 29, 2003, p10: "Shu'a' Siyahi: Banurama Harb Tishrin al-Tahririyya;" *al-Thawra*, August 1, 2012 (Army Day), "Sarh hadari yuhaki shumukh Qasyun ... Banurama Harb Tishrin al-Taharruriyya," http://thawra.alwehda.gov.sy/_print_veiw.asp?FileName=87090842220120731172937, date of ac-cess: April 23, 2013. Other Arab newspapers mentioned the connection openly but in passing: *Al-Khalij* (United Arab Emirates), October 9, 1998, p24: "'Ard li-ma'arik al-nasr wa'l-sumud 'am 1973: Injaz 'Banurama Harb Tishrin' fi Dimashq;" *al-Hayat*, October 7, 1999, p4: "'Banurama Harb Tishrin' tahki waqi' al-hal: Mu'ahadat salam qabla khamsat alaf sana ... wa-butulat Zanubiyya wa-Salah al-Din." Iranian, Turkish and Arab delegations visited the monument and were impressed: *Al-Thawra*, June 7, 2002, p4: "Al-Wafd al-Irani yazuru Banurama Harb Tishrin al-Tahririyya;" *Tishrin*, June 28, 2004, p15: "Wafd Hizb al-'Adala wa'l-Tanmiya al-Turki yazuru Banurama Harb Tishrin." The President of the Kuwaiti House for National Works Yusuf al-'Amiri visited the Panorama to profit from the Syrian experiences in his plans to erect a similar structure to commemorate the 1990 to 91 Iraqi occupation of his country. *Al-Ra'y* (Kuwait), July 27, 2008, p5: "Tadummu ajniha 33 dawla 'Arabiyya wa-ajnabiyya sharakat fi Harb al-Tahrir: Al-Kuwayt ta'tazimu iqamat "Banurama" tatadammanu tarikh al-bilad wa-hadaratiha." – The National Memorial Museum, or "Museum Against Forgetting" in Kuwait City is, according to the available in-formation, in fact not a proper panorama. It tells the story of the occupation through several dioramas and a monumental painting of 22 meters in length. It is located in the House of National Works (*Bait al-A'mal al-Wataniyya*). See *al-Watan*, August 2,

2012, "Mathaf "Ki La Nansa" .. numudhaj hayy yujassidu ahdath al-ghazw al-'Iraqi 'ala Kuwaytina al-habiba," http://kuwait.tt/articledetails.aspx?Id=212080, date of access: July 23, 2013.

38 *Tishrin*, August 1, 1999, p7: "Jawlat al-kamira wa'l-sura fi sarh Banurama Harb Tishrin al-Tahririyya ..."

39 On Luqa see http://www.syrianstory.com/e.louka.htm, date of access: July 24, 2013.

40 *Al-Thawra*, May 23, 2004, p16: "Ma'an 'ala'l-Tariq: Matahif takhassusiyya." On the Berlin exhibition see http://www.dhm.de/ausstellungen/der-erste-weltkrieg/, date of access: April 18, 2013.

41 See the article in *al-Thawra*, November 15, 2002, p7: "Da'wa li-ziyarat Banurama Harb Tishrin al-Tahririyya." (signed Hazza' 'Assaf) which starts: "My dear children: I invite you to visit the Tishrin Liberation War Panorama ..."

42 *Tishrin*, August 1, 1999, p7: "Jawlat al-kamira wa'l-sura fi sarh Banurama Harb Tishrin al-Tahririyya ..."

43 Kanan Makiya, *The Monument: Art and Vulgarity in Saddam Hussein's Iraq* (London; New York: I.B. Tauris, 2004), 6–8, 11–18, 49–57; Eric Davis, *Memories of State: Politics, History, and Collective Identity in Modern Iraq* (Berkeley: University of California Press, 2005), 191–7. For the methods of the Korean painters see *Tishrin*, August 1, 1999, p7: "Jawlat al-kamira wa'l-sura fi sarh Banurama Harb Tishrin al-Tahririyya ...;" *al-Gumhuriyya*, October 5, 1989, p4: "Banurama harb uktubir allati yushahiduha al-ra'is Mubarak al-yawm ..."

44 Thanks to Will Hanley for this wording.

45 Lisa Wedeen, *Ambiguities of Domination: Politics, Rhetoric, and Symbols in Contemporary Syria* (Chicago: University of Chicago Press, 1999), 1–18, quote on 6.

46 The latter is attested with regard to Egyptian militarism in Belli, *An Incurable Past: Nasser's Egypt Then and Now*, 70f.

47 Wedeen, *Ambiguities of Domination*, title and 40–42, quote on 10.

48 See a video presenting Syrian Army maneuvers including the firing of missiles with such telling names as "Earthquake" ("Zilzal"), "Golan," "Tishrin," and "Maysalun" on https://www.youtube.com/watch?v=wK-sBFTB0vU, date of access: July 24, 2013.

49 Michael Provence, "Ottoman Modernity, Colonialism, and Insurgency in the Interwar Arab East," *International Journal of Middle East Studies* 43 (2011): 213, 216–18.

50 *Tishrin*, August 1, 1999, p7: "Jawlat al-kamira wa'l-sura fi sarh Banurama Harb Tishrin al-Tahririyya ..."

51 As confirmed by Provence, "Ottoman Modernity," 213. Sati' al-Husri, the eminent Arab nationalist theoretician, wrote one of his most widely distributed books about Maysalun. See, for example, one of several editions: Sati' al-Husri, *Yawm Maysalun: Safha min tarikh al-'Arab al-hadith, mudhakkirat musawwira bi-muqaddima 'an tanazu' al-duwal hawla'l-bilad al-'Arabiyya wa-mudhayyala bi-watha'iq wa-suwar* (Beirut: Dar al-Ittihad, 1965); and in translation: Sati' al-Husri, *The Day of Maysalun: A Page from the Modern History of the Arabs: Memoirs* (Washington, DC: Middle East Institute, 1966).

52 *Tishrin* online, April 16, 2014: "Yusuf al 'Azma.. al-sha'la allati anarat darb al-jala' al-tawil," by Muhammad al-Rifa'i, http://tishreen.news.sy/tishreen/public/read/285152, date of access: July 24, 2013.

53 Ihsan Fu'ad Khatib, *Wamadat min 'umr al-zaman: Qabasat min hayat al-Shaykh Fu'ad al-Khatib, sha'ir al-thawra al-'Arabiyya al-kubra* (Beirut: Dar al-'Ilm li'l-Malayin, 1994), 44–5.

54 James L. Gelvin, *Divided Loyalties: Nationalism and Mass Politics in Syria at the Close of Empire* (Berkeley: University of California Press, 1998), 1–3, 51–137.

55 Khatib, *Wamadat min 'umr al-zaman*, 45–7; on unrest post-Maysalun see Gelvin, *Divided Loyalties*, 292–5; Philip S. Khoury, *Syria and the French Mandate: The Politics of Arab Nationalism, 1920–1945* (Princeton: Princeton University Press, 1987), 98–9.

56 See images in the newspaper references below. The author visited and documented the tomb on October 4, 2010.

57 Reinhart Koselleck, "Einleitung," in *Der politische Totenkult: Kriegerdenkmäler in der Moderne*, eds. Reinhart Koselleck and Michael Jeismann (München: Fink, 1994), 9.

58 Ibid., 9–19.

59 Dina Rizk Khoury, *Iraq in Wartime: Soldiering, Martyrdom, and Remembrance* (New York: Cambridge University Press, 2013), 219, 225–8.

60 Aside from the major war cemeteries that contain the graves of European soldiers who fought in the Middle East during the World Wars, there are war cemeteries near Suez and near the Golan Heights, but they are quite remote from the capitals. This author has not had a chance to visit them, yet. Compare, however, the grass-roots festival in Port Said that commemorates, among other things, Egypt's various modern wars, and the notes about the Port Said war museum in Belli, *An Incurable Past: Nasser's Egypt Then and Now*, 75–162. Names of the fallen are also engraved, regardless of rank, on the walls of the Unknown Soldier monument in Cairo: Meital, "Sadat's Grave," 230.

61 Friederike Pannewick, *Opfer, Tod und Liebe: Visionen des Martyriums in der arabischen Literatur* (München: Wilhelm Fink, 2012), 11–20. Quote in David Cook, *Martyrdom in Islam* (Cambridge; New York: Cambridge University Press, 2007), 12. See also Meir Hatina, *Martyrdom in Modern Islam: Piety, Power, and Politics* (Cambridge: Cambridge University Press, 2014), 61f, 97f, 101f, and passim. Secular nationalist examples of an ideology of self-sacrifice in the Arab lands play only a minor role in Hatina's book, though.

62 Khoury, *Syria and the French Mandate*, 248–84.

63 *Al-Qabas*, July 24, 1930, p1: "Dhikra al-karitha: Tammuz 1920–1930."

64 *Al-Qabas*, July 27, 1930, p1: "Khitab Jamil Mardam Bey fi haflat yawm Maysalun al-kubra."

65 *Al-Qabas*, July 24, 1936, p1: "Ma'sat qawmiyya! Maysalun wa-wu'ud al-hulafa'! Butulat Yusuf al-'Azma."

66 *Al-Qabas*, July 29, 1936, p1, shows a photograph of troops of Iron Shirts and "Maysalun Scouts" receiving Bloc leaders and other participants at the site of the grave, using the fascist salute, as was common at the time in youth movements in the Arab world and elsewhere.

67 *Al-Qabas*, July 28, 1937, p3: "Awwal ihtifal bi-dhikra Maysalun fi 'ahd al-hurriyya wa'l-istiqlal: Al-Ihtifal al-watani al-kabir bi-dhikra Maysalun."

68 *Al-Qabas*, July 26, 1938, p1: "Khitab al-ustadh Khalid Bakdash 'ala jadath shahid Maysalun al-'azim: La nabna amalana 'ala'l-khilafat fi'l-hay'at al-wataniyya." On Bakdash and the communists see Khoury, *Syria and the French Mandate*, 563, 606f.

69 Ibid., 248.

70 *Al-Qabas*, July 28, 1937, p6: "Awwal ihtifal bi-dhikra Maysalun ..."

71 *Al-Ayyam*, July 25, 1957, p1, 5, 8: "Yawm al-istishhad bi-Maysalun: Kalimat al-Quwatli," "Al-Ihtifal al-ra'i' fi Maysalun 'ala darih al-shahid al-'azim Yusuf al-'Azma." Quotes on p8.

72 *Al-Ba'th*, July 25, 1966, p1, 2: "Dhikra Maysalun... Fida' wa-butula," Assad's speech and quotes on pp1, 7.

73 *Al-Ba'th*, July 24, 1966, p6: "Yawm Maysalun."

74 See, for instance, http://syrianstory.com/g-alkssane.htm, date of access: July 29, 2013.

75 Jan [Jean] Aliksan, "Zaynab fi Maysalun," *al-Jundi*, April 19, 1960, 32–3. Quoted in Gelvin, *Divided Loyalties*, 4n, 214n.
76 *Al-Ba'th*, July 24, 1968, p6: "Duwar al-kadihin fi ma'arikina al-sha'biyya – wa'l-su'al al-kabir alladhi tatrahuhu 'alayna dhikra ma'rakat Maysalun." (The article is signed "jim alif," which are without a doubt Jean Aliksan's initials. *Al-Ba'th*, July 24, 1975, p8: "Hadhihi'l-mar'a harabat fi Maysalun."
77 Gelvin, *Divided Loyalties*, 213f.
78 *Al-Ba'th*, July 24, 1968, p6: "Duwar al-kadihin fi ma'arikina al-sha'biyya..."
79 Compare Nazih N. Ayubi, *Over-Stating the Arab State: Politics and Society in the Middle East* (London; New York: Tauris, 1995), 256–78.

7 Arab nationalism, fascism, and the Jews

1 For a survey of the respective literature see Gudrun Krämer, "Anti-Semitism in the Muslim World: A Critical Review," *Die Welt des Islams* 46 (2006): 246–54.
2 Ihsan Fu'ad Khatib, *Wamadat min 'umr al-zaman: Qabasat min hayat al-Shaykh Fu'ad al-Khatib, sha'ir al-thawra al-'Arabiyya al-kubra* (Beirut: Dar al-'Ilm li'l-Malayin, 1994), 99–106, 113, quotes on 99, 109. On the topic of Jews and Zionists see Krämer, "Anti-Semitism in the Muslim World," 264–5; and in more breadth and depth Alexander Flores, "Judeophobia in Context: Anti-Semitism among Modern Palestinians," *Die Welt des Islams* 46 (2006): 307–30.
3 Khatib, *Wamadat min 'umr al-zaman*, 61–5, 115–16, 148.
4 Ibid., 119–21, quotes on 121. See also Hanna Batatu, *The Old Social Classes and the Revolutionary Movements of Iraq: A Study of Iraq's Old Landed and Commercial Classes and of Its Communists, Ba'thists, and Free Officers* (Princeton: Princeton University Press, 1978), 337–44; Jennifer Marie Dueck, *The Claims of Culture at Empire's End: Syria and Lebanon under French Rule* (Oxford; New York: Oxford University Press, 2010), 118–41; Keith David Watenpaugh, *Being Modern in the Middle East: Revolution, Nationalism, Colonialism, and the Arab Middle Class* (Princeton, NJ: Princeton University Press, 2006), 255–78; Peter Wien, *Iraqi Arab Nationalism: Authoritarian, Totalitarian and Pro-Fascist Inclinations, 1932–1941* (London; New York: Routledge, 2006), 78–105.
5 Khatib, *Wamadat min 'umr al-zaman*, 134f, 147, quote on 135. On radio propaganda see Jeffrey Herf, *Nazi Propaganda for the Arab World* (New Haven: Yale University Press, 2009), 36–56, and passim. Herf's study covers the story of German radio propaganda from the perspective of Berlin only. His findings should not be used for conclusions about the reception and actual impact of this propaganda. See criticism and corrections in Alexander Flores, "The Arabs as Nazis? Some Reflections on 'Islamofascism' and Arab Anti-Semitism," *Die Welt des Islams* 52 (2012): 454–7; René Wildangel, "The Invention of 'Islamofascism'. Nazi Propaganda to the Arab World and Perceptions from Palestine," *Die Welt Des Islams* 52 (2012): 526–44.
6 Fu'ad al-Khatib, *Fath al-Andalus* (Amman, 1931), 20–6 (act three). Al-Khatib followed the general storyline that Jirji Zaydan had laid out in his novel. Zaydan, however, presented Andalusian Jews in a more positive light than al-Khatib. But even in Zaydan's account, they were prone to conspiracy, cabals and bribery. A depiction of a secret meeting of Jews in Écija is reminiscent of Masonic rituals. The lumping together of allegations of Jewish secretiveness and Free Masonry is a mainstay of anti-Semitism and features in the *Protocols of the Elders of Zion*. See Jirji Zaydan, *Fath al-Andalus* (Cairo: Dar al-Hilal, 1965), 148–98, 315–41.
7 For examples of academic works, see Sylvia G. Haim, *Arab Nationalism: An Anthology* (Berkeley, CA; Los Angeles; London: University of California Press, 1976); Reeva S. Simon, *Iraq Between the Two World Wars: The Militarist Origins*

of Tyranny (New York: Columbia University Press, 2004); Bassam Tibi, *Arab Nationalism: Between Islam and the Nation-State* (New York: St. Martin's Press, 1997). Other examples are cited below.

8 See the articles in Gerhard Höpp, Peter Wien, and René Wildangel, *Blind für die Geschichte? Arabische Begegnungen mit dem Nationalsozialismus*, ZMO-Studien 19 (Berlin: Klaus Schwarz Verlag, 2004); Arabic translation: Gerhard Höpp, Peter Wien, and René Wildangel eds. *'Umyan 'an al-tarikh?! Al-'Arab wa-Almaniya wa'l-Yahud* (Damascus: Qadmus, 2007); Wien, *Iraqi Arab Nationalism*; René Wildangel, *Zwischen Achse und Mandatsmacht: Palästina und der Nationalsozialismus*, ed. Zentrum Moderner Orient ZMO-Studien 24 (Berlin: Klaus Schwarz Verlag, 2007); Götz Nordbruch, *Nazism in Syria and Lebanon: The Ambivalence of the German Option, 1933–1945* (Milton Park; New York: Routledge, 2008); Israel Gershoni and James P. Jankowski, *Confronting Fascism in Egypt: Dictatorship Versus Democracy in the 1930s* (Stanford: Stanford University Press, 2010). These and other works are cited in two special issues of *Die Welt des Islams* that are pertinent to this chapter: 46.3 (2006), ed. Gudrun Krämer; and 52.3–4 (2012), ed. Stefan Wild.

9 A key text promoting the concept of Islamofascism as an explanatory paradigm for violence and terrorism in the Muslim world is Matthias Küntzel, *Jihad and Jew-Hatred: Islamism, Nazism and the Roots of 9/11* (New York: Telos Press, 2007); see the German original: Matthias Küntzel, *Djihad und Judenhass: Über den neuen antijüdischen Krieg* (Freiburg i.Brsg.: ça ira, 2003). A critique of the term "Islamofascism" is in Stefan Wild, "'Islamofascism'? Introduction," *Die Welt des Islams* 52 (2012): 225–41; Reinhard Schulze, "Islamofascism: Four Avenues to the Use of an Epithet," *Die Welt des Islams* 52 (2012): 290–330. A sharp criticism of Küntzel's book is in Flores, "The Arabs as Nazis?" 452–4.

10 Recent literature has shown, for instance, that it is fruitful to test the structures of Saddam Hussein's Iraq in light of a totalitarian paradigm. Achim Rohde, *State-Society Relations in Ba'thist Iraq: Facing Dictatorship* (London; New York: Routledge, 2010).

11 Gershoni and Jankowski, *Confronting Fascism*; Wien, *Iraqi Arab Nationalism*.

12 On anti-fascism see 'Abdallah Hanna, *Al-Haraka al-munahida li'l-fashiyya fi Suriya wa-Lubnan: 1933–1945. Dirasa watha'iqiyya* (Beirut: Dar al-Farabi, 1975).

13 Orit Bashkin, *The Other Iraq: Pluralism and Culture in Hashemite Iraq* (Stanford: Stanford University Press, 2008); Orit Bashkin, "The Barbarism from Within: Discourses about Fascism amongst Iraqi and Iraqi-Jewish Communists, 1942–1955," *Die Welt Des Islams* 52 (2012): 400–429; Nordbruch, *Nazism in Syria and Lebanon*; Wien, *Iraqi Arab Nationalism*; Wildangel, *Zwischen Achse und Mandatsmacht*.

14 Gershoni and Jankowski, *Confronting Fascism*. See also Israel Gershoni and Götz Nordbruch, *Sympathie und Schrecken: Begegnungen mit Faschismus und Nationalsozialismus in Ägypten, 1922–1937*, Studien/Zentrum Moderner Orient 29 (Berlin: Klaus-Schwarz, 2011); Israel Gershoni, "Egyptian Liberalism in an Age of 'Crisis of Orientation': Al-Risala's Reaction to Fascism and Nazism, 1933–39," *International Journal of Middle East Studies* 31 (1999): 551–76; Götz Nordbruch, "Islam as a 'Giant Progressive Leap': Religious Critiques of Fascism and National Socialism," *Die Welt des Islams* 52 (2012): 499–525; Nir Arielli, *Fascist Italy and the Middle East, 1933–40* (Basingstoke; New York: Palgrave Macmillan, 2010); Haggai Erlich, "Periphery and Youth: Fascist Italy and the Middle East," in *Fascism Outside Europe: The European Impulse Against Domestic Conditions in the Diffusion of Global Fascism*, ed. Stein Ugelvik Larsen (Boulder; New York: Social Science Monographs, Columbia University Press, 2001), 393–423. On Arab attitudes towards Jews in Arab lands during World War II see Robert B. Satloff, *Among the Righteous: Lost Stories from the Holocaust's Long Reach into Arab Lands* (New York: PublicAffairs, 2006), 99–137, and passim.

15 See Götz Nordbruch, "Geschichte im Konflikt. Der Nationalsozialismus als Thema aktueller Debatten in der ägyptischen Öffentlichkeit," in *Blind für die Geschichte? Arabische Begegnungen mit dem Nationalsozialismus*, eds. Gerhard Höpp, Peter Wien, and René Wildangel, ZMO-Studien 19 (Berlin: Klaus Schwarz Verlag, 2004), 269–94; Meir Litvak and Esther Webman, *From Empathy to Denial: Arab Responses to the Holocaust* (New York: Columbia University Press, 2009).

16 Omar Kamil, *Der Holocaust im arabischen Gedächtnis: Eine Diskursgeschichte 1945–1967*, Schriften des Simon-Dubnow-Instituts 15 (Göttingen: Vandenhoeck & Ruprecht, 2012), 33–5, 78–9.

17 Israel Gershoni, "'Der verfolgte Jude'. Al-Hilals Reaktionen auf den Antisemitismus in Europa und Hitlers Machtergreifung," in *Blind für die Geschichte? Arabische Begegnungen mit dem Nationalsozialismus*, eds. Gerhard Höpp, Peter Wien, and René Wildangel, ZMO-Studien 19 (Berlin: Klaus Schwarz Verlag, 2004), 39–72; Nordbruch, *Nazism in Syria and Lebanon*, 15–29; Wildangel, *Zwischen Achse und Mandatsmacht*, 121–89, 264–80.

18 Wildangel, "The Invention of 'Islamofascism'," 542–3; Wildangel quotes from Stuart Carter Dodd, *A Pioneer Radio Poll in Lebanon, Syria and Palestine* (Jerusalem: The Government Printer, 1943), quote on p26. In Jidda, Saudi Arabia, the American Legation of the United States assessed that public opinion of Germany was high during World War II as long as there were reports about German victories. As soon as they receded, the regard for Germany did so, too. See National Archives and Record Administration, College Park, RG 84 Records of the Foreign Service Posts of the Department of State, Egypt, US Embassy and Legation, Cairo, Classified and Unclassified General records, 1936–1955, Box 78, 1942: 820.02 Jidda, Saudi Arabia, to the Department of State (copy to American Legation, Cairo), October 17, 1942: Materials supplied by the Office of War Information for Distribution in Saudi Arabia, pp3–2. See also James Jankowski, "The View from the Embassy: British Assessments of Egyptian Attitudes during World War II," in *Arab Responses to Fascism and Nazism: Attraction and Repulsion*, ed. I. Gershoni (Austin, TX: University of Texas Press, 2014), 171–94.

19 Litvak and Webman, *From Empathy to Denial*, passim; Stefan Wild, "Die arabische Rezeption der 'Protokolle der Weisen von Zion,'" in *Islamstudien ohne Ende*, eds. Rainer Brunner et al., Abhandlungen für die Kunde des Morgenlandes 54.1 (Würzburg, 2002), 517–28.

20 Editor's remark in n11: the herdsmen were the Hyksos of Pharaonic times, who were Arab kings.

21 Fu 'ad al-Khatib, *Diwan al-Khatib*, ed. Riyad al-Khatib (Cairo: Dar al-Ma'arif, 1959), the poem on 359ff, the verses on 362. The time "after Prophethood" relates to the period during and after the rise of Islam.

22 Gershoni and Nordbruch, *Sympathie und Schrecken*, 152–3, 265–7, 293; Kamil, *Der Holocaust im arabischen Gedächtnis*, 15–17, 21, 34, 78–9, n119.

23 Ahmad Hasan al-Zayyat, "Rahm Allah Udulf Hitlar!" *al-Risala* 708 (1947), 1. The quotes, in a slightly different translation, are in Litvak and Webman, *From Empathy to Denial*, 209. They maintain that they prove that "the emerging conflict in Palestine led al-Zayyat to shift from his sharp criticism of Nazism of the 1930s, to longing for it." There is another (overly free) translation in Kamil, *Der Holocaust im arabischen Gedächtnis*, 18. He focuses on the anti-imperialist content, though.

24 al-Zayyat, "Rahm Allah Udulf Hitlar!" p1.

25 Assessment based on Kamil, *Der Holocaust im arabischen Gedächtnis*, passim.

26 Gilbert Achcar, *The Arabs and the Holocaust: The Arab–Israeli War of Narratives* (New York: Metropolitan Books, 2010), 5–29, 248–56, and passim. On the terminology of "islamisierter Antisemitismus" or "Islamized anti-Semitism" see Michael Kiefer, "Islamischer, islamistischer oder islamisierter Antisemitismus?," *Die Welt*

des Islams 46 (2006): 277–306; Krämer, "Anti-Semitism in the Muslim World," 275. On the importance of the Palestine conflict as a context for the occurrence of anti-Semitism in the Arab world see Flores, "Judeophobia in Context."

27 Orit Bashkin, *New Babylonians: A History of Jews in Modern Iraq* (Stanford, CA: Stanford University Press, 2012), 100–40; Nordbruch, *Nazism in Syria and Lebanon*, 89–102; Wien, *Iraqi Arab Nationalism*, 105–12. The military history is in Geoffrey Warner, *Iraq and Syria 1941* (London: University of Delaware Press, 1974).

28 Patrick Bernhard, "Behind the Battle Lines: Italian Atrocities and the Persecution of Arabs, Berbers, and Jews in North Africa during World War II," *Holocaust and Genocide Studies* 26 (2012): 425–46.

29 Klaus-Michael Mallmann and Martin Cüppers, *Halbmond und Hakenkreuz: Das Dritte Reich, die Araber und Palästina* …, Veröffentlichungen der Forschungsstelle Ludwigsburg der Universität Stuttgart 8 (Darmstadt: Wissenschaftliche Buchgesellschaft, 2006), 137–47, 199–235; see the English translation: Klaus Michael Mallmann and Martin Cüppers, *Nazi Palestine: The Plans for the Extermination of the Jews in Palestine*, trans. Krista Smith (New York: Enigma Books, 2011). Much of the book is taken up by a problematic discussion of links between Arabs and Nazism in Palestine. The authors imply that there was a logical link between German designs for the Jewish population of the Middle East and Arab resistance to Zionism during the 1930s and World War II. See the following reviews: Peter Wien, "Coming to Terms with the Past: German Academia and Historical Relations between the Arab Lands and Nazi Germany," *International Journal of Middle East Studies* 42 (2010): 311–21; Flores, "The Arabs as Nazis?" 457–62. The deployment of Muslims for Nazi Germany's war effort is covered in impressive detail in David Motadel, *Islam and Nazi Germany's War*, 2014, part III in particular. See also Satloff, *Among the Righteous*, 73–137.

30 Gerhard Höpp, "Der verdrängte Diskurs: Arabische Opfer des Nationalsozialismus," in *Blind für die Geschichte? Arabische Begegnungen mit dem Nationalsozialismus* (Berlin: Klaus Schwarz Verlag, 2004), 238–52. Höpp was able to identify around 450 Arab KZ inmates by name, but maintains that there were probably many more. Among those identified, 34 were in Auschwitz, 148 in Buchenwald, 84 in Dachau, 62 in Mauthausen, 42 in Sachsenhausen, and 4 in Lublin-Majdanek. Most were North Africans, with only a few from Egypt and the Middle East. Arabs were not targeted by the Nazi extermination policy, however. Many fell victim to the 'ordinary' terror of the Nazi regime (ibid., 252). Gerhard Höpp mentions one Moroccan inmate who died in the Mauthausen gas chamber. Many others survived. It is a matter of debate, of course, to count the Jews from Arab lands, as Gerhard Höpp does, as Arab victims, such as the so-called "Austauschjuden" ("Exchange Jews") from Libya, who the Nazis were trying to use as ransom for German POWs. See Rachel Simon, "It Could Have Happened There: The Jews of Libya During the Second World War," *Africana Journal* 16 (1994): 381–422.

31 Al-Husseini's Berlin years are best documented in Klaus Gensicke, *Der Mufti von Jerusalem, Amin el-Husseini, und die Nationalsozialisten* (Frankfurt am Main; New York: P. Lang, 1988); a revised and less balanced version is Klaus Gensicke, *Der Mufti von Jerusalem und die Nationalsozialisten: eine politische Biographie Amin el-Husseinis*, Veröffentlichungen der Forschungsstelle Ludwigsburg der Universität Stuttgart 11 (Darmstadt: Wissenschaftliche Buchgesellschaft, 2007). The Mufti reached out to British representatives for reconciliation still in the fall of 1939. See Francis R. Nicosia, *Nazi Germany and the Arab World* (New York: Cambridge University Press, 2015), 185. On Rashid 'Ali al-Kailani see Renate Dieterich, "Rashid 'Ali al-Kailani in Berlin – ein irakischer Nationalist in NS-Deutschland," *Al-Rafidayn: Jahrbuch zur Geschichte und Kultur des modernen Iraq* 3 (1995): 47–79.

32 Gensicke, *Der Mufti von Jerusalem*, 149–64; manuscripts of the speeches are edited in Gerhard Höpp, *Mufti-Papiere: Briefe, Memoranden, Reden und Aufrufe Amin al-Husainis aus dem Exil, 1940–1945*, ZMO-Studien 16 (Berlin: Klaus Schwarz Verlag, 2001); for an analysis of the actual broadcast content see Herf, *Nazi Propaganda for the Arab World*, chs. 5–7. Herf does not provide information about the reception of these speeches among Arab listeners. A critique of Herf in the form of a reassessment of the organization, goals and contents of German radio propaganda to the Middle East is in Hans Goldenbaum, "Nationalsozialismus als Antikolonialismus: Die deutsche Rundfunkpropaganda für die arabische Welt," *Vierteljahrshefte für Zeitgeschichte* 64 (2016): 449–89. The author would like to thank Hans Goldenbaum for making the manuscript available. He argues that religion played an insignificant role in the broadcasts. Secular nationalist and anti-Semitic statements received a veneer of Islamic terminology.

33 Gensicke, *Der Mufti von Jerusalem*, 164–7; Hannah Arendt, *Eichmann in Jerusalem: A Report on the Banality of Evil* (London: Penguin Books, 2006), 13 (first published in 1963); Simon Wiesenthal, *Grossmufti – Grossagent der Achse: Tatsachenbericht* (Salzburg: Ried-Verlag, 1947), 37–9. Gensicke comments that these massive allegations should be based on stronger evidence to become credulous. He refers to Alexander Schölch, "Drittes Reich, Zionistische Bewegung und Palästina-Konflikt," *Vierteljahrshefte für Zeitgeschichte* 30 (1982): 672.

34 USHMM, Kempner Materials, RG-71.005.06, Box 235 (Auswärtiges Amt, Section/Abteilung PolVII, 6447g and gII). The documents contain a correspondence between Envoy Fritz Grobba, who at the time was the Foreign Office's liaison with al-Kaylani, and his superiors in the ministry. June 26, 1942: Grobba indicates to Unterstaatssekretär Luther that both al-Husayni and al-Kaylani had dispatched a representative to participate in Secret Service (*Sicherheitsdienst, SD*) training sessions. A visit to Sachsenhausen was part of the session. Al-Kaylani had expressed the wish to participate in this visit to see if similar institutions could be used in Iraq ("… ob er Einrichtungen eines solchen Konzentrationslagers als Muster für entsprechende Anlagen im Irak verwenden könne.") Grobba wrote that the *SD* had inquired whether the Foreign Office had any objections to this visit. Luther's reply on July 12 was that he had serious reservations ("erheblichste Bedenken") not only about the visit, but about the general idea of participation in *SD* trainings. On July 14, Grobba informed Luther that he had called off the endeavor after he had had second thoughts about it himself. Grobba, however, reported to Luther on July 17 that he had received notice from the Reich Security Main Office (*Reichssicherheitshauptamt, RSHA*) that three of al-Kailani's and one of al-Husayni's associates had already visited the camp. (I would like to thank Stefan Hördler for pointing me to this reference.) See also Mallmann and Cüppers, *Halbmond und Hakenkreuz*, 153.

35 Astrid Ley and Günter Morsch, *Medizin und Verbrechen: Das Krankenrevier des KZ Sachsenhausen 1936–1945* (Berlin: Metropol, 2007), 379–93.

36 Amin al-Husayni, *Mudhakkirat al-Hajj Muhammad Amin al-Husayni*, ed. 'Abd al-Karim 'Umar (Damascus: al-Ahali, 1999), 126f.

37 Wildangel, *Zwischen Achse und Mandatsmacht*, ch. 5.

38 On internal competition in German foreign policy see Milan Hauner, "The Professionals and the Amateurs in National Socialist Foreign Policy: Revolution and Subversion in the Islamic and Indian World," in *Der "Führerstaat": Mythos und Realität. Studien zur Struktur und Politik des Dritten Reiches*, eds. Gerhard Hirschfeld and Lothar Kettenacker, Veröffentlichungen des Deutschen Historischen Instituts London 8 (Stuttgart, 1981), 305–28; Peter Wien, "Arab Nationalists, Nazi-Germany and the Holocaust: An Unlucky Contemporaneity," in *Der Völkermord an den Armeniern und die Shoah/The Armenian Genocide and the Shoah*, eds. Hans Lukas Kieser and Dominik J. Schaller (Zurich: Chronos, 2002), 599–614. Nazi foreign

policy never included plans to let Arab national interests overrule the imperialist claims of its French, Italian and Spanish allies over the southern and eastern rim of the Mediterranean; see Nicosia, *Nazi Germany and the Arab World*, passim. Nazi German *Islam Politics* focused on Muslims in the Soviet Union rather than on Arabs as can be seen in David Motadel, *Islam and Nazi Germany's War* (Cambridge, MA: The Belknap Press of Harvard University Press, 2014), passim.

39 This is in line with a general, steep decline of numbers of foreign students in Germany after 1933. The largest group of foreign students during the war was of South-East European origin. Michael Grüttner, *Studenten im Dritten Reich* (Paderborn: Ferdinand Schöningh, 1995), 108f; see also Gerhard Höpp, "Zwischen Universität und Straße: Ägyptische Studenten in Deutschland 1849–1945," *Würzburger Geographische Manuskripte* 60 (2002): 40f and passim.

40 Wildangel, "The Invention of 'Islamofascism'," 532–7; Munir Hamida, "Amin al-Husayni in der deutschen Kriegspropaganda des Zweiten Weltkrieges – eine Studie zur arabischsprachigen Zeitschrift 'Barid ash-Sharq'" (Berlin: M.A. Thesis, Free University, 2007), 12ff, 35ff.

41 Gensicke, *Der Mufti von Jerusalem*, 134ff; Gerhard Höpp, "Muslime unterm Hakenkreuz: Zur Entstehungsgeschichte des Islamischen Zentralinstituts zu Berlin e.V.," *Moslemische Revue* 14.1 (1994): 16–27; Höpp, *Mufti-Papiere: Briefe, Memoranden, Reden und Aufrufe Amin al-Husainis aus dem Exil, 1940–1945*, 123–6. On radio propaganda, see Goldenbaum, "Nationalsozialismus als Antikolonialismus."

42 See *Al-Dalil al-'Iraqi al-rasmi (The Iraq Directory)* (Baghdad, 1936), 604. It says that he went to Hamburg.

43 Zentrum Moderner Orient, Berlin, Archiv, Nachlass Gerhard Höpp (Gerhard Höpp papers, henceforth: ZMOHöpp), 1.21.64: photocopy of Djabir Omar, *Grundstruktur einer zukünftigen arabischen staatsbürgerlichen Erziehung* (Zurich: PhD thesis, 1940), title page, table of contents, introduction, and curriculum vitae.

44 Gerhard Höpp, "Ruhmloses Zwischenspiel: Fauzi al-Qawuqji in Deutschland, 1941–1947," *Al-Rafidayn: Jahrbuch zur Geschichte und Kultur des modernen Iraq* 3 (1995): 23, 25, 33; 'Abd al-Razzaq al-Hasani, *Al-Asrar al-khafiyya fi harakat al-sana 1941 al-taharruriyya.* (Sayda: Matba'at al-'Irfan, 1958), 203. ZMOHöpp, 1.21.60: Universitätsarchiv Jena, Matrikelbuch, entry "Omar, Jabir" ["Djabir" is erroneously deleted and replaced with "Yahir"].

45 ZMOHöpp, 1.12.50: photocopy of Djabir Omar, "Arabien und England," in *Völkischer Beobachter*, July 19, 1939: p8 (slightly truncated).

46 "Bei unserer Verteidigung handelt es sich also um die Bekämpfung der Engländer, die uns unsere Freiheit nahmen, und um die Abwehr der Juden, die als fremdrassige Eindringlinge kein Heimatrecht [in Palästina] haben dürfen."

47 ZMOHöpp, 1.21.64: Omar, *Grundstruktur*, 5ff.

48 Wien, *Iraqi Arab Nationalism*, 19–24; Simon, *Iraq Between the Two World Wars*, 7–40.

49 Ludmila Hanisch, "Akzentverschiebung – Zur Geschichte der Semitistik und Islamwissenschaft während des 'Dritten Reichs'," *Berichte zur Wissenschaftsgeschichte* 18 (1995): 217–26; Ursula Wokoeck, *German Orientalism: The Study of the Middle East and Islam from 1800 to 1945* (New York: Routledge, 2009); Ekkehard Ellinger, *Deutsche Orientalistik zur Zeit des Nationalsozialismus 1933–1945* (Edingen-Neckarhausen: Deux Mondes, 2006). See also Stefan Wild, "Wissenschaft im Zwielicht. Orientalisten im 'Dritten Reich'," *Orientalistische Literaturzeitung* 103.4–5 (2008): 478–85. The latter is a review of Ellinger.

50 ZMOHöpp, 1.21.34: Universitätsarchiv Jena, Bestand BA 2132: Nationalsozialistische Deutsche Arbeiterpartei, Gauleitung Thüringen, NSD-Dozentenbund, Gaudozentenbundführer, signed i.V. Dr. Knoche: Rundschreiben an alle Professoren, Dozenten

und Assistenten der Friedrich-Schiller-Universität; Nationalsozialistische Deutsche Arbeiterpartei, Gauleitung Thüringen, NSD-Dozentenbund, Gaudozentenbundführer, signed i.V. Dr. Knoche, Betrifft: "Arbeitsgemeinschaft über arabische Lebensfragen," An Se. Magnifizenz, den Herrn Rektor der Friedrich-Schiller-Univ. Jena; [Nationalsozialistische Deutsche Arbeiterpartei, Gauleitung Thüringen, NSD-Dozentenbund, Gaudozentenbundführer] signed i.V. Dr. Knoche, Leiter der Arbeitsgemeinschaft, An Se. Magnifizenz, den Herrn Rektor der Friedrich-Schiller-Univ. Jena, Staatsrat Professor Dr. Astel. The *Arbeitsgemeinschaft* was also instrumental in securing the publication of some of its Arab participants' papers in German newspapers and journals. This is probably how 'Umar's article made it into the *Völkische Beobachter*; see ZMOHöpp, 1.21.49: Arbeitsgemeinschaft über arabische Lebensfragen an der Friedrich-Schiller-Universität, Bericht über die erste Vortragsreihe im Sommer-Semester 1939, Jena, Auslandsamt der Dozentenschaft, Auslandsstelle der Universität [photocopy of the report]: p5f.

51 Title: "Die Verbreitung der Araber in der Welt." ZMOHöpp, 1.21.49: Arbeitsgemeinschaft über arabische Lebensfragen an der Friedrich-Schiller-Universität, Bericht über die erste Vortragsreihe im Sommer-Semester 1939, Jena, Auslandsamt der Dozentenschaft, Auslandsstelle der Universität [photocopy of the report]: 8–10. Krückmann (1904–1984), who held a chair for studies of the ancient Orient (*Altorientalistik*) at Freiburg University after the war, was dispatched to Baghdad as a translator for the *Abwehr* military intelligence service in May 1941. ZMOHöpp, 1.21.67: BArchB, AA, F13300, Telegramm, [sent:] Bagdad, den 18. Mai 1941, [received Berlin] Pol I M 1313, Nr 51 vom 18.5., auf Telegramm [from AA] vom 15. Nr. 18, Verschlusssache [ten copies distributed in AA, Berlin].

52 Albert Habib Hourani, *Arabic Thought in the Liberal Age, 1798–1939* (Cambridge: Cambridge University Press, 1983), 260–73; Bashkin, *The Other Iraq*, 170–1.

53 Jeffrey Herf, *The Jewish Enemy: Nazi Propaganda During World War II and the Holocaust* (Cambridge, MA: The Belknap Press of Harvard University Press, 2006), 134f, 180f. Von Leers also published articles in *Barid al-Sharq*. See Hamida, "Amin al-Husayni in der deutschen Kriegspropaganda," 41f. An example for Leers' conflation of racism, anti-Semitism, and geostrategic analysis: Johann von Leers, *Rassen, Völker und Volkstümer* (Langensalza, Berlin, Leipzig: Julius Beltz, 1938), passim; on Jews and Arabs see pp181–90, 400–8.

54 "Politische Kraftlinien im vorderen Orient," in: ZMOHöpp, 1.21.49: Arbeitsgemeinschaft: 11–13.

55 "Islam und Judentum," in: ZMOHöpp, 1.21.49: Arbeitsgemeinschaft: 20–3. On similar debates in the Middle East about concerns that Nazi anti-Semitism might include the Arabs, and specifically about the ambivalence with regard to translations of *Mein Kampf* and its racial terminology into Arabic see Stefan Wild, "National Socialism in the Arab Near East Between 1933 and 1939," *Die Welt des Islams* 25 (1985): 139–41; Nordbruch, *Nazism in Syria and Lebanon*, 32–4.

56 "Lebensform und Führung bei den Arabern." ZMOHöpp, 1.21.49: Arbeitsgemeinschaft: 24–6. Kannuna, born 1913, had enrolled at Jena University in 1937 for pedagogy. He left after the summer semester of 1939 without graduating. ZMOHöpp, 1.21.60: Universitätsarchiv Jena, Matrikelbuch, entry "Kannûna, Karim." See also Höpp, "Der verdrängte Diskurs," 237.

57 "Die arabische Jugendbewegung." ZMOHöpp, 1.21.49: Arbeitsgemeinschaft: 29–30.

58 Batatu, *The Old Social Classes*, 812; Marion Farouk-Sluglett and Peter Sluglett, *Iraq since 1958: From Revolution to Dictatorship* (London; New York: I.B. Tauris, 2003), 73.

59 Jabir 'Umar, *Hawla al-qawmiyya al-'Arabiyya: Muhadarat* (Damascus: Matba'at al-Nidal, 1948).

60 Tobias C. Bringmann, *Handbuch der Diplomatie, 1815–1963: Auswärtige Mission-schefs in Deutschland und deutsche Missionschefs im Ausland von Metternich bis Adenauer* (München: K.G. Saur, 2001), 227.

61 "Nazarat fi'l-qawmiyya al-'Arabiyya," in 'Umar, *Hawla al-qawmiyya al-'Arabiyya*, 3–33.

62 The curricula were developed by the eminent Arab nationalist thinker Sati' al-Husri. See William L. Cleveland, *The Making of an Arab Nationalist: Ottomanism and Arabism in the Life and Thought of Sati' Al-Husri* (Princeton: Princeton University Press, 1971), 85ff; Tibi, *Arab Nationalism: Between Islam and the Nation-State*, 127–38.

63 'Umar, *Hawla al-qawmiyya al-'Arabiyya*, 3–5.

64 The Damascus daily *al-Qabas* nevertheless reported in a short note that "Nazarat fi'l-qawmiyya" had been a very "valuable" lecture, February 2, 1947, p4.

65 'Umar, *Hawla al-qawmiyya al-'Arabiyya*, 9.

66 "Al-Qadiyya al-'Arabiyya fi'l-tarikh al-hadith," in ibid., 89–97.

67 Ibid., 91f. See also Veccia Vaglieri, L., "Khaybar." Encyclopaedia of Islam, 2nd edn, eds. P. Bearman, Th. Bianquis, C.E. Bosworth, E. van Donzel, W.P. Heinrichs Brill Online, 2016. Reference. University of Maryland – College Park. http://refer-enceworks.brillonline.com/entries/encyclopaedia-of-islam-2/khaybar-COM_0503, date of access: January 21, 2016. The Prophet Muhammad and his followers con-quered Khaybar, at the time the largest Jewish settlement in the region, in 628CE, but granted its inhabitants the right to stay and cultivate the land. Caliph 'Umar, however, reverted this decision, according to some traditions, because of an order given by Muhammad shortly before his death that there was no place for more than one religion in this part of Arabia. In recent times, the name *Khaybar* has become a battle cry for Arabs and Muslims rejecting the State of Israel.

68 Herf, *Nazi Propaganda for the Arab World*, 197f.

69 The focus of the literature about the second half of the twentieth century has been on Arab responses to the Holocaust, as in Achcar, *The Arabs and the Holocaust*; Kamil, *Der Holocaust im arabischen Gedächtnis*.

70 Rudolf Augstein ed. *Historikerstreit: Die Dokumentation der Kontroverse um die Einzigartigkeit der Nationalsozialistischen Judenvernichtung*, 2nd edn. (Munich: Piper, 1987).

71 Zeev Sternhell, "How to Think about Fascism and Its Ideology," *Constellations* 15 (2008): 280–90.

72 For a critique of the lack of rigidity in Nolte's terminology see Martin Kitchen, "Ernst Nolte and the Phenomenology of Fascism," *Science & Society* 38 (1974): 131–48.

73 Ilham Khuri-Makdisi, *The Eastern Mediterranean and the Making of Global Radi-calism, 1860–1914* (Berkeley: University of California Press, 2010), 3–11.

74 For a concrete example see Wien, *Iraqi Arab Nationalism*, 41f. See also the works by Wildangel, Nordbruch, Gershoni referenced in this chapter. The Effendiyya has recently been conceptualized again by Lucie Ryzova, *The Age of the Efendiyya: Passages to Modernity in National-Colonial Egypt* (Oxford; New York: Oxford University Press, 2014), 10–26, and passim.

75 Wien, *Iraqi Arab Nationalism*, 78–105; on Jews in Futuwwa see Bashkin, *New Baby-lonians*, 79.

76 Watenpaugh, *Being Modern*, 255–78; Philip S. Khoury, *Syria and the French Mandate: The Politics of Arab Nationalism, 1920–1945* (Princeton: Princeton University Press, 1987), 471–6. On Egypt see James P. Jankowski, *Egypt's Young Rebels: "Young Egypt": 1933–1952* (Stanford: Hoover Institution Press, Stanford University, 1975).

77   Labib Zuwiyya Yamak, *The Syrian Social Nationalist Party: An Ideological Analysis*, Harvard Middle Eastern Monographs 14 (Cambridge: Distributed for the Center for Middle Eastern Studies of Harvard University by Harvard University Press, 1966), 77–88.

78   Christoph Schumann, *Radikalnationalismus in Syrien und Libanon: Politische Sozialisation und Elitenbildung 1930–1958* (Hamburg: Deutsches Orient-Institut, 2001), 282–5; Christoph Schumann, "Symbolische Aneignungen. Antun Sa'adas Radikalnationalismus in der Epoche des Faschismus," in *Blind für die Geschichte? Arabische Begegnungen mit dem Nationalsozialismus*, eds. Gerhard Höpp, Peter Wien, and René Wildangel, ZMO-Studien 19 (Berlin: Klaus Schwarz Verlag, 2004), 155–89.

79   On the elite co-opting the youth see Wien, *Iraqi Arab Nationalism*, 33. See also Rashid Khalidi, "Arab Nationalism: Historical Problems in the Literature," *American Historical Review* 96.5 (1991): 1364f.

80   As in Watenpaugh, *Being Modern*.

81   See Stein Larsen, "Was There Fascism Outside Europe? Diffusion from Europe and Domestic Impulses," in *Fascism Outside Europe: The European Impulse Against Domestic Conditions in the Diffusion of Global Fascism*, ed. Stein Ugelvik Larsen (New York: Columbia University Press, 2001), 720–2.

82   Roger Griffin, ed. *International Fascism: Theories, Causes and the New Consensus* (London; New York: Arnold; Oxford University Press, 1998), 1–20.

83   Roger Griffin, *Modernism and Fascism: The Sense of a Beginning under Mussolini and Hitler* (Basingstoke: Palgrave Macmillan, 2007), 6–10.

84   Roger Eatwell, "Universal Fascism? Approaches and Definitions," in *Fascism Outside Europe: The European Impulse Against Domestic Conditions in the Diffusion of Global Fascism*, ed. Stein Ugelvik Larsen (New York: Columbia University Press, 2001), 15–45.

85   Sternhell, "How to Think about Fascism," 280–90.

86   Gershoni and Jankowski, *Confronting Fascism*; Bashkin, *The Other Iraq*; Nordbruch, *Nazism in Syria and Lebanon*; Wien, *Iraqi Arab Nationalism*.

87   Elizabeth Thompson, *Colonial Citizens: Republican Rights, Paternal Privilege, and Gender in French Syria and Lebanon* (New York: Columbia University Press, 2000), 19–57.

88   An overview and critique of this argument, debated by such scholars as N. Safran, P.J. Vatikiotis, C. Smith, and A. Lutfi al-Sayyid Marsot, is in Israel Gershoni, "The Theory of Crisis and the Crisis in a Theory: Intellectual History in Twentieth-Century Middle Eastern Studies," in *Middle East Historiographies: Narrating the Twentieth Century*, eds. Israel Gershoni, Amy Singer, and Y. Hakan Erdem (Seattle: University of Washington Press, 2006), 131–82.

89   Ernst Nolte, *Die Krise des liberalen Systems und die faschistischen Bewegungen* (München: Piper, 1968). Quotes in Horst Möller, "Ernst Nolte und das 'Liberale System,'" in *Weltbürgerkrieg der Ideologien: Antworten an Ernst Nolte: Festschrift Zum 70. Geburtstag*, eds. Thomas Nipperdey, Anselm Doering-Manteuffel, and Hans-Ulrich Thamer (Berlin: Propyläen, 1993), 60. See also the model of a connection between degrees of liberalization and the potential for the development of fascist movements in Larsen, "Was There Fascism Outside Europe?" 812–15.

90   Wien, *Iraqi Arab Nationalism*, 14–51, 105–12.

91   Federico Finchelstein, *Transatlantic Fascism: Ideology, Violence, and the Sacred in Argentina and Italy, 1919–1945* (Durham: Duke University Press, 2010), 4–11; Maria Framke, *Delhi-Rom-Berlin: Die indische Wahrnehmung von Faschismus und Nationalsozialismus, 1922–1939*, Veröffentlichungen der Forschungsstelle Ludwigsburg der Universität Stuttgart 21 (Darmstadt: Wissenschaftliche Buchgesellschaft, 2013), 38–40, and passim; Markus Daechsel, "Scientism and

Its Discontents: The Indo-Muslim 'Fascism' of Inayatullah Khan Al-Mashriqi," *Modern Intellectual History* 3 (2006): 443–72; Benjamin Zachariah, "Rethinking (the Absence of) Fascism in India, C. 1922–45," in *Cosmopolitan Thought Zones: South Asia and the Global Circulation of Ideas*, ed. Sugata Bose and Kris Manjapra (Houndmills, Basingstoke; New York: Palgrave Macmillan, 2010), 178–209; see also the various contributions in Stein Ugelvik Larsen, *Fascism Outside Europe: The European Impulse Against Domestic Conditions in the Diffusion of Global Fascism* (New York: Columbia University Press, 2001).

92 Not of reasoning altogether, though. Fascism was "anti-rational," not "irrational." Eatwell, "Universal Fascism," 27.

93 Daechsel, "Scientism and Its Discontents," 443.

94 See Sami Zubaida, "Islam and Nationalism: Continuities and Contradictions," *Nations and Nationalism* 10 (2004): 409.

95 Gershoni and Jankowski, *Confronting Fascism*, 214–18; Nordbruch, "Islam as a 'Giant Progressive Leap,'" 521–25.

96 Finchelstein, *Transatlantic Fascism*, 118–37.

97 Ibid., 42, 112–13.

98 The German historian and Islamicist Fritz Steppat used the term "faschistoid." Fritz Steppat, "Das Jahr 1933 und seine Folgen für die arabischen Länder des Vorderen Orients," in *Die Große Krise der dreißiger Jahre: Vom Niedergang der Weltwirtschaft zum Zweiten Weltkrieg*, ed. Gerhard Schulz (Göttingen, 1985), 274.

99 This is also true for the Muslim Brotherhood: I. Gershoni and James P. Jankowski, *Redefining the Egyptian Nation, 1930–1945* (Cambridge; New York: Cambridge University Press, 1995), 15–16.

100 Finchelstein, *Transatlantic Fascism*, 62. On Hourani and his role in mid-twentieth-century Syria see Elizabeth Thompson, *Justice Interrupted: The Struggle for Constitutional Government in the Middle East* (Cambridge, MA; London: Harvard University Press, 2013), 207–35.

101 Akram Fouad Khater, ed. "Antun Sa'adeh Declares His Vision of 'Greater Syria' or Regional Nationalism, June 1, 1935," in *Sources in the History of the Modern Middle East*, 2nd edn. (Boston: Houghton Mifflin, 2011), 128–30.

102 Robert O. Paxton, "The Five Stages of Fascism," *Journal of Modern History* 70 (March 1998): 14–21.

103 This trend is the topic of Eric Davis, *Memories of State: Politics, History, and Collective Identity in Modern Iraq* (Berkeley: University of California Press, 2005); and Lisa Wedeen, *Ambiguities of Domination: Politics, Rhetoric, and Symbols in Contemporary Syria* (Chicago: University of Chicago Press, 1999).

8 Epilogue and conclusion

1 Source: https://www.youtube.com/watch?v=Jl0Jf17r3BI, date of access: April 17, 2015.

2 See an interview on BBC Arabic on https://www.youtube.com/watch?v=GHBRUM kB9kM, date of access: April 17, 2015.

3 A report on the funeral is in *al-Jumhuriyya*, June 27, 1989, p1: "Wada'an faqid al-umma: Al-Qa'id Saddam Husayn wa-dhawu al-faqid wa-a'da' qiyadat al-hizb yahmuluna al-na'sh – Dafn al-faqid al-rahil fi-hada'iq al-qiyada al-qawmiyya li'l-hizb." See also the images and reports in other issues of the newspaper.

4 *Al-Jumhuriyya*, June 25, 1989, p1: "Al-Qiyadatan al-qawmiyya wa'l-qutriyya tan'ayan mu'assi al-hizb wa-aminahu al-'amm al-rafiq Mishil 'Aflaq…"

5 *Al-Jumhuriyya*, June 27, 1989, p1: "Wada'an faqid al-umma …"

6 See the blog-entry on http://hdiggity.blogspot.com/2006/05/foosball-and-baathism. html, date of access: March 21, 2016.

7 William Granara, "Nostalgia, Arab Nationalism, and the Andalusian Chronotope in the Evolution of the Modern Arabic Novel," *Journal of Arabic Literature* 36 (2005): 57f.

8 http://www.joshualandis.com/blog/syrian-regime-loses-last-credible-ally-among-the-sunni-ulama-by-thomas-pierret/; http://www.bbc.com/news/world-middle-east-22086230;http://www.annahar.com/article/22476-دفـن-بوطـي-يجـوار-قـبر-صـلاح-ديـن...; معارضـين-بعـض-غضـب-اثـار; https://www.youtube.com/watch?v=lnaEGs4tuxs. Date of access for all: December 15, 2015.

Bibliography

Archives

Centre des Archives diplomatiques de Nantes (CADN)
Dar al-Watha'iq al-Qawmiyya, Cairo (DWQ, Egyptian National Archives)
Zentrum Moderner Orient/Centre for Modern Oriental Studies, Library: Prof. Dr. Gerhard
    Höpp Estate, Berlin (ZMOHöpp)

Periodicals

Egypt:
al-Ahali
al-Ahram
al-Ahram al-Masa'i
al-Akhbar
'Aqidati
al-Balagh
al-Fath
al-Gumhuriyya
al-Hilal
al-Muqattam
al-Risala

Iraq:
al-Istiqlal
al-Jumhuriyya

Kuwait:
al-Ra'y
al-Watan

Lebanon:
al-Nahar

Palestine:
al-Difa'
Filastin

Syria:

al-Ayyam
al-Ba'th
al-Jundi
al-Qabas
al-Thawra
Tishrin

United Arab Emirates:

al-Khalij

International:

al-Hayat

Europe and USA:

The Christian Science Monitor
The Guardian
Jeune Afrique
The New York Times
Der Standard

Books and scholarly articles

'Abbadi, Ahmad Mukhtar 'Abd al-Fattah. *Fi Tarikh al-Maghrib wa'l-Andalus.* Alexandria: Mu'assasat al-Thaqafa al-Jami'iyya, 1975.

'Abd al-'Alim, Abu Bakr 'Ali. *Al-Lugha al-'Arabiyya: Iqra' wa-naqish. Al-Saff al-khamis al-ibtida'i, al-fasl al-dirasi al-auwal.* Edited by Jumhuriyyat Misr al-'Arabiyya, Wizarat al-Tarbiyya wa'l-Ta'lim. Cairo: Al-Mu'assasa al-'Asriyya li'l-Nashr wa'l-Tarjama, 2001.

'Abd al-Qadir al-Jaza'iri. *Kitab al-mawaqif fi'l-tasawwuf wa'l-wa'z wa'l-irshad.* Damascus: Dar al-Yaqza al-'Arabiyya li'l-Ta'lif wa'l-Tarjama wa'l-Nashr, 1966.

'Abd Muhammad, Sawadi. *Tariq Ibn Ziyad: Hayatuhu, zuhuruhu, nasabuhu, khitatuhu al-'askariyya wa-waqa'i'uhu fi'l-Andalus wa'l-Maghrib.* Baghdad: Dar al-Shu'un al-Thaqafiyya al-'Amma "Afaq 'Arabiyya," 1988.

Achcar, Gilbert. *The Arabs and the Holocaust: The Arab-Israeli War of Narratives.* New York: Metropolitan Books, 2010.

Achrati, Nora. "Following the Leader: A History and Evolution of the Amir 'Abd Al-Qadir Al-Jazairi as Symbol." *The Journal of North African Studies* 12 (2007): 139–52.

'Aflaq, Michel. *Dhikra al-Rasul al-'Arabi.* Beirut: Al-Mu'assasa al-'Arabiyya li'l-Dirasat wa'l-Nashr, 1972.

Amin, Muzaffar 'Abd Allah al-. *Jama'at al-Ahali: Munshi'uha, 'aqidatuha, wa-dawruha fi'l-siyasa al-'Iraqiya, 1932–1946.* Beirut: Al-Mu'assasa al-'Arabiyya li'l-Dirasat wa'l-Nashr, 2001.

Anderson, Benedict. *Imagined Communities: Reflections on the Origin and Spread of Nationalism.* New edn. London: Verso, 2006.

Anderson, Betty S. *The American University of Beirut: Arab Nationalism and Liberal Education.* Austin: University of Texas Press, 2011.

Antonius, George. *The Arab Awakening: The Story of the Arab National Movement.* New York: Capricorn Books, 1965.

Antun, Farah. *Al-Sultan Salah al-Din wa-mamlakat Urshalim: Riwaya tamthiliyya dhat arba'at fusul*. Cairo: [s.n.], 1923.

———. *Al-Sultan Salah al-Din wa-mamlakat Urshalim*. [Beirut]: Dar Marun 'Abbud, 1981.

Arendt, Hannah. *Eichmann in Jerusalem: A Report on the Banality of Evil*. London: Penguin Books, 2006.

Arielli, Nir. *Fascist Italy and the Middle East, 1933–40*. Basingstoke, New York: Palgrave Macmillan, 2010.

Arslan, Shakib. *Al-Hulal al-sundusiyya fi'l-akhbar wa'l-athar al-Andalusiyya*. Vol. 1. Cairo: Al-Matba'a al-Rahmaniyya, 1936.

———. *Al-Hulal al-sundusiyya fi'l-akhbar wa'l-athar al-Andalusiyya*. Vol. 3. Cairo: Matba'at 'Isa al-Babi al-Halabi wa-shuraka'uhu, 1939.

Asad, Talal. *Formations of the Secular: Christianity, Islam, Modernity*. Stanford: Stanford University Press, 2003.

Aschbach, Joseph. *Geschichte der Ommaijaden in Spanien, nebst einer Darstellung des Entstehens der spanischen christlichen Reiche*. Frankfurt/Main: Franz Barrentrapp, 1829.

———. *Tarikh al-Andalus*. Translated by Muhammad 'Abd Allah 'Inan. Cairo: Matba'at Lajnat al-Ta'lif wa'l-Tarjama wa'l-Nashr, 1940.

Aubin-Boltanski, Emma. "Salah al-Din, un héros à l'épreuve: Mythe et pèlerinage en Palestine." *Annales* 60 (2005): 91–107.

Augstein, Rudolf, ed. *Historikerstreit: Die Dokumentation der Kontroverse um die Einzigartigkeit der Nationalsozialistischen Judenvernichtung*. 2nd edn. Munich: Piper, 1987.

Ayalon, Ami. *The Press in the Arab Middle East: A History*. New York, Oxford: Oxford University Press, 1995.

Ayubi, Nazih N. *Over-Stating the Arab State: Politics and Society in the Middle East*. London, New York: Tauris, 1995.

'Azm, Sadiq Jalal. *Naqd al-fikr al-dini*. Beirut: Dar al-Tali'a, 1969.

Badawi, Muhammad Mustafa. *Early Arabic Drama*. Cambridge; New York: Cambridge University Press, 1988.

Bashkin, Orit. *The Other Iraq: Pluralism and Culture in Hashemite Iraq*. Stanford: Stanford University Press, 2008.

———. *New Babylonians: A History of Jews in Modern Iraq*. Stanford: Stanford University Press, 2012.

———. "The Barbarism from Within: Discourses about Fascism amongst Iraqi and Iraqi-Jewish Communists, 1942–1955." *Die Welt Des Islams* 52 (2012): 400–29.

Batatu, Hanna. *The Old Social Classes and the Revolutionary Movements of Iraq: A Study of Iraq's Old Landed and Commercial Classes and of Its Communists, Ba'thists, and Free Officers*. Princeton: Princeton University Press, 1978.

———. *Syria's Peasantry, the Descendants of Its Lesser Rural Notables, and Their Politics*. Princeton: Princeton University Press, 1999.

Baud, Marcelle, and Magdelaine Parisot. *Les Guides Bleus: Égypte. Le Nil égyptien et soudanais du Delta à Khartoum*. Paris: Hachette, 1956.

Bauer, Thomas. *Die Kultur der Ambiguität: Eine andere Geschichte des Islams*. Berlin: Verlag der Weltreligionen, 2011.

Be'eri, Eliezer. *Army Officers in Arab Politics and Society*. Jerusalem: Israel University Press, 1969.

Behrens-Abouseif, Doris. *Islamic Architecture in Cairo: An Introduction*. Studies in Islamic Art and Architecture, v. 3. Leiden, New York: E.J. Brill, 1989.

Beinin, Joel, and Zachary Lockman. *Workers on the Nile: Nationalism, Communism, Islam, and the Egyptian Working Class, 1882–1954*. Cairo: The American University in Cairo Press, 1998.

Belghazi, Taieb. "Festivalization of Urban Space in Morocco." *Critique: Critical Middle Eastern Studies* 15 (2006): 97–107.

Belli, Mériam N. *An Incurable Past: Nasser's Egypt Then and Now*. Gainesville: University Press of Florida, 2013.

Ben Halima, Hamadi. *Un demi siècle de théâtre arabe en tunisie, 1907–1957*. Publications de l'Université de Tunis, Faculté des lettres et sciences humaines de Tunis: 6. sér., Philosophie-littérature; v. 6. [Tunis: Université de Tunis], 1974.

Ben-Amos, Avner. *Funerals, Politics, and Memory in Modern France, 1789–1996*. Oxford, New York: Oxford University Press, 2000.

Bengio, Ofra. *Saddam's Word: Political Discourse in Iraq*. New York: Oxford University Press, 1998.

Bennett, Tony. *The Birth of the Museum: History, Theory, Politics*. London, New York: Routledge, 1995.

Bernhard, Patrick. "Behind the Battle Lines: Italian Atrocities and the Persecution of Arabs, Berbers, and Jews in North Africa during World War II." *Holocaust and Genocide Studies* 26 (2012): 425–46.

Bernhardsson, Magnus Thorkell. *Reclaiming a Plundered Past: Archaeology and Nation Building in Modern Iraq*. Austin: University of Texas Press, 2005.

Bloom, Michelle E. *Waxworks: A Cultural Obsession*. Minneapolis: University of Minnesota Press, 2003.

Braae, Christel. "The Early Museums and the Formation of Their Publics." In *Middle Eastern Cities, 1900–1950: Public Places and Public Spheres in Transformation*, edited by Hans Chr. Korsholm Nielsen and Jakob Skovgaard-Petersen, 112–32. Aarhus: Aarhus University Press, 2001.

Bringmann, Tobias C. *Handbuch der Diplomatie, 1815–1963: Auswärtige Missionschefs in Deutschland und deutsche Missionschefs im Ausland von Metternich bis Adenauer*. München: K.G. Saur, 2001.

Brockelmann, Carl. *Geschichte der Arabischen Literatur*, Vol. 1 and 2; Suppl. 2 and 3. Leiden: E.J. Brill, 1938–49.

Brown, Nathan J. *Constitutions in a Nonconstitutional World: Arab Basic Laws and the Prospects for Accountable Government*. Albany: State University of New York Press, 2002.

Brugman, J. *An Introduction to the History of Modern Arabic Literature in Egypt*. Studies in Arabic Literature 10. Leiden: E.J. Brill, 1984.

Brunner-Traut, Emma, and Vera Hell. *Aegypten: Studienreiseführer mit Landeskunde*. 2nd edn. Führer für Studienreisen 1. Stuttgart: Günther, 1966.

Burke, Edmund. "Middle Eastern Societies and Ordinary People's Lives." In *Struggle and Survival in the Modern Middle East*, ed. Edmund Burke, 1–27. Berkeley: University of California Press, 1993.

Campos, Michelle U. *Ottoman Brothers: Muslims, Christians, and Jews in Early Twentieth-Century Palestine*. Stanford: Stanford University Press, 2011.

Carlyle, Thomas. *On Heroes, Hero-Worship, and the Heroic in History*. New York: Wiley and Putnam, 1846.

Çelik, Zeynep. *Displaying the Orient: Architecture of Islam at Nineteenth-Century World's Fairs*. Comparative Studies on Muslim Societies, 12. Berkeley: University of California Press, 1992.

Chahine, Youssef. *Al-Nasir Salah al-Din.* Film. 1963.

Chahine, Youssef, and Joseph Massad. "Art and Politics in the Cinema of Youssef Chahine." *Journal of Palestine Studies* 28 (1999): 77–93.

Chivers, T.H. "Count Julian, or the Virgin of the First Fond Love. A Tragedy, in Five Acts." In *The Unpublished Plays of Thomas Holley Chivers,* 1–112. Delmar: Scholars' Facsimiles & Reprints, 1980.

Choueiri, Youssef M. *Arab Nationalism: A History. Nation and State in the Arab World.* Oxford, Malden: Blackwell, 2000.

Clancy-Smith, Julia A. *Rebel and Saint: Muslim Notables, Populist Protest, Colonial Encounters (Algeria and Tunisia, 1800–1904).* Berkeley: University of California Press, 1994.

Cleveland, William L. *The Making of an Arab Nationalist: Ottomanism and Arabism in the Life and Thought of Sati' Al-Husri.* Princeton: Princeton University Press, 1971.

———. *Islam Against the West: Shakib Arslan and the Campaign for Islamic Nationalism.* Austin: University of Texas Press, 1985.

———. "The Arab Nationalism of George Antonius Reconsidered." In *Rethinking Nationalism in the Arab Middle East,* eds. James P. Jankowski and Israel Gershoni, 65–86. New York: Columbia University Press, 1997.

Cohn, Bernard S. *Colonialism and Its Forms of Knowledge: The British in India.* Princeton: Princeton University Press, 1996.

Cole, Juan Ricardo. *Colonialism and Revolution in the Middle East: Social and Cultural Origins of Egypt's 'Urabi Movement.* Princeton Studies on the Near East. Princeton: Princeton University Press, 1993.

Colla, Elliott. *Conflicted Antiquities: Egyptology, Egyptomania, Egyptian Modernity.* Durham: Duke University Press, 2007.

Commins, David Dean. *Islamic Reform: Politics and Social Change in Late Ottoman Syria.* New York: Oxford University Press, 1990.

Cook, David. *Martyrdom in Islam.* Cambridge, New York: Cambridge University Press, 2007.

Cooke, Steven, and Lloyd Jenkins. "Discourses of Regeneration in Early Twentieth-Century Britain: From Bedlam to the Imperial War Museum." *Area* 33 (2001): 382–90.

Daechsel, Markus. "Scientism and Its Discontents: The Indo-Muslim 'Fascism' of Inayatullah Khan Al-Mashriqi." *Modern Intellectual History* 3 (2006): 443–72.

Dahn, Felix. *König Roderich: Ein Trauerspiel in fünf Aufzügen.* 2nd edn. Leipzig: Breitkopf und Härtel, 1876.

Al-Dalil al-'Iraqi al-rasmi (The Iraq Directory). Baghdad, 1936.

Dalil al-Mathaf al-Harbi bi'l-Qal'a wa-'Abidin. Cairo: Matba'at al-Tahrir, 1958.

Dam, Nikolaos van. *The Struggle for Power in Syria: Sectarianism, Regionalism, and Tribalism in Politics, 1961–1978.* 1st edn. New York: St. Martin's Press, 1979.

Damir-Geilsdorf, Sabine. "Politische Utopie und Erinnerung: Das 'Goldene Zeitalter' in islamischen Diskursen heute." In *Geschichte und Erinnerung im Islam,* ed. Angelika Hartmann, 75–94. Formen der Erinnerung 15. Göttingen: Vandenhoeck & Ruprecht, 2004.

Das Schweizerische Landesmuseum, 1898–1948: Kunst, Handwerk und Geschichte. Festbuch zum 50. Jahrestag der Eröffnung. Zurich: Atlantis, 1948.

Davis, Eric. *Memories of State: Politics, History, and Collective Identity in Modern Iraq.* Berkeley: University of California Press, 2005.

Dawisha, Adeed. *Arab Nationalism in the Twentieth Century: From Triumph to Despair.* Princeton: Princeton University Press, 2003.

Dawn, C. Ernest. *From Ottomanism to Arabism: Essays on the Origins of Arab National-ism.* Urbana: University of Illinois Press, 1973.

Deheuvels, Luc-Willy. "Le Saladin de Farah Antun du mythe littéraire arabe au mythe politique." *Revue des mondes musulmans et de la Méditerranée*, no. 89–90 (2000): 189–203.

Di-Capua, Yoav. *Gatekeepers of the Arab Past: Historians and History Writing in Twentieth-Century Egypt.* Berkeley: University of California Press, 2009.

Dieterich, Renate. "Rashid 'Ali al-Kailani in Berlin – ein irakischer Nationalist in NS-Deutschland." *Al-Rafidayn: Jahrbuch zur Geschichte und Kultur des modernen Iraq* 3 (1995): 47–79.

Dodd, Stuart Carter. *A Pioneer Radio Poll in Lebanon, Syria and Palestine.* Jerusalem: The Government Printer, 1943.

Dozy, Reinhart Pieter Anne. *Spanish Islam: A History of the Moslems in Spain.* London: Chatto & Windus, 1913.

Drayson, Elizabeth. *The King and the Whore: King Roderick and La Cava.* New York: Palgrave Macmillan, 2007.

Dueck, Jennifer Marie. *The Claims of Culture at Empire's End: Syria and Lebanon under French Rule.* Oxford, New York: Oxford University Press, 2010.

Duncan, Carol. "Art Museums and the Ritual of Citizenship." In *Exhibiting Cultures: The Poetics and Politics of Museum Display*, ed. Ivan Karp and Steven Lavine, 88–103. Washington: Smithsonian Institution Press, 1991.

Dupont, Anne-Laure. "Le grand homme, figure de la 'Renaissance' arabe." In *Saints et héros du moyen-orient contemporain: actes du colloque des 11 et 12 décembre 2000, à l'institut universitaire de France*, ed. Catherine Mayeur-Jaouen, 47–73. Paris: Maisonneuve et Larose, 2002.

Durkheim, Emile. *The Elementary Forms of the Religious Life.* London: George Allen & Unwin Ltd., 1968.

Eatwell, Roger. "Universal Fascism? Approaches and Definitions." In *Fascism Outside Europe: The European Impulse Against Domestic Conditions in the Diffusion of Global Fascism*, ed. Stein Ugelvik Larsen, 15–45. New York: Columbia University Press, 2001.

Eich, Thomas. "The Forgotten Salafi – Abul-Huda as-Sayyadi." *Die Welt des Islams* 43 (2003): 61–87.

———. "Abu l-Huda l-Sayyadi: Still Such a Polarizing Figure (Response to Itzchak Weismann)." *Arabica* 55 (2008): 433–44.

Eickelman, Dale F. and Armando Salvatore. "Muslim Publics." In *Public Islam and the Common Good*, eds. Armando Salvatore and Dale F. Eickelman, 3–27. Social, Economic, and Political Studies of the Middle East and Asia, 95. Leiden, Boston: Brill, 2004.

El Shakry, Omnia S. *The Great Social Laboratory: Subjects of Knowledge in Colonial and Postcolonial Egypt.* Stanford: Stanford University Press, 2007.

El-Alfy, Amal M. Safwat, ed. *al-Mathaf al-Harbi al-Qawmi.* Cairo: Jumhuriyyat Misr al-'Arabiyya, Wizarat al-Difa', Hay'at al-Athar al-Misriyya, 1987.

El-Rouayheb, Khaled. "Was There a Revival of Logical Studies in Eighteenth-Century Egypt?" *Die Welt des Islams* 45 (2005): 1–19.

———. *Islamic Intellectual History in the Seventeenth Century: Scholarly Currents in the Ottoman Empire and the Maghreb.* Cambridge: Cambridge University Press, 2015.

Ellinger, Ekkehard. *Deutsche Orientalistik zur Zeit des Nationalsozialismus 1933–1945.* Edingen-Neckarhausen: Deux Mondes, 2006.

Elshakry, Marwa. *Reading Darwin in Arabic, 1860–1950.* Chicago, London: The University of Chicago Press, 2013.

Ende, Werner. *Arabische Nation und islamische Geschichte: Die Umayyaden im Urteil arabischer Autoren des 20. Jahrhunderts.* Beirut, 1977.

———. "Wer ist ein Glaubensheld, wer ist ein Ketzer? Konkurrierende Geschichtsbilder in der modernen Literatur islamischer Länder." *Die Welt des Islams* 23/24 (1984): 70–94.

———. "Der Mihrab in der Kathedrale: Die Mezquita in Cordoba und der muslimisch-christliche Dialog." In *Zwischen Orient und Okzident: Studien zu Mobilität von Wissen, Konzepten und Praktiken,* eds. Anke Bentzin, Henner Fürtig, Thomas Krüppner, and Riem Spielhaus, 104–20. Freiburg im Breisgau: Herder, 2010.

Epalza, Mikel de. "Dos literatos arabes viajan por sharq al-Andalus: Shakib Arslan (1939) y Husain Mones (1963)." *Sharq Al-Andalus: Estudios Árabes* 1 (1984): 173–84.

Eppel, Michael. "The Elite, the Effendiyya, and the Growth of Nationalism and Pan-Arabism in Hashemite Iraq, 1921–1958." *International Journal of Middle East Studies* 30 (1998): 227–50.

Erlich, Haggai. "Periphery and Youth: Fascist Italy and the Middle East." In *Fascism Outside Europe: The European Impulse Against Domestic Conditions in the Diffusion of Global Fascism,* ed. Stein Ugelvik Larsen, 393–423. Boulder, New York: Social Science Monographs, Columbia University Press, 2001.

———. "The Tiger and the Lion: Fascism and Ethiopia in Arab Eyes." In *Arab Responses to Fascism and Nazism: Attraction and Repulsion,* ed. I. Gershoni, 271–88. Austin: University of Texas Press, 2014.

Esposito, Matthew D. "The Politics of Death: State Funerals as Rites of Reconciliation in Porfirian Mexico, 1876–1889." *The Americas* 62.1 (2005): 65–94.

Fahmy, Khaled. *All the Pasha's Men: Mehmed Ali, His Army, and the Making of Modern Egypt.* Cambridge Middle East Studies 8. Cambridge, New York: Cambridge University Press, 1997.

Fahmy, Ziad. *Ordinary Egyptians: Creating the Modern Nation Through Popular Culture.* Stanford: Stanford University Press, 2011.

Faroqhi, Suraiya. *Pilgrims and Sultans: The Hajj under the Ottomans, 1517–1683.* London: Tauris, 1994.

Farouk-Sluglett, Marion, and Peter Sluglett. *Iraq since 1958: From Revolution to Dictatorship.* London; New York: I.B. Tauris, 2003.

Farrukh, Mustafa. *Rihla ila bilad al-majd al-mafqud,* [s.n.], 1933.

Fauvel, Jean Jacques, Dimitri Meeks, and Christine Favard-Meeks. *Égypte: le Nil égyptien et soudanais, du delta à Khartoum.* Les Guides bleus. Paris: Hachette, 1976.

Fawaz, Leila Tarazi. *An Occasion for War: Civil Conflict in Lebanon and Damascus in 1860.* Berkeley: University of California Press, 1994.

Fay, Mary Ann, ed. *Auto/biography and the Construction of Identity and Community in the Middle East.* New York: Palgrave, 2001.

Finchelstein, Federico. *Transatlantic Fascism: Ideology, Violence, and the Sacred in Argentina and Italy, 1919–1945.* Durham: Duke University Press, 2010.

Flores, Alexander. "Judeophobia in Context: Anti-Semitism among Modern Palestinians." *Die Welt des Islams* 46 (2006): 307–30.

———. "The Arabs as Nazis? Some Reflections on 'Islamofascism' and Arab Anti-Semitism." *Die Welt des Islams* 52 (2012): 450–70.

Fortna, Benjamin C. *Imperial Classroom: Islam, the State, and Education in the Late Ottoman Empire.* Oxford, New York: Oxford University Press, 2002.

———. "Islamic Morality in Late Ottoman 'Secular' Schools." *International Journal of Middle East Studies* 32 (2000): 369–93.

Framke, Maria. *Delhi-Rom-Berlin: Die indische Wahrnehmung von Faschismus und Nationalsozialismus, 1922–1939.* Veröffentlichungen der Forschungsstelle Ludwigsburg der Universität Stuttgart 21. Darmstadt: Wissenschaftliche Buchgesellschaft, 2013.

Gana, Nouri. "In Search of Andalusia: Reconfiguring Arabness in Diana Abu-Jaber's *Crescent.*" *Comparative Literature Studies* 45 (2008): 228–46.

Gelvin, James L. "The Other Arab Nationalism: Syrian/Arab Populism and Its Historical and International Contexts." In *Rethinking Nationalism in the Arab Middle East*, eds. James P. Jankowski and Israel Gershoni, 231–48. New York: Columbia University Press, 1997.

———. *Divided Loyalties: Nationalism and Mass Politics in Syria at the Close of Empire.* Berkeley: University of California Press, 1998.

———. "Pensée 1: 'Arab Nationalism' Meets Social Theory." *International Journal of Middle East Studies* 41 (2009): 10–12.

Gensicke, Klaus. *Der Mufti von Jerusalem, Amin el-Husseini, und die Nationalsozialisten.* Ethnien, Regionen, Konflikte. Frankfurt am Main, New York: P. Lang, 1988.

———. *Der Mufti von Jerusalem und die Nationalsozialisten: eine politische Biographie Amin el-Husseinis.* Veröffentlichungen der Forschungsstelle Ludwigsburg der Universität Stuttgart 11: Darmstadt: Wissenschaftliche Buchgesellschaft, 2007.

Gershoni, Israel. "Rethinking the Formation of Arab Nationalism in the Middle East, 1920–1945. Old and New Narratives." In *Rethinking Nationalism in the Arab Middle East*, eds. James P. Jankowski and Israel Gershoni, 3–25. New York: Columbia University Press, 1997.

———. "Egyptian Liberalism in an Age of 'Crisis of Orientation': Al-Risala's Reaction to Fascism and Nazism, 1933–39." *International Journal of Middle East Studies* 31.4 (November 1, 1999): 551–76.

———. "'Der verfolgte Jude'. Al-Hilals Reaktionen auf den Antisemitismus in Europa und Hitlers Machtergreifung." In *Blind für die Geschichte? Arabische Begegnungen mit dem Nationalsozialismus*, eds. Gerhard Höpp, Peter Wien, and René Wildangel, 39–72. ZMO-Studien 19. Berlin: Klaus Schwarz Verlag, 2004.

———. "The Theory of Crisis and the Crisis in a Theory: Intellectual History in Twentieth-Century Middle Eastern Studies." In *Middle East Historiographies: Narrating the Twentieth Century*, eds. Israel Gershoni, Amy Singer, and Y. Hakan Erdem, 131–82. Seattle: University of Washington Press, 2006.

———. "Eine Stimme der Vernunft: Muhammad Abdallah Inan und die Zeitschrift Al-Risala." In *Konstellationen: Über Geschichte, Erfahrung und Erkenntnis. Festschrift für Dan Diner zum 65. Geburtstag*, eds. Nicolas Berg, Omar Kamil, Markus Kirchhoff, and Susanne Zepp, 105–24. Göttingen: Vandenhoeck & Ruprecht, 2011.

Gershoni, Israel, and Götz Nordbruch. *Sympathie und Schrecken: Begegnungen mit Faschismus und Nationalsozialismus in Ägypten, 1922–1937.* Studien/Zentrum Moderner Orient 29. Berlin: Klaus-Schwarz, 2011.

Gershoni, Israel, and James P. Jankowski. *Egypt, Islam, and the Arabs: The Search for Egyptian Nationhood, 1900–1930.* Oxford, New York: Oxford University Press, 1987.

———. *Redefining the Egyptian Nation, 1930–1945.* Cambridge, New York: Cambridge University Press, 1995.

————, eds. *Rethinking Nationalism in the Arab Middle East*. New York: Columbia University Press, 1997.

————. "Print Culture, Social Change, and the Process of Redefining Imagined Communities in Egypt; Response to the Review by Charles D. Smith of Redefining the Egyptian Nation." *International Journal of Middle East Studies* 31 (1999): 81–94.

————. *Confronting Fascism in Egypt: Dictatorship Versus Democracy in the 1930s*. Stanford: Stanford University Press, 2010.

Ghazal, Amal N. *Islamic Reform and Arab Nationalism: Expanding the Crescent from the Mediterranean to the Indian Ocean (1880s–1930s)*. London: Routledge, 2010.

Ghurbal, Shafiq. *Muhammad 'Ali al-Kabir*. New edn. Kitab Al-Hilal 430. Cairo: Dar al-Hilal, 1986.

Gilman, Nils. *Mandarins of the Future: Modernization Theory in Cold War America*. Baltimore: Johns Hopkins University Press, 2003.

Glanville, S.R.K. "Reginald Engelbach." *The Journal of Egyptian Archaeology* 32 (1946): 97–99.

Goldenbaum, Hans. "Nationalsozialismus als Antikolonialismus: Die deutsche Rundfunk-propaganda für die arabische Welt." *Vierteljahrshefte für Zeitgeschichte* 64 (2016): 449–89.

Goldschmidt, Arthur. *Biographical Dictionary of Modern Egypt*. Boulder: Lynne Rienner, 2000.

Goode, James F. *Negotiating for the Past: Archaeology, Nationalism, and Diplomacy in the Middle East, 1919–1941*. Austin: University of Texas Press, 2007.

Gordon, Joel. *Nasser's Blessed Movement: Egypt's Free Officers and the July Revolution*. New York: Oxford University Press, 1992.

————. *Revolutionary Melodrama: Popular Film and Civic Identity in Nasser's Egypt*. Chicago Studies on the Middle East. Chicago: Middle East Documentation Center, 2002.

Gran, Peter. *Islamic Roots of Capitalism: Egypt, 1760–1840*. 2nd edn. Syracuse: Syracuse University Press, 1998.

Granara, William. "Nostalgia, Arab Nationalism, and the Andalusian Chronotope in the Evolution of the Modern Arabic Novel." *Journal of Arabic Literature* 36 (2005): 57–73.

Grau, Oliver. *Virtuelle Kunst in Geschichte und Gegenwart: Visuelle Strategien*. Berlin: Reimer, 2001.

————. *Virtual Art: From Illusion to Immersion*. Leonardo. Cambridge, MA: MIT Press, 2003.

Griffin, Roger, ed. *International Fascism: Theories, Causes and the New Consensus*. London, New York: Arnold; Oxford University Press, 1998.

————. *Modernism and Fascism: The Sense of a Beginning under Mussolini and Hitler*. Basingstoke: Palgrave Macmillan, 2007.

Grüttner, Michael. *Studenten Im Dritten Reich*. Paderborn: Ferdinand Schöningh, 1995.

Güçlü, Yücel. "The Role of the Ottoman-Trained Officers in Independent Iraq." *Oriente Moderno* 21.2 n.s. (2002): 441–58.

Haddad, Mouloud. "Sur les pas d'Abd el-Kader: la hijra des Algériens en Syrie au XIXe siècle." In *Abd el-Kader, un spirituel dans la modernité*, edited by Ahmed Bouyerdene, Éric Geoffroy, and Setty G. Simon-Khedis, 51–68. Damascus: Presses de l'Ifpo, 2012.

al-Haddad, Najib. *Riwayat Salah al-Din al-Ayyubi*. Alexandria, 1893.

Hagen, Gottfried, and Tilman Seidensticker. "Reinhard Schulzes Hypothese einer islamischen Aufklärung. Kritik einer historiographischen Kritik." *Zeitschrift der Deutschen Morgenländischen Gesellschaft* 148 (1998): 83–110.

Haim, Sylvia G. *Arab Nationalism: An Anthology*. Berkeley, Los Angeles, London: University of California Press, 1976.

Halim, Hala. "The Signs of Saladin: A Modern Cinematic Rendition of Medieval Heroism." *Alif: Journal of Comparative Poetics* 12 (1992): 78–94.

Halliday, Fred. "Pensée 3: The Modernity of the Arabs." *International Journal of Middle East Studies* 41 (2009): 16–18.

Hamida, Munir. "Amin al-Husayni in der deutschen Kriegspropaganda des Zweiten Weltkrieges – eine Studie zur arabischsprachigen Zeitschrift 'Barid ash-Sharq.'" Berlin: M.A. Thesis, Free University, 2007.

Hanisch, Ludmila. "Akzentverschiebung – Zur Geschichte der Semitistik und Islamwissenschaft während des 'Dritten Reichs.'" *Berichte zur Wissenschaftsgeschichte* 18 (1995): 217–26.

Hanna, Nelly. *In Praise of Books: A Cultural History of Cairo's Middle Class, Sixteenth to the Eighteenth Century*. Syracuse: Syracuse University Press, 2003.

Hanna, 'Abdallah. *Al-Haraka al-munahida li'l-fashiyya fi Suriya wa-Lubnan: 1933–1945. Dirasa watha'iqiyya*. Beirut: Dar al-Farabi, 1975.

———. *'Abd al-Rahman al-Shahbandar, 1879–1940: 'Alam nahdawi wa-rajul al-wataniyyah wa'l-taharrur al-fikri*. Damascus: Al-Ahali li'l-Tiba'a wa'l-Nashr wa'l-Tauzi', 1989.

Hanssen, Jens. *Fin de Siècle Beirut: The Making of an Ottoman Provincial Capital*. Oxford, New York: Oxford University Press, 2005.

Hartmann, Angelika. "Einleitung." In *Geschichte und Erinnerung im Islam*, ed. Angelika Hartmann, 9–30. Formen der Erinnerung 15. Göttingen: Vandenhoeck & Ruprecht, 2004.

Hasani, 'Abd al-Razzaq al-. *Al-Asrar al-khafiyya fi harakat al-sana 1941 al-taharruriyya*. Sayda: Matba'at al-'Irfan, 1958.

———. *Tarikh al-wizarat al-'Iraqiyya*. Vol. 4. Baghdad: Dar al-Shu'un al-Thaqafiyya al-'Amma, 1988.

Hashimi, Taha al-. *Mudhakkirat 1919–1943*. Beirut: Dar al-Tali'a, 1968.

Hatina, Meir. *Martyrdom in Modern Islam: Piety, Power, and Politics*. Cambridge: Cambridge University Press, 2014.

Hauner, Milan. "The Professionals and the Amateurs in National Socialist Foreign Policy: Revolution and Subversion in the Islamic and Indian World." In *Der "Führerstaat": Mythos und Realität. Studien zur Struktur und Politik des Dritten Reiches*, eds. Gerhard Hirschfeld and Lothar Kettenacker, 305–28. Veröffentlichungen des Deutschen Historischen Instituts London 8. Stuttgart, 1981.

Haykal, Muhammad Husayn. *Hayat Muhammad*. Cairo: Matba'at Dar al-Kutub al-Misriyya, 1936.

Heidemann, Stefan. "Memory and Ideology: Images of Saladin in Syria and Iraq." In *Visual Culture in the Modern Middle East: Rhetoric of the Image*, eds. Christiane Gruber and Sune Haugbolle, 57–81. Bloomington: Indiana University Press, 2013.

Hendrich, Geert. *Islam und Aufklärung: Der Modernediskurs in der arabischen Philosophie*. Darmstadt: Wissenschaftliche Buchgesellschaft, 2004.

Herf, Jeffrey. *The Jewish Enemy: Nazi Propaganda During World War II and the Holocaust*. Cambridge: The Belknap Press of Harvard University Press, 2006.

———. *Nazi Propaganda for the Arab World*. New Haven: Yale University Press, 2009.

Hermes, Nizar F. "Nostalgia for al-Andalus in Early Modern Moroccan *Voyages en Espagne*: Al-Ghassani's *Rihlat al-wazir fi iftikak al-asir* (1690–91) as a Case Study." *The Journal of North African Studies* 21 (2016): 433–52.

Hillenbrand, Carole. *The Crusades: Islamic Perspectives*. Chicago: Fitzroy Dearborn Publishers, 1999.

Hodgson, Marshall G. S. *The Venture of Islam: Conscience and History in a World Civilization*. Vol. 1. Chicago: University of Chicago Press, 1974.

Hooper-Greenhill, Eilean. *Museums and the Shaping of Knowledge*. London, New York: Routledge, 1992.

Höpp, Gerhard. "Muslime unterm Hakenkreuz: Zur Entstehungsgeschichte des Islamischen Zentralinstituts zu Berlin e.V." *Moslemische Revue* 14.1 (1994): 16–27.

———. "Ruhmloses Zwischenspiel: Fauzi al-Qawuqji in Deutschland, 1941–1947." *Al-Rafidayn: Jahrbuch zur Geschichte und Kultur des modernen Iraq* 3 (1995): 19–46.

———. *Mufti-Papiere: Briefe, Memoranden, Reden und Aufrufe Amin al-Husainis aus dem Exil, 1940–1945*. ZMO-Studien 16. Berlin: Klaus Schwarz Verlag, 2001.

———. "Zwischen Universität und Straße: Ägyptische Studenten in Deutschland 1849–1945." *Würzburger Geographische Manuskripte* 60 (2002): 31–42.

———. "Der verdrängte Diskurs: Arabische Opfer des Nationalsozialismus." In *Blind für die Geschichte? Arabische Begegnungen mit dem Nationalsozialismus*, eds. Gerhard Höpp, Peter Wien, and René Wildangel, 215–68. Berlin: Klaus Schwarz Verlag, 2004.

Höpp, Gerhard, Peter Wien, and René Wildangel, eds. *Blind Für Die Geschichte? Arabische Begegnungen Mit Dem Nationalsozialismus*. ZMO-Studien 19. Berlin: Klaus Schwarz Verlag, 2004.

———, eds. *'Umyan 'an al-tarikh?! Al-"Arab wa-Almaniya wa"l-Yahud*. Damascus: Qadmus, 2007.

Hourani, Albert Habib. *Arabic Thought in the Liberal Age, 1798–1939*. Cambridge: Cambridge University Press, 1983.

Hudson, Kenneth. *Museums of Influence*. Cambridge, New York: Cambridge University Press, 1987.

Husayni, Amin al-. *Mudhakkirat al-Hajj Muhammad Amin al-Husayni*, ed. 'Abd al-Karim 'Umar. Damascus: al-Ahali, 1999.

Husri, Sati' al-. *Yawm Maysalun: Safha min tarikh al-'Arab al-hadith, mudhakkirat musawwira bi-muqaddima 'an tanazu' al-duwal haula'l-bilad al-'Arabiyya wamudhayyala bi-watha'iq wa-suwar*. Beirut: Dar al-Ittihad, 1965.

———. *The Day of Maysalun: A Page from the Modern History of the Arabs: Memoirs*. Washington, DC: Middle East Institute, 1966.

Hyde, Ralph. *Panoramania! The Art and Entertainment of the "All-Embracing" View*. London: Trefoil, Barbican Art Gallery, 1988.

Ibn Habib, 'Abd al-Malik. *Kitab Al-Ta'rij: (La Historia)*. Ed. Jorge Aguadé. Fuentes Arábico-Hispanas 1. Madrid: Consejo Superior de Investigaciones Científicas, Instituto de Cooperación con el Mundo Arabe, 1991.

Ibn Khaldun. *Histoire des Berbères et des dynasties musulmanes de l'Afrique septentrionale*. Ed. Paul Casanova. Translated by William MacGuckin Slane. Vol. 1. Paris: P. Geuthner, 1968.

Ibn 'Abd al-Hakam. *The History of the Conquest of Egypt, North Africa and Spain, Known as the Futuh Misr of Ibn 'Abd Al-Hakam*. Ed. Charles Cutler Torrey. Yale Oriental Series. Researches 3. New Haven: Yale University Press, 1922.

'Inan, Muhammad 'Abdallah. *Dawlat al-Islam fi'l-Andalus min al-fath ila nihayat mamlakat Gharnata*. Cairo: Matba'at Lajnat al-Ta'lif wa'l-Tarjama wa'l-Nashr, 1943.

Iqbal, Muzaffar. *The Making of Islamic Science*. Sclangor, Malaysia: Islamic Book Trust, 2009.

Irving, Washington. *Legends of the Conquest of Spain*. London: John Murray, 1836.

Jankowski, James P. *Egypt's Young Rebels: "Young Egypt": 1933–1952*. Stanford: Hoover Intitution Press, Stanford University, 1975.

Jankowski, James. "Egyptian Responses to the Palestine Problem in the Interwar Period." *International Journal of Middle East Studies* 12 (1980): 1–38.

———. "The View from the Embassy: British Assessments of Egyptian Attitudes during World War II." In *Arab Responses to Fascism and Nazism: Attraction and Repulsion*, ed. I. Gershoni, 171–94. Austin, TX: University of Texas Press, 2014.

Jayyusi, Salma Khadra, ed. *Modern Arabic Poetry: An Anthology*. New York: Columbia University Press, 1987.

Kadhim, Abbas K. *Reclaiming Iraq: The 1920 Revolution and the Founding of the Modern State*. Austin: University of Texas Press, 2012.

Kamil, Mustafa. *Fath al-Andalus: al-nass al-kamil lil-masrahiyya al-wahida allati katabaha al-za'im al-khalid Mustafa Kamil*. Ed. Rishad Rushdi. Masrahiyyat Mukhtara 19. Cairo: Matabi' al-Hai'a al-Misriyya al-'Amma li'l-Kitab, 1973.

Kamil, Omar. *Der Holocaust im arabischen Gedächtnis: Eine Diskursgeschichte 1945–1967*. Schriften des Simon-Dubnow-Instituts 15. Göttingen: Vandenhoeck & Ruprecht, 2012.

Karpat, Kemal H. *The Politicization of Islam: Reconstructing Identity, State, Faith, and Community in the Late Ottoman State*. Oxford: Oxford University Press, 2001.

Kavanagh, Gaynor. *Museums and the First World War: A Social History*. London, New York: Leicester University Press, St. Martin's Press, 1994.

———. "Making Histories, Making Memories." In *Making Histories in Museums*, edited by Gaynor Kavanagh, 1–14. London, New York: Leicester University Press, 1996.

Kayali, Hasan. *Arabs and Young Turks: Ottomanism, Arabism, and Islamism in the Ottoman Empire, 1908–1918*. Berkeley, Los Angeles, London: University of California Press, 1997.

———. "Elections and the Electoral Process in the Ottoman Empire, 1876–1919." *International Journal of Middle East Studies* 27 (1995): 265–86.

Khadduri, Majid. "The Alexandretta Dispute." *American Journal of International Law* 39 (1945): 406–25.

Khalidi, Rashid. "Arab Nationalism: Historical Problems in the Literature." *American Historical Review* 96.5 (1991): 1363–73.

———. "Ottomanism and Arabism in Syria Before 1914: A Reassessment." In *The Origins of Arab Nationalism*, eds. Rashid Khalidi, Lisa Anderson, Muhammad Muslih, and Simon, Reeva S., 50–71. New York: Columbia University Press, 1991.

Khalil, Samir al-. *Republic of Fear: The Politics of Modern Iraq*. Berkeley, Los Angeles: University of California Press, 1989.

Khater, Akram Fouad, (Ed.) "Sadiq Al-'Azm, an Arab Intellectual, Critiques the Arab State and Clergy for Their Use of Religion, 1968." In *Sources in the History of the Modern Middle East*, 2nd edn, 225–28. Boston: Houghton Mifflin, 2011.

———. *Sources in the History of the Modern Middle East*. 2nd edn. Boston: Houghton Mifflin, 2011.

———. "Antun Sa'adeh Declares His Vision of 'Greater Syria' or Regional Nationalism, June 1, 1935." In *Sources in the History of the Modern Middle East*, 2nd edn, 125–30. Boston: Houghton Mifflin, 2011.

Khatib, Fu'ad al-. *Diwan al-Khatib*, ed. Riyad al-Khatib. Cairo: Dar al-Ma'arif, 1959.

————. *Fath al-Andalus.* Amman: [s.n.], 1931.

Khatib, Ihsan Fu'ad. *Wamadat min 'umr al-zaman: Qabasat min hayat al-Shaykh Fu'ad al-Khatib, sha'ir al-thawra al-'Arabiyya al-kubra.* Beirut: Dar al-'Ilm li'l-Malayin, 1994.

Khouri, Malek. *The Arab National Project in Youssef Chahine's Cinema.* Cairo; New York: The American University in Cairo Press, 2010.

Khoury, Dina Rizk. *Iraq in Wartime: Soldiering, Martyrdom, and Remembrance.* New York: Cambridge University Press, 2013.

————. "Ambiguities of the Modern: The Great War in the Memoirs and Poetry of the Iraqis." In *The World in World Wars: Experiences, Perceptions and Perspectives from Africa and Asia,* eds. Heike Liebau, Katrin Bromber, Katharina Lange, Dyala Hamzah, and Ravi Ahuja, 313–40. Studies in Global Social History 5. Leiden, Boston: Brill, n.d.

————. "Looking for the Modern: A Biography of an Iraqi Modernist." In *Auto/biography and the Construction of Identity and Community in the Middle East,* ed. Mary Ann Fay, 109–24. New York: Palgrave, 2001.

————. "History and Historiography of Modern Iraq." *Middle East Studies Association Bulletin* 39 (2005): 64–78.

Khoury, Philip S. *Urban Notables and Arab Nationalism: The Politics of Damascus, 1860–1920.* Cambridge, New York: Cambridge University Press, 1983.

————. *Syria and the French Mandate: The Politics of Arab Nationalism, 1920–1945.* Princeton, NJ: Princeton University Press, 1987.

Khuri-Makdisi, Ilham. *The Eastern Mediterranean and the Making of Global Radicalism, 1860–1914.* Berkeley: University of California Press, 2010.

Kiefer, Michael. "Islamischer, islamistischer oder islamisierter Antisemitismus?" *Die Welt des Islams* 46 (2006): 277–306.

Kiernan, Maureen. "Cultural Hegemony and National Film Language: Youssef Chahine." *Alif: Journal of Comparative Poetics* 15 (1995): 130–52.

Kitchen, Martin. "Ernst Nolte and the Phenomenology of Fascism." *Science & Society* 38 (1974): 130–49.

Koselleck, Reinhart. *Vergangene Zukunft: Zur Semantik geschichtlicher Zeiten.* Frankfurt am Main: Suhrkamp, 1979.

————. "Einleitung." In *Der Politische Totenkult: Kriegerdenkmäler in der Moderne,* eds. Reinhart Koselleck and Michael Jeismann, 9–19. München: Fink, 1994.

Kostyuchenko, Svetlana. "Die Geschichte der sowjetischen Dioramenkunst." In *Panorama: Virtualität und Realitäten: 11. Internationale Panoramakonferenz in Altötting 2003,* ed. Gebhard Streicher, 64–66. Amberg: SPA Stiftung Panorama Altötting, 2005.

Kreiser, Klaus. "Public Monuments in Turkey and Egypt, 1840–1916." *Muqarnas* 14 (January 1, 1997): 103–17.

Kretzler, Wilhelm. "Glückauf im Bergwerk: Das Besucherbergwerk im Deutschen Museum." *Kultur & Technik – das Magazin aus dem Deutschen Museum* 12.1 (1988): 2–7.

Krämer, Gudrun. "Anti-Semitism in the Muslim World: A Critical Review." *Die Welt des Islams* 46 (2006): 243–76.

Köhbach, Markus. "Die osmanische Gesandtschaft nach Spanien in den Jahren 1787/88: Begegnung zweier Kulturen im Spiegel eines Gesandtschaftsberichts." *Wiener Beiträge zur Geschichte der Neuzeit* 10 (1983): 143–52.

Küntzel, Matthias. *Djihad und Judenhass: Über den neuen antijüdischen Krieg.* Freiburg i.Brsg.: ça ira, 2003.

———. *Jihad and Jew-Hatred: Islamism, Nazism and the Roots of 9/11*. New York: Telos Press, 2007.

La Cava the Musical. CD. [London]: Dress Circle, 2000.

Larsen, Stein. "Was There Fascism Outside Europe? Diffusion from Europe and Domestic Impulses." In *Fascism Outside Europe: The European Impulse Against Domestic Conditions in the Diffusion of Global Fascism*, ed. Stein Ugelvik Larsen, 705–818. New York: Columbia University Press, 2001.

Lauzière, Henri. "The Construction of Salafiyya: Reconsidering Salafism From the Perspective of Conceptual History." *International Journal of Middle East Studies* 42 (2010): 369–89.

Lawson, Fred H. "Pensée 4: Out With the Old, in With the New." *International Journal of Middle East Studies* 41 (2009): 19–21.

Le Chatelier, A. "Les Musulmans algériens au Maroc et en Syrie." *Revue du monde musulman* 2 (1907): 499–512.

Leers, Johann von. *Rassen, Völker und Volkstümer*. Langensalza, Berlin, Leipzig: Julius Beltz, 1938.

Lefèvre, Raphaël. *Ashes of Hama: The Muslim Brotherhood in Syria*. New York: Oxford University Press, 2013.

Léna, Annette. "Algérie: Le Retour d'Abdel Kader." *Jeune Afrique* 290 (July 17, 1966): 14–15.

Levtzion, Nehemia, and John Obert Voll eds. *Eighteenth-Century Renewal and Reform in Islam*. Syracuse: Syracuse University Press, 1987.

Lewis, Bernard. *History – Remembered, Recovered, Invented*. Princeton: Princeton University Press, 1975.

Ley, Astrid, and Günter Morsch. *Medizin und Verbrechen: Das Krankenrevier des KZ Sachsenhausen 1936–1945*. Berlin: Metropol, 2007.

Liqani, Ahmad Husayn al-, ʿAbd al-ʿAziz, Saif al-Din, Farraj, ʿAbd al-Wahid Ahmad, Muhammad, Fariʿa Hassan, Ghandur, Fuʾad Muhammad al-, and Al-Sayyid Jamil, Muhammad. *Al-Dirasat al-Ijtimaʿiyya. Biʾat wa-shakhsiyyat Misriyya. Al-Saff al-khamis al-ibtidaʾi. Al-Fasl al-dirasi al-awwal*. Edited by Jumhuriyyat Misr al-ʿArabiyya, Wizarat al-Tarbiyya waʾl-Taʿlim. Cairo: Dar al-Tawfiqiyya liʾl-Tibaʿa, 2001.

———. *Al-Dirasat al-Ijtimaʿiyya. Biʾat wa-shakhsiyyat Misriyya. Al-Saff al-khamis al-ibtidaʾi. Al-Fasl al-dirasi al-thani*. Edited by Jumhuriyyat Misr al-ʿArabiyya, Wizarat al-Tarbiyya waʾl-Taʿlim. Cairo: Sharikat al-Islam Misr liʾl-Tibaʿa, 2001.

———, and Jumhuriyyat Misr al-ʿArabiyya, Wizarat al-Tarbiyya waʾl-Taʿlim. *Al-Dirasat al-Ijtimaʿiyya. Al-Saff al-rabiʿ al-ibtidaʾi (muhafazati juzʾ min Misr). Al-Fasl al-dirasi al-awwal*. Cairo: ʿAmr Ibn al-ʿAs liʾl-Tibaʿa, 2001.

Litvak, Meir, and Esther Webman. *From Empathy to Denial: Arab Responses to the Holocaust*. New York: Columbia University Press, 2009.

Luna, Miguel de. *La verdadera historia del rey Don Rodrigo*. Valencia: En casa de P. P. Mey, a costa de B. Simon, 1606.

Maffi, Irene. *Pratiques du patrimoine et politiques de la mémoire en Jordanie: Entre histoire dynastique et récits communautaires*. Lausanne: Payot Lausanne, 2004.

———. "The Intricate Life of Cultural Heritage: Colonial and Postcolonial Processes of Patrimonialisation in Jordan." In *The Politics and Practices of Cultural Heritage in the Middle East: Positioning the Material Past in Contemporary Societies*, edited by Rami Daher and Irene Maffi, 66–103. Library of Modern Middle East Studies 101. London: Tauris, 2014.

Makiya, Kanan. *The Monument: Art and Vulgarity in Saddam Hussein's Iraq*. London, New York: I.B. Tauris, 2004.

Mallmann, Klaus-Michael, and Martin Cüppers. *Halbmond und Hakenkreuz: Das Dritte Reich, die Araber und Palästina*. Veröffentlichungen der Forschungsstelle Ludwigsburg der Universität Stuttgart 8. Darmstadt: Wissenschaftliche Buchgesellschaft, 2006.

———. *Nazi Palestine: The Plans for the Extermination of the Jews in Palestine*. Translated by Krista Smith. New York: Enigma Books, 2011.

Mals, Muhammad Bassam. *Fath al-Andalus fi adab al-atfal: dirasa naqdiya*. Buhuth fi thaqafat al-tifl al-Muslim 8. Riyadh: al-Mamlaka al-'Arabiyya al-Sa'udiyya, Wizarat al-Ta'lim al-'Ali, Jami'at al-Imam Muhammad ibn Sa'ud al-Islamiyya, Idarat al-Thaqafa wa'l-Nashr, 1994.

Malvern, Sue. "War, Memory and Museums: Art and Artefact in the Imperial War Museum." *History Workshop Journal* 49 (2000): 177–203.

al-Mamlaka al-Maghribiyya, Wizarat al-Tarbiyya al-Wataniyya. *Al-Qira'a: Kitab al-Talmidh. Al-Sana al-khamisa min al-ta'lim al-asasi*. Rabat: Dar Nashr al-Ma'rifa, 2001.

Manna', Muhammad 'Abd al-Raziq. *Batal al-Andalus Tariq Ibn Ziyad*. Abtal al-Islam. Benghazi: Mu'assasat Nasir li'l-Thaqafa, 1978.

Maqqarī, Aḥmad ibn Muḥammad. *The History of the Mohammedan Dynasties in Spain; Extracted from the Nafhu-T-Tíb Min Ghosni-L-Andalusi-R-Rattíb Wa Táríkh Lisánu-D-Dín Ibni-L-Khattíb*. London: Printed for the Oriental translation fund of Great Britain and Ireland, 1840.

al-Maqqari, Ahmad Ibn Muhammad. *Nafh al-tib*. Ed. Muhammad Muhyi al-Din 'Abd al-Hamid. Vol. 1, 1967.

Marr, Phebe. "Yasin Al-Hashimi: The Rise and Fall of a Nationalist (A Study of the Nationalist Leadership in Iraq, 1920–1936)." Harvard University: PhD thesis, History and Middle Eastern Studies, 1966.

Massad, Joseph. *Desiring Arabs*. Chicago: University of Chicago Press, 2007.

Mayeur-Jaouen, Catherine. *Saints et héros du moyen-orient contemporain: actes du colloque des 11 et 12 décembre 2000, à l'institut universitaire de France*. Paris: Maisonneuve et Larose, 2002.

McDougall, James. *History and the Culture of Nationalism in Algeria*. Cambridge, New York: Cambridge University Press, 2006.

Meeks, Dimitri, and Jean Jacques Fauvel. *Les Guides bleus: Égypte. le Nil égyptien et soudanais, du delta à Khartoum*. Les Guides bleus. Paris: Hachette, 1971.

Meital, Yoram. "Sadat's Grave and the Commemoration of the 1973 War in Egypt." In *National Symbols, Fractured Identities: Contesting the National Narrative*, ed. Michael E. Geisler, 222–40. Middlebury: Middlebury College Press, 2005.

Messick, Brinkley Morris. *The Calligraphic State: Textual Domination and History in a Muslim Society*. Comparative Studies on Muslim Societies 16. Berkeley: University of California Press, 1993.

Micklewright, Nancy. "An Ottoman Portrait." *International Journal of Middle East Studies* 40.3 (2008): 372–3.

Mitchell, Richard P. *The Society of the Muslim Brothers*. London: Oxford University Press, 1969.

Mitchell, Timothy. *Colonising Egypt*. Berkeley, Los Angeles, London: University of California Press, 1991.

Motadel, David. *Islam and Nazi Germany's War*. Cambridge: The Belknap Press of Harvard University Press, 2014.

Mubarak, 'Ali. *Khulasat Tarikh Al-'Arab*. Cairo: Matba'at Muhammad Afandi Mustafa, 1309 AH (1891–2CE).

Mucha, Ludvík. *Webster's Concise Encyclopedia of Flags & Coats of Arms*, ed. W.G. Crampton. Translated by Jiří Louda. New York: Crescent Books: Distributed by Crown Publishers, 1985.

Musil, Robert. "Monuments." In *Selected Writings*, edited by Burton Pike, 320–23. The German Library 72. New York: Continuum, 1986.

Möller, Horst. "Ernst Nolte und das 'Liberale System.'" In *Weltbürgerkrieg Der Ideologien: Antworten an Ernst Nolte: Festschrift Zum 70. Geburtstag*, ed. Thomas Nipperdey, Anselm Doering-Manteuffel, and Hans-Ulrich Thamer, 57–72. Berlin: Propyläen, 1993.

Nicosia, Francis R. *Nazi Germany and the Arab World*. New York: Cambridge University Press, 2015.

Nieto Cumplido, Manuel, and Carlos Luca de Tena y Alvear. *La Mezquita de Córdoba: planos y dibujos*. Córdoba: Colegio Oficial de Arquitectos de Andalucía Occidental, 1992.

Nolte, Ernst. *Die Krise des liberalen Systems und die faschistischen Bewegungen*. München: Piper, 1968.

Noorani, Yaseen. "The Lost Garden of Al-Andalus: Islamic Spain and the Poetic Inversion of Colonialism." *International Journal of Middle East Studies* 31.2 (May 1, 1999): 237–54.

Nordbruch, Götz. "Geschichte im Konflikt. Der Nationalsozialismus als Thema aktueller Debatten in der ägyptischen Öffentlichkeit." In *Blind für die Geschichte? Arabische Begegnungen mit dem Nationalsozialismus*, eds. Gerhard Höpp, Peter Wien, and René Wildangel, 269–94. ZMO-Studien 19. Berlin: Klaus Schwarz Verlag, 2004.

———. *Nazism in Syria and Lebanon: The Ambivalence of the German Option, 1933–1945*. Milton Park; New York: Routledge, 2008.

———. "Islam as a 'Giant Progressive Leap' – Religious Critiques of Fascism and National Socialism." *Die Welt des Islams* 52 (2012): 499–525.

al-Nusuli, Anis. "Al-Tamthil." In *Asbab al-nahda al-'Arabiyya fi'l-qarn al-tasi' 'ashar*, 196–200. Beirut: Dar Ibn Zaydun, 1985.

———. *Asbab al-nahda al-'Arabiyya fi'l-qarn al-tasi' 'ashar*, ed. 'Abd Allah Anis Tabba'. Beirut: Dar Ibn Zaydun, 1985.

Oettermann, Stephan. *Das Panorama: Die Geschichte eines Massenmediums*. Frankfurt/Main: Syndikat, 1980.

———. *The Panorama: History of a Mass Medium*. New York: Zone Books, 1997.

Ormos, István. *Max Herz Pasha 1856–1919: His Life and Career*. Cairo: Institut français d'archéologie orientale, 2009.

Owen, Roger. *The Middle East in the World Economy, 1800–1914*. London; New York: Methuen, 1981.

O'Fahey, R.S. *Enigmatic Saint: Ahmad Ibn Idris and the Idrisi Tradition*. Evanston: Northwestern University Press, 1990.

O'Fahey, R.S., and Bernd Radtke. "Neo-Sufism Reconsidered." *Der Islam* 70 (1993): 52–87.

Pannewick, Friederike. *Opfer, Tod und Liebe: Visionen des Martyriums in der arabischen Literatur*. München: Wilhelm Fink, 2012.

Paxton, Robert O. "The Five Stages of Fascism." *Journal of Modern History* 70 (March 1998): 1.

Pelckmans, Paul. "Walter Scott's Orient: The Talisman." In *Oriental Prospects: Western Literature and the Lure of the East*, eds. C.C. Barfoot and Theo d'Haen, 97–109. Amsterdam, Atlanta: Editions Rodopi, 1998.

Peled, M. "Annals of Doom: 'Palestinian Literature – 1917–1948.'" *Arabica* 29.2 (1982): 143–83.

Peters, Rudolph. "Reinhard Schulze's Quest for an Islamic Enlightenment." *Die Welt des Islams* 30 (1990): 160–62.

Pérès, Henri. *L'Espagne vue par les voyageurs musulmans de 1610 à 1930*. Publications de l'Institut d'études orientales, Faculté des lettres d'Alger 6. Paris: Librairie d'Amerique et d'Orient, A. Maisonneuve, 1937.

Philipp, Thomas. *Gurgi Zaidan, His Life and Thought*. Beiruter Texte und Studien 3. Beirut, Wiesbaden: Orient-Institut der Dt. Morgenländischen Gesellschaft; Steiner, 1979.

Pierret, Thomas. *Religion and State in Syria: The Sunni Ulema under the Ba'th*. Cambridge: Cambridge University Press, 2013.

Podeh, Elie. "The Symbolism of the Arab Flag in Modern Arab States: Between Commonality and Uniqueness." *Nations and Nationalism* 17 (2011): 419–42.

Pollard, Lisa. *Nurturing the Nation: The Family Politics of Modernizing, Colonizing and Liberating Egypt, 1805–1923*. Berkeley: University of California Press, 2005.

Prakash, Gyan. *Another Reason: Science and the Imagination of Modern India*. Princeton, Chichester: Princeton University Press, 1999.

Provence, Michael. *The Great Syrian Revolt and the Rise of Arab Nationalism*. Austin: University of Texas Press, 2005.

———. "Ottoman Modernity, Colonialism, and Insurgency in the Interwar Arab East." *International Journal of Middle East Studies* 43 (2011): 205–25.

Rabbat, Nasser O. *The Citadel of Cairo: A New Interpretation of Royal Mamluk Architecture*. Islamic History and Civilization, v. 14. Leiden, New York: E.J. Brill, 1995.

Rabinovich, Itamar. *Syria under the Ba'th, 1963–66: The Army Party Symbiosis*. Jerusalem: Israel Universities Press, 1972.

Radtke, Bernd. "Erleuchtung und Aufklärung: Islamische Mystik und europäischer Rationalismus." *Die Welt des Islams* 34 (1994): 48–66.

———. "Sufism in the 18th Century: An Attempt at a Provisional Appraisal." *Die Welt des Islams* 36 (1996): 326–64.

Raymond, André. *Artisans et commerçants au Caire au XVIIIe siècle*. Vol. 2. Damas: Institut français de Damas, 1974.

Reeve, John. "Making the History Curriculum." In *Making Histories in Museums*, edited by Gaynor Kavanagh, 228–39. London, New York: Leicester University Press, 1996.

Reid, Donald M. *The Odyssey of Farah Antun: A Syrian Christian's Quest for Secularism*. Studies in Middle Eastern History, no. 2. Minneapolis: Bibliotheca Islamica, 1975.

———. "Cultural Imperialism and Nationalism: The Struggle to Define and Control the Heritage of Arab Art in Egypt." *International Journal of Middle East Studies* 24.1 (1992): 57–76.

———. "The Egyptian Geographical Society: From Foreign Laymen's Society to Indigenous Professional Association." *Poetics Today* 14.3 (October 1, 1993): 539–72.

———. "Nationalizing the Pharaonic Past: Egyptology, Imperialism, and Egyptian Nationalism, 1922–1952." In *Rethinking Nationalism in the Arab Middle East*, edited by Israel Gershoni and James P. Jankowski, 127–49. New York: Columbia University Press, 1997.

———. *Whose Pharaohs? Archaeology, Museums, and Egyptian National Identity From Napoleon to World War I*. Berkeley: University of California Press, 2002.

———. *Contesting Antiquity in Egypt: Archaeologies, Museums & the Struggle for Identities from World War I to Nasser*. Cairo: American University in Cairo Press, 2015.

Reynolds, Dwight F. "Musical 'Membrances of Medieval Muslim Spain." In *Charting Memory: Recalling Medieval Spain*, ed. Stacy N. Beckwith, 229–62. New York: Garland, 2000.

Reynolds, Nancy Y. *A City Consumed: Urban Commerce, the Cairo Fire, and the Politics of Decolonization in Egypt*. Stanford: Stanford University Press, 2012.

Rogan, Eugene. *The Arabs: A History*. New York: Basic Books, 2009.

Rogozen-Soltar, Mikaela. "Al-Andalus in Andalusia: Negotiating Moorish History and Regional Identity in Southern Spain." *Anthropological Quarterly* 80 (2007): 863–86.

Rohde, Achim. *State-Society Relations in Ba'thist Iraq: Facing Dictatorship*. London; New York: Routledge, 2010.

Rohr, Isabelle. *The Spanish Right and the Jews, 1898–1945: Antisemitism and Opportunism*. Brighton; Portland: Sussex Academic Press, 2007.

Ruedy, John. *Modern Algeria: The Origins and Development of a Nation*. 2nd edn. Bloomington: Indiana University Press, 2005.

Russell, Mona L. *Creating the New Egyptian Woman: Consumerism, Education, and National Identity, 1863–1922*. New York: Palgrave Macmillan, 2004.

Ryad, Umar. "New Episodes in Moroccan Nationalism Under Colonial Role: Reconsideration of Shakib Arslan's Centrality in Light of Unpublished Materials." *The Journal of North African Studies* 16 (2011): 117–42.

Ryzova, Lucie. *The Age of the Efendiyya: Passages to Modernity in National-Colonial Egypt*. Oxford, New York: Oxford University Press, 2014.

Sade. "Rodrigue ou la tour enchantée: Conte allégorique." In *Les crimes de l'amour: nouvelles héroïques et tragiques; précédées d'une Idée sur les romans*, 257–71. Dix-huit. Cadeilhan: Zulma, 1995.

Said, Edward W. *Orientalism*. New York: Pantheon Books, 1978.

Salim, Mahmud. *Qisas tarikh al-Islam li'l-fityan wa'l-fatayat*. Beirut: al-Mu'assasa al-'Arabiyya li'l-Dirasat wa'l-Nashr, 1977.

Salvatore, Armando, and Dale F. Eickelman. "Preface." In *Public Islam and the Common Good*, eds. Armando Salvatore and Dale F. Eickelman, xi–xxv. Social, Economic, and Political Studies of the Middle East and Asia 95. Leiden, Boston: Brill, 2004.

Samadi, Imtinan al-. *Shi'r Fu'ad al-Khatib fi'l-thawra al-'Arabiyya al-kubra wa'l-Hashimiyya*. Amman: Wizarat al-Thaqafa, 2010.

Satloff, Robert B. *Among the Righteous: Lost Stories from the Holocaust's Long Reach into Arab Lands*. New York: PublicAffairs, 2006.

Schulze, Reinhard. "Das islamische achtzehnte Jahrhundert: Versuch einer historiographischen Kritik." *Die Welt des Islams* 30 (1990): 140–59.

———. "Islamofascism: Four Avenues to the Use of an Epithet." *Die Welt des Islams* 52 (2012): 290–330.

———. "Was ist die islamische Aufklärung?" *Die Welt des Islams* 36 (1996): 276–325.

Schumann, Christoph. *Radikalnationalismus in Syrien und Libanon: Politische Sozialisation und Elitenbildung 1930–1958*. Hamburg: Deutsches Orient-Institut, 2001.

———. "The Generation of Broad Expectations: Nationalism, Education and Autobiography in Syria and Lebanon, 1930–1958." *Die Welt Des Islams* 41 (2001): 174–205.

———. "Symbolische Aneignungen. Antun Sa'adas Radikalnationalismus in der Epoche des Faschismus." In *Blind für die Geschichte? Arabische Begegnungen mit dem*

Nationalsozialismus, eds. Gerhard Höpp, Peter Wien, and René Wildangel, 155–89. ZMO-Studien 19. Berlin: Klaus Schwarz Verlag, 2004.

Schölch, Alexander. "Drittes Reich, Zionistische Bewegung Und Palästina-Konflikt." *Vierteljahrshefte Für Zeitgeschichte* 30 (1982): 646–74.

Schwartz, Vanessa R. *Spectacular Realities: Early Mass Culture in Fin-de-Siècle Paris.* Berkeley: University of California Press, 1998.

Scott, Walter. *Tales of the Crusaders.* Philadelphia: James Crissy, 1825.

Sedgwick, Mark. "Modern and Islamic Icons in Arab-Islamic Popular Historical Memory." In *Islamic Myths and Memories: Mediators of Globalization*, eds. Itzchak Weismann, Mark Sedgwick, and Ulrika Mårtensson, 15–33. Surrey, Burlington: Ashgate, 2014.

Sédillot, L.-A. *Histoire des Arabes.* Paris: L. Hachette et Cie, 1854.

Sedra, Paul. "Imagining an Imperial Race: Egyptology in the Service of Empire." *Comparative Studies of South Asia, Africa and the Middle East* 24 (2004): 249–59.

Seikaly, Samir. "Shukri Al-'Asali: A Case Study of a Political Activist." In *The Origins of Arab Nationalism*, eds. Rashid Khalidi, Lisa Anderson, Muhammad Muslih, and Reeva S. Simon, 73–96. New York: Columbia University Press, 1991.

Shafir, Gershon, and Mark LeVine. "Introduction: Social Biographies in Making Sense of History." In *Struggle and Survival in Palestine/Israel*, eds. Mark LeVine and Gershon Shafir, 1–20. Berkeley: University of California Press, 2012.

Shalabi, Mahmud. *Hayat Tariq Ibn Ziyad, Fatih al-Andalus.* Beirut: Dar al-Jil, 1992.

Shannon, Jonathan Holt. *Among the Jasmine Trees: Music and Modernity in Contemporary Syria.* Middletown: Wesleyan University Press, 2006.

———. "Performing al-Andalus, Remembering al-Andalus: Mediterranean Soundings from Mashriq to Maghrib." *Journal of American Folklore* 120 (2007): 308–34.

———. "There and Back Again: Rhetorics of al-Andalus in Modern Syrian Popular Culture." *International Journal of Middle East Studies* 48 (2016): 5–24.

Sharkey, Heather J. *Living with Colonialism: Nationalism and Culture in the Anglo-Egyptian Sudan.* Colonialisms 3. Berkeley: University of California Press, 2003.

Shaw, Wendy M.K. *Possessors and Possessed: Museums, Archaeology, and the Visualization of History in the Late Ottoman Empire.* Berkeley: University of California Press, 2003.

Shawqi, Ahmad. *Al-Shawqiyyat.* Vol. 2 and 3. Cairo: Matba'at al-Istiqama, 1964.

———. *Duwal al-'Arab wa-'uzama' al-Islam.* Beirut: Dar al-Kitab al-'Arabi, 1970.

Sheehi, Stephen. *Foundations of Modern Arab Identity.* Gainesville: University Press of Florida, 2004.

Shields, Sarah D. *Fezzes in the River: Identity Politics and European Diplomacy in the Middle East on the Eve of World War II.* Oxford; New York: Oxford University Press, 2011.

Shinqiti, Muhammad Mahmud. *Al-Hamasa al-saniyya al-kamila al-maziyya fi'l-rihla al-'ilmiyya al-Shinqitiyya al-Turkuziyya.* Ed. Muhammad Wuld Khabbaz. Mauritania: [s.n.], 2000.

Shoup, John. "As It Was, and As It Should Be Now: Al Andalus in Contemporary Arab Television Dramas." *Transnational Broadcasting Studies* 15 (Fall 2005), http://www.tbsjournal.com/Archives/Fall05/Shoup.html, date of access: May 19, 2015.

Simon, Rachel. "It Could Have Happened There: The Jews of Libya During the Second World War." *Africana Journal* 16 (1994): 391–422.

Simon, Reeva S. *Iraq between the Two World Wars: The Militarist Origins of Tyranny.* New York: Columbia University Press, 2004.

Sinno, Abdel-Raouf. "The Emperor's Visit to the East as Reflected in Contemporary Arabic Journalism." In *Baalbek: Image and Monument 1898–1998*, eds. Helene Sader,

Thomas Scheffler, and Angelika Neuwirth, 115–33. Beiruter Texte und Studien, Bd. 69. Stuttgart: Steiner, 1998.

Sivan, Emmanuel. "Modern Arab Historiography of the Crusades." *Asian & African Studies* 8.2 (1972): 109–49.

———. "Arab Nationalism in the Age of the Islamic Resurgence." In *Rethinking Nationalism in the Arab Middle East*, eds. Israel Gershoni and James P. Jankowski, 207–28. New York: Columbia University Press, 1997.

Smith, Anthony D. *The Ethnic Origins of Nations*. Oxford, Malden: Blackwell, 1986.

Smith, Charles D. *Islam and the Search for Social Order in Modern Egypt: A Biography of Muhammad Husayn Haykal*. Albany: State University of New York Press, 1983.

———. "'Imagined Identities, Imagined Nationalisms: Print Culture and Egyptian Nationalism in Light of Recent Scholarship.' A Review Essay of Israel Gershoni and James P. Jankowski, *Redefining the Egyptian Nation, 1930–1945*." *International Journal of Middle East Studies* 29 (1997): 607–22.

———. "'Cultural Constructs' and Other Fantasies: Imagined Narratives in Imagined Communities; Surrejoinder to Gershoni and Jankowski's 'Print Culture, Social Change, and the Process of Redefining Imagined Communities in Egypt.'" *International Journal of Middle East Studies* 31 (1999): 95–102.

Smith, Whitney Jr. "Arab National Flags." *Middle East Forum* 36.8 (1960): 19–25.

Snir, Reuven. "'Al-Andalus Arising from Damascus': Al-Andalus in Modern Arabic Poetry." In *Charting Memory: Recalling Medieval Spain*, ed. Stacy N. Beckwith, 263–93. New York: Garland, 2000.

Sourdel-Thomine, Janine. "Les anciens lieux de pèlerinage damascains d'après les sources arabes." *Bulletin d'études orientales* 14 (1952–1954): 65–85.

Southey, Robert. *Roderick: The Last of the Goths*. Vol. 1. London: Longman, Hurst, Rees, Orme, and Brown, 1816.

Steppat, Fritz. "Das Jahr 1933 und seine Folgen für die arabischen Länder des Vorderen Orients." In *Die Große Krise der dreißiger Jahre: Vom Niedergang der Weltwirtschaft zum Zweiten Weltkrieg*, ed. Gerhard Schulz, 261–78. Göttingen, 1985.

Sternhell, Zeev. "How to Think about Fascism and Its Ideology." *Constellations* 15 (2008): 280–90.

Sulaiman, Mustafa Ahmad, Ahmad Ahmad Mutawalli Jad, and Nasif Mustafa 'Abd al-'Aziz. *Al-Lugha al-'Arabiyya: Iqra' wa-ta'allam. Al-Saff al-thalith al-ibtida'i, al-fasl al-dirasi al-awwal*, ed. Jumhuriyyat Misr al-'Arabiyya, Wizarat al-Tarbiyya wa'l-Ta'lim. Cairo: Sharikat al-Islam Misr li'l-Tiba'a, 2001.

———. *Al-Lugha al-'Arabiyya: Iqra' wa-ta'allam. Al-Saff al-thalith al-ibtida'i, al-fasl al-dirasi al-thani*, ed. Jumhuriyyat Misr al-'Arabiyya, Wizarat al-Tarbiyya wa'l-Ta'lim. Cairo: Sharikat al-Islam Misr li'l-Tiba'a, 2001.

Suleiman, Yasir. *The Arabic Language and National Identity: A Study in Ideology*. Edinburgh: Edinburgh University Press, 2003.

Swedenburg, Ted. *Memories of Revolt: The 1936–1939 Rebellion and the Palestinian National Past*. Minneapolis: University of Minnesota Press, 1995.

Tabari, al-. *The Sasanids, the Byzantines, the Lakhmids, and Yemen*. Translated by Clifford Edmund Bosworth. The History of Al-Tabari 5. Albany: State University of New York Press, 1999.

Tae Sun, Ryom. "Panoramas in the Democratic People's Republic of Korea." In *Die Welt der Panoramen: Zehn Jahre Internationale Panorama Konferenzen*, eds. Gabriele Koller and Gebhard Streicher, 86–87. Amberg: SPA Stiftung Panorama Altötting, 2003.

Tarbush, Mohammad A. *The Role of the Military in Politics. A Case Study of Iraq to 1941.* Vol. 2. London: Kegan Paul International, 1983.

Tariq Ibn Ziyad, Fatih al-Andalus. Abtal al-'Arab 10. Beirut: Dar al-'Awda, 1975.

Tariq Ibn Ziyad, Fatih al-Andalus. Beirut: Dar al-'Ilm li'l-Malayin, 2000.

Taylor, Charles. *A Secular Age.* Cambridge: Belknap Press of Harvard University Press, 2007.

Teitelbaum, Joshua. "The Muslim Brotherhood in Syria, 1945–1958: Founding, Social Origins, Ideology." *Middle East Journal* 65 (2011): 213–33.

"The New Flag of the Kingdom of the Hedjaz." *The Muslim World* 8.1 (January 1918): 190.

Thomas, Martin C. "French Intelligence-Gathering in the Syrian Mandate, 1920–40." *Middle Eastern Studies* 38, no. 1 (2002): 1–32.

Thompson, Elizabeth. *Colonial Citizens: Republican Rights, Paternal Privilege, and Gender in French Syria and Lebanon.* New York: Columbia University Press, 2000.

———. *Justice Interrupted: The Struggle for Constitutional Government in the Middle East.* Cambridge MA; London: Harvard University Press, 2013.

Tibi, Bassam. *Nationalismus in der Dritten Welt am arabischen Beispiel.* Frankfurt a.M. 1971.

———. *Arab Nationalism: A Critical Enquiry*, eds. Marion Farouk-Sluglett and Peter Sluglett. New York: St. Martin's Press, 1981.

———. *Arab Nationalism: Between Islam and the Nation-State.* New York: St. Martin's Press, 1997.

Todd, Frederick P. "The Military Museum in Europe." *Military Affairs* 12 (1948): 36–45.

Tripp, Charles. *A History of Iraq.* 3rd edn. Cambridge: University Press, 2007.

Troutt Powell, Eve. *A Different Shade of Colonialism: Egypt, Great Britain, and the Mastery of the Sudan.* Colonialisms 2. Berkeley: University of California Press, 2003.

al-Tu'ma, Salih Jawad. *Salah al-Din fi'l-shi'r al-'arabi al-hadith: dirasa wa-nusus.* 2nd edn. Damascus: Dar Kutha, 1997.

'Umar, Jabir. *Hawla al-qawmiyya al-'Arabiyya: Muhadarat.* Damascus: Matba'at al-Nidal, 1948.

'Uways, 'Abd al-Halim. *Qadiyat ihraq Tariq Ibn Ziyad li'l-sufun: Bayna al-ustura wa'l-tarikh.* Cairo: Dar al-Sahwa, 1987.

Vatikiotis, P.J. *Nasser and His Generation.* New York: St. Martin's Press, 1978.

Verdery, Katherine. *The Political Lives of Dead Bodies: Reburial and Postsocialist Change.* New York: Columbia University Press, 1999.

Voll, John O. "Linking Groups in the Networks of Eighteenth-Century Revivalist Scholars: The Mizjaji Family in Yemen." In *Eighteenth-Century Renewal and Reform in Islam*, eds. Nehemia Levtzion and John Obert Voll, 69–92. Syracuse: Syracuse University Press, 1987.

———. "Neo-Sufism: Reconsidered Again." *Canadian Journal of African Studies* 42 (2008): 314–30.

Walker, Dennis. "Egypt's Arabism: Mustafa Kamil's 1893 Play (Fath al-Andalus) on the Muslim Conquest of Spain." *Islamic Studies* 33.1 (1994): 49–76.

al-Wardani, 'Ali Ibn Salim. *Al-Rihla al-Andalusiyya.* Ed. al-Habib 'Awwadi. Tunis: Matba'at Fann al-Tiba'a, 2008.

Warner, Geoffrey. *Iraq and Syria 1941.* London: Davis Poynter, 1974.

Watenpaugh, Keith D. "'Creating Phantoms': Zaki Al-Arsuzi, the Alexandretta Crisis, and the Formation of Modern Arab Nationalism in Syria." *International Journal of Middle East Studies* 28 (1996): 363–89.

————. *Being Modern in the Middle East: Revolution, Nationalism, Colonialism, and the Arab Middle Class*. Princeton: Princeton University Press, 2006.

Weber, Stefan. *Damascus: Ottoman Modernity and Urban Transformation (1808–1918)*. 2 vols. Proceedings of the Danish Institute in Damascus 5. Aarhus: Aarhus Universitetsforlag, 2009.

Wedeen, Lisa. *Ambiguities of Domination: Politics, Rhetoric, and Symbols in Contemporary Syria*. Chicago: University of Chicago Press, 1999.

Wehr, Hans, and J. Milton Cowan. *A Dictionary of Modern Written Arabic (Arab.-Engl.)*. 4th edn. Wiesbaden: Harrassowitz, 1979.

Weismann, Itzchak. *Taste of Modernity: Sufism, Salafiyya, and Arabism in Late Ottoman Damascus*. Islamic History and Civilization 34. Leiden, Boston: Brill, 2001.

————. "Abu l-Huda l-Sayyadi and the Rise of Islamic Fundamentalism." *Arabica* 54 (2007): 586–92.

————. "Genealogies of Fundamentalism: Salafi Discourse in Nineteenth-Century Baghdad." *British Journal of Middle Eastern Studies* 36 (2009): 267–80.

Wien, Peter. "Arab Nationalists, Nazi-Germany and the Holocaust: An Unlucky Contemporaneity." In *Der Völkermord an den Armeniern und die Shoah/The Armenian Genocide and the Shoah*, eds. Hans Lukas Kieser and Dominik J. Schaller, 599–614. Zurich: Chronos, 2002.

————. *Iraqi Arab Nationalism: Authoritarian, Totalitarian and Pro-Fascist Inclinations, 1932–1941*. London, New York: Routledge, 2006.

————. "Coming to Terms with the Past: German Academia and Historical Relations between the Arab Lands and Nazi Germany." *International Journal of Middle East Studies* 42 (2010): 311–21.

————. "The Culpability of Exile. Arabs in Nazi Germany." *Geschichte und Gesellschaft* 37 (2011): 332–58.

————. "The Long and Intricate Funeral of Yasin al-Hashimi: Pan-Arabism, Civil Religion, and Popular Nationalism in Damascus, 1937." *International Journal of Middle East Studies* 43 (2011): 271–92.

————. "Arabs and Fascism: Empirical and Theoretical Perspectives." *Die Welt des Islams* 52 (2012): 331–50.

Wiesenthal, Simon. *Grossmufti – Grossagent der Achse: Tatsachenbericht*. Salzburg: Ried-Verlag, 1947.

Wild, Stefan. "Gott und Mensch im Libanon: Die Affäre Sadiq al-'Azm." *Der Islam* 48 (1972): 206–53.

————. "Der Generalsekretär und die Geschichtsschreibung: Saddam Husayn und die irakische Geschichtswissenschaft." In *The Challenge of the Middle East. Middle Eastern Studies at the University of Amsterdam*, ed. Ibrahim A. El-Sheikh et al., 161–72. Amsterdam, 1982.

————. "National Socialism in the Arab Near East Between 1933 and 1939." *Die Welt des Islams* 25 (1985): 126–73.

————. "Islamic Enlightenment and the Paradox of Averroes." *Die Welt des Islams* 36 (1996): 379–90.

————. "Die arabische Rezeption der 'Protokolle der Weisen von Zion.'" In *Islamstudien ohne Ende*, eds. Rainer Brunner, Monika Gronke, Jens Peter Laut, and Ulrich Rebstock, 517–28. Abhandlungen für die Kunde des Morgenlandes 54,1. Würzburg, 2002.

————. "Wissenschaft im Zwielicht. Orientalisten im 'Dritten Reich.'" *Orientalistische Literaturzeitung* 103.4–5 (2008): 478–85.

————. "'Islamofascism'? Introduction." *Die Welt des Islams* 52 (2012): 225–41.

Wildangel, René. *Zwischen Achse und Mandatsmacht: Palästina und der Nationalsozialismus*. Ed. Zentrum Moderner Orient. ZMO-Studien 24. Berlin: Klaus Schwarz Verlag, 2007.

———. "The Invention of 'Islamofascism'. Nazi Propaganda to the Arab World and Perceptions from Palestine." *Die Welt des Islams* 52 (2012): 526–44.

Wilson, Christopher S. *Beyond Anıtkabir: The Funerary Architecture of Atatürk*. Farnham: Ashgate Publishing, 2013.

Wizarat al-Ma'arif al-'Umumiyya. *Mathaf al-Hadara al-Misriyya 1949*. Cairo, 1949.

Wokoeck, Ursula. *German Orientalism: The Study of the Middle East and Islam from 1800 to 1945*. New York: Routledge, 2009.

Zachariah, Benjamin. "Rethinking (the Absence of) Fascism in India, C. 1922–45." In *Cosmopolitan Thought Zones: South Asia and the Global Circulation of Ideas*, eds. Sugata Bose and Kris Manjapra, 178–209. Houndmills, Basingstoke, New York: Palgrave Macmillan, 2010.

Zaki, Ahmad. *Rapport sur les manuscrits arabes conservés à l'Escurial en Espagne*. Cairo, (1894), 14.

———. "Sur les relations entre l'Egypte et l'Espagne pendent l'occupation musulmane." In *Homenaje á D. Francisco Codera en su jubilación del profesorado: Estudios de erudición oriental con una introducción de D. Eduardo Saavedra*, ed. Eduardo Saavedra, 456–81. Zaragoza: M. Escar, tipógrafo, 1904.

———. *Rihla ila'l-Andalus, 1893*. Ed. Muhammad Kamil al-Khatib. Damascus: Wizarat al-Thaqafa fi'l-Jumhuriyya al-'Arabiyya al-Suriyya, 1990.

———. *Al-Safar ila'l-mu'tamar*. Cairo: Al-Dar al-Misriyya al-Lubnaniyya, 2000.

Zaydan, Jirji. *Dibawah Rajuan Setan*. Translated by A. Fuad Said. Medan: Dian, 1964.

———. *Fath al-Andalus*. Cairo: Dar al-Hilal, 1965.

———. *Penaklukan Andalus*. Translated by A. Fuad Said. Medan: Pustaka "Budaja," 1964.

———. *Pengantin Fergana*. Translated by A. Fuad Said. Medan: Dian, 1965.

———. *Rahasia Tjintjin Nukman. Roman Sedjarah Karya Djirdji Zaidan, Alih Bahasa A. Fuad Said*. Translated by A. Fuad Said. Medan: Firma Harris, 1965.

———. *Salah al-Din al-Ayyubi*. Cairo: Dar al-Hilal, 1965.

Zubaida, Sami. *Islam, the People and the State: Essays on Political Ideas and Movements in the Middle East*, 2nd edn. London, New York: I.B. Tauris, 1993.

———. "Islam and Nationalism: Continuities and Contradictions." *Nations and Nationalism* 10 (2004): 407–20.

Zuwiyya Yamak, Labib. *The Syrian Social Nationalist Party: An Ideological Analysis*. Harvard Middle Eastern Monographs 14. Cambridge: Distributed for the Center for Middle Eastern Studies of Harvard University by Harvard University Press, 1966.

Index